BORDER BOSS

Number One: The Canseco-Keck History Series
Jerry Thompson, General Editor

BORDER BOSS

Manuel B. Bravo and Zapata County

J. GILBERTO QUEZADA

Texas A&M University Press
College Station

Copyright © 1999 by J. Gilberto Quezada
Manufactured in the United States of America
All rights reserved
First edition
The paper used in this book meets the minimum requirements of the American National
Standard for Permanence of Paper for Printed Library Materials, z39.48-1984.
Binding materials have been chosen for durability.
∞

Library of Congress Cataloging-in-Publication Data

Quezada, J. Gilberto, 1946–
    Border boss : Manuel B. Bravo and Zapata County / J. Gilberto Quezada. — 1st ed.
        p.   cm. — (The Canseco-Keck history series ; no. 1)
    Includes bibliographical references (p.   ) and index.
    ISBN 0-89096-865-9 (cloth)
    1. Bravo, Manuel B., d. 1984.   2. Mexican-American judges—Texas—Zapata
County—Biography.   3. Judges—Texas—Zapata County—Biography.   4. Zapata
County (Tex.)—Politics and government.   5. Democratic Party (Tex.)—History—
20th century.   6. Zapata County (Tex.)—Biography.   I. Title.   II. Series.
F392.Z3Q49   1999
976.4'48306'092—dc21
    [B]   98-42635
                                                                              CIP

For my parents, Eloisa L. Quezada and the late Pedro Quezada,
and for my beloved wife, Jo Emma Bravo,
whose infinite love and wisdom have been a constant
source of inspiration

CONTENTS

Illustrations

TABLES

PREFACE

I first met Zapata County Judge Manuel B. Bravo in 1970 at an Easter family picnic to which my fiancée, the judge's granddaughter, had invited me. By then he had been retired from active politics for some time. On first impression, I held him to be a generous, warm-hearted man, possessing a simple demeanor, a good sense of humor, and an innate trait of humility. Anyone knowing the judge would scarcely have considered him a historic personage or suspected that he had amassed a considerable archival collection unknown to researchers. At no time would one have guessed that Bravo and Lyndon B. Johnson had shared a close friendship that spanned more than thirty years.

It was not until the summer of 1990, six years after his death, that I began taking an interest in his political career. Prior to that date, his public and private papers remained obscure and forgotten, resting silently inside an old four-drawer, metal filing cabinet, which for more than twenty years had remained largely unnoticed by my in-laws. The rusty greenish depository seemed to blend with the canned foods, detergents, dried goods, and other household products that filled the small pantry room at the Bravo home.

Bravo's entire collection, classified in a well-organized manner, chronicled his involvement in politics from about 1929 to 1979, including his twenty years as county judge (1937–57). In the collection were more than fifty letters between Johnson and Bravo, most of which are still not available at the LBJ Library. The two men's close friendship and association began during Johnson's first bid for the Senate in 1941 and continued after Bravo retired from public office in 1957.[1]

Following a lengthy discussion in 1990 that included myself, my wife, and her paternal grandmother—the judge's ninety-two-year-old widow, Mrs. Josefa V. Bravo—the family agreed and granted me permission to open the judge's personal and private papers. Mrs. Bravo felt that since many of the old political avant-garde were no longer around to provide us with an oral history, the younger generation needed to have a sense of their own heritage, something that they might gain by study of the contributions Judge Bravo made to Zapata County.

After reviewing the judge's papers, I felt that Bravo was a figure worthy of a biography and important to Texas history for the following reasons. First, his story would be the first biography of a Tejano county judge. Second, of the five bosses who controlled South Texas counties (Webb, Starr, Zapata, Jim Wells, and Duval) during the 1930s through the 1950s, Judge Bravo was the only boss who left behind a paper trail that could clarify political, social, and economic issues. Third, a major study could analyze, from the perspective of those involved, the complexity of border politics at the local, state, and national levels. Last, the different personalities and diverse problems involved in Zapata County politics could well offer a deeper understanding of county administrative and networking practices. For example, the Bravo collection includes correspondence with James V. Allred, Lloyd Bentsen, Jr., Eligio "Kika" de la Garza, Coke Stevenson, George Parr, Ralph W. Yarborough, José T. Canales, Joe M. Kilgore, George Bush, Tom Connally, Alonso Perales, Rogers Kelley, and others. Topically, the papers contain information related to the construction of Falcon Dam, the Democratic Party, El Chamizal settlement, soil conservation, drought relief, the Félix Longoria episode, foot-and-mouth disease projects, education, and much more.

The following chapters elaborate on Zapata County involvement in election campaigns as well as in local, state, and national matters. Chapter 1 examines Bravo's formative years and his initial encounter in politics with the A. Y. Baker regime in Hidalgo County. Chapter 2 chronicles his first term as county judge of Zapata County. Under his leadership, the Democratic political machine initiated a series of changes in the administration of county affairs. In state politics, W. Lee O'Daniel won his bid for governor in 1938 with the border counties supporting different candidates. This was obviously an indication that the local bosses controlled their own bailiwicks. An in-house fight that took place within the 49th District Court had serious political consequences for Zapata, Webb, Dimmit, and Jim Hogg counties. It brought outgoing Governor James V. Allred to interfere with the border leaders and settle the dispute. The special Senate election of 1941 served as the prelude to a long-lasting, mutual friendship between Judge Bravo and Lyndon B. Johnson.

The onset of World War II and Bravo's active participation in several patriotic activities sets the stage for chapter 3. An interesting 1942 race for the Senate seat between incumbent O'Daniel and two former governors, James Allred and Dan Moody, found Judge Bravo and other county bosses undecided about which candidate to support. The oil companies, collecting on past political favors, demanded that Judge Bravo support their candidate for Texas railroad commissioner.

Judge Bravo took a firm stand against discrimination when it reached an all-time high against Tejanos and Mexican citizens during the early 1940s. He was the product of a generation who witnessed human rights violations in the Lower Río Grande Valley, especially by the Texas Rangers (*los rinches*). Even though Zapata, Webb, and Starr counties did not experience discrimination, this was certainly not the case in other South and Central Texas counties.

The turbulent political campaigns of 1948 are the main focus of chapter 4. In the infamous runoff Senate election between Lyndon Johnson and Coke Stevenson, the Bravo Papers provide an alternate explanation to the traditional one for the missing or lost election results from Ballot Box No. 3. Since the federal investigation targeted box 3 in Zapata County and box 13 in Jim Wells, there is no doubt that the border bosses and George Parr gave Johnson a dubious narrow victory. Moreover, this study supports historian Robert Dallek's thesis that the runoff election for the 15th Congressional District seat between Philip A. Kazen and Lloyd M. Bentsen, Jr., directly impacted the voter turnout for the Johnson/Stevenson campaign.

Chapter 5 documents Judge Bravo's strong feelings against racial discrimination during the Félix Longoria incident. The episode, capable of exploding into an international crisis, brought to the forefront the GI Forum. Documents found in the Bravo papers and at the LBJ Library revealed that during the 1952 Democratic election campaign, the FBI, Senator Johnson, and the Attorney General's office became involved in the local political maelstrom.

Chapters 6 and 7 discuss Judge Bravo's administrative efforts and boss-style politics in dealing with the relocation issues and the bureaucratic red tape of the International Boundary and Water Commission (IBWC) during construction of the international Falcon Dam. In vying for political power and hegemony, the ruling Partido Viejo struggled with the Partido Nuevo during negotiations with the IBWC. In some instances, this internal strife delayed the relocation process and positioned Judge Bravo and his cohorts for taking a defensive course during the 1954 election. Further, this study shows that the federal agencies involved should have taken a more humane approach in dealing with the social, economic, and cultural heritage of the displaced people of Zapata County.

The last chapter begins when Judge Bravo resigned from public office and, thanks to Lyndon Johnson, started a second career with Brown & Root in South America. During his five-year absence from active politics, he continued to exert his political influence from afar, responding to requests for assistance with several projects. After his return, as correspondence in the Bravo papers indicates, partisan and nonpartisan citizens sought Judge Bravo's advice on local and state issues, causing him to consider the county judgeship again. However, the "Big Four" had retired from the political arena, and the machine no longer existed. Unable to establish a power base, he gracefully bowed out of the campaign. Soliciting help from Senator Johnson again, he ironically found employment with the IBWC, and was assigned to work in Zapata County. In his capacity as claims adjuster, Judge Bravo negotiated a fair and just settlement for his constituents, and all the pending claims against the federal government finally came to a close. Later, the IBWC transferred him to El Paso, where he assisted in the official settlement of El Chamizal Treaty in 1967. Throughout his retirement, Judge Bravo remained a staunch Democrat, offered whatever assistance he could provide to fledgling politicians, and always maintained an unflinching loyalty to the Democratic Party.

Acknowledgments

Over the span of almost eight years that the research and writing phase of this project consumed, I met many people who shared my enthusiasm for and interest in Judge Manuel B. Bravo, and their support and cooperation made the journey gratifying and rewarding. I am forever grateful to the judge's widow, Mrs. Josefa V. Bravo, who at ninety-two, when I interviewed her, still had a keen recollection of places, people, and events. Mrs. Bravo was always available to reminisce about the judge's political and social life and cheerfully allowed me the use of his public and private papers. I further want to give special recognition to Virginia B. López, who assisted me by visiting libraries in the Lower Río Grande Valley in search of useful documents relating to Zapata County. In addition, I wish to express my appreciation to Eddie Bravo, Sr., and Ana María Casso Bravo.

In a very special way, I am eternally indebted to Dr. Arnoldo De León of Angelo State University, who took much time from his teaching and research schedule to take my manuscript under his wing. Without his painstaking assistance, this project would have never made it to publication. He meticulously reviewed every single page of the entire work, provided expert technical advice, and offered encouraging words of support and inspiration throughout the editing process. Similarly, I owe much to Dr. Félix D. Almaráz, Jr., of the University of Texas at San Antonio, who from the inception of the undertaking encouraged its development; Dr. Lewis L. Gould, of the University of Texas at Austin, who offered helpful guidance about the literature on voting fraud in American history and who continuously believed in the story of Judge Bravo from our first meeting in the spring of 1992; Dr. Claudia Anderson, archivist at the LBJ Library, who placed at my disposal the Pre-Presidential Confidential, Senate and House files; Bill Richter, former archivist at the Barker Texas History Center; Laura K. Seagert and Michael R. Green with the Texas State Archives; and Laura Gutiérrez-Witt, head librarian at the Benson Latin American Collection.

My special thanks go to Janice Weber and Juanita Valls, librarians at the Laredo Public Library; the late Luciano Guajardo; Omelia Villarreal with the Zapata County Historical Commission; Adán Gutiérrez, former librarian at the Zapata County Public Library; Consuelo Villarreal and Dora Ramírez with the Zapata County Clerk's Office; Dr. Hubert J. Miller, professor emeritus at the University of Texas—Pan American; and Belinda Bravo, for reproducing old family photos and xeroxing pertinent documents.

My greatest debt and gratitude I owe to my wife, Jo Emma, who in her unflinching role as research assistant, typist, and proofreader, labored diligently over the entire manuscript and reviewed it for accuracy, consistency, cohesiveness, and clarity. Of course, I assume full responsibility for all omissions and shortcomings in the final product.

BORDER BOSS

Introduction

A case study of County Judge Manuel B. Bravo as a political boss in South Texas merits writing for the following reasons. First, Bravo's personal and private papers, which are not yet available to the public, combined with other archival sources and oral histories, bring to light a new and fuller understanding of the role political bosses played in shaping the future of local, state, national, and sometimes even international politics. Second, there is a serious lack of analysis and interpretation of boss rule in South Texas during the Great Depression, World War II, and the postwar epoch. Bravo, heretofore, has been a figure often mentioned in biographies and studies of Lyndon B. Johnson and other Texas politicos, yet no one has taken time to give him a full length study. Third, it is important to have a solid Tejano biography that examines a South Texas political boss and his leadership record from the 1930s to the 1950s—the time when the "Mexican American generation" played important leadership roles. Fourth, Bravo's boss-style politics need to be assessed in light of the broad generalizations other researchers have attributed to South Texas bosses. Fifth, a revisionist view of South Texas politics must dispel the myth that one political boss controlled and/or influenced a vast geopolitical area. The more realistic scenario in the region resembled a "political quilt": a network in which bosses in specific counties formed alliances and coalitions with their counterparts in surrounding counties. Countless times these county bosses met in smoke-filled rooms in Laredo, decided which regional or state candidates to endorse and support, and then tried to deliver the Tejano bloc vote. Seldom did these several bosses, as is commonly believed, submit to the dictates of George Parr (the so-called Duke of Duval County), who allegedly ruled ten or more counties by himself; indeed, there has never been any direct evidence to prove Parr's regional domination. Finally, South Texas politics must be presented from the perspective of insiders who actually participated, and not from the point of view of outsiders who write detached academic tomes.

The several questions pursued and analyzed in the present work place Judge Bravo's politics within the recent scholarship on bossism and the Chicano literature on politics. To wit: How does Bravo's twenty-year reign as county judge conform to the characteristics generally associated with South Texas bosses? How does this case study fit the contemporary Chicano literature on politics? How do Bravo's politics in Zapata County differ from those discussed in Evan Anders's *Boss Rule in South Texas: The Progressive Era?* What was Judge Bravo's political ideology? What was the impact of the construction of Falcon Dam and the relocation process on the economic, social, and political life of the people in Zapata County and on the residents of the Lower Río Grande Valley? Did the federal government treat Hispanics in Zapata County similarly to or differently than Native Americans also displaced by dams? What structural and functional service did the Zapata County political machine perform during the relocation process? The pages that follow elaborate on all these questions in an effort to define Judge Bravo's place as a political boss.

A rose is a rose is a rose may be a truism all the time, but a boss is a boss is a boss may not have the same meaning all the time. An underlying consideration for the present study may be giving a clear definition of what is meant by a "political boss." Political analysts, historians, social scientists, and others use "political boss" rather loosely and even disagree on its meaning and interpretation. Historians have attributed the origins of the terms *boss*, the *ring*, and the *machine* to the periods known in American history as the Industrial Age and the Gilded Age, that era from about the middle of the nineteenth century to about the early 1900s.[1] It was these turbulent times—when local municipal governments were unable to provide the needed public services due to the tremendous population growth of cities and urban centers—that "encouraged the emergence of political machines and bosses. . . . In city after city, it was exactly this fragmented political life that brought the bosses to power." [2] A review of the scholarship shows that historians hold divergent insights and notions on the subject of political bosses.

Frank R. Kent, in his 1930 classic, *The Great Game of Politics,* asserted that all political bosses are not dishonest, nor are they in politics to get wealthy or make business profits for personal gains.[3] The boss, however, relies on patronage to maintain the existence of his political machine and to exert loyalty from its members. In city politics, the boss typically moves up the bureaucratic ladder, starting at the lowest rung. The boss in a county, Kent argues, follows a different pattern, ascending to the top of the local party: "Leadership in a county comes to him, in most cases, not because he has won his spurs as a machine politician, but because he is the dominant man in other ways in his county." [4] The reason for this scenario is that in rural counties, the population is much smaller than in the city, and most of the people tend to know each other. The county boss has more personal contact with the people than does the big city boss.

Robert Merton in *Social Theory and Social Structure* presented an analytical model for examining the political boss and his machine in the contextual complexity of an urban setting. Other researchers have relied on his model to understand the key structural functions of the boss in different environments. In Merton's study, the boss's main function is "to organize, centralize and maintain in good working condition" his political machine through the different subgroups living in the precincts.[5] The survival of the boss and his machine rests on a grassroots approach of accommodating the basic social and economic needs of the people living in each precinct. After all, this is where elections are won. To meet the social needs of the voters, the boss's lieutenants in each precinct developed personal relationships with those who had "specific personal problems and personal wants." [6]

Evan Anders, previously mentioned, used Merton's model to examine South Texas politics. Anders looked at the political machines in Cameron, Hidalgo, Duval, and Starr counties during the 1890s and early 1900s and found a political structure similar to the ones described by Merton. While the big city political boss worked with business titans, real estate brokers, and stock market investors, the rural boss dealt primarily with family-owned small businesses, ranchers, and farmers. In Anders's study, the boss assumed a paternalistic role and, through per-

sonal interrelationships, provided economic and social welfare for the
people. Corruption and violence as general patterns of behavior ruled
the four counties, and "all the bosses systematically violated the election
laws of the state by paying for the poll taxes of their Hispanic followers,
recruiting ineligible aliens to vote, marking the ballots of illiterate voters,
and tampering with the results when necessary."[7]

The practice of graft, for both personal and political gain, was common among these South Texas bosses, according to Anders. Simply
stated, the county treasury became a slush fund for the misappropriation
of thousands of dollars. Archie Parr, the first Duke of Duval County, for
example, embezzled public funds to the tune of $315,000. Even though
Parr survived many investigations, other border bosses who engaged in
similar practices were forced to resign.[8]

In his M.A. thesis, "James B. Wells and the Brownsville Patronage
Fight, 1912–1917," Anders attributed Wells's political power to the control of the Tejano vote; manipulation of the ineligible votes from Mata-
moros, Mexico; alliances with other well-known bosses; acquisition of
huge real estate acreage; paternalism and benevolence on Wells's part;
and to a quasi-informal method of welfare for the economically disad-
vantaged Tejanos.[9] Wells's political behavior, in many ways, was similar
to that exhibited by the city bosses from the East and Midwest.[10] For the
most part, they tended to blend politics and business in pursuit of personal gain, relying on patronage and graft to maintain their political machine in power. These bosses "viewed politics as an avenue of upward
mobility, a means of achieving status, power, and wealth. They usually
worked their way up through the hierarchical ranks of the local political
organization," and "provided jobs, social services, and special favors in
return."[11]

While the urban bosses flourished during the Gilded Age, in South
Texas the political machines relied on the manipulation and control of
the Tejano and illegal Mexican votes to remain in power. It was not uncommon for them also to use the tombstone vote. In essence, border
bosses were no different than their city counterparts, exerting their paternalistic authority through similar means. Douglas Weeks, in "The
Texas-Mexican and the Politics of South Texas," saw the *patrón* (boss),
"not as a boss but as a type of patriarch. . . . The inhabitants recognized
him as their supreme leader socially and politically."[12]

South Texas bosses exhibited the same personal traits and characteristics as their counterparts from the East and the Midwest. As Edgar Shelton put it in his *Political Conditions among Texas Mexicans Along the Río Grande,* "it is common knowledge that all of these bosses are well off financially. Whether they participate in the old political custom of graft or not is not known."[13] In the border counties, whether the patrón was Anglo or Tejano, control of the Tejano vote was paramount for election success. In Webb County, for instance, Judge Manuel J. Raymond, a Brownsville native who adopted Laredo as his hometown, ruled with such an iron fist that his machine earned the nickname, "Judge Raymond's gang."[14] Some well-known bosses who ruled over the Lower Río Grande Valley for decades included Jim Wells in Cameron County; John Closner and A. Y. Baker in Hidalgo County; Archie Parr and later his son, George, in Duval County; the Klebergs of the King Ranch, whose influence overlapped into other counties; and the Guerra brothers in Starr County. During a state investigation over misappropriation of county funds in Starr County, Commissioner Manuel Guerra was described as "a man of dominating character, inordinate ambition, and soulless purpose," who by "virtue of his political dictatorship, controls the elections of the county and places in office those and only those agreeable to his purposes."[15]

The boss was the dominant person who operated many aspects of county affairs, and control was made easier in rural South Texas since generally folks knew each other and in some cases were related by marriage. People profited from the practices of patronage and graft, keeping the machine in power. According to Douglas Foley and co-workers in *From Peones to Politics: Ethnic Relations in a South Texas Town, 1900–1977,* if a person needed a job with the county, the local boss was the person to see.[16] During election time, the patrón was also underhand in a unique way. If an election became a close one, he or his supporters working the polls would reach into Mexico and obtain the necessary votes. In state elections, the county bosses sometimes supported each other through alliances and mutual agreements. The downside to this arrangement was that in all probability, some state officials sought and bought these political machines. Each candidate selected received the Tejano bloc vote, which raised suspicion about the similar voting patterns among the political machines in the various counties.[17]

John R. Peavey in *Echoes From the Río Grande* summarized the definition of a border county boss as "a past master of every trick in or out of the book. The boss was always a very proud character with an engaging personality, conversant in both languages [English and Spanish]; an unscrupulous prevaricator when necessary to accomplish his purpose and to establish himself and hold his position of power and control." [18] According to Peavey, it was common practice to count votes cast by Mexican citizens. In many cases, Tejanos had relatives living in the Mexican border towns, and this connection made it feasible to solicit their votes. When a person got on the wrong side of the law, the family members of the malefactor requested the boss to intervene on their behalf. Of course, the boss collected on the favor at election time. [19]

Recently, John E. Clark wrote *The Fall of the Duke of Duval*, a firsthand insight into the political boss seemingly the most corrupt in the history of South Texas. Clark, a former U.S. attorney for the Western District of Texas, served as the prosecutor during the George B. Parr investigation in the 1970s. He succinctly delineated three major components that generally characterized successful boss rule in South Texas. First, the local boss relied on corruption and coercion to assure the successful outcome of every local election. Second, the political machine, in order to survive and maintain its control, practiced patronage to the fullest. Finally, the boss and his cohorts used public funds to augment their personal wealth. [20]

So what do the various historical interpretations tell us about political bossism? Generally speaking, they describe the political boss as a person who is dishonest; practices graft; uses patronage to keep the political machine in control; is an organizer, compromiser, and negotiator; assumes a paternalistic role; uses violence and fraud to win elections; forms alliances with businesses and other political leaders; acquires huge amounts of real estate; takes a leadership role in solving pertinent local issues; communicates skillfully in the language of the voters; provides for the social and economic welfare of constituents; and manipulates people. The boss was the leader of a small partisan group, which consisted of the party organization's movers and shakers, also known as the local ring or machine. [21] Loyalty to the *jefe político* and to the Democratic Party was essential for the survival of the coterie's dominance and hegemony over election returns and county affairs. In some exceptions, the political boss is depicted as honest and trustworthy.

Judge Bravo certainly embodied some of the attributes generally associated with a political boss, and one way to portray him is as a shrewd politician. In his role as county judge, Bravo assumed total responsibility for the political, social, and economic affairs of the county. Without the bureaucracy of a city council, a city manager, or a mayor, the only governmental entity in Zapata County centered around the county judge and the commissioners' court.[22] Therefore, his decision-making authority, which rested on his public office in the form of county government, constituted considerable power and control over local affairs. Judge Bravo's actions, thus, fit the stereotypical image of a political boss. Even though he did not grow up in the slums to become a ruthless, evil, and greedy demagogue, when it came to politics, he nevertheless operated an allegedly corrupt political machine.

Like the other bosses in South Texas, Judge Bravo also assumed a paternalistic role. He "helped the county patrons with his own money and without hesitation. People believed that a county judge was their landlord and their Savior . . . they would knock at his door, during the day or night, and ask for favors, . . . for money to take somebody to the hospital or to get them out of jail. . . . He was kind of their father for them . . . he knew everyone by their name, last name, . . . who all the relatives were, all the cousins." [23] In the small towns and on the ranches of the county, politics took on a more personal flavor, being much closer to the people.

In Zapata County, Judge Bravo and his political machine operated, controlled, and survived every Democratic primary election from 1937 to 1957. To maintain the machine in good working condition, he relied on patronage—the lifeblood of the organization. Those who supported the machine received jobs with the three largest employers in the county: the county offices, the school district, or the oil and gas companies. Often the judge recommended political foes for employment, working to win them over for the next election.[24] When reelection time came around, these workers were the same people who actively campaigned for the incumbents. Another form of patronage involved the granting of contracts to businesses from which the county would then purchase supplies and materials.

From published works, one gets a similar but more generalized view on Bravo and South Texas politics. This literature documents the corruption that existed among the border bosses, notably George B. Parr, the most notorious and best known of them. Using newspaper articles, Seth McKay in his 1954 monograph *Texas and the Fair Deal, 1945–1952* referred to Parr as "the ruling power of the 18-county twenty-seventh Senatorial District," which included Zapata County.[25] George Norris Green, in *The Establishment in Texas Politics, 1938–1957,* also makes reference to Parr's influence and describes Judge Bravo as a petty despot: "Over the years the Parrs dominated Duval County and exerted heavy influence over petty despots in Zapata, Jim Hogg, Jim Wells and Starr counties, among others." [26]

Recent biographies of Lyndon B. Johnson have been more descriptive and detailed in arriving at basically the same conclusion regarding South Texas political operations. Ronnie Dugger in *The Politician: The Life and Times of Lyndon Johnson,* asserted that Judge Bravo and the Laredo bosses took orders from Parr. According to Bravo, "George Parr was calling up here . . . very enthusiastically pushing for Lyndon." [27]

In 1990, in his controversial biography *The Years of Lyndon Johnson: Means of Ascent,* Robert Caro described Judge Bravo, among others, as "less well known, petty despots who ruled along the Rio Grande," and one whom Parr controlled "through alliances." [28] Moreover, Caro states that Parr had absolute command over six counties, including Zapata County.[29]

A year later, Robert Dallek in *Lone Star Rising: Lyndon Johnson and His Times, 1908–1960,* followed the same interpretive line regarding South Texas politics. Historically speaking, Dallek notes, "the Valley was notorious for selling its votes to the highest bidder, with the buyer usually receiving over 90 percent of the ballots," and Judge Bravo was among the "South Texas political bosses" who masterminded this effort.[30] Dallek also asserted that during the federal investigation that followed the 1948 Senate election, Bravo "did everything possible" to cover his own tracks.[31]

Though there is no documentation, it appears highly probable that Judge Bravo's association with the politicos in Hidalgo County helped him to crystallize his own ideas about administering county politics. His alliance with George Parr and his fellow *compadres* from the surrounding border counties usually, but not always, perpetuated the delivery of a Tejano bloc vote majority to the candidate of their choice.[32] Nonetheless, Bravo operated an apparently corrupt political machine, assisted by the *pistoleros* Sheriff Leopoldo Martínez assigned to make sure that the people voted for the right candidate.[33]

A second way to present Judge Bravo's boss style politics is to see it as a product of its times and political environment. A native of Hidalgo County, and a resolute liberal Democrat, Bravo saw bossism entrenched in the entire social and economic fabric of South Texas. From the beginning of his political involvement with the Democratic Party in the 1920s, his experience in Hidalgo County proved to be the training ground for continuing machine politics in Zapata County, some fifteen years later.[34]

Under the tutelage of his uncle John L. Box—a staunch Democrat, who owned the Edinburg Drug Company and who at one time had served as a public official—Bravo, as an ambitious young aspiring politician, became a strong supporter of the infamous Hidalgo County political machine known as the "Baker Ring," named for Sheriff Anderson Yancy (known as "A. Y.") Baker, who inherited it from Boss John Closner in 1918.[35] Early in his involvement with the Democratic Party, Bravo and Hidalgo County Judge A. W. Cameron, one of Baker's lieutenants, had become close friends and political allies of Parr's.[36] The foundation for their camaraderie started in 1919, when Bravo was eighteen years old. Through the influence of his uncle John, the young Manuel found a job with the Valley Abstract Company, owned by W. R. Montgomery, who was also vice president of the Edinburg State Bank and Trust Company, and where—by no coincidence—A. Y. Baker served as president.[37]

Bravo's association with Montgomery and Baker had paid big dividends. Being on the inside of the Baker ring, Bravo, after working for Montgomery for two years, found employment in the county tax assessor/collector's office. Joe Alamía, the county tax collector, who happened to be one of Baker's henchman, gave Bravo the job. Working in the Hidalgo County Courthouse for nine years helped Bravo establish a long-lasting relationship with another Baker cohort, A. E. Chávez, the county clerk.[38]

Bravo experienced firsthand many of the political intrigues that eventually led to Baker's downfall. Documentation does not exist showing whether Bravo actually participated in the corrupt voting practices, for his name is not mentioned in any of the allegations. Unfortunately, one can only assume that as a close member of Baker's ring, young Bravo collaborated with Boss Baker and his lieutenants. Bravo had to have known what was going on, and if nothing else, he learned as a politician-in-waiting what to do and what not to do.

A third way to view Bravo is to note that he had a particular acumen for the political game. In 1936, after he had been a Zapata County resident for just three years, the local Democratic political machine asked Bravo to accept the top political position—that of county judge. Bravo was an outsider from Hidalgo County and did not belong to the ruling families, even though his brother-in-law, Hesiquio Cuéllar, was involved in politics. The county judgeship came to him not because he had worked his way up the political rungs but because he was the dominant person in other ways. In all probability, Bravo's personality paved the way for his meteoric rise to power. He had an indispensable personality trait, an essential characteristic of any successful politician: the ability to communicate well with people, including political foes.[39] Bravo's strong command of both English and Spanish gave him a definite edge in the political cauldron.

According to Eddie Bravo, Sr., the judge's oldest son, "He had an innate sense (*un don*) to win the opposition to his side. Even though he knew that they had voted against him, he would still shake his opponents' hand, pat them on the back, and write letters of recommendations for them. If they needed assistance, he helped them, and had coffee or lunch with them—that, I think is politics . . . he was a heck of a darn politician."[40]

Bravo had numerous redeeming qualities that also put him in a separate category from other political bosses. For instance, he did not use his influence and position to steal from the county treasury. On the contrary, he established a system for maintaining fiscal records. At the time of his death in 1984, he left behind a plain will that included a simple, one-story, four-bedroom stucco house, a Ford automobile, and a modest savings and investment account.[41]

Judge Bravo never boasted about himself, even though he garnered many accolades. As a matter of fact, he rarely talked about politics in particular, but those close to him knew that he kept up with events through the local newspaper and television. During one Thanksgiving reunion, a family member asked him (in my presence) to tell the rest of us the story of the missing election returns from Ballot Box No. 3 (which contained the alleged fraudulent votes giving Johnson additional ballots in the 1948 Senate election), and what had happened in Jim Wells County with Ballot Box No. 13. The judge, then about seventy-five years old, just smiled and refused to say a word. He knew more than he was willing to say, but he preferred not to talk about it.

James C. Parish, a retired columnist for the *Laredo Times,* interviewed Judge Bravo and wrote numerous articles about him during the 1970s. He discovered that Bravo was an easy person to interview and found personal qualities in him that other political bosses lacked:

> He liked to say that he began his political career with a determination to never become *amargo* (Spanish for "embittered") when political developments were disappointing. He kept that resolution and his memorable sense of humor and fairness until the end of his life. He never bad-mouthed, or talked bad about political opponents. That approach towards politics caused him to be respected and appreciated by Hispanics and Anglos alike. He was often sought out for advice by State officials because they knew he had an inborn understanding of South Texas politics.[42]

Aside from placing this case study of Judge Bravo within the scholarship on bossism, this monograph also fits him into the Chicano literature on politics for that era. Judge Bravo's activities in Zapata County, for example, conform to what the "Mexican-American generation," would have advocated.[43] Tejanos who experienced the anti-Mexican prejudice of the 1920s, the Great Depression, and World War II emerged as a generation who fought for civil rights and for equal treatment as first-class citizens.[44] Bravo was a product of these times. He provided leadership and the politics of direct action in behalf of Mexican Americans.

In *Not Room Enough: Mexicans, Anglos, and Socio-Economic Change in Texas, 1850–1900*, Kenneth L. Stewart and Arnoldo De León survey the historical origins of machine politics and the rise of bossism within the context of Tejano and Anglo politics. Taking issue with the literature in which it is claimed that the basis for a feudalistic origin for bossism in Texas rested on a "relationship of subservience on the part of the peon and paternalism on behalf of the *patrón*," Stewart and De León argue that not enough documentation exists to support the assumption that Tejanos "viewed themselves as peons and retreated into political submission of their own accord."[45]

The present case study of Judge Bravo is in harmony with the above interpretations of South Texas Tejano politics. I contend, as Stewart and De León do, that the electorate in Zapata County accepted the principles of democracy and pledged their loyalty and allegiance to a political leader as an avenue for achieving full participation in the democratic system.[46] Support for Bravo and his cohorts was not because of ignorance, fear, or intimidation (although these factors applied in some cases) but rather because the Partido Viejo (Bravo's political party) provided the economic means of survival. The competing Partido Nuevo in Zapata County viewed Bravo's machine as evil and corrupt. Its campaign slogans of "Honesty, Progress, Equal Opportunities" were abstractions and made little sense to the people who were trying to cope with the harsh realities of the period.[47] In return for the machine's material assistance and other benefits, therefore, Tejanos in Zapata County voted for Democratic Party candidates at election time.

More to the point, my research indicates that Judge Bravo's politics were shaped not so much by the temptations of bossism as by the geography, history, economy, demography, and social structure of Zapata County. Physically, the county was isolated from the course of events that transpired in South Texas. Its relative isolation allowed politicians to run local government without too much meddling from neighboring bosses and members of the business community, or by civic reformers such as those who had managed to end boss rule in the farm counties. Historically, political bossism had been a way of life in Zapata County for generations, so that the judge simply perpetuated political relationships that reached a long way back.

The agrarian economy also affected the manner in which politics were conducted in Zapata County. As late as the 1950s, poor folks depended on ranch and farm owners not only for their salaries but for food, homes, security, and other things received for year-round performance of essential agricultural chores. This mutual reliance spilled over into politics, as the larger ranchers and farmers, many of whom doubled as political leaders, provided county benefits and perquisites to workers in return for the vote.

The overall demographic structure of the county further affected the style of local governance. The county remained predominantly Hispanic, so that people placed faith in the *amo* (boss) as a figure who could provide them with needed services. The old social structure similarly remained unchanged, again reinforcing boss politics. Well-to-do folks had traditionally ruled, and as Bravo belonged to such an elite class, he probably believed that it was encumbent upon him to govern as others of his social rank had done in the past.

My findings also show that Bravo's politics were based on his experiences and his belief that bossism, being a way of life in the county, was the best way to pursue goals that benefitted the entire community. He felt that the political machine should try to maintain the status quo, as it was much better at achieving this objective than were other forces. The judge perceived politics not as a business for personal wealth but as a public service. He did not acquire extensive real estate, yet he could have. He did not manipulate the county treasury as his own slush fund, though he could have.

This biography further demonstrates that Bravo's politics were never unidimensional, as is generally believed. His actions both fit and deviate from the ones associated with the stereotypical boss. Being an integral player in the dynamics that resulted when the two opposing factions (the Partido Viejo and the Partido Nuevo) confronted different socioeconomic issues, Judge Bravo acted as the mediator, striving to achieve the best results for the county. He possessed superior interpersonal skills that permitted him to pursue honesty in government and to befriend people in high places as well as befriending his enemies. Judge Bravo avoided badmouthing his opponents either privately or publicly, despite philippic attacks on him. On the contrary, as noted, he tried to win them over and even recommended them for government jobs.

But the judge could be a cunning intriguer who turned to shady, dubious practices in the belief that it was essential for him and his party to remain the provider of services to the people. In effect, Bravo's boss style embodied the different leadership approaches typically associated with bossism. It combined benevolence, manipulation, persuasion, and connivance to chart the course of Zapata County politics.

In the end, this biography presents a revisionist interpretation of bossism. While the book illustrates the judge's positive attributes, something necessary in order to obtain another perspective on machine politics, this study is not a hagiography of Judge Bravo. In the pages that follow are assessments of his political style; of the impact of his tenure on Zapata County and the success or failure of his reforms; of his leadership role during the construction of Falcon Dam and the relocation process; and of his continued political influence as a retired county judge over South Texas politics.

THE HIDALGO COUNTY EXPERIENCE

Manuel B. Bravo's early years in Hidalgo County politics prepared him well for later becoming the political boss of
Zapata County. His active association in the A. Y. Baker
Democratic ring gave him the exposure to learn firsthand how a political
machine worked. His involvement in the Knights of Columbus and the
League of United Latin American Citizens (LULAC) during the 1920s
provided the visibility Bravo needed to establish a political base in South
Texas. In the course of this period, several social, educational, and economic issues also helped shape his ideological and pragmatic outlook on
future policymaking.

FAMILY BACKGROUND

Manuel's parents, Emma Box and David Bravo, came from two distinguished pioneer families. Emma's father, Lina H. Box, left his hometown
of Crockett in the piney woods of East Texas and migrated to Hidalgo
County shortly after the conclusion of the Civil War.[1] He entered politics,
purchased *porción* 72, and established El Rancho Sauz, a remote border
ranch in the southern part of the county. David's family moved from
northeastern Mexico to the border town of Reynosa (in Mexico), a suitable place to continue their farming and ranching interests. The Bravos
owned grazing land on both sides of the Río Grande. David and Emma
met at El Rancho Sauz and, after due courtship, obtained their marriage

license on May 24, 1900.[2] Luckily for David, who spoke only Spanish, Emma was bilingual.

Born on May 2, 1901, at El Rancho Sauz, Manuel, the oldest of eight children, spent his early years in a rugged frontier environment. He used a kerosene lamp to do his homework and brought water from the Río Grande for cooking, washing, bathing, and keeping down the dust on the dirt floor.[3] When he finished the daily chores, Manuel went by horseback to watch the steamboats chugging up and down the river. In the Bravos' modest one-room adobe house, he learned both English and Spanish and was exposed to Emma's devout Methodism and to David's zealous Catholicism.[4]

In 1910, the Río Grande flooded the Bravo ranch property, forcing David to move his family and belongings, by mule-driven wagons, to McAllen, a newly established town located a few miles inland and on higher ground.[5] Having begun his rudimentary primary education at El Rancho Sauz, Manuel now continued studying in a one-room segregated Mexican school for Tejano children in the McAllen public school system.[6]

When he had finished the eighth grade in McAllen, Manuel's schooling came to an unfortunate halt. Factors at home played a critical role in determining Manuel's educational fate. The Bravos' economic situation deteriorated during the turmoil of the Mexican revolution, especially since they had familial ties in Mexico. Moreover, his father was not a great believer in books; David was more of a hands-on worker.[7] In trying to make ends meet, Manuel had no choice but to drop out of school and seek employment.

He found a temporary job as a soda jerk in a drugstore in nearby Pharr. In 1917, when he was sixteen years old, his mother arranged for him to leave and work at the drugstore belonging to her brother, John Leslie Box, in Edinburg, the new Hidalgo County seat.[8] Emma was also concerned about Manuel's safety: the increased number of Mexicans migrating to escape the wrath of Porfirio Díaz made the Anglos feel fearful, uncomfortable, and suspicious; but at the same time, the farmers welcomed the cheap labor.

Emma made the right decision in sending young Manuel to live with Uncle John. After the discovery of the Plan de San Diego (a revolutionary plot hatched in 1915 to liberate Tejanos and other minorities from Anglo oppression), Texas Rangers intensified their atrocities, and in some cases, the "executions of 'escaped' suspects were not the only evidence of Anglo retribution. Posses burned homes of suspected raiders and sympathizers, disarmed all Mexicans, and forced them to move into towns where they could be better controlled."[9] Manuel's father was not immune to this type of racial harassment. On one occasion, Emma wrote a letter to the Inspector of Immigration: "This is to certify that my husband David Bravo owns land and livestock on the Mexican side of the Río Grande, which needs his attention, which makes it imperative for him to go and come as he provides for my living and our children too . . . and for that reason I explain the matter to you so you may act fairly towards us."[10] For months, David stayed in Reynosa, Mexico, to avoid being persecuted by the Texas Rangers. He relished the idea of carrying a gun for protection and the Rangers did not fancy this notion.[11]

The pharmacist John Leslie Box may be credited with introducing young Manuel to the machinations of local politics—the Democratic ring. By the time Manuel arrived at his pharmacy, Box had already served as a trustee for five years on the school board. Along with Alfredo N. Vela, A. E. Chávez, and others, John L. Box signed the original application for the incorporation of the city of Edinburg in 1919. Under political boss John Closner's influence, he had even benefitted from political graft.[12]

Box was a strong supporter of the A. Y. Baker Democratic ring. Baker was a ruthless, greedy, and powerful boss in Hidalgo County, just as Archie Parr was in Duval and Jim Wells in Cameron County. His reputation as a tough and mean Texas Ranger preceded him, causing terror among the lower-class Tejanos. He was brought to trial for brutally killing Ramón de la Cerda and his brother in cold blood in 1903, but Jim Wells convinced the jury that Baker had acted in self-defense and won an acquittal for the defendant.[13]

Sheriff Baker blossomed into a kind of urban boss. His ideology of combining politics and business garnered him huge amounts of real estate; a Chrysler dealership; presidency of the Edinburg State Bank and Trust Company, Edinburg Improvement Association, Edinburg Building Company, and Edinburg Hotel Company; and ownership of several large irrigation districts.[14] Critics added the label of "millionaire" to his title of sheriff, and Baker's lavish lifestyle and huge fortune substantiated the accusations.[15]

During his twelve-year reign (1918–30), Baker established alliances with Archie Parr, Jim Wells, Manuel Guerra, and other South Texas bosses. In addition to using patronage and graft for personal gain, the Hidalgo County strongman resorted to all sorts of illegal tactics during elections, controlling people in every county office, city council, school board, road and irrigation district, and county precinct. Corrupt voting practices included paying poll taxes, transporting illegal Mexicans from Reynosa, stuffing ballot boxes, tampering with election returns, and using deputy sheriffs to intimidate voters.[16]

Baker's one-man rule "had gathered into his hands domination of all legislative, executive and judicial functions of the county government."[17] In addition, he controlled two of the county's newspapers: the *McAllen Daily Press* and the *Edinburg Valley Review*. He assumed a paternalistic manner toward his constituents, especially the Tejano laboring class, whose votes he could count on at election time. Farmers were forced to support the Baker ring, otherwise they did not receive the needed irrigation water, and teachers had to purchase school supplies from his approved list of vendors.[18]

Working at his uncle's drugstore produced two fortuitous connections for Manuel. First, he met his future wife, Josefa Villarreal, the sister of John L. Box's second wife, Braulia. Josefa worked as a clerk at the county courthouse, situated directly across the street from the drugstore. When Josefa visited her sister, whether at work or at home, Manuel developed an interest in her.[19] Second, he connected with the A. Y. Baker machine in 1919, when his uncle got him a job with the Valley Abstract Company, a business owned by W. R. Montgomery, who happened to be one of Baker's trusted cohorts. Baker, as president of the Edinburg State Bank and Trust Company, had appointed Montgomery, a one-time state representative for Hidalgo County, to be bank vice president.[20] The job gave Manuel a steady source of income and, after two years of courtship, Manuel married Josefa on October 24, 1919, at the Sacred Heart Catholic Church in Edinburg.

After leaving the Abstract Company, Manuel used the political camaraderie that existed among his Uncle John and Baker's cohorts to obtain a better-paying job. In 1921, Joe Alamía, the county tax collector and a Baker henchman, gave Bravo a job in the county tax assessor and collector's office. Working in the Hidalgo County Courthouse for nine years helped him to establish political ties with more of Baker's lieutenants, in particular with A. E. Chávez, the county clerk. Eventually, Manuel received a promotion to chief deputy in the delinquent tax department. Throughout the decade of the 1920s, Manuel and Josefa worked at the courthouse, and when the family started growing, she quit her job to spend more time rearing their four children, James Edward, Joseph, Aurora, and Manuel, Jr.[21]

EXPANDING HIS POLITICAL BASE

His father had secretly baptized Manuel at the age of three in Mission, Texas, though the lad's mother raised him in the Methodist faith.[22] In due time, Josefa, a devout Catholic, converted Manuel to Catholicism. On April 17, 1921, he officially became a charter member of the Knights of Columbus, Keralum Council No. 2252, in McAllen. Manuel and Joe Alamía, the county tax collector, were the only Hispanics among the forty-three members. Maintaining an active role in the Knights of Columbus and organizing Catholic youth organizations garnered him by 1930 a promotion to district deputy of the 18th district in Texas and grand knight of the local council.[23]

During his tenure as district deputy, Manuel attended many conventions, officiated at degree ceremonies, and initiated new councils throughout the 18th district. Consequently, on Easter Sunday, April 20, 1930, the Knights of Columbus elevated him to a fourth degree, the highest rank of the order. Two fellow knights from McAllen, along with 108 other knights from throughout South Texas, were also promoted at a special ceremony held at St. Peter's Catholic Church in Laredo.[24]

Manuel's involvement with the Knights of Columbus coincided with his active participation in the League of Latin American Citizens, founded in Harlingen in the summer of 1927. The group's ideological purpose was to organize Tejano leaders in an effort to address the issue of racial discrimination so pervasive throughout South Texas on the educational, social, and economic fronts. Along with Manuel, the leadership from the Edinburg Council included J. Alamía, José Barrera, and J. A. Guerra. Prominent leaders from the Lower Río Grande Valley included J. T. Canales, A. Uribe, F. C. Garza, Andrés Longoria, Lazaro Hinojosa, J. Luz Sáenz, and Amado Vera.[25] Soon, councils were established in McAllen, Peñitas, Grulla, Encino, La Salle, Laredo, and Brownsville.

On February 17, 1929, in Corpus Christi, Manuel and other Tejano leaders representing the League of Latin American Citizens met with the leaders of the Order of Sons of America and the Order Knights of

America to merge and coordinate efforts toward founding a statewide organization called the United Latin American Citizens League, later changed to the League of United Latin American Citizens.[26] Manuel became a member of its Supreme Council since he was the leader of the Edinburg chapter, and thus joined the distinguished body that constituted the Executive Board: Ben Garza, president; M. C. González, secretary; J. T. Canales; and J. Luz Sáenz. Before adjourning, the delegates scheduled the first annual convention of LULAC at Corpus Christi for May 18 and 19, 1929, for the purpose of drafting its constitution and by-laws.

The weekend convention at Corpus Christi in May promised a full agenda of business meetings and lectures as well as musical entertainment and a first-class banquet and dance to close the day's activities.[27] On Saturday morning, President Ben Garza appointed a committee of twenty-one delegates to draft the constitution and by-laws. Manuel B. Bravo and J. A. Guerra were selected from the Edinburg council; J. T. Canales from Brownsville; J. Luz Sáenz, McAllen; R. E. Austin and Tristán Longoria, La Grulla; Eugenio Longoria and J. M. Longoria, Encino; and others from San Antonio, Alice, Robstown, Falfurrias, and Corpus Christi. On Sunday afternoon, the convention delegates approved several resolutions before adjourning. Among these were ones naming Alonso S. Perales an honorary president of the organization, selecting Laredo as the next convention site for May 1, 1930, and approving an act of appreciation to J. T. Canales for all his work and dedication to the principles of the organization.[28]

At a special meeting held on Sunday afternoon, June 23, 1929, in McAllen, the LULAC Supreme Council delegates met to approve the by-laws, which were supposed to have been adopted at the May convention in Corpus Christi. Bravo gave the welcome address to twenty-six members representing thirteen councils. Music followed, and next J. T. Canales gave an explanation of the LULAC constitution and by-laws. Prior to the end of the meeting, President Ben Garza appointed the following five-member committee to assist the local councils with developing club by-laws: Manuel B. Bravo, Edinburg; J. T. Canales, Brownsville; Andrés de Luna, Corpus Christi; E. H. Martín, Robstown; and J. Luz Sáenz, McAllen.[29]

Within the next three years, twenty-three LULAC councils were organized throughout the state. The Edinburg council elected Bravo as its president, and with a seven-member planning committee prepared to host the league's third annual convention. Assisting Manuel with preparations for it were J. G. Barrera, P. de la Vina, A. Cavazos, Jr., J. A. Guerra, J. Alamía, D. Candía, and G. E. García. Scheduled for May 3–4, 1931, at the Edinburg College auditorium, the two-day summit provided a mix of business with a little pleasure. In keeping with the tradition of the two previous conventions, a banquet and dance topped the evening agenda. During the day, Alonso Perales, general president of LULAC, delivered the keynote address to more than a thousand delegates. Lecture topics during the course of the gathering ranged from the plight of Tejano children in the public schools to the cultural and historical heritage of Tejanos.[30] The presence of J. T. Canales and J. Luz Sáenz, as always, added a special touch to the overall ambience of the convention since both were highly respected Tejano leaders.

THE ELECTION OF 1932

Manuel's visibility at the leadership helm of the Knights of Columbus and of LULAC expanded his network of Democratic friends throughout Hidalgo County. On a personal level, his loyal support of the Baker regime had paid big dividends when his monthly salary jumped from $60 to $175.[31] However, the Baker ring suffered its first setback during the federal investigation of the November 6, 1928, county election, an episode known in local history as the "Hidalgo County Rebellion."[32] Since the early 1900s, a new influx of northern and midwestern farmers and other residents had questioned Baker's corrupt stranglehold over county politics. These newcomers and anti-Baker Democrats initially organized as the Citizens' Republican League but later became known as the Good Government League (GGL).[33] The Citizens' Republican League charged that Baker, County Judge A. W. Cameron, County Clerk Cam E. Hill, and other public officials had thrown out the whole Weslaco ballot box, allegedly because the envelope containing the ballots had not been sealed, as required by law. The group vehemently argued that discarding the votes deprived the citizens of their civil rights, and thus, Baker had stolen the election from their favorite son, Gordon Griffin—the GGL candidate for district judge. Baker and his cohorts responded by stating that many of the ballots had been mutilated and were no longer valid, and that the GGL intimidation tactics had prevented hundreds of Tejanos from voting.[34]

The scandal brought state and national attention to Hidalgo County politics and, most important, exposed the political shenanigans of Sheriff Baker and his regime. Two significant events boosted the Citizens' Republican League cause. One was Owen P. White's June 22, 1929, article in *Collier's* magazine, entitled "High-handed and Hell-bent," which brought the corrupt county practices of Boss Sheriff Baker to a national audience. In particular, it focused on an eight-mile paved road from McAllen to Hidalgo, dubbed the "Nickel Plated Highway to Hell," because it cost taxpayers an exorbitant one hundred thousand dollars per mile and "ended at a sixty-cent toll bridge, an exclusive franchise owned mostly by A. Y. Baker, which came to a full stop at a saloon and dance hall owned by one of Hidalgo County's public officials."[35]

The other event that attracted statewide publicity against the Baker machine was a dramatic automobile caravan of more than four hundred GGL members, who traveled from Edinburg to the state capitol. Their purpose was to protest Baker's disposal of the Weslaco ballot box and to prove that fraud had been committed in the 1928 election.[36] A congressional committee, pressured by the GGL to investigate the election irregularities, concluded that the evidence against Baker was overwhelming.[37] On February 30, 1930, a federal grand jury indicted Baker and other county officials for depriving citizens (GGL voters) of their right to vote.

Several loyal Democrats jumped ship and supported the Good Government League in the election of 1930. Former staunch Baker backer and Bravo friend Santiago Guzmán, the deputy tax collector, and Joe Alamía, county tax collector, were among those who switched sides. The GGL ran on a reform platform designed to clean up Baker's political machine and rid county politics of bossism. Many Democrats in the GGL and in the Democratic Party tried to settle their differences and reorganize the Democratic Party. Sheriff Baker's stranglehold, however, still allowed him to control nearly every county office. The only recourse available for the dissident Democrats was to remain with the GGL.[38]

On November 1, 1930, just three days from the general election, Baker died unexpectedly at the age of fifty-five, following a stroke. His untimely death coupled with a GGL landslide victory in all county offices signaled the end of boss-controlled politics in Hidalgo County. When the GGL county officials took office on January 1, 1931, Manuel, who had remained loyal to Baker, lost his job at the courthouse.[39] With a wife and four small children to support and unable to find work in the midst of the depression, he became self-employed by representing large and small taxpayers who owed delinquent taxes to the state and/or county. Clients paid him a fee based on the settlement he was able to procure for them. He supplemented his income by selling life insurance for the Southland Life Insurance Company.

At the insistence of J. C. Looney, A. W. Cameron, and A. E. Chávez (former Baker henchmen), his Uncle John, and several prominent Democratic Party leaders, Manuel accepted the nomination in 1932 as a candidate for the office of district clerk, a position his grandfather, Lina H. Box, had occupied sixty-six years earlier.[40] His opponent was the GGL incumbent L. C. Lemen. With Baker dead, the remaining less assertive Democratic Party leaders prepared for the next election. After their humiliating defeat two years earlier, they promptly sought ways to restructure the party into a formidable competitor. By attracting new candidates and portraying an image devoid of bossism, the members wanted to remove Baker's fingerprints from party politics. They worked at restoring trust and confidence in the former supporters who had defected, hoping to win them back into the Democratic fold. In the meantime, the GGL continued its rigorous campaign efforts where it had left off in 1930—exposing the evils of Bakerism and its association with the once ruling party. Some Democrats who had won offices under the GGL ticket switched back to run under the Democratic ticket. D. C. Earnest, the tax assessor, and Santiago Guzmán, county treasurer, both of whom had won in the previous election, ran as Democrats.[41] However, other former Baker lieutenants, sensing the lack of stability in the party, changed sides and now supported the GGL.

Manuel's political career officially began on April 8, 1932, when the *Edinburg Valley Review* announced his candidacy on the Democratic ticket: "I am not a politician, but am making this race on the basis of qualification to serve the people of the county. . . . I believe my previous experience has fitted me to look after the records which are in charge of the district clerk's office."[42] Prior to the July primary, two other Democratic candidates filed against Manuel—H. P. Griffin and Harry Merts.

During the following months, Manuel campaigned vigorously across the county and attended all the political rallies. To broaden his visibility, he assisted other prominent Tejano party leaders in organizing the Latin-American Democratic Women of Hidalgo County. At their first organizational meeting on May 6, 1932, in Edinburg, Manuel spoke on the group's objectives and goals. Then the membership elected new officers: his wife, reporter; Berta Vela, president; Celia T. de Guerra, vice president; Amelia Vela, secretary; and Timotea Cavazos, treasurer.[43] The Women's Good Government League also played a prominent role in campaigning for the GGL candidates and their platform. On May 24, 1932, Manuel joined fellow delegates at the state Democratic convention in Houston.

The July 23 primary election results indicated that Manuel defeated his two fellow Democrats with 3,130 votes, while his opponent, Lemen, easily won the GGL nomination by an overwhelming majority. Out of the many (106) aspiring candidates in both political parties, the Democrats offered six Tejano candidates, while the Good Government League had no Tejanos on its ticket.[44] Along with Bravo, A. E. Chávez, the only other Tejano and former Baker cohort, won his nomination for county treasurer. The general election, scheduled for November 8, 1932, had Manuel campaigning under the catchy slogan—"Elect these Democrats for a New and Better Deal in Hidalgo County. They Stand for Honesty, Economy, Lower Taxes."[45] Manuel, considered one of the leading Tejano contenders, had been carefully handpicked to represent the new, clean, uncorrupted, and boss-free Democratic Party. Even though he had been associated with the Baker ring, he had never been accused of any political wrongdoing. His fellow candidates on the Democratic slate symbolized the reform movement within the party.

Bravo campaigned vigorously among the Tejano communities throughout the county. His liberal political ideology served the party's purposes in attracting the Mexican voters. Already known in Hidalgo County for his LULAC activities, Manuel stood as a stalwart leader and a spokesperson against the conservative Anglo establishment. However, his liberal tendencies did not sit well with the GGL and conservative Democrats, who wanted to maintain control over the social, economic, and political well-being of the Tejano population. The GGL counterpunched by reminding voters about past corrupt elections held by the Baker regime: "Can Hidalgo County Face Such Things as This Nonchalantly and Not Rise Up in 1932 against Boss Control as We Did in 1930," and "Let's finish the job."[46]

The 1932 general election produced a voter turnout among the largest in Hidalgo County's history, with a total of 15,134 votes cast; the Hispanic vote reached a record high of almost 5,000, almost doubling the figure of the 1930 election. Feeling comfortable with the voter turn-out, Democratic Party Chair J. C. Looney optimistically predicted a sweeping Democratic victory in almost all of the county's twenty-one voting precincts.[47] At the national and state levels, key Democrats won electoral races, led by Franklin D. Roosevelt, governor of New York, for president and, in Texas, Miriam "Ma" Ferguson for governor.

In Hidalgo County, however, the Democrats lost every countywide office and precinct post. Incumbent Bill Lemen crushed Bravo by 2,479 votes, while C. H. Pease beat the other Tejano candidate, Chávez, by 1,819 votes.[48] Manuel was defeated in his first political race because, according to Josefa, "a close friend and *compadre,* Humberto Ramírez betrayed Manuel by distributing flyers throughout Hidalgo County, tell-ing people not to vote for Bravo in the general election. . . . He was envi-ous because Manuel won the primary election . . . besides, the [GGL] were anti-Mexican in Edinburg . . . they didn't want a Mexican in the courthouse."[49] Unfortunately for Manuel, there were still some Tejanos who voted for the incumbent, not considering race to be a deciding fac-tor. A key point was that the GGL electorate, composed mainly of wealthy Anglo farmers and growers, businesspersons, and professionals, was thoroughly committed to perpetuating conservative politics. Thus Manuel lost not only because of his liberal principles in racial issues but also because of his past connection with Baker's political machine. Both he and Chávez had been strong Baker supporters and the GGL made sure that the voters were constantly reminded of the corruption and political shenanigans associated with bossism.

Shortly after the election, hard times fell on Manuel and his family. His job was seriously hampered by the Great Depression. He could not make the payments on the new house and ranch he had mortgaged heav-ily to finance his campaign; eventually he lost everything.[50] Disconsolate and in need of work to support his family, Manuel asked former County Judge A. W. Cameron to intercede on his behalf. Cameron wrote to their influential cohort Archie Parr: "Our mutual friend, M. B. Bravo, of Edin-burg, desires to talk some matters over with you and I would appreciate it very much if you will do what you can for him. . . . He has a hard row to travel for the past few months and needs a job as badly as any one I know. He is capable and deserving and I would like to be of some help in getting him something to do. . . . Anything you may be able to do for Bravo will be greatly appreciated by me."[54]

DEPARTURE TO ZAPATA COUNTY

Assistance from Parr and Cameron never came through, and Manuel remained in dire need of employment. In August, 1933, he accepted the suggestion of Josefa's oldest sister, María and her husband, Hesiquio Cuéllar, to move to the town of Zapata, Texas, where the couple lived.[52] Since the Cuéllars owned a profitable mercantile business, they offered him employment and financial assistance. Without any other recourse, Manuel accepted their help and relocated his family to Zapata. He worked part-time in his brother-in-law's business and, on weekends, transported cattle to area markets. From 1933 to 1937, Manuel supplemented the family income by working in several self-employed business ventures, while his two oldest sons helped by working at the Cuéllar mercantile store. At one point in 1935, the sheriff/tax collector of Zapata County, Ygnacio Sánchez, asked him to operate a restaurant and bar called the White House, which Manuel turned into a profitable and successful business operation.[53]

Zapata County is situated between Webb and Starr counties to the north and south respectively, the Río Grande to the west, and Jim Hogg County to the east. Then as now, Zapata County was one of the smallest counties along the Río Grande, having only 1,090 square miles.[54] Created in 1858 from Starr and Webb counties, the unit had undergone two geographical changes: in 1911, a section of Zapata County was politically removed to create part of Brooks County, and in 1913, another chunk was taken to establish Jim Hogg County.

When Bravo arrived—and, for that matter, throughout the time that he served as county judge—Zapata County remained relatively isolated from the rest of South Texas. A high-suspension international bridge, finished in 1931, connected the town of old Zapata to Mexico. The closest Mexican town, Ciudad Guerrero, was about seven miles away on the banks of the Salado River. The construction of railroads during the latter part of the nineteenth century had totally bypassed the county, which therefore, never developed as a commercial port of entry with Mexico. A paved highway connecting the town of Zapata to Laredo—the "gateway to Mexico" in terms of international trade—and to the Lower Río Grande Valley was not constructed until the early 1940s. Until that time, Zapata County was disconnected from the major commercial cities.

In the early 1930s, the settlement of Zapata had a population of about 500 people. Zapata County's population growth had reached its

Table 1. Population Growth by Counties

	Zapata	Starr	Hidalgo	Webb
1860	1,248	2,406	1,182	1,397
1870	1,488	4,154	2,387	2,615
1880	3,636	8,304	4,347	5,273
1890	3,562	10,749	6,534	14,842
1900	4,760	11,469	6,837	21,851
1910	3,809	13,151	13,728	22,503
1920	2,929	11,089	38,110	29,152
1930	2,867	11,409	77,004	42,128
1940	3,916	13,312	106,059	45,916
1950	4,405	13,948	160,446	56,141
1960	4,393	17,137	180,904	64,791
1970	4,352	17,707	181,535	72,859
1987	8,228	36,473	376,558	123,761

Source: Texas Almanac, 1936, 1941–42, 1943–44, 1956–57, 1961–62, 1990–91

peak of over 4,500 inhabitants in 1900, following two decades during which the number of residents had remained stable at about 3,500.[55] At the onset of the depression, many residents had migrated north to the U.S. Midwest and others moved back to Mexico, although none were illegally deported, as was the case in other Río Grande Valley counties. The overall county population in 1930 included approximately 2,967 residents, of whom about six were blacks, forty-five were whites (Anglos), and the rest were native-born Tejanos and Mexican nationals.[56] Some of the few whites had remained from the days of the Mexican American War and the Civil War, while others had recently come to work in the oil fields. From the 1950s to the 1970s, the population would increase to around 4,300 residents; by the 1990s, the population has doubled to about 8,000.[57]

The landscape that greeted the Bravos upon their arrival in 1933 resembled the area where they had lived in Hidalgo County, but was still somewhat different. Mesquite, cacti, ebony, blackbrush, cenizo, catclaw, and huisache covered rolling to broken terrain with hilly areas where the flora thrived on a gray and sandy soil; in the lowlands was reddish chocolate clay. Most of the county's acreage was situated away from the Río Grande and was natural terrain for widespread ranching.[58]

The Zapata County economy during the time when Judge Bravo was politically active (1937–57) was based on irrigation farming, dry-land farming, ranching, businesses, and oil and gas production. Utilizing the Río Grande for irrigation, the farmers tilled about 12,000 acres of lowlands along the Texas-Mexico border, cultivating tomatoes, onions, canteloupes, green peppers, and eggplants. Additional lands located away from the river and toward the center of the county were used for some dry-land farming, and there ranchers took risks, depending on a rainy season in their attempts to harvest cotton, broom corn, rain sorghums, and peanuts. For five years (1935–40), the total cropland remained steady at 11,832 acres, representing about 450 farms altogether.[59] Depending on annual rainfall, the number of farms and tillable acreage fluctuated. For example, there were 329 farms in 1940, 275 between 1945 and 1950, and 310 in 1954. Land under agronomic production went from 9,066 acres in 1940 to 6,195 in 1944; but by 1954, much of the 12,000 acres of farm land along the river had been inundated by the Falcon Dam reservoir.[60] Of the county's approximately 691,200 acres of land area, close to 3 percent was devoted to both types of farming during the period from the 1930s to the mid-1950s.

By contrast, the remaining 97 percent of the county, situated at some distance from the river, accommodated the dominant industry—cattle ranching. Even though sheep ranching was a profitable pursuit, the main source of income was beef cattle with Brahman crosses. The 1940 census data reported a total of 15,332 head of cattle (including calves), 769 sheep and lambs, 62 turkeys, and 2,464 chickens.[61] Five years later, the number of bovine stock had jumped to 33,656, and goats and sheep had increased to 1,897.[62] Some ranchers diversified by investing time and money in dairying, poultry, and the marketing of swine.

More than sixty ranches, varying in acreage, functioned throughout Zapata County during the time Bravo was judge. Some dated back to the eighteenth and nineteenth centuries. Among the best-known ranches from the 1700s were La Lajita, Corralitos, and El Tigre. The most important ones established in the 1800s included Bustamante (Las Comitas), El Clareño, Miraflores, La Perla, El Capitaneño, San Francisco, San Antonio, and San Bartolo.[63]

Ranchers and farmers, as well as other community members, bought their supplies, groceries, and implements at local businesses establishments. Many family-owned stores were scattered throughout the county, with about sixteen of them located in Zapata, the county seat.[64] In the

Table 2. Assessed Valuation and County Tax Rate

	1935	1940	1954–55
Zapata	2,949,530 – $ .95	3,857,953 – n/a	4,532,755 – $1.25
Starr	4,012,109 – 1.61	5,661,095 – n/a	28,487,030 – 1.50
Webb	19,414,958 – .75	21,397,102 – n/a	41,848,092 – 2.65
Hidalgo	34,661,657 – .86	35,150,139 – n/a	102,690,252 – 1.10

Source: Texas Almanac, 1936, 1941–42, 1956–57

---

early 1930s, these small enterprises included five grocery stores, two gasoline service stations, one blacksmith shop, a small hotel, and assorted businesses. In 1938, the yearly retail sales amounted to $140,000; two years later, they dropped to $116,000, but after World War II, sales jumped from $222,000 to $330,000.[65] After the completion of Falcon Dam in 1953, the construction of new homes and an increase in business caused retail sales to skyrocket to almost $1,154,000.

The last important contributor to Zapata County's economy during Judge Bravo's tenure was oil and gas production. When the judge took office in 1937, the oil companies were producing 991,068 barrels a year. By 1944, the number of barrels had fallen to 847,539, and it continued to decrease; two years later, it was 573,672 barrels annually. However, by 1954, the oil fields yielded 870,489 barrels. There are no census data available on gas drilling or the revenues realized.[66]

For many years, Zapata County's ranchers, merchants, and farmers were among the leading families, influencing all aspects of life in the county. Many Zapata families were direct descendants of the original Spanish land grant recipients who settled the colonial town of Revilla, renamed Ciudad Guerrero in 1827, and over the course of time these families had helped shape frontier life by actively participating in all the endeavors that contributed to the growth and development of the area on the east bank of the Río Grande.[67]

Therefore the leading families—the Cuéllars, Treviños, Velas, Yzaguirres, Uribes, González, Ramírez, Martínez, Flores, Medina, Garza, and others—exerted a considerable influence over the social, economic, and political structure of the county. In terms of social classes, the ranchers, landowners, merchants, and farmers comprised the upper crust; from this stratum came the people who were actively involved in the social and civic activities of the county and of South Texas. They did not have to contend with discrimination. The few white males married into the elite Tejano families, and to a great degree became culturally and linguistically Mexicanized.[68] If any social discrimination existed, it was between the landowners and the lower class laborers.

The sociological features of Zapata County conform to what social scientists have ascertained about political life there. In his study of South Texas counties, for example, David Montejano categorized Zapata County in 1930, as well as Jim Hogg, Brooks, Webb, Duval, and Starr, as "Mexican counties," mainly because Tejano landowners dominated them and ranching was the primary activity. Conversely, the "Anglo counties" were dominated by whites and included Hidalgo, Cameron, Kenedy, Kleberg, Jim Wells, Willacy, and Nueces counties.[69] In the Mexican counties, the Tejano majority dominated local politics and were elected to public offices. The reverse was true of Anglo counties, where few if any Tejanos held public office. Zapata County's social, political, and economic history appears to validate Montejano's thesis.

William Curtis Bryson in "The Social Basis of South Texas Bossism" draws another interesting comparison between South Texas counties that depended on irrigated agriculture and those where people's livelihood was based on a ranching economy. For the most part, he noted, the irrigated agriculture counties have remained "boss-free," while the ranching counties have a reputation for being "boss-ridden."[70]

Bryson categorized Zapata County as a boss-ridden county, along with Duval, Starr, Webb, and Kenedy. Among boss-free South Texas counties, he included Hidalgo, Cameron, and eight others.[71] Bryson used several criteria based on sixty-one election returns between 1887 and 1966 to arrive at his conclusions. The boss-controlled counties had more participation by Tejanos in local politics, showed a greater increase in purchases of the poll tax, and had an absence of discrimination and racial segregation of students.[72] The opposite was true of the boss-free counties.

Thus, it appears that bossism thrived mainly in Tejano counties where Mexican Americans were involved in holding public office and active in the electorate process. The political machines in Zapata, Webb, and Starr counties viewed the Tejanos (whom they had integrated along with the Anglos and other groups into the mainstream of politics, education, and business), as a bloc political force, which they could deliver in the range of 80 to 95 percent for their candidates. In Anglo counties that did not have bossism (Dimmit, Zavala, and Nueces), Tejanos were in the minority, socially and educationally segregated, viewed as an economic commodity to be exploited by way of cheap farm labor, and discouraged from participating in politics. These counties usually gave their candidates about 50 to 60 percent of the votes, which reflected a more equitable distribution of votes (as compared to the boss-controlled counties).

Despite Bryson's observations, politics in the Mexican or boss-ridden counties could vary. In many ways, Zapata County resembled Webb and Starr. Both of these latter counties had influential ruling families. In Webb County, the Benavides, Sánchez, Martin, Puig, Casso, Guerra, Leyendecker, Bruní, Montemayor, and other families controlled social, political, and economic affairs. In Starr County, the Guerra family ruled almost like an oligarchy for generations. All three counties were predominantly Tejano and had high illiteracy rates and excessive poverty levels, features that enabled the political machine to dictate voting practices. These several ranching counties also had a high number of Tejano landowners.

In contrast with Zapata County, however, Webb and Starr were not geographically isolated from the mainstream of American business enterprises. Both counties had railroads connecting them with major cities, which expanded their mercantile, farming, and ranching industries. Especially in Webb County, the railroad extended not only to San Antonio and Corpus Christi but also into Mexico by way of Nuevo Laredo. With many Anglo newcomers entering into the business sector, the economy gradually expanded to other ventures: oil and gas fields and the import-export business.

Zapata County had its first political boss in Angus Peter Spohn, an adventurous Canadian-born young man who worked as a ranch hand and later joined the United States Customs Service. In the 1880s, he married Juana Estrada in Encinal, Texas. Spohn was the last Anglo to serve as county judge (1898–21) after the state created Zapata County. Prior to his election, four other Anglos had intermittently served in that capacity for much shorter terms.[73]

During his reign, the county "went consistently Republican at every election, state, national and local . . . with himself as its undisputed king, an oligarchy in a rock-ribbed Democratic state."[74] With the support of the leading Tejano families, Spohn often opposed the influence of well-known Democratic boss Jim Wells. It was during Spohn's tenure that the county underwent realignment of its geographical boundaries. This was a political maneuver by Anglo ranchers in the northern section of Starr and Hidalgo counties, who wished to remove themselves from the Tejano influence.[75] The border-ruling Tejano families of Zapata and Starr counties controlled the public offices, and Anglos refused subordination.

After Spohn died on May 30, 1921, at the age of sixty-seven, the political machine returned to the Democratic Party under the leadership of newly appointed County Judge José M. Sánchez, and supported Democrat John W. Davis over Calvin Coolidge in the 1924 presidential race. Sánchez had served as district and county clerk for ten years before his appointment. He performed the duties of county judge for about seven years (1921–28), until he was succeeded by Antonio Victor Navarro on November 6, 1928.[76] The Democratic-controlled faction kept a close, tight grip on local politics. From the 1922 election until 1937 when Manuel Bravo became county judge, the political machine consisted of Primitivo Uribe, José M. Sánchez, Benjamin Martínez, Federico Cuéllar, Leopoldo Martínez, Proceso Martínez, Jr., Guillermo González, Manuel Medina, Ygnacio Sánchez, and Santos Yzaguirre.[77]

The death of Angus Peter Spohn marked the decline of the Republican party as a competitive faction in local politics. It was not until the 1952 election, thirty-one years later, that the Republican Santiago González finally defeated Guillermo González (his uncle) for county commissioner of precinct 3.[78] Santiago won the election but had run on the Democratic party ticket, reverting to his Republican Party affiliation after the election. Over the years, many hopeful Republicans tried to crack the Democratic political machine by running on the ballot as Democrats, but voters saw through their tactic and voted against them. Zapata County waited fifty-three years for the next Republican county judge. Jake Rathmell, a well-known Republican and chairman of the Republican Party, won the November 5, 1974, election unopposed. He too ran as a Democrat on the Democratic Party ticket but disclosed his true loyalty upon winning.

Cautiously at first, but with mounting confidence, Manuel Bravo became active in Zapata community activities and in local Democratic Party politics. In Zapata County, the Democratic Party was synonymous with the Partido Viejo (Old Party). In the early 1920s discontented Democrats joined forces with the Republican Party to form the Partido Nuevo (New Party). Both parties attracted sympathizers from the leading families as well as from the laboring class, but the Partido Viejo always remained stronger. The few whites divided their allegiance between the two camps.

The political ideologies of the parties were markedly different. The Partido Viejo's platform during the 1930s consisted of several realistic, down-to-earth objectives: more jobs; better farm roads; improved education; greater federal assistance; newer progressive ideas; and an efficient, experienced, and honest administration.[79] Conversely, the Partido Nuevo's platform pushed for lofty, idealistic and often quixotic goals: adherence to democratic principles; better government and less politics; equal opportunities for all, regardless of social status; accountability; an all-out offensive on bossism and the political machine; and unity.[80]

In terms of party identification, the Partido Nuevo played the Mexican song of "Las Coronelas" at every election. The Partido Viejo also had its own identifiable musical piece to rally the voters in every campaign. The *Botas* and the *Guaraches* in Webb County were recognized by their respective symbols (boots and sandals), and in the Lower Río Grande Valley, the Democrats identified with the color blue and the Republicans with red.

The Partido Viejo managed to survive elections and maintain its hegemony over local politics by employing creative political strategies. First, the party leaders brought new blood into the political machine. In the late 1920s, the Democratic ring recruited A. V. Navarro, Ygnacio Sánchez, Santos Yzaguirre, and Juventino Martínez. By the early 1930s, Guillermo González, Adán Gutiérrez, and Manuel Medina got elected to the county commissioners' court.[81] Second, the political leaders changed offices frequently, and some pulled double duty in two positions. This maneuver helped them to control their political base. The third strategy of the Partido Viejo was to fill the precinct offices with trusted acquaintances and/or relatives (sometimes women) of the elected officials. Patronage, equal gender participation, and loyalty at the grassroots level assured the party of controlling, and if necessary, manipulating, the election returns. Finally, the four county commissioners also sat on the Zapata County Independent School District board of trustees. They controlled not only county workers but also the vote of the school district employees. At the helm of the school district board was the county judge, acting as the ex-officio superintendent. The commissioners were even appointed to manage the improvements of the roads in their own precincts! The same members, including the judge, also assigned themselves to the Board of Equalization.[82]

Through his brother-in-law's political ties, Bravo started associating with the county's Partido Viejo leaders, earning their confidence and gradually fitting into their local political circle. It was not easy for him to forget his friends and the political setback he had experienced in Hidalgo County, especially when one close friend reminded him that he had "more friends in Hidalgo County, than . . . in Zapata. You do not know this, but you are very well thought of in Hidalgo county, more so among the people that remember the double-cross that you got from you[r] *compadre.*" [83]

In the 1934 Democratic primary, nonetheless, he actively campaigned for the incumbents, who easily won reelection to all county and precinct offices. A year later, he was selected to serve as secretary of the Zapata Athletic Club, of which Rafael San Miguel, Jr., was president and Manuel Medina treasurer. The thirteen-member club board included the political leaders Matías Cuéllar, county judge; A. V. Navarro, county/district clerk; Leopoldo Martínez, sheriff/tax collector; Ygnacio Sánchez; and former county judge J. M. Sánchez. Moreover, Manuel's fifteen-year experience with delinquent taxes in Hidalgo County proved to be an asset, as his help was frequently requested in the county tax office.[84] He maximized his position within the Partido Viejo's inner political circle by using his oral and written fluency in English and Spanish, an asset the ruling politicos liked, since not all of them were bilingual. Bravo witnessed that bossism also existed in Zapata County, mainly because as in Hidalgo County, a small group of politicos formed a ring to control the infrastructure. But in Zapata County, the ruling families were related by blood and marriage to the founding settlers, whereas in Hidalgo County, the ruling Anglo politicians were not related to the descendants of the original Spanish or Mexican landowners. This major difference led the Democratic factions in the respective counties to take on distinctively different political ideologies.

In the early part of January, 1936, the county qualified for participation in the Works Progress Administration (WPA), a federally funded effort designed to stimulate the national economy by providing employment for the construction of public buildings, bridges, and hard-surfaced roads. The county commissioners approved $3,000 in matching funds in order to apply for a $25,800 grant to upgrade the quality of three roads that led out in an easterly direction from Zapata, San Ygnacio, and Lopeño.[85] Without any opposition, the county commissioners approved Manuel's application for the position of road supervisor, a post that was a WPA prerequisite for funding, effective February 1, 1936. Faced with impending deadlines, the new appointee prepared and submitted the required paperwork to the Texas Planning Board of the WPA. After a period of negotiations, the county received approval of $28,000 for the road projects, another $22,000 for improvements to school buildings, and an additional $15,000 to renovate the courthouse and jail.[86] Periodically, Bravo presented status reports on the projects at commissioners' court meetings.

THE 1936 ELECTION CAMPAIGN

In the fall of 1936, the most influential Democratic leaders in Zapata County—J. M. Sánchez, Leopoldo Martínez, Ygnacio Sánchez, and Manuel Medina (known as the "Big Four")—strongly cajoled thirty-five-year-old Bravo to accept the candidacy for county judge, even though Judge Antonio V. Navarro, the incumbent, had easily won the party's primary election. Of the Big Four, Medina, a businessman, was the youngest at twenty-six, followed by Martínez, a rancher, at thirty-seven, Sánchez, another rancher with extensive landholdings, at forty-three, and the elder Ygnacio, a merchant with oil interests, at forty-eight years of age. This was the political machine, a close-knit organization that, using patronage and alleged corruption at the polls, maintained control over the county's sociopolitical and economic network. Despite Navarro having been county judge since 1926, the rank and file of the Democratic Party along with the Big Four expressed dissatisfaction with his administration.[87] On the eve of the November 3 general election, the fifty-year-old Navarro, quietly and without offering the media any explanation, withdrew from the election. Bravo's name was a write-in on the ballot. In almost anticlimactic fashion, Bravo easily won the election with 227 votes. Navarro garnered forty-one, and León Ramírez only one vote.[88]

Exactly what happened in the local political cauldron that caused Judge Navarro to resign hours before the general election? He had won the Democratic primary in July, faced no opposition, and offered no explanations, except that he wanted to retire from politics. Given the timing of his resignation, the people voted exactly how the machine had wanted, with no confusion at the polls. Not knowing the internal political situation, leaders in neighboring Webb County expressed total surprise at Navarro's last-minute decision.[89] Judge Navarro's "sudden" resignation was certainly not the norm in South Texas politics, and perhaps historians will never know the truth about it. The *Laredo Times* did not publish a follow-up story after the general election. After his resignation, Navarro and his family relocated to Laredo, Texas.

Manuel's meteoric rise to the top of the Zapata County's Democratic machine deserves some theoretical explanation. First, Navarro no longer fulfilled the future needs of the county. The machine—the Big Four—wanted Bravo to be the successor and told Navarro to go public officially with his resignation just before the election. This scheme prevented other contenders outside the machine from politicking for the position. Second, Bravo represented "new blood" for the betterment of the political machine. Moreover, his own vision and purpose as regards where and how he wanted to lead the county were congruent with the plans of the Big Four. Third, Bravo's family ties with Hesiquio Cuéllar had opened social, economic, and political contacts with the political machine. Fourth, Bravo's background fitted him out well. His experience in Hidalgo County's ruthless and corrupt Baker regime might have led him to become more perceptive, ambitious, and opportunistic, forcing Navarro to resign. His successful handling of the WPA projects impressed the county leaders. His previous active involvement as leader of the Edinburg LULAC council and the Knights of Columbus gave him credibility, visibility, and a reputation as a charismatic and articulate spokesperson. Finally, according to the 1920 U.S. Census, Navarro spoke only Spanish, and the county leaders needed a more assertive, bilingual leader to carry them through upcoming changes in the county.[90] Bravo's proficiency in both English and Spanish, oral and written, added a leadership quality that the political machine needed to bring more jobs, to seek federal assistance for needed rural projects, and to represent the county in the transactions with the federal government in the impending construction of Falcon Dam.[91]

BOSSISM AND LULAC

Bravo's association with the A. Y. Baker machine and his rise within the Democratic Party in Hidalgo County ultimately paved the way for his successful 1936 election run in Zapata County. Although he had by then lived in Zapata County for just three years, he had already developed linkages to the Big Four and he was soon part of the ruling Partido Viejo. As the newly elected county judge, Bravo now assumed total responsibility and control over the local political machine.

Certainly Bravo's career had profited from South Texas bossism, and his participation in it begs the question: What was his political outlook or philosophy toward boss rule? Growing up in a segregated society in Hidalgo County, the goals of LULAC had appealed to him as a means for fighting racism, school segregation, and bossism, among other social and political problems. If LULAC "explicitly rejected such conventional activities as participation in electoral politics, bloc voting, or the formation of an ethnic political machine," then what explanation is there for Judge Bravo's involvement with the Baker regime and with the Zapata's Big Four?[92] Did he subscribe to the LULAC perspective that bossism was unethical? Or did he see bossism as a vehicle to deal with the same issues that LULAC wanted to resolve?

At first, Bravo's personal ambition—to become associated with the Baker ring and later with Zapata's Big Four—did not contradict LULAC tenets. The restrictions against bossism and involvement in partisan politics were meant for the organization as a collective group, and not for individual members. As one student of the organization notes: "Ultimately political decision making and participation were properly an individual affair. . . . At most the league's purpose was to prepare individual Mexican Americans to participate in electoral politics and community affairs, but only as individuals."[93] Bravo's personal approach was to use bossism to reach some of LULAC's goals.

Second, he became involved with bossism as a way of dealing with the same issues that LULAC wanted to address. Running as a reformed Democrat in the 1932 election, he truly felt that the Democratic Party, which consisted of both Anglos and Tejanos, would serve Mexican American social, economic, educational, and political needs, given the realities of racial discrimination. In Zapata County, none of the discriminatory practices that Bravo had experienced in Hidalgo County existed (subconsciously, he may have wanted acceptance by the dominant Anglo society in Texas; after all, his mother and his uncle John were Anglos). But the Zapata LULAC council also supported all the statewide efforts that the parent organization advocated. Therefore, his association with the Big Four was an opportunity not only to advance his own political career but also to work within the established power structure to bring about much needed relief from the economic and educational problems the county and its predominantly Mexican American citizens were experiencing.

POLITICS OF PERSUASION AND CHANGE

D uring his first two terms in office, Judge Bravo accomplished a number of projects and initiated a series of improvements in county affairs. This chapter sheds light on the complex political intrigues that occurred inside the Zapata and Webb county machines. Despite vicious attacks from the Partido Nuevo (PN), Bravo succeeded in consolidating his power and streamlining his political machine. Moreover, he used the "Frontier Hilation," an event that combined politics with social activities, to place Zapata County on the map. Most important, he helped bring about completion of the highway that connected Webb with Starr County. Finally, Bravo established a long-lasting mutual friendship with Lyndon B. Johnson.

In the early years of his tenure as county judge, from 1937 to 1941, Judge Bravo faced many challenges in county affairs that necessitated the use of different leadership approaches. Contrary to the stereotypical boss who delved into the taxpayers' money for personal gain, he sought to maintain an image of financial incorruptibility in the county. In dealing with the politics of the 49th district and Webb County's powerful Independent Club, on the other hand, Judge Bravo played the role of a Machiavellian manipulator. He stood ready to do whatever it took to keep the Partido Viejo (PV) in power. He learned to reciprocate with neighboring county judges; the Frontier Hilation was an excellent example of three county heads working together in a harmonious political triumvirate. Judge Bravo quickly familiarized himself with the politics of the oil and

gas companies and through his persuasive approach allowed these interest groups to continue financing and supporting the Partido Viejo. Conversely, correspondence in the Bravo Papers provides a small but
interesting glimpse into the judge's paternalistic approach toward the local citizens.

CHANGES IN EDUCATION

On January 1, 1937, Manuel B. Bravo at the age of thirty-five officially
became the twelfth Zapata County judge and ex-officio county superintendent of schools, with an annual combined salary set at fifteen hundred
dollars plus a three-hundred-dollar travel allowance. From his office, located on the second floor of the two-story sandstone county courthouse
in Zapata, Judge Bravo, in tandem with the other county officials,
planned, coordinated, and set into motion a series of countywide improvements to upgrade the operation of county government and to keep
it within the law.[1] He had learned such lessons from his political career
in Hidalgo County.

The Zapata County Democratic political machine controlled county
business affairs through the county commissioners, and educational matters by way of the school board. Judge Bravo was head of both public
entities. As the ex-officio superintendent of schools, he had a partisan
county school board, whose members also sat on the commissioners'
court.

At the county school board's first meeting after Judge Bravo's installation, he "pointed out to this Board the fact that there existed no Record
of School Districts, Minutes of this Boards of County School Trustees,
and Records of School Funds . . . nor a Register of Vouchers issued and
approved for the several School Districts of this County."[2] Consequently,
Judge Bravo requested the purchase and use of the following items: a
journal to be used by the secretary to keep the minutes of all meetings, a
ledger for funds and vouchers, and another record book to keep track of
any work orders affecting the two school districts. The trustees agreed
on a procedure for maintaining sound financial responsibility in all expenditures incurred by the county, and adopted a system for monitoring
the inventory of school equipment and supplies, since there was no financial management system.[3] To guarantee good management practices
and to ensure the machine's control over business vendors, the board
appointed Judge Bravo to serve as the county's purchasing agent.

Next on the judge's agenda was upgrading the deplorable condition of the one-room schoolhouses throughout the county. These academies were no more than *jacales* (huts), often with rotting wood and cracked floors and walls. They lacked heaters and inside plumbing, used old desks (sometimes benches served as escritoires), and had a limited supply of blackboards.[4] To make matters worse, there were some isolated ranches and farms that had ten or more eligible children but no instructional facilities. As the need for additional classroom space arose, especially in remote settlements that were miles away from the nearest existing educational edifice, the county board of trustees established one-room schoolhouses. For instance, with enough students identified in grades one through seven at the Primavera Ranch, another elementary building was erected on October 4, 1937.[5] Throughout the 1940s, more and improved places of learning replaced the deteriorating one-room structures.

In order to meet state statutory requirements, Judge Bravo on May 10, 1937, reclassified the county schools, arranging them into the elementary "common school" grades of one through seven and the high school grades of eight through eleven. The boundaries of the two school districts were simultaneously geographically redrawn.[6]

Four years later, Bravo initiated the planning process to hold Zapata County's first bond election for constructing additional schools and upgrading the existing ones in Common School District No. 1.[7] On September 8, 1941, the citizens of precincts 1, 3, and 4 overwhelmingly supported the bond election by 117 to 64 votes. Unfortunately for the children, the outcome of the bond election was held up in litigation for over a year. This was because Cesario P. Flores, a successful rancher with extensive landholdings, and eleven other influential taxpayers filed suit against Judge Bravo, the four county commissioners, and the trustees of the school board, protesting an order that had redefined the boundaries of Common School District No. 1. The suit contested "the legality of the district as it existed and now exists, which was based on orders that should have been recorded by the Commissioners Court back in 1895 and 1911, but which were not recorded."[8] If the school district boundaries were not legal, the plaintiffs argued, then the bond election was null and void.

The 49th District Court ruled in favor of Judge Bravo and the commissioners and trustees. This was anticipated since the prosecuting district attorney, Philip A. Kazen, and Manuel J. Raymond, Webb County's judge and attorney for the Zapata school officials, belonged to the political ring in Webb County that had ties to the machine in Zapata County. On appeal, the Court of Civil Appeals and the Texas Supreme Court ruled in favor of the plaintiffs.[9] At their October 21, 1942, meeting, the Board of County School Trustees authorized Tax Collector Leopoldo Martínez to refund to taxpayers the 1941 school taxes paid to Common School District No. 1. With the oil companies, however, Judge Bravo thought of a clever scheme. He would refund the oil companies and then they in turn could endorse the checks back to the county "to be used for the benefit of the schools and to apply on the cost of litigation to the time of the dismissal of the suit."[10]

Judge Bravo wrote letters to all the oil companies explaining the status of the suit and how his idea of using their 1941 taxes could still benefit the students. All the companies agreed and expressed a need to support the county: "It is our desire to cooperate with you in this matter, because we have confidence in your judgement in this matter and in the things you are trying to accomplish."[11] Judge Manuel J. Raymond's suggestion to have the contributions made out in his name (for unknown reasons) was not well received by the oil companies; they preferred to follow the arrangements as previously agreed upon with Judge Bravo. This charitable act on the part of the oil companies was not totally out of the goodness of their hearts. The donations were more than likely tax deductions and write-offs. In good faith, they wanted to support the judge's efforts to improve the educational system. As one oil company man noted, "The County had, up to a few years ago, had practically no schools; however, since Judge Bravo became interested in the school situation there had been a distinct change for the better."[12] But their more realistic rationale for returning the checks as a contribution was in gratitude, "in so much as the assessment of oil properties has been handled without the necessity of the Board of Equalization and since the County had been run so economically."[13]

On other educational fronts, Judge Bravo implemented more improvements, which proved less time-consuming and expensive than the bond election lawsuit. Though he was forced to hire college students as teachers because of the lack of funds required to pay teachers' salaries, the college students eventually worked toward their degrees in the summer and continued teaching in Zapata. Further, Judge Bravo surrounded himself with three key educators whose extensive knowledge and work experience in public education was invaluable. He contracted the services of Miss Florence Baker, who was A. Y. Baker's sister; Mrs. Jewel Walker, who later was named principal; and Leo J. Leo, all from Hidalgo County. Moreover, the school district hired more certified teachers, in the process improving the quality of learning and gaining full accreditation from the Texas Education Agency (TEA) in the 1950s. Judge Bravo's vision for a better education system had finally materialized. As Mercurio Martínez, county historian, succinctly concluded in 1953 of the Zapata County school system, "Judge Bravo lifted [it] from a third-rate, poorly-housed and poorly managed system. . . . One who knew the schools in Zapata twenty years ago cannot help but marvel at the changes here today."[14]

County voters had by then unified the two common school districts— 190 votes to zero—into the present Zapata County Independent School District. At a county school board meeting on August 2, 1949, Judge Bravo appointed his political allies as the first trustees for the new district: Leopoldo Martínez, president; Proceso Martínez, secretary; Manuel Medina, treasurer; Guillermo González; and Félix Ramos.[15] All were powerful friends and important figures in the county. They came from old founding families whose economic interests involved farming, ranching, and business. As such, these people exerted political and economic weight throughout the area.

REFINING COUNTY AFFAIRS

Since the early 1920s, the county treasurer had made no attempts to maintain records of or to report on the financial status of the county treasury. No records existed to show the taxpayers how much revenue came in or how much was spent on what projects.[16] This accountability dilemma placed Judge Bravo and the Democratic party leaders in a delicate and vulnerable situation. One-page political flyers published by the Partido Nuevo exposed these countywide shortcomings. Bravo was well aware that similar dubious practices used in Hidalgo County had cost the Democratic Party the elections in 1930 and 1932.

As a result of Judge Bravo's efforts to convince the Democratic leaders to make the necessary changes, on August 12, 1940, the county commissioners approved his recommendation to employ an independent auditor "to make an audit of all money received and paid by the County Treasurer . . . [and] of warrants issued by the County clerk."[17] Bravo contacted Charles D. Turner, his old political ally from Hidalgo County and A. Y. Baker's independent county auditor. Baker had originally hired Turner to oversee and monitor the expenditures of the Hidalgo County treasury. Turner's contract was terminated in 1932 when the GGL took over all county offices, but he continued to house his office at Baker's State Bank building in Edinburg.

About a month later, the county commissioners approved Judge Bravo's recommendation of contracting with the accounting firm of Charles D. Turner to perform an independent audit of all county financial transactions from January 1, 1939, to July 31, 1940. The commissioners also asked Turner to suggest a system for maintaining auditable and accurate records which "will be helpful to the officers of Zapata County in serving the best interests of its taxpayers and citizens." [18] Judge Bravo wanted Turner to set up a finance ledger for the county clerk and to bring the county into the twentieth century and out of the old practice of paying for expenditures (mostly in cash) with no receipts to allow for an audit trail. The commissioners agreed unanimously to pay Turner five hundred dollars for his services. If the county bosses had anything to hide, at least they would now have to do it legally.

After Turner had completed the audit, a political rift occurred between him and Manuel Medina, the co-owner of the Zapata bank. Medina reneged on the contractual agreement and suggested that Turner be paid four hundred dollars.[19] District Attorney Philip Kazen had convinced some of the commissioners that Turner was not a qualified public accountant capable of conducting county audits.[20] As a matter of fact, Turner was on the state-approved list of public accountants and one of the few permitted to handle federal income tax cases.

Where did Judge Bravo stand during this raucous encounter? It appears that the judge was neutral in this awkward situation since Turner, on two occasions, asked for his advice: "I would appreciate it Manuel if you would be kind enough to write me and tell me if you would prefer that I bring suit. Or let me know what you think I should do." [21] Judge Bravo requested Leo C. Buckley, the county attorney, to render an opinion on the matter. There is no record in the commissioners' court minutes or in the Bravo Papers of this issue being settled or of the whereabouts of the audit report. This encounter, however, marked the beginning of a lasting political relationship between the Kazen brothers from Laredo and Zapata County's Partido Viejo.

The judge also found questionable practices in the bookkeeping used by the county/district clerk. In an effort to acquire technical assistance and guidance, Judge Bravo called upon the Laredo Bar Association to appoint a special select committee, chaired by Nat B. King, and to include Frank Y. Hill and Bismark Pope.[22] In a meeting held on May 4, 1942, the county commissioners and the judge asked Matías Cuéllar, the county/district clerk, to inform them on "the methods by which your office safeguards and files the records of the District and County Courts and instruments delivered to you as recorder."[23]

In the area of delinquent property taxes, Judge Bravo's previous experience in the Hidalgo County delinquent tax department helped him to establish solutions to what might otherwise have remained a political hot potato. In prior years the county had been lax in collecting taxes and many county citizens did not make an effort to pay them. An unsuccessful attempt at collecting back taxes had been made in 1929, when commissioners solicited the legal services of Laredo attorney Manuel J. Raymond. When he requested 20 percent of the collected taxes, however, the county leaders backed out.[24] Judge Bravo thus took another approach—employed from July 31, 1937, to December 31, 1938—to collecting delinquent taxes: with the approval of the county commissioners, he appointed Laredo attorney Charles H. Kazen (the oldest of the Kazen brothers) to assist in the matter. This unexpected announcement brought a flurry of criticisms from the opposing Partido Nuevo faction.

In a one-page propaganda flyer, the PN felt strongly that the citizens of Zapata should be given at least one year's tax notice. This grace period would allow taxpayers enough time to find the necessary funds to pay their delinquent debts. Under the PV guidelines, property owners were given only thirty days in which to meet their obligations.[25] The flyer concluded by telling they were being governed in a callous manner and asking them to vote at the next election for those candidates who would free them from bossism. While the opposition blamed the ruling Democratic Party leaders for the injustice in the plan of collecting delinquent taxes, Judge Bravo, who had been in office for only one year, received much of the criticism.[26]

Another area of improvement that benefitted the entire county was a program of road construction. The need for building and maintaining an effective road system throughout the county prompted Hesiquio Cuéllar and fifty-seven other prominent ranchers and farmers to submit a petition to the county commissioners for a road bond election scheduled for December 12, 1940.[27] Unlike the ill-fated school construction bond, this one was a huge success (240 votes for the bond and 27 against). Judge Bravo next appointed the county commissioners as ex-officio road super-intendents and to the Board of Equalization.[28] As supervisors of the county roads, they approved jobs for their loyal supporters in their own precincts and also awarded work contracts.

In health-related matters, the judge convinced county officials that there existed a dire need for a county doctor. This idea was not new. From time to time the county did hire a physician to oversee all health-related issues. However, this position had not been filled for some time, mainly because few doctors were willing to establish a practice in a rural county. It simply was not a profitable market. On May 10, 1937, the commissioners approved Judge Bravo's recommendation and renewed Dr. W. A. Harper's contract as the county health officer.[29] Three years later, the county faced the same dilemma when Dr. Harper resigned. But it obtained the services of Dr. Lauro Montalvo, who served in this capac-ity until his induction into the armed forces during World War II. After his tour of military duty ended in 1945, Montalvo returned to his old office of county doctor.

Judge Bravo also made changes in the administration of the county commissioners' proceedings. Immediately upon taking office, he sched-uled the commissioners' meetings to occur once a week. His predecessor, Judge Navarro, had held these every fortnight. Another important im-provement was the specification in the minutes that expenses be itemized and that the funding source be identified. On yellow notepads, he kept handwritten minutes of all the commissioners court meetings. These were later typed and filed in the courthouse. The commissioners estab-lished several new budget line-item categories, such as the general fund, road and bridge, courthouse and jail, etc. In August, 1937, the commis-sioners' court authorized itself to transfer surplus monies from one ac-count to another.[30] Judge Bravo had met in Austin in June with the Board of County and District Road Indebtedness to obtain an excess amount of over two thousand dollars, and he now wished to transfer these re-sources to the general fund. Though J. M. Sánchez questioned the proce-dure, the commissioners agreed with Bravo.

ELECTION CAMPAIGN OF 1938

Both political factions started their campaign almost nine months before the July 23, 1938, Democratic primary. The ruling Democratic PV filled the slate with prominent citizens. The PN candidates (also mainly ranchers and merchants but including some common folks) were Republicans, but their only chance of winning was as Democrats during the primary; when the general election came around in November, they—as Republicans—had little opportunity of getting elected against the powerful ruling Democratic Party machine. It was Judge Bravo's first reelection campaign, and already he had to avert the attacks against his administration. Through their propaganda flyers, the PN kept hammering on the issues of misuse of county taxes and lack of accountability from the county treasurer. They accused the machine of being antiquated, incompetent, and self-centered. Using a platform titled "Better Government and Less Politics," they promised if elected to have responsible public officials and to run an accountable and fair administration.[31]

PV members gathered their strong supporters as they braced for a rough, tough, and dirty political campaign. All the PV county officials faced PN opponents. The latter slate included Conrado Lozano for county judge; Alberto Treviño, county/district clerk; J. M. Salinas, sheriff/tax assessor; Trinidad Uribe, treasurer; Adán Gutiérrez, commissioner, precinct 1; Amado Ramírez, commissioner, precinct 2; León J. Ramírez, commissioner, precinct 3; Tomás McDermott, commissioner, precinct 4; and all four justices of the peace. These politicians were also related to the county's influential families.

Wasting no time, Bravo's political machine hurried to finish up county improvements and to defuse their opponents' criticisms. The PV candidates campaigned energetically throughout the county, soliciting votes from WPA workers and even threatening them with losing their jobs if they voted for the opposition.[32] A month before the primary, the PN's campaign against the political machine got so heated that Judge Bravo contemplated the possibility of carrying a firearm for protection.[33]

Rumors of voting improprieties and fraud by PN members prompted Judge Bravo to obtain advice from Leo C. Buckley, the county attorney, on the best legal methods to choose election supervisors for each of the four voting precincts.[34] The machine of course wanted to make sure the supervisors were from the PV, and it succeeded in getting two of the supervisors—chosen by one-fourth of the PV candidates on the official ballot—to represent the four precincts. Still, Judge Bravo felt that he needed some outside special overseers to monitor the precincts at election time; observers had predicted a tumultuous election. He petitioned George H. Sheppard, Texas comptroller of public accounts, for help, and Sheppard partly approved: "I am pleased to advise it has been the policy of this department to leave such matters up to the local authorities, however, in this particular I do not object to joining with you in the selection of these supervisors, but it would be impossible for me to contact the candidates you suggest that I see for you." [35]

Despite showers predicted for election day, the voter turnout in Zapata County was high. When the final votes were counted, tabulated, and reported to the Texas Election Bureau, all the incumbents at the local level had won easy victories, Judge Bravo leading the way with a margin of 283 votes. The machine favorites, Manuel Medina, Ygnacio Sánchez, and Leopoldo Martínez, received huge margins of 564, 328, and 368 respectively. After more than thirty years in power, the PV, as expected, again came out triumphant. Despite the mudslinging, a slew of accusations, and a barrage of verbal personal attacks, the *Laredo Times* reported only that "Zapata Names Old Officers Again" and that things had been quiet on election day. [36]

For the gubernatorial race, twice Governor James V. Allred, upon receiving a federal district judgeship appointment from President Roosevelt, decided not to seek reelection. This left the field open for thirteen candidates; W. Lee O'Daniel, in his first bid for public office, received the electorate's approval over the next three leading contenders: Attorney General William McGraw, Railroad Commissioner Ernest O. Thompson, and oil operator Tom Hunter. The Fort Worth businessman had been expected to win, and it was the first time in history that a nonincumbent had won the primary without a runoff. In the so-called boss-controlled counties, only Webb and Starr counties gave Thompson lopsided victories, with 71 and 96 percent of the votes respectively. Parr's Duval County voted for McGraw with 84 percent of the votes. [37] An interesting scenario developed in Zapata County, where the machine split between Thompson with 42 percent of the votes, and McGraw, with 43 percent. As expected, the boss-free counties voted for O'Daniel, these being Dimmit (62%), Hidalgo (51%), Cameron, (55%), Brooks (53%),

Table 3. Zapata County Election Results for Democratic Primary, July 23, 1938

County Judge
  (I) M. B. Bravo   778
      Conrado Lozano   495
Sheriff
  (I) Ygnacio Sánchez   796
      J. M. Salinas   468
District/County Clerk
  (I) Leopoldo Martínez   821
      Alberto Treviño   453
County Treasurer
  (I) Primitivo Uribe   764
      Trinidad Uribe   506
County Attorney
  (I) Leo C. Buckley   1,277
      (ran unopposed)
County Commissioner, Precinct #1
  (I) Manuel Medina   351
      Adán Gutiérrez   200
County Commissioner, Precinct #2
  (I) Proceso Martínez   190
      Amado Ramírez   145
County Commissioner, Precinct #3
  (I) Guillermo González   194
      León J. Ramírez   91
County Commissioner, Precinct #4
  (I) Santos Yzaguirre   59
      Tomás McDermott   36

Note: (I) - Incumbent
Source: Primary Election Returns, July 23, 1938, Zapata County Courthouse

Zavala (68%), and Frio (59%).[38] Parr's neighboring county—Jim Wells—opted to disagree with the Duval boss, and instead went 52 percent for O'Daniel. It seems that not all the political bosses agreed on a candidate, and Parr was the only one who gave McGraw a huge majority.

The state Senate race for the 27th district, between the incumbent

James Neal, a lawyer from Laredo, and Rogers Kelley from Hidalgo County, ended in a runoff election scheduled for August 27, 1938. This proved an interesting race since the Webb County political machine preferred to support Kelley, an outsider, rather than their native son. The reason was that back in 1934, O. W. Killam, an influential business leader from Laredo, had financially supported Neal to defeat Archie Parr, an election the Laredo politicos did not forget. According to the Laredo newspaper, Killam had heralded himself as the "undisputed chief of Laredo, Webb County and Zapata Counties."[39] Even though Kelley received 59 percent of the votes in Webb County, and Neal a respectable 41 percent in Zapata County, both Neal and Killam convinced Judge Bravo and some members of the machine to carry Neal, who garnered 52 percent over Kelley's 45 percent.[40] In Starr and Duval counties, Kelley won with huge victories of 97 and 89 percent of the votes respectively; however, Jim Wells County gave Neal 66 percent of the votes: another split in the Parr controlled counties! Overall, Kelley led by more than five thousand votes over Neal.

The runoff election between Kelley and Neal took a totally different political path. The South Texas counties that had voted for Kelley in the primary remained loyal in the runoff. In Zapata County, John A. Valls, district attorney for the 49th District Court and a Parr supporter, flexed his political muscle over Killam, and this time the machine responded with 81 percent of the votes for Kelley.[41] Parr's connections to Valls and the Zapata machine may have had an impact on this election. Also, Bravo and Kelley were old political allies who had served under the Baker regime and had campaigned together on the same Democratic ticket in Hidalgo County in 1932. When the tabulations were counted, leading contender Rogers Kelley emerged as the victor by a majority of 4,242 votes.

At about the same time the general election took place, 49th District Judge J. F. Mullally decided to retire after thirty-three years of service to a district that included Webb, Zapata, Dimmit, and Jim Hogg counties. The decision caused an internal political rift among the jefes políticos of Webb County's ruling Independent Club, a faction founded in 1894 by leading Republicans, but which had gone on to become a powerful Democratic machine in Laredo after the Progressive era. After several prolonged meetings behind closed doors, the Laredo Bar Association and the Independent Club endorsed 49th District Attorney John A. Valls to succeed Mullally. Valls's nomination received support from the rank and file. Then Joe and Albert Martin, the real powers behind the Independent Club, selected Webb County Judge Manuel J. Raymond for the district attorney's post over the incumbent Assistant District Attorney Philip Kazen. An almost synchronized outcry of "dirty politics" swept across the four counties.[42] Bill Quilliam, former Jim Hogg county attorney, and Kazen, among other aspiring contenders, had expressed an interest in the vacant position for district attorney. They made their concerns known by forwarding their complaint to Governor Allred and Governor-Elect O'Daniel. Quilliam and Kazen, both staunch Democrats, differed in their philosophical ideologies from the majority position in the Independent Club and adamantly opposed the Martin-Raymond domination of the group.[43]

Judge Bravo, new to Webb County politics and not totally familiar with the Raymond, Valls, or Kazen political tactics, remained neutral and waited patiently for the outcome. Four days later, on November 11, 1938, at 8:30 in the evening, Governor Allred, after much deliberation and discussion with Judge Robert Lee Bobbitt and with William Prescott Allen, publisher of the *Laredo Times,* appointed John A. Valls to succeed Judge Mullally and promoted Philip Kazen to the district attorney's post.[44] Governor Allred pondered the matter until he personally met with Allen, whose newspaper was pro-Kazen. Both Valls and Kazen were Allred's strong political supporters and friends.

Thus ended the political turmoil that engulfed the entire 49th District Court. Since Quilliam supported O'Daniel for governor, there was strong speculation that if Governor Allred had postponed his decision, then O'Daniel, as the new governor, would have appointed Quilliam over Valls or even over Kazen. What a terrible blow to the Webb County Independent Club! Two years later, Philip Kazen ran for his own post in what would become one of the most colorful campaigns in South Texas politics.

THE FRONTIER HILATION

During the summer of 1940, Zapata County hosted one of the biggest sociopolitical celebrations ever held in South Texas. This was the first time in history that the three border political machines of Webb, Zapata, and Starr counties collaborated in planning an event. After years of construction, the State Highway Department had completed the last strip, from Arroyo Veleño to the Starr County line, of the more than two-hundred-mile-long U.S. Highway 83. This new road now connected Webb County with the Lower Río Grande Valley. The project was a significant accomplishment not only for the border counties but for the entire state. The increased flow of traffic promised to bring future economic development to South Texas and Mexico, and the border counties celebrated with festivities. What started out as a small *fiesta* for Zapata County residents soon mushroomed into a "Frontier Hilation" of large-scale proportions, promoted throughout the state as "the Old West Will Live Again" and "Famous Frontier Hospitality Will Reign Supreme."[45]

The Frontier Hilation was chaired by Judge Bravo, Webb County Judge Raymond, and Starr County Judge H. Garza, Jr., supported by many committee chairpersons representing chamber of commerce presidents and business and political leaders from Brownsville to Del Rio. The one-day celebration, rescheduled several times because of the preparation time needed to accommodate some twenty thousand participants, was planned for Saturday, July 20, 1940, on a vast field about one mile north of the Zapata international bridge.[46]

Many state officials and aspiring candidates seeking public office for the 1940 Democratic primary took advantage of the opportunity and accepted the county's invitation. This widely publicized occasion was an excellent time to solicit last minute votes, since the primary would take place a week later on July 27. Judge Bravo predicted that there would be "more important office seekers assembled in Zapata . . . than have ever been gathered at one affair in the history of the state," with the presence of such notables as Clyde E. Smith, Ernest Thompson, J. E. McDonald, Judge James Norvell, L. A. Woods, Bascon Giles, Robert Lee Bobbitt, Charley Lockhart, Pierce Brooks, Senator Van Zandt, and Jerry Sadler, among others.[47]

A full day of entertainment, food (over five thousand pounds of barbecue meat), and games for everybody followed the ribbon-cutting ceremonies that took place at the Zapata–Starr County line. Webb County Judge Raymond presided as emcee, and Judge Bobbitt, the state highway commissioner, delivered the keynote speech. Hailed by many observers as the "greatest day in the history of Zapata County" and the "biggest, most interesting and most exciting show in the history of border country," the grandiose event allowed the participating political candidates an opportunity to network, socialize, and solicit votes.[48]

"Blackout" Politics in Zapata— the 1940 Campaign

The contested race for 49th district judge and district attorney surged to the forefront of border politics during the spring of 1940 when the Independent Club, as expected, endorsed the reelection of Judge Valls but refused to support the incumbent district attorney, Philip Kazen. Instead, the machine opted for a newcomer, Bill Neblett, for the district attorney seat.[49] Left to run on a separate ticket, Bill Quilliam and Philip Kazen campaigned as candidates without a party, for district judge and district attorney respectively.

During Kazen's first political rally, held on Sunday evening, July 21, 1940, in Zapata's public plaza (opposite the county courthouse), Delis Negrón, a well-known Republican supporter and editor of the partisan Laredo Spanish newspaper *El Día,* addressed about two thousand people to convey support for Kazen's candidacy.[50] Earlier in the day, rumors had spread throughout the county that supporters from Webb County's Independent Club were going to break up Kazen's rally. Coincidentally, an electrical blackout occurred when Kazen was introduced.[51] Loyal supporters and sympathizers came to the rescue by turning on their cars headlights and illuminating the whole plaza. The rally proceeded as planned, but the memorable event left a deep and questionable impression on those present.

Almost as if orchestrated, the electricity came back on just as Kazen had concluded his speech. Was this a clear message that Judge Bravo and his cohorts were supporting Webb County's Independent Club? Was Kazen an independent Democrat or a Republican campaigning as a Democrat? Who was responsible for the blackout, or was it a mere coincidence? Did the Zapata political machine support Valls and Kazen but not Neblett? Kazen blasted the tactics of the "dictatorial politicians of the district set-up."[52] Moreover, he fulminated against Webb County's ruling Independent Club, which had allegedly spread its influence to Zapata County.[53]

When the 1940 Democratic primary election results were tabulated, Philip Kazen, the energetic red-haired lawyer, had conquered overwhelming odds, cracking the Independent Club by winning three of the four counties. In Zapata County, he garnered 599 to 393 votes. Dimmit County voted 809 to 535 for Kazen, and Jim Hogg County voted 1,056 to 132 for Kazen. However, in Webb County, Neblett won with 3,258 votes to 2,324, but not with enough votes to defeat the incumbent district attorney. In the final countdown, Neblett received 4,417 votes and Kazen won by a margin of 371 votes.[54] The pro-Kazen Laredo newspaper, elated at the way Zapata County citizens had voted, applauded their efforts, stating that "for years [Zapata County] was merely a rubber stamp for the now impotent Independent Club machine." Now it had "rared [sic] back and asserted its independence by thumbing its nose at the Laredo machine."[55] Perhaps the three counties where voters favored Kazen were retaliating against the Independent Club's effort to force Valls and Raymond down their throats back in 1938. Two days after the primary, an elated Judge Bravo and the county commissioners, in a spirit of camaraderie, sent Kazen a congratulatory telegram.[56]

A day after the election, the *Laredo Times* captured all the euphoria of Kazen's victory with a three- by five-inch photo of Kazen on the front page and the headline, "People's Choice!" Kazen, said the *Times,* "took it directly to a people that for more than half a century had been taught that the office holders of the political machine kowtowed only to the bosses of the machine and the bosses—they kowtowed to nobody—not even to God."[57] For district judge, the popular and well-respected Independent Club candidate Judge Valls won in all four counties by a huge majority of 2,761 votes. The 1940 primary election results for the two 49th district posts showed that border politics were controlled neither by the Webb County Independent Club nor by George Parr.

OIL AND POLITICS

Oil interests and the state's oil lobby played a key role in South Texas during the 1940 election campaign for railroad commissioner. It was considered an acceptable practice for the oil companies to become actively involved in local politics during election time to support Democratic Party candidates who looked after their interests. In his study *The Politics of Oil,* Robert Engler concluded that "oil increasingly accepts politics as an integral and continuing part of management practices. . . . Some industry executives speak frankly of their insurance policies, that is, the financial assistance given to all possible victories in primaries [and] runoffs."[58] In other words, the oil representatives paid the political machine to obtain votes for their candidates!

Webb County's Independent Club supported Olin W. Culberson in the 1940 primary for the position of railroad commissioner, primarily because he had the backing of influential Judge Robert Lee Bobbitt, who had strong ties with the Laredo machine. Zapata County opted for Clyde E. Smith, one of Culberson's opponents, giving him a majority of 346 votes, 24 to Culberson, and 38 to Pierce Brooks, a third candidate in the race. Smith had come across as a champion for education and had pledged to regulate the oil industry for the financial benefit of the state's education system.[59] Support from other county superintendents probably influenced Bravo to support Smith. Transwestern Oil Company lobbied on behalf of Brooks and found a favorable response from Judge Bravo, but to no avail as Brooks came in a distant second, "We are counting on having you [Lamar Seeligson] and your partners present . . . , and also other officials . . . , and when you are here we will take up the candidacy of Mr. Brooks, with my *compadres*."[60] Statewide results pitted Olin Culberson against Pierce Brooks in a runoff scheduled for August 24, 1940.

During the runoff election campaign, J. R. Hill, a representative of the H-Y Oil Company in Fort Worth, tried to coerce Bravo into supporting Culberson: "Now he [Pierce Brooks] is the wrong man for the oil industry. We want Culberson. He will make us a real efficient Railroad Commissioner, he knows the oil business. I would take it as a special favor if you would line up Zapata County to vote for Mr. Culberson. I don't know where Zapata County got the idea of voting for this Dallas fellow so I am going to depend on you to carry Zapata County for Culberson. . . . Now you put the word out that he is the man. That is all that is necessary. All of your people have utmost confidence in you."[61]

Hill followed up with specific instructions to his production supervisor assigned to the Zapata area, advising him to make sure the word got out on Culberson. One can safely assume that similar tactics were employed in other oil-producing counties. However, Judge Bravo had already begun campaigning for Culberson before he received Hill's letter.[62] In prior elections, the oil companies in Zapata had contributed financially to the Democratic Party, and they also utilized their field workers to campaign actively throughout the county. Judge Bravo was vigorously supporting Culberson over Brooks even before he received a generous personal contribution from one oil company, "and this evening when I got in I find your letter with a nice contribution for my campaign, and this makes me feel very happy and confident of a successful election."[63] The H-Y Oil Company also promised to assist in every way possible: "I

want to thank you for your cooperation and work for Mr. Culberson. . . . Why in the Sam Hill haven't you told me before that you were
in a run-off primary? Enclosed you will find my check. . . . I am sure
Zapata County will go for him. . . . I am writing my boys this morning
to get out and work for you." [64]

The Texas Election Bureau's final statewide runoff election results
had Culberson ahead with 458,061 votes and 410,656 for Brooks. In
Zapata County, the machine delivered 160 votes for Culberson, and 18
for Brooks. The same machine voting patterns existed in Webb County,
where Culberson got 1,578 votes to 162 for Brooks; Starr County voted
824 for Culberson and 31 for Brooks; and Duval County also had a
lopsided 3,578 for Culberson, with Brooks receiving 72.

Politics aside, Olin Culberson was the better qualified candidate for
the position of railroad commissioner. Pierce Brooks's background was
in the business sector, and while he had a working knowledge of the
state's bureaucracy, he had never held public office. His actual experience
was with safety activities that involved the different transportation agencies. Culberson, on the other hand, had worked for eight years with the
Railroad Commission as chief examiner and then as chief of the gas utilities division. In 1939, his tenacious and thorough investigations of several gas companies caused gas lobby groups to have him removed from
office. [65]

THE 1940 GENERAL ELECTION

For the November 5, 1940, general election in Zapata County, a full slate
of Republican candidates, comprising ranchers, farmers, and even some
Democrats running on the Republican ticket, campaigned vigorously
against Judge Bravo and his fellow incumbents for not supporting Bill
Neblett during the primary. Bravo, however, remained steadfast in his
loyalty to the Democratic Party and to the local machine, who confiden-
tially told J. R. Hill, spokesperson for the H-Y Oil Company, "This situation can be blamed directly to the District Attorney's opposition in the
primaries." [66] Some PV supporters had sided with Webb County's Independent Club and supported Neblett and were upset at Bravo for going
with Kazen. Zapata County officials had faced no opposition during the
primary, but now they were up against a strong field of Republican chal-
lengers, among them Juan Manuel Vela for county judge, L. E. Vela for
county clerk, Trinidad Uribe for sheriff and tax assessor/collector, and

Table 4. Retail Sales by Counties, 1940 Census

County	Sales
Duval	$3,700,000
Hidalgo	19,632,000
Jim Wells	5,757,000
Starr	1,193,000
Webb	10,444,000
Zapata	116,000

Source: Texas Almanac, 1943–44

Table 5. Assessed Taxable Property, 1940 Census

County	Assessed Valuation	Pct. of true Valuation	True Valuation
Starr	$11,126,080	65	$17,117,046
Webb	21,363,202	50	42,726,404
Zapata	3,746,130	70	5,353,614

Source: Texas Almanac, 1943–44

Delfino Lozano for county treasurer. The four Republican county commissioner candidates included Lauro Garza for precinct 1; Amado Ramírez for precinct 2; Salvador García for precinct 3; Manuel Yzaguirre for precinct 4.

The Laredo newspaper predicted a hot and exciting election that guaranteed to "keep Zapata politics at the boiling point from now on." [67] Bravo and his supporters planned an all-out election campaign. They asked the teachers to vote on election day, to contribute two dollars each, and to provide voters with transportation to the rally. The judge and the county commissioners donated twenty-two dollars each, while the other county officials gave ten dollars per person. [68] On October 13, 1940 at the courthouse plaza, the Democratic Party staged an extravagant political rally that included two orchestras for entertainment, lots of food and beer, and speakers such as Judge J. T. Canales, M. J. Raymond, and John Valls, and from Hidalgo County, José V. Alamía and Ramón Garza.

On October 5, the Zapata County Democratic Executive Committee, made up of the county's ruling families, had accepted the resignation of José M. Sánchez, who had won in the primary for sheriff and tax assessor/collector. In his place, the committee approved the selection of his nephew, Leopoldo Martínez, to fill the vacancy and campaign for the position. In addition, the Big Four quickly promoted Matías Cuéllar to Martínez's post of county and district clerk.[69] Since 1933, Cuéllar had held the office of deputy county and district clerk, a position created then by Leopoldo Martínez, and he had also served as chair of the Democratic Executive Committee. This internal political strategic maneuver did not sit well with many loyal supporters because Leopoldo and his uncle controlled the county's tax office. One influential citizen, in particular, expressed dissatisfaction with the change. He further stated that to remain friends with the candidates from the Partido Nuevo, he had divided his family's eight votes equally between the parties.[70]

With one month left in the campaign, Judge Bravo traveled throughout the county, visiting as many ranches as possible to solicit votes. In addition, he mailed to every county resident a one-page typed letter (written in Spanish), displaying a black-and-white photo of him in the upper left-hand corner. In the course of his itinerary, Judge Bravo listed by individual name the families he found living at each ranch. Next to the names, he marked the number of votes that each family would contribute—husband and wife = 2 votes, one individual = only 1 vote, etc. He noted which voters had expressed dissatisfaction with the political machine, for these were the voters whom the judge needed to win over to his side.[71] He was a firm believer in the absentee vote and traveled long distances—to Corpus Christi, Hebbronville, Freer, San Antonio, and Eagle Pass—to find the county's migrant workers.[72]

About a week before the general election, Judge Valls ruled against a writ of mandamus requested by John Rathmell, chairperson of the Zapata County Republican Party, and his attorney, Bismark Pope. According to Pope, Judge Bravo and his cohorts had denied the Republican Party's petition, submitted in February, 1940, to place two of their judges in each of the voting precincts.[73] Webb County Judge M. J. Raymond, representing Judge Bravo and the other incumbents, responded by stating that the Republican candidates had participated in the Democratic primary and therefore were Democrats when they filed the petition. Assisting Raymond was a team of lawyers that included county attorney

Leo C. Buckley, U. S. Algee, and A. A. Alvarado from Laredo. In rendering his decision, Judge Valls questioned the Republican candidates "who take the Democratic pledge and vote the Democratic ticket in the July primaries and then seek protection of the court as Republicans in the general election," and concluded that he had no authority to render a judgment because the 49th District Court in Zapata, where the case originated, was now on vacation; a resolution would have to wait until the next term.[74] The outcome of Judge Valls's decision was highly predictable since both he and Judge Raymond were staunch Democrats and loyal supporters of Zapata County's political machine. Not by chance, the district court's next scheduled session would be after the general election.

The Republican Party supporters were outraged at Judge Valls's decision and at the Democratic machine's maneuvers against their members. The partisan Laredo daily newspaper, *El Día,* compared Judge Bravo and the commissioners' court to political gangsters controlling and manipulating the electoral process.[75] The judge had been in office for barely four years, yet had already earned the following colorful cognomens: "*Su Majestad*" (Your Majesty), "*maestro político*" (master politician), "flamboyant judge," "*sangre fría*" (cold-blooded), and "*dictador,*" (dictator).[76] At the heart of the controversy was Bravo's denying the Republican Party equal access to representation at the polling precincts. According to his opponents, the action taken by Judge Bravo and the Big Four was totally incomprehensible and illegal and made Hitler, Stalin, and Mussolini come across as angels.[77]

On the eve of the general election, a heated rally by both parties at the county courthouse lasted from 8:00 P.M. to past 1:00 A.M. Republican representatives spoke first, including several eloquent orators from Laredo, such as Republican leader Cullee Mann. *El Día* editor Delis Negrón, Assistant District Attorney E. D. Salinas, Philip and Charles Kazen, and Conrado Lozano attacked the Democratic Party for corrupt activities. One hot issue was the use of county equipment to fix roads and small dams on the Mexican side.[78] The Democrats followed, led by Judge Bravo, Judge Raymond, and J. V. Alamía from Hidalgo County. Speaking in Spanish, Judge Raymond attacked Philip Kazen for politiking with both parties and for "not having the courage of his convictions in as much as he was helping the Republicans who had in turn helped him by voting for him in the July primaries as Democrats, and who now were running for office on the Republican ticket." Kazen was "afraid to come out in the open [to help the Republicans] but was sending his office boy, Mr. E. D. Salinas, the Assistant Attorney, to speak at Republican rallies."[79]

When all the general election ballots had been counted, the incumbent frontrunners emerged as victors: Judge Bravo, Matías Cuéllar, Leopoldo Martínez, Primitivo Uribe, Manuel Medina, Proceso Martínez, Jr., and Santos Yzaguirre. The political machine's total control of the county offices was marred by the loss of three posts in precinct 3 (Lopeño) to the Republicans: Salvador García for county commissioner, Dagoberto López for justice of the peace, and Abel Ramírez for constable.[80] All three were successful ranchers, especially García, who had vast landholdings and many gas wells. García edged González by 22 votes, 152 to 130. By no coincidence, all three candidates were strong Democrats who chose to run as Republicans in the general election, since this approach was the only avenue available for them to win against the incumbents. The new county commissioner, Salvador García, was a well-known rancher and an influential member of his community. He and the other two candidates took a page from Philip Kazen's tactics and made a small crack in the political machine's stronghold.

AFTERMATH OF THE 1940 ELECTION

On January 1, 1941, Judge Bravo began his third term in office amidst a controversy over the election in the 49th District Court. The Republican Party had filed an election contest suit questioning the validity of the election on the grounds that only Democrats had been permitted to serve as election judges and clerks, that ineligible people had voted, and that absentee voting procedures were improperly handled. All votes, they argued, were thus fraudulent.[81] For years, bitter rivalry feuds had been going on between the ruling Democratic Party and the Republican faction, with family members even campaigning against each other. This cannibalistic mentality was deeply rooted in the history of the county, and topped with cries of fraud, it became the underlying issue in the election contest suit.[82]

On February 4, 1941, when the issue of the pending court hearing resurfaced, 49th District Judge John A. Valls and the Laredo attorneys again purposely delayed the trial, until February 24, 1941. The lawyers began to be concerned because Judge Bravo could not produce the election returns needed for his defense. In desperation, Judge Raymond pleaded with Judge Bravo, "We can do nothing without the facts. We must have complete facts on all contested voters both for and against you and unless you can bring or send said information to our office immediately, we will be unable to best represent you in this matter." [83] Again, Judge Raymond used delay tactics, postponing the trial until May 26, and according to the 49th District Court minutes, the trial was rescheduled for a third time, for August 11, 1941. On this date, however, the court minutes showed that no trial took place. [84] In the meantime, Judge Valls, who had long suffered from a heart ailment, was hospitalized. Two days later, on August 13, he died of double pneumonia. The four counties that made up the 49th District then endorsed the Webb County Independent Club's selection of District Judge R. D. Wright of the 111th Judicial District (Webb County) to succeed Valls. Almost a year later, on September 28, 1942, District Judge Wright dismissed the case "for want of prosecution at case of plaintiff," adding, "with the costs adjusted against the respective plaintiffs in each case." [85] This was a convenient way to cover up the fact that the election results had allegedly been destroyed and hence no case existed.

Special 1941 Senate Election

On April 9, 1941, Senator Morris Sheppard, who had been in Congress since 1903 and had high hopes of seeking reelection in 1942, suddenly and unexpectedly died. Texas Governor Lee "Pappy" O'Daniel called for a special Senate election to be held on Saturday, June 28, 1941. In the interim, Governor O'Daniel appointed Sam Houston's son, Andrew Jackson Houston, a frail eighty-seven-year-old, to fill the unexpired term. Shortly after his appointment, complications following stomach surgery resulted in Houston's death. [86]

Twenty-seven aspiring contestants filed for a place on the ballot, with only four contenders emerging at the top: Martin Dies, Lyndon B. Johnson, Gerald C. Mann, and Governor O'Daniel. Congressman Lyndon Johnson from the 10th Congressional District entered the senatorial race with President Franklin D. Roosevelt's full blessings. Johnson was considered one of the New Dealers in Washington, particularly with his experience in Texas as the director of the National Youth Administration Program. Roosevelt's backing became apparent from the start when both appeared shaking hands as part of Johnson's campaign literature. County Judge Roy Hofheinz, from Harris County, sent Judge Bravo a letter with a photograph of Johnson and Roosevelt together, requesting his support for Johnson. The caption underneath the photograph stated, "He is my very old and close friend.—F.D.R." [87]

John Duncan, a close friend of both Judge Bravo and Johnson, suggested that the congressman notify Bravo immediately about his candidacy and seek his support in the campaign. Following Duncan's advice, on June 11, 1941, Johnson encouraged the Zapata judge to campaign on his behalf. With just seventeen days left in the campaign, LBJ felt positive about winning the election with the judge's support in Zapata County. [88]

Apparently, the judge had made up his mind to support Johnson because on June 13, 1941, he informed Judge Hofheinz that Lyndon was the candidate of his choice. Judge Bravo did not sound very optimistic about rounding up support for him, mainly because the majority of the migrant farm families were away at work. Yet he was hopeful that there could still be enough votes to help Johnson. [89] President Roosevelt's radio campaign speech for Johnson on June 15 reaffirmed Bravo's commitment to support the congressman: "Am going to get what few votes I can for you, made my mind up when our Comander [sic] in Chief spoke." [90]

At about the same time, County Judge Merritt H. Gibson from Gregg County and Mose J. Harris, a prominent businessman from McAllen, representing the Gerald C. Mann campaign headquarters, approached Judge Bravo for his support. The former attorney general was also considered one of the top contenders in the Senate race. But the request came too late because Bravo had already decided to campaign for Johnson. In his reply to Harris, Bravo indicated his strong commitment to campaign for Johnson; however, he said that if the request had come sooner, he might have given it "serious consideration." [91]

During the previous election year, Bravo had successfully campaigned for Gerald C. Mann's reelection as attorney general. There is a strong possibility that had the Mann headquarters reached Judge Bravo about a week earlier, the outcome of the special Senate election in Zapata County would have taken a different route. As Bravo indicated, "May be [sic] next time we can get together on candidates." [92]

Twelve days before the election, on June 16, Judge Bravo, anxious to have the Democratic Party complete its campaign for Johnson across the county, requested additional materials. "Please send me two hundred circulars of Roosevelt and Unity, as I intend to mail that many letters to voters in this County."[93] As the special Senate election approached, Johnson enthusiastically encouraged Judge Bravo on Thursday, June 19, to work even harder:

> I can't tell you how happy it made me to receive your card telling me that I can depend on your continued efforts in this election. . . . We're going to win this election. Every day we gain strength and more support. Let's redouble our efforts and work harder than ever from now until election day. There can't be any question about the results. If you will continue working as you have been, LYNDON JOHNSON WILL BE YOUR NEXT SENATOR. You can depend on it that he will never forget what you have done to help. Keep in touch with me and let me have your suggestions.[94]

A day later, Johnson, obviously grateful for the judge's all-out efforts in Zapata County, mailed Bravo another letter, this time to thank him in advance for his support in the Senate election campaign.[95] However, this was not the case in neighboring Webb County, where District Judge Valls had urged Leopoldo Martínez, Zapata County sheriff/tax assessor to persuade Zapata public officials to support the candidacy of Governor O'Daniel, stating in Spanish, "Nos conviene que sea electo" (It is to our advantage that he be elected).[96] In the 1940 Democratic primary, Zapata County had voted unanimously for Governor O'Daniel. Apparently, certain key Democratic public officials in Webb County wanted Governor O'Daniel to win the Senate seat so that Lt. Governor Coke R. Stevenson could become governor. In a tactful and diplomatic response, Martínez reminded Valls that they had started campaigning for Johnson after Judge Raymond told Zapata County's boss that prior to the governor's entry into the race, he had had no specific candidate in mind.[97] Almost apologetically, Martínez assured Valls that "I am going to straighten out those closest friends to vote for the Governor. Hope that this will meet with your approval."[98]

Although statewide election results declared Governor O'Daniel the winner by 1,311 votes over Johnson, in Zapata County a mere three hundred people went to the polls out of 2,147 eligible voters. Congressman Johnson garnered 273 votes in comparison to 21 votes cast for the governor, while Gerald C. Mann received 5 votes and Martin Dies only 1 vote. Unofficial returns from the Texas Election Bureau showed that statewide, O'Daniel had received 175,602 votes; Johnson, 174,279;

Mann, 140,707; and Dies, 78,551. In Webb County, Johnson received 978 votes; Mann, 81; O'Daniel, 257; and Dies, only 77 votes.

In other South Texas counties, Johnson was not the favorite Democratic candidate. For example, in Jim Wells County, O'Daniel defeated Johnson, 344 to 322; Dies garnered 257 votes and Mann just 200. However, in Duval County, Parr's machine delivered 93 percent of the votes, 1,506, for Johnson; O'Daniel, the closest opponent, received only 65 votes. Likewise in Starr County, the Guerra machine voted almost unanimously for Johnson with 615 votes; O'Daniel received 12, Mann 10, and Dies 7. Dimmit County did not follow the other three counties in the 49th District Court, and gave O'Daniel 239 votes, Johnson 129, Mann 127, and Dies 53 votes.[99]

There has never been any direct evidence proving or confirming the allegations that the bloc votes delivered by the machines resulted from Johnson purchasing the votes of "corrupt South Texas Border bosses" or that George B. Parr, Duke of Duval County, spread his political influence over the "border bosses" in dictating which candidate to support.[100] Johnson was the victim of his own enemies. Four out of the five border counties voted for Johnson—Zapata and Starr with 91 and 96 percent respectively. Zapata was the only county with a round number of 300 votes, almost as if the number was preplanned. Webb followed with 70 percent and Cameron with 33 percent for Johnson. Hidalgo was the only county that voted for the governor. According to Belia Peña Cooper, Judge Bravo's secretary, the judge and Lyndon Johnson communicated quite often by telephone.[101] The prevailing popular myth that Parr controlled all the South Texas border bosses is questioned by the judge's widow and by Santos Medina, who was closely involved in local politics and who later succeeded Bravo as county judge. He stated that "Parr had no control over Zapata County, but [they] helped each other because of their friendship," and "George Parr no se metia con Zapata, pueda [ser] que con Webb" (George did not get involved with Zapata, maybe with Webb County).[102] Mrs. Bravo remembered that Parr and Bravo were political friends and helped each other; they communicated by telephone but seldom wrote to each other.[103]

A few days after the election results were officially certified on July 3, 1941, Judge Bravo expressed his feelings to Johnson about the outcome of the special election. "We have been disheartened with the final count, but on the other hand we hope to in the future be able to again help your candidacy. You did not lose the election, it was the State of Texas, who lost it. The Latin-vote of Zapata County was almost unanimous and they are proud that they voted for you. May you continue to enjoy health and carry on your good work in behalf of Roosevelt-America." [104]

Johnson led by over five thousand votes but lost by corrected returns from East Texas counties; this lesson came in handy when he ran again for the Senate in 1948. About a week later, on July 10, Johnson replied to Judge Bravo, "One of the great compensations in the situation which has arisen in the last few days is the letter you sent me on July the third. We cannot win every fight every time we go into it. But we can continue to fight for the principle we have adhered to and we can look to the future when those principles may prevail fully. You are generous and kind in your comments about me and my work. I feel an added responsibility in that work because of your confidence." [105]

Even though he lost his first attempt at a statewide political election, Johnson thanked all the people who supported and voted for him. Always a shrewd and clever politician, and just in case he ran again in 1948, Johnson wanted to let the bosses know how much he appreciated their friendship for delivering the huge Tejano bloc votes. From his office in the House of Representatives, Johnson sent a thank-you note to every member of Zapata's political machine, with a personal message to Judge Bravo: "For your own fine spirit of loyalty and cooperation, I will ever be grateful and I want you to call on me when there is anything I can do to be of assistance to you and your friends. . . . You did your part and we will work together again." [106] The 1941 election campaign was the beginning of a lasting friendship between the two politicos. A bond between them had been established and would return to the fore seven years later during Johnson's second bid for the Senate seat, in the 1948 election campaign.

Meanwhile, other business proceeded as usual. Soon after the special Senate election, Judge Bravo turned his attention briefly to a transportation business venture that involved operating a bus line to Moore Air Field (then recently established), about twelve miles from Mission, Texas. On July 30, 1941, he inquired of his friend Major Sidney D. Grubbs, who was stationed at Randolph Field in San Antonio, about a possible franchise. Approximately a week later, on August 15, Major Grubbs conveyed the good news that "the permit from the Railroad Commission of Texas is all that is necessary providing you have the permission of the Commanding officer of the field to operate within the gates." [107]

Judge Bravo never followed through with his plans to request a permit to operate the bus service line. In all probability, he found out that Senator Rogers Kelley, Judge J. C. Looney (from Hidalgo County), and Vance D. Raimond had already formed a corporation and submitted an application for a permit from the Texas Railroad Commission. The application received approval on September 1, 1941, and in 1942, the Valley Airfield Bus Company became operational, providing services from Edinburg, Pharr, McAllen, and Mission to Moore Air Field. [108] This company became the first commercial bus line to benefit the Lower Río Grande Valley.

More personal kinds of benefits routinely required Judge Bravo's attention. A common practice confronting him—something that occurred almost immediately after getting his reelection—was county citizens requesting personal financial assistance. As the major political figure in the county, he practiced a paternalistic style of bossism toward needy people who had no financial recourse and came to seek his help. The widow of an old political crony from Hidalgo County requested fifty dollars a month for six months to help her out of financial hardship. [109] During the latter part of January, 1941, a Partido Viejo supporter asked the judge for fifteen dollars to defray medical costs. Judge Bravo graciously acknowledged the request but could only send five dollars due to his own financial circumstances. [110] A loyal supporter of the Democratic Party needed the judge to be cosignatory on a bank loan of thirty dollars for final payments on a car; Bravo gladly obliged, counting on the constituent's entire family for support at election time. [111] Another constituent of the Partido Viejo had just been to the doctor's office in Laredo and wanted the county to pay for a series of prescribed injections. [112]

Then the Japanese sudden attack on Pearl Harbor on December 7, 1941, broke the quiet and slow-paced lifestyle of the local residents. For the first time in a long while, politics took a temporary back seat.

POLITICAL SURVIVAL TACTICS

What may be said about Judge Bravo's politics from the material presented in this chapter? The Democratic Party's political machine was already in power by the time he came in and took over the administration of the county. For fifteen or more years, the Big Four had had in place a partisan clique that controlled local government and local participation in state politics. After he won the 1936 election as a write-in candidate, Bravo fell back on his experience with bossism to guide county affairs through his first two terms of office. No sooner had he begun his term as county judge than the machine's opponents started labeling him a "boss." During his first two reelection campaigns in 1938 and 1940, the Partido Nuevo attacked the Democratic Party's style of bossism and blamed the Big Four for its corruption and incompetency.

During his first four years in office, Judge Bravo promptly learned about the county's political nuances and the necessary *movidas* (wheeling and dealing) to keep the Partido Viejo in power. His own experiences in Hidalgo County, coupled with his personal traits of honesty and trustworthiness, molded Bravo's concept of running an effective county administration. But he was also blessed with a leadership and management style that allowed him not only to deal effectively with Zapata County politics but also to operate either harshly or compassionately with his political foes, depending on the circumstances. His strong command of English and Spanish, in conjunction with his love for the game of politics, further allowed him to become a successful and effective county administrator.

In the role of boss, he helped upgrade the entire educational system with adequate facilities, more schools, sound fiscal management, better prepared teachers, and accreditation status. Seeing a great need to make changes in the county treasurer's department, Bravo established an accountability system, hired an independent auditor, and developed provisions for collection of delinquent taxes. He knew from experience that a weak and inefficient tax office would continue to be a pivot of criticism by the Partido Nuevo and could eventually lead to the machine's downfall. Pursuing efficiency further, he solicited technical assistance from the Laredo Bar Association to improve the practices and management of the county/district clerk's office. Through a successful road bond, he improved the county's highway construction program.

In the political arena, Judge Bravo's capacity to negotiate skillfully the affairs within his jurisdiction helped to perpetuate Zapata County's influential machine. Through already established alliances with the oil and gas companies, the 49th District Court, and Webb County's Independent Club, he made sure the Partido Viejo remained in power and in control over county and state affairs. On two court cases—the legality of the geographical boundaries for Common School District No. 1 and the Republican Party's petition after the 1940 election—his mentor Judge Valls ruled in favor of the political machine, though the school lawsuit decision was later overturned by the Fourth Court of Civil Appeals.

The judge further relied heavily on patronage to sustain the loyalty of machine supporters, utilizing county offices, the school system, and the oil and gas companies for rewards. Through political appointments, Judge Bravo assured the survival of the machine. He named the same powerful and influential Partido Viejo members who were county commissioners to serve on the county school board of trustees, as ex-officio road superintendents of the county, and to the important Board of Equalization.

WORLD WAR II EPOCH

During the years between 1941 and 1945 Zapata County got heavily involved in the war effort, more so than other surrounding counties. At one point, Judge Bravo tried to join the armed forces, while his opponents who sat on the county selective service board tried (unsuccessfully) to embarrass him by not giving him the proper and correct draft status. He felt that his patriotic duty was above politics and pondered leaving his political career behind. The 1942 Senate race between the incumbent O'Daniel and two former governors produced turmoil within the Zapata County PV, as the party wavered over which candidate to support. The issue of racial discrimination against Tejanos and Mexican citizens in Texas reached an all-time high during this period. Zapata, Webb, and Starr counties experienced the least prejudice because of their predominantly Tejano populations, but in other counties in South and Central Texas discrimination was overt and flagrant. Judge Bravo sought assistance from José T. Canales in provoking Governor Coke Stevenson to address this inhumane practice. Toward the latter 1940s, Zapata County played a significant role, along with other border counties, in an international effort to eradicate foot-and-mouth disease. A highly contagious virus affecting cloven-hoofed animals, it causes blisters in the mouth and around the hoof area, the pain so severe that the animals starve to death.

THE WAR EFFORT IN ZAPATA COUNTY

At the onset of World War II, Zapata County did more than its fair share to support the war effort, both at home and abroad. Even though the population of the county was small, a high percentage of citizens from both political parties enlisted in the armed forces. At every possible opportunity, Judge Bravo gave eloquent patriotic speeches to support the war effort and to recruit men and women into the military. Judge Bravo as chairperson and Manuel Medina as treasurer headed the county's United Service Organizations (USO) War Fund Campaign, and at the end of the fundraising drive, the citizens of Zapata had contributed over 45 percent more than the county quota designated by the state.[1] Zapata County during the month of July, 1942, also established a state record unequaled by any other county of its size in the sale of war bonds and stamps. The county's War Savings Committee—a nonpartisan group headed by Manuel Medina in the chair, Alberto Treviño, Judge Bravo, rancher Guadalupe Martínez, and John Rathmell, another landholder—exceeded its quota by purchasing about two and one-half times more bonds than the assigned allotment.[2] Zapata County's unique efforts did not go unnoticed by the Laredo newspaper: "While its population of American citizens may have less Anglo-Saxon names than other counties of Texas, [Zapata County] has shown that the people of that county are 100 percent American," and "has the true spirit of patriotism and the desire to help the war effort of its country."[3]

Since two of his sons were in the air corps, the judge felt a sense of obligation to place patriotism above politics. On March 11, 1942, he wrote to military headquarters in San Antonio, Texas: "Would appreciate very much any information or application blanks wherein I could volunteer to the services of my country, with a chance to an appointment in our United States Army. . . . Notwithstanding that I feel I can get elected for another term as County Judge for Zapata County, I would prefer an opportunity as an officer in the Army."[4] A month later, the judge traveled to Randolph Field and applied to officers' training school. After passing the physical examination, he submitted four letters of recommendation and two photographs.[5] To write the letters of support, he selected the county attorney Leo Buckley, used-car dealer and president of the local LULAC council René A. Garza, County Commissioner and Vice President of the Zapata Bank Manuel Medina, and Sheriff/Tax Assessor Leopoldo Martínez. Simultaneously, he applied to the Civil Service Commission to work as a translator. The judge did not feel optimistic about taking the qualifying exam, confiding to his son Eddie (the oldest of four children) "that I do not have much hope. Of course there is nothing much pushing me out of office, but sometimes I think a little recess, may boost a mans [sic] chance to come and get for a little longer time after the war."[6]

This was not the first time he had wanted to work for the government. On October 24, 1941, he had solicited the assistance of his friend Congressman Milton West, who represented the 15th district, to secure employment in a consular office in South America.[7] Judge Bravo considered a hiatus from politics and felt that his bilingual linguistic skills could be better utilized working in a Latin American country. The lure of working abroad, with the travel and the adventure involved, appealed to him.

By the end of May, 1942, Captain W. F. Schreiner informed Judge Bravo that he had not been selected for officers' training school. Only a few applicants were nominated to the special kind of administrative work that needed to be performed.[8] Much to Bravo's amazement, the civil service application was approved, but with stipulations. The offer to work on a semipermanent status for less than two thousand dollars a year disappointed Bravo since his present salary and other compensations amounted to more than four thousand dollars. Ideally, he wished to work either for fewer days (thirty or sixty days), regardless of salary, or to work part-time but with an annual salary to exceed two thousand dollars.[9] Consequently, the judge did not accept the offer.

In the meantime, René A. Garza, chairing the Zapata County Rationing Board, implemented the federal rationing program. For the most part, the plan itself caused little opposition, with the exception of gasoline rationing. Given the geographic size of the state and, in particular, the great distance between rural towns in South Texas, gasoline allocation restrictions did prove disruptive to economic activity along the border. Especially hard hit were the representatives of the oil companies, whose own quota was reduced to an allotment of six or seven hundred miles per month. J. R. Hill, who represented the H-Y Oil Company (with headquarters in Fort Worth, Texas), requested Judge Bravo's assistance in pleading his case with the rationing board: "If we cannot get gasoline to carry our business this State will soon get in a heck of a mess. . . . It is absurd. For instance, next week I have to go 15 miles north of Beeville, a trip of about 350 miles, and then another trip on to Zapata County, and then my mileage is all gone! . . . If we have no gasoline to look over these properties, how are we going to stay in the oil business? So you see how important the oil business is to your community." [10]

During the middle of the gasoline controversy, Garza submitted a letter of resignation from his position on the county rationing board. Unable to find a replacement, Mark McGee, the state director, asked Judge Bravo's intercession in persuading Garza to stay or to recommend a successor.[11] Fortunately, the commissioners' court convinced Garza to stay for an indefinite period. The Zapata County officials also ran into gasoline rationing problems when their quota was reduced. For years they had to use their personal vehicles for county business trips, so at their regularly scheduled meeting on October 12, 1942, the county commissioners voted unanimously to purchase a new car for the business use of the sheriff, the county judge, and the commissioners, given "the difficulties of transportation on account of rationing of tires and gasoline for the members of the Court and the Sheriffs' office."[12] Garza found a sympathetic ear and some future relief when Governor Coke Stevenson, after his reelection in 1942, said, "I know this rationing stuff is uncalled for . . . a moral depressant."[13]

As the war escalated in Europe and in the Pacific, tighter security along the United States–Mexico border received high priority. It may have been coincidental that additional border patrol inspectors were needed at this time for the Southwest Customs Patrol in the border area—the Mexican government had after all allied itself with the United States—but Homer Garrison, Jr., director of the Texas Department of Public Safety, sent out requests to the border counties soliciting applications for persons to join the border patrol service. Judge Bravo took advantage of this opportunity to recommend one of the Guerra boys from Starr County and two former employees of an oil company from Zapata County.[14] For the latter duo, both of them Anglos, this was the payback for past political favors.

THE 1942 DEMOCRATIC PRIMARY

With the Democratic primary election scheduled for July 25, 1942, candidates started filing their applications as early as May for a place on the official ballot. Since the chairman of the Democratic Executive Committee, Francisco J. Martínez (Leopoldo Martínez's brother), had joined the armed forces, Judge Bravo accepted applications in the interim and made sure that the candidates' names appeared on the ballot. A few days later, Leopoldo Martínez appointed his sister, Josefa Martínez Gutiérrez, a school teacher, to replace their brother Francisco.[15]

Now that he had been a county judge for five years, Bravo's sphere of political influence extended beyond local and county boundaries. Letters seeking the endorsement of the political machine in the upcoming primary election came from Edward W. Smith, chief justice of the Fourth Supreme Judicial District; Milton West, congressman from the 15th Congressional District; Rogers Kelley, state representative from the 27th district; and from many more candidates. Ernest O. Thompson, running for railroad commissioner, wrote, "I will greatly appreciate your support and hope you can find time to talk around a bit and let me know what you hear and think about things."[16] Judge Smith commented, "I am very grateful to you for your letter of the 6th [May, 1942], and particularly for your friendly assurance which, I am afraid, I had already taken for granted because of the friendship and support good old Zapata has always given me so generously."[17]

For the U.S. Senate race, incumbent W. Lee O'Daniel from Fort Worth faced tough opposition from two former governors: Dan Moody of Austin and James V. Allred from Houston. On June 2, 1942, Allred officially requested Judge Bravo's support. "As you know I have resigned as Federal Judge and am a candidate for the United States Senate. It was a momentous decision to make, but I feel that the present situation offers an opportunity for service greater than any which has come to me in the past. I have not had occasion to contact you since my announcement; however, I would appreciate your support in this campaign," said Allred. Wanting to know which candidate the political machine was supporting, he added, "A note from you telling me the true picture in your area and how you are situated will be welcome."[18]

A day after receiving Allred's letter, Bravo got correspondence from Leslie McKay, one of Moody's personal friends, requesting the judge's endorsement for the other former governor. Unlike Allred, Moody himself never asked for the judge's support, but instead McKay wanted the county to give him consideration: "Of course, I have no idea how you stand in the present race for the United States Senate, but want to put in a few words for my good friend."[19] The political machine in Zapata got together with George Parr, the Independent Club in Laredo, the Guerras from Starr County, and the leaders from Jim Hogg County, and collectively they decided to support Allred. On June 5, Judge Bravo notified Allred about Zapata's plans: "It is with pleasure I want to advise you that your friends in Zapata County, are already working in behalf of your candidacy. . . . It was their desire to take advantage of a personal interview to advise you of same." [20]

On June 12, 1942, Allred responded to the judge's previous letter, stating, "I . . . am indeed grateful for the assistance you and my other friends down there are giving me. . . . Please let me have any suggestions you may care to make at any time, and from time to time advise me as to your reaction on the general situation. If you know of any down there you feel I should write, let me know." [21] As the July 25 Democratic primary drew to a close, the local Democrats reminded all registered voters to submit their absentee ballots as soon as possible. They wanted to make sure that every vote got counted. With two days left before the election, the judge informed his son Eddie, who was stationed in Waco, that he had received Eddie's absentee ballot, but that it was not notarized. "So now I will have to try some friend in Laredo to acknowledge it. It cannot be done in Zapata because if you had voted in Zapata then the County Clerk would have to be the acknowledging officer. The same thing happened to the affidavit that you sent with the application for a ballot, it should have been signed by a Notary Public, but in that case I went ahead and signed as a Notary, although it probably is not so ethical. Well anyway will try to get your vote counted." [22]

For U.S. senator, statewide election results indicated a runoff between Allred (317,501 votes) and O'Daniel (475,541 votes); Dan Moody ran a distant third with 178,471. In Zapata County, as expected, Allred received 436 votes and O'Daniel 30 votes, while Dan Moody and Floyd E. Ryan got 1 vote apiece. [23] The two Lower Río Grande counties, Cameron and Hidalgo, voted for O'Daniel with Allred in a close second place. Other results indicated that Webb and Starr counties supported Allred, with the strong backing of Philip Kazen and the Independent Club (he and they had settled their political differences and were now on the same side) and the Guerra family in Starr County. [24] However, in the other "Parr-controlled" counties, a split occurred. Jim Wells County voted for O'Daniel, 1,741 to 1,116 for Allred. Duval County voted for Allred by a huge margin of 2,777 votes to O'Daniel's 148. Jim Hogg County voted for Allred, but Dimmit County opted for O'Daniel.

Why did Parr and the border political machines of Webb, Zapata, and Starr counties give Allred lopsided victories in the primary? There are several possible explanations. First, according to George N. Green in *The Establishment in Texas Politics,* Allred "could deliver dams and other projects for their region."[25] Second, during the 1941 special Senate election, Parr and the rest of the border machines voted overwhelmingly for Johnson over O'Daniel. Third, President Franklin D. Roosevelt supported Allred, and the Zapata Democratic Party was a staunch supporter of the president, as were the other machines. These counties had greatly benefitted economically from New Deal programs, especially when the WPA provided opportunities during the mid-1930s. During Allred's campaign in San Antonio, he stated his all-out support of "'1,000 percent' to President Roosevelt's war leadership . . . [and] was cheered again and again as he declared 'our Commander-in-Chief is the greatest leader in the world today.'"[26] Finally, neither O'Daniel nor Moody personally sought Judge Bravo's support, nor did they solicit help from the other bosses.

For railroad commissioner, Judge Bravo and the Laredo Independent Club did not agree on the same candidate. In Zapata County, the machine's influence over county voters gave James E. Kilday 382 votes compared to a total of 29 for the other ten candidates. In neighboring Webb County, the machine strongly backed the other leading contender, Beauford Jester, with 2,216 votes, while Kilday came in second with 471 votes and Pierce Brooks received only 62 votes.[27] Statewide results indicated that Kilday was out of the race but that Brooks and Jester would face each other in a runoff. Four days after the election, on July 29, 1942, Judge Bravo wrote apologetically to Jimmy Kilday on the outcome: "We are very sorry that the light vote of Zapata County was not enough to help your candidacy, however we were very glad to give you all we had. We are very proud of the service given by the Kilday's and whenever we can we shall continue to do our part."[28] On the bottom part of the same letter, Kilday responded with a friendly salutation in Spanish, "Mi Querido Amigo," and the following postscript, "The Kildays will never forget you. Without friends like you, life would not be worth while. When you need me, call me and I will come to you, day or night."[29]

At the local level, Judge Bravo and the rest of the PV slate ran unopposed, with the exception of Guillermo González, the candidate for county commissioner for precinct 3. González won the power struggle and defeated the incumbent, Salvador García, by a slender margin of 121 to 116 votes. Triumphant without opposition were Manuel Medina, county commissioner for precinct 1; Proceso Martínez, county commissioner for precinct 2; Santos Yzaguirre, county commissioner for precinct 4; Matías Cuéllar for county and district clerk; Leopoldo Martínez for sheriff and tax assessor/collector; and Primitivo Uribe for treasurer.[30] The PV retained tight control over Zapata's political life and it spilled over into social affairs. For example, Judge Bravo appointed himself, Leopoldo Martínez, and J. M. Sánchez (Leopoldo's uncle) to represent Zapata County on Laredo's International Fair and Stock Show Committee.[31]

STATE RUN-OFF ELECTION, 1942

An interesting matter surfaced in the August 22 runoff election for Texas railroad commissioner between Beauford Jester from Navarro County and Pierce Brooks from Dallas County. The debate over regulating the oil companies in the state became an important oil issue, including for the oil companies drilling and exploring in Zapata County. C. O. Maddox, an independent oilman and owner of Shary-Maddox Oil Company in Mission, Texas, and with oil interests in Zapata, urged Judge Bravo to make a concerted effort to defeat Brooks in the runoff election.

> I am writing this letter in behalf of Beauford Jester for R.R. Commissioner and I am very happy to learn that you fellows are supporting him, but, Bravo, I am writing to urge you to get out as many votes as you can, because it is extremely important to the independent oil man that we elect him, but it is also of much greater importance that we defeat Pierce Brooks, because we could be in no end of trouble with Brooks in that office.
>
> Therefore, I ask that you fellows do your very best up there and if I can do anything, let me hear from you.[32]

The independent oil companies exerted their lobbying power on the judge for past political favors. In past elections, they had campaigned on his behalf with manpower and financial contributions. Since becoming county judge, Bravo had supplemented his salary by providing the oil companies with oil and gas leases obtained from the landowners. He checked around the county for suitable sites, developed lease proposals, and submitted these to the oil companies for their approval.[33] After a company reviewed and accepted his recommendation, the judge filed the necessary title papers with the Henry Abstract Company in Laredo. In return, the oil companies provided Judge Bravo with monetary compensation for his personal services, an arrangement considered legal but perhaps questionable.[34]

With just five days left before the runoff election of August 22, Allred, concerned about not being ahead in the Senate race, made doubly sure that Bravo delivered the hefty Tejano bloc vote in Zapata. "I want you to do everything within your power until the polls close on Saturday night to get as many Allred people to the polls as possible—let's get a big majority while we are at it," wrote Allred, urging Bravo to adopt the slogan: "CARRY YOUR COUNTY FOR ALLRED."[35]

Since there were no local candidates in the runoff election, the voting at Zapata County's four precincts went rather uneventfully. The runoff election paired Allred against O'Daniel for U.S. Senator; John Lee Smith against Harold Beck for lieutenant governor; and Jesse James against W. Gregory Hatcher for state treasurer. A total of 639 county residents cast their votes: they favored Allred for senator (615 to 24), Smith for lieutenant governor (613 to 15), James for state treasurer (615 to 14), and Beauford Jester for Texas railroad commissioner (615 to 12). The remaining boss-controlled counties voted for the same candidates—Webb, Jim Hogg, and Starr counties likewise supporting Allred, Smith, James, and Jester—except that as before, Jim Wells supported O'Daniel, while Duval went with Allred.[36]

The boss-free South Texas counties split between Allred and O'Daniel. Hidalgo County voted for O'Daniel, Smith, James, and Jester; Cameron County voted for Allred, Beck, James, and Jester. Dimmit, Kenedy, and Willacy counties voted for O'Daniel, while Brooks, Nueces, and Kleberg counties went with Allred. Allegedly, Parr controlled ten or more counties in South Texas, but out of a total of fourteen counties, nine voted for Allred, and five supported O'Daniel.

As indicated, counties with influential political machines (Jim Wells, Zapata, Webb, Starr, Duval, and Jim Hogg) gave the winning candidates whopping support, indicating that the local machines controlled the votes. Conversely, in counties with less political hegemony, the votes were evenly distributed among the candidates. This latter outcome indicated more freedom at the polls, honest election judges, and considerable disagreement among the voters. The 1942 runoff Senate race for South

Table 6. 1942 Runoff Senate Race

	O'Daniel	Allred
Hidalgo	4,406	4,037
Jim Wells	1,690	1,348
Zapata	23	615
Webb	291	4,254
Starr	32	982
Jim Hogg	86	578
Dimmit	396	364
Duval	115	2,770
Cameron	3,255	3,313
Brooks	226	391
Kenedy	61	27
Willacy	1,217	461
Nueces	4,327	5,836
Kleberg	488	672

Source: Mike Kingston et al., *The Texas Almanac's Political History of Texas,* pp. 126–29

Texas illustrated that one political boss did not control the leaders of other counties but rather that a political mosaic existed, in which local leaders determined their own positions and formed alliances and coalitions with surrounding counties if needed.

When the statewide election tabulations were announced, incumbent O'Daniel had defeated Allred for the Senate seat by 451,359 votes to 433,203. The *Laredo Times* described the close election as being like a "political horse race ... it appeared that the one that stuck out his tongue would win the race." [37] To close out the election year, Governor Stevenson issued a proclamation announcing Tuesday, November 3, 1942, as the date for the general election.

With the conclusion of the runoff election, the local politicos set their eyes on the Democratic State Convention, scheduled to begin on September 8, 1942, at the Gregory gymnasium on the University of Texas campus in Austin. The Zapata County delegation elected to represent the four voting precincts consisted of the leaders of the political machine— J. M. Sánchez, Leopoldo Martínez, Manuel Medina, and County Judge Bravo. [38] A few weeks before the convention, John J. O'Hern, representing Rogers Kelley's 27th District of Texas, had sent Judge Bravo some proxy forms to use in case a delegate, at the last minute, would be unable to attend the convention. O'Hern proceeded to inform the judge that "inasmuch as . . . Senator Rogers Kelley has joined the Armed Forces and is not going to be there, it is necessary that we do everything we can to protect his interests while he is fighting for ours."[39]

Two days after the convention, the Zapata County Commissioners' Court convened at a specially called meeting to discuss the vacancy for district and county clerk left open by the induction of Matías Cuéllar into the army. Matías had neither requested a leave of absence nor appointed a deputy clerk to handle the business affairs.[40] Judge Bravo asked Salvador García, who had lost to Guillermo González in the primary, to resign his remaining time as commissioner and consider taking Cuéllar's post. Four days later, on September 14, Bravo appointed González to fill García's unexpired term. The truism that politicians make strange bedfellows is no less true in South Texas counties than the Lone Star State as a whole.

SELECTIVE SERVICE SYSTEM FIASCO

As the general election drew closer, Judge Bravo's political opponents (even though he had no competitor for his post) sought dubious ways to embarrass him, to reduce his political influence, and eventually to remove him from office. In a politically motivated scheme, the Zapata County Selective Service Board (composed of three ranchers and a businessperson, all but one were staunch Republican supporters) on August 21, 1942, intentionally classified Bravo in class III-A, a deferment for dependency, which implied that if he were drafted, his family would suffer hardships.[41] The local board members were aware of the various selective service system draft categories but refused his request for reclassification. Judge Bravo, well-known for his patrotism, was deeply annoyed. On the advice of the county attorney, he wrote a lengthy letter to the local board, not appealing his classification but asking the board to correct it. His argument cited the Selective Service Act, section 24, volume 3, which indicated that the proper classification should have been class IV-B, "a judge of a court of record."[42] His intentions all along were to set the record straight (rumors that he was trying to evade military duty notwithstanding); he still had hopes of pursuing the possibility of acceptance at the officers' training school.

Bravo sent a similar letter to the state selective service system head-quarters in Austin, requesting an interpretation of the regulations. An attached letter from County Attorney Leo C. Buckley stated, "Judge Bravo has never shown any inclination to evade military service, but on the contrary has made several bona fide, sustained attempts to secure a commission."[43] On September 3, 1942, Bravo was aptly vindicated. Captain Fred Upchurch with the selective service division of appeals answered, "Without going into detail, it is not even a debatable question that a County Judge is a Judge of a 'court of record' and as such, should be placed in classification IV-B."[44] Captain Upchurch sent a copy of his reply to the Zapata County local board and to Judge Bravo.

DON LEOPOLDO'S ELECTION CAMPAIGN

At the local level, the general election escalated to the heated campaign the Laredo newspaper had predicted. Judge Bravo faced no opposition, but Sheriff Leopoldo Martínez was right in the middle of all the mud-slinging and personal insults. His opponent, Lauro Garza, bombarded the county with a political propaganda flyer entitled "La Voz del Amo y Don Leopoldo" (The Boss's Voice and Mr. Leopoldo), with Garza's photograph centered in the upper middle section.[45] Garza, a well-known rancher from a prominent South Texas family, operated the family's Zapata County estate, comprising of over thirty thousand acres and some twenty five hundred head of cattle. Using rhetorical elegance in attacking Martínez in Spanish, Garza accused him of occupying several public offices for the economic and political benefit of his uncles (José M. Sánchez and Ygnacio Sánchez) and other relatives; of running the county like a concentration camp, for all the corrupt politicians seemed to be concentrated there; of recognizing no boundaries in his political ambition, for since childhood the sheriff had been a political parasite draining the county; and of sending agents from the political machine to Laredo to solicit illegal absentee votes.[46] In another political flyer, Garza referred to his opponent's family as the Royal Family of Zapata, headed by none other than King Leopoldo![47]

To protect his seat, the sheriff assigned additional deputy sheriffs, at times described as *pistoleros*, to watch the elections. According to the opposition, their presence was to intimidate the Partido Nuevo party voters. Understandably, the county political machine rallied behind Leopoldo Martínez to reinforce his chances of keeping his post. Election results indicated that the incumbent defeated Lauro Garza by 699 to 375 votes. Allegations surfaced claiming that many votes for Garza were lost or destroyed by the presiding judges, who, it was claimed, intentionally tampered with the ballots. During the election, Judge Bravo resorted to outside political influences to gather support for the candidate of the Democratic Party. In combination with the usual speakers from Edinburg, he contracted the services of A. Y. Baker's sister, Florine Baker, as a motivational speaker. He wrote to her "Enclosing a cashable warrant for your service but which does not cover your sacrifice in making time to attend. . . . my sincere thanks to you, for your good will and desire to help us out election day."[48]

RACIAL DISCRIMINATION

Shortly after the general election, Judge Bravo and his family visited his son, Joseph, who had been transferred to South Plains Army Air Field near Lubbock. On their trip, they observed large signs posted outside restaurants warning Tejanos to stay away: "We do not serve Mexicans." In discussing his observations with his son, the judge also found out that other business establishments, such as barbershops, practiced similar discriminatory policies.[49]

As already noted, the issue of discrimination was seldom a problem in Zapata, Webb, or Starr counties, as the population was predominantly Hispanic. But in many South and Central Texas communities, discrimination against Tejanos, even those who wore military uniforms, increased to an all-time high. They were treated as inferior, as second-class citizens. People of Mexican descent born in Texas and citizens of Mexico were equally discriminated against in public places—especially people whose skin was a dusky shade of brown.

Obviously angered by the overt display of racial prejudice against the Hispanic race in general, including Tejano soldiers, Judge Bravo solicited the assistance of his old friend, José T. Canales, a prominent Brownsville attorney and civil rights advocate, to look into the matter. Together they drafted a letter to Governor Stevenson, with courtesy copies to State Senator Kelley and Representatives West and Kleberg, stating in part, "Suppose my people in Zapata County would put up signs that they would not serve 'Gringos'; I know what you would do in such a case; and I believe that you would not hesitate to act likewise. I merely request that you, as our Governor should do likewise and protect our Latin American soldier citizens from humiliation and prevent these demoralizing conditions to exist in any section of the State." [50] The judge further recommended that at the next session of the legislature, the governor initiate some legislation to stop the practice of discrimination.

On December 4, 1942, after reviewing and revising a draft copy of the letter, Judge Bravo advised Judge Canales about collecting additional documentation, "Am expecting my son from Lubbock on the 14th of this month, so I am holding the writing of the letter until said time as I want to have the name of the barbershop where the incident happened and I would also like to have the evidence on other cases, and that way in case of an investigation we can produce the evidence." [51]

Constant political pressure—from Judge Bravo, J. T. Canales, Alonso S. Perales, and other Tejano civil rights advocates—and Mexico's strong stand against discrimination affecting Mexican nationals caused Governor Stevenson to approve House Concurrent (Caucasian Race) Resolution 105 on May 6, 1943. In developing the statement to discourage discrimination against Hispanics, state officials took into account the Hispanic community's involvement in the war; Mexico's friendly diplomatic gesture to continue the Bracero program (whereby Mexican workers were temporarily hired in the United States to perform farm labor); and the mounting pressure from Tejano civil rights activists. [52] In essence, the resolution stated that all Caucasians, including Tejanos and Mexican nationals, had equal access to public facilities, and it strongly discouraged discrimination in all such places as violation of the state's Good Neighbor policy. Unfortunately, the legal and judicial empowerment to enforce it statewide did not exist. Consequently, racial discrimination against Tejanos and Mexican citizens continued unabated.

Shortly after the passage of the Caucasian race resolution, proponents who endorsed Governor Stevenson's Good Neighbor policy adopted similar positions in their own counties, condemning any type of racial discrimination against Hispanic citizens. The Cameron County Commissioners' Court, led by J. T. Canales, adopted such a plan on August 23, 1943, becoming the first county in South Texas to do so. [53] Canales sent copies of the Cameron County resolution to Judge Bravo, Judge Garza of Starr County, and Judge Looney of Hidalgo County. Canales vehemently suggested to Bravo "that whatever we fail to do now in order to wipe out and destroy this prejudice against Mexicans and Latin Americans it will never be done after the War. The time to strike is now."[54]

As a member of the Zapata County LULAC Council No. 123, Judge Bravo reviewed Canales's statement with the council president, René A. Garza, and added changes. After a final draft had been prepared, the LULAC council presented it to the county commissioners for review and discussion. Officials reacted immediately to Canales's proposal, modified the Cameron County resolution by substituting dates and their names, and struck out the word *county* and replaced it with *State* to signify that discrimination did not exist in Zapata but was more prevalent in other parts of Texas.[55] In Zapata County, Hispanics occupied most public offices and owned local businesses and consequently had better interracial understanding with Anglos than in Hidalgo or Cameron County.

On September 13, 1943, at their regularly scheduled monthly meeting, the Zapata County Commissioners' Court unanimously approved going on record "as condemning any discrimination against our fellow citizens of Latin American extraction, and/or our fellow Americans of the Republic of Mexico or of the other United Nations on account of racial differences."[56] They went one step further and submitted a copy of the resolution to Governor Stevenson, who on October 7, 1943, responded, "I was very pleased to have the copy of the Resolution adopted by the Commissioner's Court of Zapata County in reference to our Latin-American relations. This is such an interesting and encouraging action that I am having it brought to the attention of the Good Neighbor Commission which I recently named in Texas."[57]

About a week later, Bravo notified Canales about the governor's reply and included a copy of the Zapata County resolution. He also mentioned regretting not having reported several discriminatory incidents that he had witnessed while traveling to Lubbock. Had he included them in his report to the governor, Bravo informed Canales, his letter "would have been very timely, and further it would have hit said Governor right in the *Llaves*, [a Mexican expression similar to the English idiom of getting hit between the eyes] as he is from that section of which it referred."[58]

In the spring of 1946, during a business trip to San Antonio (about 150 miles from Zapata), Bravo ran up against the problem more dramatically. As he took a brief rest at a small eating place in Dilley on Interstate 35, several Anglo men assaulted him, but failed in their burglary attempt.

These men had on numerous occasions reportedly manhandled other Hispanics who stopped for a coffee break.[59] Other complaints of racial intimidation soon reached prominent civil rights attorney Alonso Perales, who was in the process of collecting affidavits to present before the Grand Jury in San Antonio. Aware that Judge Bravo had been one of the victims, Perales requested his assistance in identifying the Anglos and describing the incident in full detail. Perales collected enough data to show that discrimination against Hispanics had escalated alarmingly after the war.[60]

Bravo and Perales were contemporaries. The judge was well aware of Perales's reputation as the most influential Tejano advocate for civil rights. Both had been involved during the initial struggles to organize LULAC in South Texas during the late 1920s. The judge felt that going to Perales for assistance could bring about changes. Perales, along with J. T. Canales, could do something to curtail legally the discrimination against Tejanos. This issue did not appear again in Judge Bravo's agenda until 1949, when Lyndon Johnson and Hector P. García became involved in the Félix Longoria incident—though he was a native of Three Rivers, Texas, the Rice Funeral Home denied burial services for the hometown war hero.

RURAL MAIL DELIVERY

Constituents from the small farming town of Falcon pressured Judge Bravo to submit petitions to government officials requesting the establishment of a post office for their convenience. The judge recommended Victoria Ramírez as the postmistress if the Post Office Department approved the application.[61] Mail delivery in rural communities was crucial to the needs of the farmers, who in many instances lived in isolated settings along the Río Grande. According to the established mail route, delivery came from Río Grande City to the post office at Lopeño, about twelve miles from Falcon, and residents had to travel there to pick up their mail. After almost eight months (January to August, 1943) of corresponding with government officials, the response was not favorable. Based on the findings of an investigation report, First Assistant Postmaster General K. P. Aldrich ruled against the request on grounds that "Falcon is a very small farm community and the only business establishments are two small stores."[62] However, Judge Bravo continued his lobbying efforts with Congressman Milton West. Finally, after another field re-

view, the second assistant postmaster general, who supervised this particular mail route, accommodated the Falcon residents by delivering mail
to their mailboxes along the route from Río Grande City to Lopeño. At
least for the moment, the farmers and ranchers of the town were satisfied
and maintained their strong support to the PV, while the congressman
kept on good terms with the machine.

The post office at Lopeño had been established during the early part
of the twentieth century and served as the midpoint station between
Roma and Zapata. The first post office in the county, founded in 1854,
was located in the county seat, and another post office had been created
in San Ygnacio in 1876, with rancher Fernando Uribe as the first postmaster.[63] Toward the end of 1943, Judge Bravo supported the appointment of Ernesto M. Uribe, a grandson of Fernando, for postmaster at
San Ygnacio. Through the political assistance of Congressman West and
Judge Bravo, Ernesto got the job.[64] Besides the postal stations at San
Ygnacio, Lopeño, and Zapata, the ranching communities of Bustamante
and Escobas also obtained mail service stations.

POLITICAL INTERLUDE

In neighboring Webb County, the year of 1943 saw the four Kazen broth-
ers plunge into the political limelight. Three years earlier, the second oldest brother, Philip, had defeated the candidate from the Webb County
Independent Club for district attorney of the 49th Judicial District.[65] In
August 1942, Philip resigned his post to pursue an appointment with the
Foreign Economic Administration in South America, where he played a
pivotal role in securing needed materials for the war effort. Governor
Stevenson needed to fill the vacancy for district attorney, and as with
other key political appointments, Zapata's Partido Viejo publicly endorsed and supported Philip's next sibling, Emil James (Jimmy). After
confirmation by the Texas Senate on January 22, 1943, Jimmy found
time to send an appreciative letter to Judge Bravo and the political machine of Zapata County.[66] Charles, the oldest brother, was Webb County
clerk. The youngest of the four was Abraham Jr., state representative for
the 75th Congressional District during the 1940s.

Bravo also worked in behalf of other political aspirants. After losing
in the 1942 runoff senatorial election to O'Daniel, James V. Allred had
returned to private practice in Houston. But his sights had remained set
on returning to the federal bench. He constantly made business trips to

Table 7. South Texas Counties Census, 1940–43

County	April 1, 1940	November 1, 1943	Change
Duval	20,565	14,500	−6,065
Hidalgo	106,059	94,270	−11,789
Jim Wells	20,239	16,942	−3,297
Starr	12,793	11,426	−1,367
Webb	45,423	45,729	+306
Zapata	3,916	3,259	−657

Source: Texas Almanac, 1945–46

Washington, D.C., and Bravo kept putting in a good word for him, especially with Senator Tom Connally. On one occasion, Allred wrote to Bravo: "Upon my return today from Washington I find a copy of your telegram to Senator Connally. I want you to know how very much I appreciate this action on your part, all the more since it was voluntary."[67] The trips to the nation's capital paid off six years later, when President Truman appointed Allred to the federal judiciary.

Toward the latter part of 1943, Zapata County again became totally immersed in the Second War Loan Drive. The U.S. Treasury War Finance Committee presented a certificate of recognition to Judge Bravo for the increased number of armed forces volunteers from Zapata County, for the number of citizens abiding by the gasoline rationing requirements, for the amount of U.S. Savings Bonds sold, and for the receipts resulting from selling salvage supplies and iron parts. The document stated in part that Bravo had "rendered in a time of national crises outstanding service to the United States of America" and was being recognized for "an unselfish and patriotic volunteer participation in the nation's war program."[68] Despite all the campaigning and political fund-raisers during the 1942 election, Zapata County never lost its emotional and patriotic intensity in the war effort. During the 1945 American Red Cross War Fund drive, the citizens of Zapata County contributed more than their share and even surpassed state quotas. As a result, the American National Red Cross presented Judge Bravo with a special recognition award for "Outstanding Loyalty, Patriotism, and Public Spirit."[69]

In addition to his active participation in different committees, the judge wrote many letters of recommendation for Zapata soldiers who were seeking promotion in rank or wanted to attend officers' training school. On April 15, 1943, at the request of County Treasurer Primitivo Uribe, Judge Bravo wrote a letter of support for his friend's son—Pvt. Pedro P. Uribe.[70] At other times, the judge also intervened with the selective service board to have men deferred from military duty because of farming or ranching responsibilities.

D-DAY AND 1944 POLITICS

Two major events highlighted the 1944 election year—D-Day on June 6 and President Roosevelt's unprecedented election to a fourth term in office. At the state level, Judge Bravo received requests for endorsements from several leading incumbents who sought reelection. Petitions for his support and influence came from Congressman Milton H. West; Richard Critz, associate justice of the Texas Supreme Court; and Grover Sellers, Texas attorney general.[71] The judge also wrote letters for those seeking appointments. He and Leopoldo Martínez strongly endorsed Brian S. Odem of the U.S. Attorney General's office for United States attorney to the Southern District Court, perhaps because of his liberal stand on racial issues. Odem seemed to be the best qualified to oversee the judicial system that had direct legal jurisdiction over Zapata County in particular and South Texas in general.[72] The Southern District of Texas had its district court office in Corpus Christi.

About a month before the July 22, 1944, Democratic primary, the United States launched its biggest military offensive on Normandy. All political activities were set aside during this important historic day of World War II, as people all over the country stayed tuned to their radios. Both of Judge Bravo's sons, Eddie and Joseph, stationed in different air force bases, commented about it. While Joseph dated his letter "D-Day," Eddie simply stated, "June 6, 1944," and wrote: "Have been listening in all day on D-Day news. Maybe things will start happening now . . . its [sic] two o'clock. Will hear Pres. Roosevelt tonite."[73] Meanwhile, partisan talks of suspending the 1944 national election for the duration of the war never materialized.

An odd twist of events in Zapata County just before the primary was that Sgt. Matías Cuéllar, the short, spectacled incumbent district and county clerk then stationed in Hebron, Nebraska, just a few miles from the Kansas border, forgot to tender his application for placing his name on the ballot. Instead, his wife, Elena Cuéllar, submitted her own name. The political machine reacted furiously to Elena's action and quickly sent Matías a stern telegram with specific and succinct instructions: "WE WILL SUPPORT YOU AS AGREED BUT WILL NOT SUPPORT YOUR WIFE. MAIL YOUR APPLICATION BEFORE SATURDAY AND YOUR WIFE WITHDRAWAL OF APPLICATION. OTHERWISE REGRET ADVISE WE WILL SUPPORT OTHER CANDIDATE. WE ARE SENDING THIS MESSAGE TO GIVE YOU AN OPPORTU-NITY TO COMPLY WITH YOUR AGREEMENT." [74] Obviously wanting an im-mediate response, the county sent Matías another firm telegram five days later. This time, they strongly demanded his wife's immediate withdrawal from the election, or else they would support another candidate. They assured him that collecting twenty-five endorsements from voters would get him on the slate.[75] Matías wisely convinced his wife to withdraw from the race, allowed his friends to place his name on the ballot, and regained political credibility with the county jefes. The notion of having a woman in public office was probably not the issue, and the action taken by the county leaders cannot be construed as discriminatory since the county, perhaps only one of a few in the state, had a woman as chairperson of the county Democratic Executive Committee. What marital repercussions, if any, emanated from this family quandary, may never be known.

Leading up to the primary, the temperature of the election campaign remained tepid, as all the incumbents at the local and state levels were certain to be reelected. Neither Judge Bravo nor his political coterie faced any serious opposition. The calm caused Judge Bravo to forewarn Asso-ciate Justice Richard Critz that "Zapata County is not voting near its strength next Saturday, but by what I have been able to observe all votes will be cast for your candidacy." [76] As expected, Zapata County sup-ported all the state incumbents with large majorities. At the guber-natorial level, Governor Stevenson received 317 votes, while Alex M. Ferguson garnered 1 vote. Other South Texas counties, including Webb, also gave Stevenson and the other incumbents similarly big margins.[77]

With just a month before the November 7, 1944, general election, the "Roosevelt-Truman Campaign for Texas," spearheaded by both the Democratic National Committee and the State Democratic Executive Committee, got into high gear statewide with an aggressive campaign aimed at involving county judges. Within a span of almost two weeks, Myron G. Blalock, National Committeeperson for Texas, sent Judge Bravo many letters urging him to accept the chairmanship of the Finance

Committee for Zapata County: "As a loyal Democrat who has always unselfishly served your party, the Democratic National Committee and the State Democratic Executive Committee are asking you to assume the Chairmanship, . . . we are relying on you, as one of our State's leading Democrats." [78] Harry L. Seay, chairman of the State Democratic Executive Committee, was more demanding in his request, instructing Mrs. Josefa Gutiérrez to replace precinct chairpersons with people who were pro–Roosevelt-Truman Democrats. [79] The Laredo newspaper carried large political advertisements letting the voters know that the Webb County Independent Club was supporting the Roosevelt-Truman ticket. On the front page of one newspaper article, the enlarged photos of the Webb County machine leaders—M. J. Raymond, Peter P. Leyendecker, Hugh S. Cluck, and Albert Martin—urged the people to vote a straight Democratic ticket. [80]

The statewide campaign goal for Texas was to collect $150,000 and one million votes for Roosevelt and Truman. In terms of the financial quota assigned to Zapata County, the county political machine contributed one hundred dollars, and on October 21, 1944, Judge Bravo unequivocally assured the Democratic Party of the county's support: "You may rest assured that Zapata County will vote its strength for the Democratic Party. . . . Although this is one of the State's poorest counties we have gladly sacrificed ourselves to contribute the $100.00 quota assigned to us. Hoping that our Commander in Chief the greatest leader in the World shall be elected by a large majority." [81]

At the national level, President Roosevelt won a sweeping victory over the Republican candidate from New York, Thomas E. Dewey, with 432 electoral votes. Meanwhile, at the state level, the Democrats' diligent efforts fell short of their statewide goal of one million votes. In Zapata County, all the incumbents easily won reelection. The electorate returned Judge Bravo to a fourth term along with his ticket of fellow Democrats. [82]

THE 1946 DEMOCRATIC PRIMARY

In making future plans for financing the upcoming 1946 campaign year, the Democratic Party held an elaborate fund-raising dinner in Austin, Texas, on April 20, 1945, on the occasion of Thomas Jefferson's birthday. Senator Tom Connally gave the keynote speech, while Tom Miller, Edward Clark, and members of the planning committee undertook the monumental task of raising over fifty thousand dollars. [83] The county's machine, consisting of M. Bravo, M. Cuéllar, G. González, L. Martínez, M. Medina, L. Ramírez, and P. Uribe, again demonstrated its active and loyal support to the Democratic Party by a contribution of fifty dollars. This fund-raising in 1945 became indispensable for dealing with the rising popularity of the Republican Party.[84]

Generally speaking, the Democratic primary on July 27, 1946, offered no major controversial issues or candidates, with the exception of the gubernatorial race, which overshadowed those for other state offices. Governor Stevenson decided not to seek reelection, thus opening the field to fourteen aspiring contenders. At the head of the group were three leading candidates: former Attorney General Grover Sellers; Dr. Homer Rainey, ousted president of the University of Texas; and Beauford Jester. At a meeting held nine days before the primary, Judge Bravo and other political bosses from Duval, Webb, Jim Hogg, and Starr counties gathered in Laredo to endorse the following candidates: Tom Connally for senator, Milton West for congressman, Grover Sellers for governor, Boyce House for lieutenant governor, Pat Neff, Jr., for attorney general, and Jesse James for treasurer.[85] Election results indicated that Zapata, Webb, Starr, and Jim Hogg counties, together with George Parr's Duval County, gave Sellers the Tejano bloc votes. The votes, however, showed big percentages in Duval (97%), Webb (89%) and Starr (67%). Zapata (55%) and Jim Hogg (44%) had a more evenly distributed count. Zapata County went with Sellers with 224 votes; Dr. Rainey came in second with 159 and Jester a distant third with a mere 23. The Lower Río Grande counties of Hidalgo, Dimmit, Jim Wells, and Cameron voted for Jester.

RUN-OFF ELECTION, 1946

Webb County's powerful Independent Club held a meeting on August 10, 1946, in Laredo with George Parr, David Carrillo Chapa of Duval County, Gus Guerra of Starr County, Judge Bravo, and other politicos from South Texas. After much deliberation, the bosses reached a consensus to support Jester and Shivers for governor and lieutenant governor respectively. However, the results from the August 24, 1946, runoff election for governor between Jester and Dr. Rainey presented an interesting dilemma. When the returns were received, the voters of Zapata County were evenly split for the first time when they gave Rainey a narrow ten-vote victory over the favorite Jester (282 to 272 votes). Parr must have been fuming, since Zapata County was supposed to support Jester. Admittedly, political machines do not always persuade the independent voter. Their operations do break down once in a while.[86]

The runoff results indicated that the boss counties (Webb, Starr, Duval, and Jim Hogg) that had supported Sellers in the primary had now voted for Jester. The counties that had initially voted for Jester (Hidalgo, Cameron, Dimmit, and Jim Wells) maintained their steadfast loyalty. But Zapata, Kleberg, and Willacy counties voted for Rainey. Perhaps Willacy County Judge Charles R. Johnson owed Bravo a political favor or vice versa, and they campaigned for Rainey. A more plausible explanation, albeit philosophical at best, is that Dr. Rainey's promises fell more in line with Judge Bravo's plank: more money for county schools; soil conservation; improved farm-to-market roads; a good hospital closer to farm families; and significant improvements in farm-family cooperatives.[87]

In the end Jester defeated Rainey overwhelmingly, polling 66 percent of the statewide vote (701,018 to 355,654) while Shivers easily defeated House.[88] In the runoff race for the 15th congressional seat, incumbent Milton West triumphed over Colonel Ellis by almost 500 votes. Within the thirteen counties that comprised the 15th district, six voted in favor of West—Zapata, Webb, Maverick, Zavala, La Salle, and Cameron. Conversely, Dimmit, Jim Hogg, Starr, Hidalgo, Willacy, Frio, and Medina counties supported the colonel.[89] It was a close race all the way; an unofficial count had West ahead by over 55 votes (20,707 to 20,152). This voting pattern among the South Texas counties again suggests that Parr did not control or manipulate all the counties all the time. In this particular election, two of the boss counties—Starr and Jim Hogg—did not follow Webb or Zapata, or vice versa.

FOOT-AND-MOUTH DISEASE
INTERNATIONAL PROJECT

Shortly after the conclusion of the 1946 election campaign, Zapata County and other border counties became involved in an international collaborative effort between the United States and Mexico known as the Foot-and-Mouth Disease Eradication Program *(La Comisión Mexico-Americana Para la Erradicación de la Fiebre Aftosa).*[90] The responsibility for recommending qualified people to supervise the cattle-crossing activities along the border fell on the county judges. At the onset, guards assigned to Zapata, Webb, and Starr counties were not from there but from neighboring areas.[91] Judge Bravo, representing the judges from the three border counties, expressed his concern by telegram to State Senator Rogers Kelley about hiring capable men from their own counties: "BELIEVE THAT WE SHOULD HAVE GIVEN OPPORTUNITY FOR OUR RESIDENT VETERANS WHO ARE QUALIFIED FOR THIS WORK. . . . IT IS MY UNDERSTANDING THAT [THE] MAJORITY OF GUARDS IN ZAPATA COUNTY ARE FROM HEBBRONVILLE."[92]

Senator Kelley interceded on behalf of the border counties by writing letters, sending telegrams, and making phone calls to the commission members, but to no avail, since all the positions had already been filled.[93] The commission had quietly bypassed the political protocol of going through the county judges. Caught in an economic crunch of trying to find jobs for returning veterans, the border leaders urged Judge Bravo to continue the letter-writing campaign. For many returning World War II veterans, the employment opportunities in Mexico came at a very opportune time. Even though his efforts with the state commission seemed fruitless, Bravo sent a letter to one of the commission members stationed in Laredo, requesting that serious employment consideration be given to six county residents, "and all of them are fully qualified to perform the duties required to guard the Mexican border against the spread of Foot and Mouth disease, and will I am sure serve you as well or better than any that you may employ anywhere."[94] Senator Kelley responded to Bravo's plea, "I have also had several telephone conversations with both Roy Loventhal and Tom Lasater (Livestock Sanitary Commission members) in an effort to see that we get jobs on the commission for our friends from Starr, Zapata, and Webb Counties."[95]

With inside confidential information that the federal government might soon take over the state's Livestock Sanitary Commission, Judge Bravo sensed the possibility of additional jobs. He immediately notified Congressman West about the status of the border situation. "Within the last 30 days the Texas Legislature authorized the expenditure of $150,000. . . . However it turned out that no individual was employed from Starr, Zapata or Webb go [sic] [to] guard the river within said Counties, instead, the[y] shipped a flock of men from Jim Hogg and La Salle Counties."[96]

During the spring of 1947, Congressman West requested a list of names for possible employment with the Bureau of Animal Industry. Qualifications for employment consisted of fluency in Spanish, experience with and knowledge of livestock, and ability to ride horses. For the next few months, news of job openings with the Bureau of Animal Industry spread throughout the border region. Judge Bravo wasted no time in coordinating this effort with René Garza of the American Legion Post and identified nine prospective candidates from each of the four voting precincts.[97] In March and April, Judge Bravo worked diligently to ensure that West supported both his brother Robert's application and that of his own oldest son, Eddie, which indeed were later approved.

During the summer months, Judge Bravo continued to submit names for employment. The judge recommended Jacob Rathmell, a rancher and son of the Zapata County Republican chairperson, who was married to Guadalupe Martínez, daughter of County Sheriff Leopoldo Martínez. For about two months, Judge Bravo, Leopoldo Martínez, and Congressman West communicated on Rathmell's application for employment as an appraiser.[98] The process of eradication of foot-and-mouth disease in Mexico continued for another five years. The project came to a successful conclusion in 1952.

PRELUDE TO THE 1948 POLITICAL CAMPAIGN

During the summer of 1947, strategic plans for the upcoming 1948 election had been placed in motion, with potential candidates feeling out the opposition and assessing the political climate of hopeful supporters before officially deciding to throw their hat into the political ring. As a postscript to one of his letters, Congressman West alarmingly questioned Judge Bravo's choice: "I have just received a report to the effect that you have agreed to support Judge Lloyd Bentsen, Jr. of Hidalgo County for Congress next year."[99] In reference to his alleged support for Judge Bentsen in the approaching race, Bravo assured West that it was only a rumor. Furthermore, Bentsen did not expect any commitments because Bravo had explicitly expressed his wholehearted endorsement for West: "I advised him [Bentsen] that if you ran for said office that I would support you because in addition of being an old reliable friend, I owed you lots of favors."[100] Besides, Zapata's political machine was being coy about making any premature commitments until it was clear which candidate Webb County would support, and "possibly Laredo would put out a candidate and . . . Zapata County depended a whole lot on the attitude that Webb County would take, with the exception that in case you ran, it might split up the vote."[101]

Bravo confirmed what other supporters had already expressed—that they would not support Bentsen if Congressman West ran for reelection. At any rate, political changes in the 15th Congressional District did happen, primarily because of the unexpected resignation of Representative West, whose failing health caused him to give up his seat of fifteen years in the early part of 1948. Months later, the election of Hidalgo County Judge Lloyd Bentsen, Jr., to the vacant post left a vacuum in the relationship between Zapata County and that district's office. Judge Bravo did not have the same confidence and trust in Congressman Bentsen and could not rely on him for political favors because Zapata County had gone on to vote against him in both the July 24 Democratic primary and the August 28, 1948, runoff election. The judge, however, did find another friend and ally in Lyndon Johnson, who acted as the intermediary for the border counties and continued assisting them in obtaining more jobs in the foot-and-mouth program.[102] Gradually, Johnson began to fill the void and establish the rapport that Representative West had so successfully established with the Zapata political machine. The relationship between Judge Bravo and Lyndon Johnson, as political allies and personal friends, would solidify during the hotly debated 1948 senatorial election campaign (discussed in the next chapter).

POLITICAL CONNECTIONS PAY OFF

From the onset of World War II in 1941 to the Foot-and-Mouth Disease International Project in 1947, Judge Bravo, functioning as the *jefe político* of Zapata County, worked diligently in addressing many different county needs and in seeing to it that the county contributed to the nation's general welfare. In the process, he enabled the Post Office Department to accommodate the needs of one of the ranching communities. As chairperson of several committees during the war effort, he helped surpass the county quotas allotted by the state for the USO War Fund Campaign, the Second War Loan Drive, and the American Red Cross War Fund.

In addition, he used to his advantage his ties to state public officials from outside the county. But how did Zapata County profit from these connections? Judge Bravo strongly believed in the political adage "You scratch my back, I scratch yours" and in using the principle to the maximum extent possible. He took special care to establish close collaboration with those who represented the interests of the county. He cultivated and courted the friendship of Milton West, Rogers Kelley, Lyndon Johnson, Abraham Kazen, Jr., and Jimmy Kazen. Judge Bravo endorsed other state officials (Edward Smith, John Lee Smith, Bascom Giles, George H. Sheppard, and others) because of their alliance with those politicians who produced tangible results for Zapata County. In other campaigns, he supported those upon whom the area bosses had collectively agreed or, as in the 1942 runoff between Jester and Brooks, those whom the independent oil companies pressured the judge to back in return for past political favors.

For those endorsements, Judge Bravo expected reciprocation now and in the future. Sometimes this assistance was for individuals; sometimes for the benefit of the county. For example, his close association with Congressman West and Johnson resulted in obtaining jobs for county residents (and for family members) during the foot-and-mouth disease eradication project. In the case of the construction of Falcon Dam and the relocation process (covered in chapters 6 and 7), the Bravo Papers and the LBJ Library contain a plethora of correspondence indicating that public officials and government bureaucrats conceded to the requests of Judge Bravo because of his knowledge about running county matters. Judge Bravo's ties with state public officials who were not directly involved with the county were more symbolic, mainly because they were associated with the same Democratic political party. He supported and campaigned for them but did not expect reciprocation through patronage or graft.

The relationship between the judge and state and federal government officials in part contributed to the Partido Viejo's resiliency, but so did the results he produced for his constituents. In return for the voters' loyalty, he provided more jobs, a better educational system with improved facilities, accessible farm-to-market roads, and new social services, especially during World War II. If anything stands out in the judge's ability to collect on past favors, it is his success in finding jobs for returning veterans. He helped place many of them in the foot-and-mouth project in Mexico. For those veterans who opted to stay in the county, Judge Bravo established a Veterans Vocational Training School. For those who could not attend high school or vocational classes because of their limited proficiency in English, he founded basic preparatory courses, acting in his capacity as the ex-officio superintendent. Those veterans eager to find employment or get an education after the war became loyal supporters of the Partido Viejo, extending their allegiance to Judge Bravo.

While Zapata County was not a focus for the racial discrimination that plagued other South Texas counties, Judge Bravo nonetheless used his influence as a political boss to seek relief for other Tejanos and Mexican citizens. His active involvement in civil rights issues during the 1930s and 1940s reflected his own sentiments regarding conditions facing *la raza*. He firmly believed, as did his fellow LULACers, that discrimination was wrong and that Tejano civil rights ought to be upheld. From growing up in Hidalgo County, he knew by firsthand experience about the injustices and atrocities committed against Tejanos by the Texas Rangers. Thus, as a product of the "Mexican American generation" who had experienced the anti-Mexican discrimination of the 1920s, the Great Depression, and World War II, Judge Bravo took a leadship role to change the socioeconomic and educational status quo of la raza.

Even so, Judge Bravo's administration, and the Partido Viejo, had an unsavory side. At times, voters kept the judge in power because of the friendly persuasion generated by the Big Four, who, understandably enough, happened to be well satisfied with Bravo's leadership role. Sheriff Don Leopoldo Martínez used his many family members to work the campaigns and, when necessary, placed more deputies on the payroll to intimidate the voters and influence the outcome of elections. The power elite in the county habitually reminded common folks, either subtly or overtly, that they should vote according to the dictates of the Partido Viejo.

THE TURBULENT POLITICAL CAMPAIGNS OF 1948

In the 1948 election, Judge Bravo sought a seventh term for county judge and faced a strong contender in PN candidate Emilio Dilley. No PN opponents since the 1940 candidacy of Juan M. Vela and his slate had seriously challenged the powerful political machine. Once more, the PN would find Bravo and company unbeatable.

The judge's ring was so efficient by the late 1940s that it could conceivably swing state and national races. When Congressman Lyndon B. Johnson made another bid for the United States Senate, the PV came through for him, allegedly changing the number of certified votes just days after the polls had closed. Collectively, Bravo and fellow border bosses delivered the Tejano bloc votes, which were crucial to Johnson's election victory. In a quintessential example of political collaboration, the South Texas bosses of Webb, Duval, Zapata, and Starr counties gave Johnson the narrow margin of 87 votes.

The aftermath of the runoff election resulted in a federal investigation involving Zapata, Duval, and Jim Wells counties (and possibly Webb County), which left an ugly mark in South Texas politics. Allegedly fraudulent elections, illegal voters, and stuffing ballot boxes became part of the lore underscoring bossism in these counties. Then, when the federal investigators hurled accusations of voting irregularities, the judge joined the other border leaders in demonstrating their effectiveness as skillful strategists, master manipulators, and shrewd operators.

THE 1948 DEMOCRATIC PRIMARY

Incumbent Lee "Pappy" O'Daniel decided not to seek another term as senator in 1948. Soon a tide of prospects filed for the post, so that when the deadline for applying drew to a close, a total of eleven hopeful candidates had placed their names on the ballot for the July 24 Democratic primary.[1] Among these were Lyndon B. Johnson and Coke Stevenson.

As soon as Johnson announced his candidacy for the Senate on May 12, 1948, Judge Bravo began politiking on his behalf. Former Governor Stevenson, considered by many Texans to be a leading contender for the Senate seat, had come out of retirement five months earlier. The bosses from the four counties in the 49th Judicial District (Jim Hogg, Dimmit, Zapata, and Webb) decided not to support Stevenson because he had declined to fill a vacancy in the district attorney's post with one of their favorite candidates. Instead, Stevenson had appointed S. Truman Phelps.[2]

Even though Johnson's campaign trail was cut short by unexpected surgery for the removal of kidney stones during the summer of 1948 at the Mayo Clinic in Rochester, Minnesota, Judge Bravo continued conducting a countywide effort on his behalf. While preparing to resume electioneering during mid-June, Johnson sent the judge two letters within a one-week period, thanking him for his all-out endorsements in the campaign to carry Zapata County. Encouraged by the support of the Partido Viejo, Johnson felt confident of becoming a Senator.[3]

As an integral part of the election strategy, Judge Bravo involved the Women Democratic Club of Zapata County, which consisted mostly of middle-class housewives. This group played a significant and active role at the grassroots level in obtaining crucial absentee votes. Josefa M. Gutiérrez, chairing the county's Democratic Executive Committee, belonged to a statewide organization called the Women's Division of the Lyndon Johnson for Senator Campaign; the local group included Josefa V. Bravo (Judge Bravo's wife), María V. Cuéllar (Bravo's sister-in-law), Elena Cuéllar (Matías's wife), Belia Benavides Muñoz, Elia González, Anita Ramírez, Petra V. Bustamante, and Josefa Ramos. These influential and loyal community volunteers implemented the tasks assigned them by Mrs. R. Max Brooks, chairperson of the statewide organization.

Their instructions from Mrs. Brooks were quite specific: obtain a poll tax list, mail campaign literature to each voter, and place pro-Johnson stickers on vehicle windshields, with the owner's approval of course. If time permitted, they were to make house visits and distribute additional campaign materials.[4] Throughout the campaign, Mrs. Brooks sent more instructions, along with encouraging remarks, suggesting that they maintain their efforts all over the county and, if necessary, contact the local chairperson for additional duties.[5]

On July 10, with ten days left for absentee voting, Josefa Gutiérrez received an urgent letter from Bess O. Beeman, cochair of the Women's Division for Johnson, stating in bold letters, "WE MUST NOT FORGET THE ABSENTEE VOTES," and reminding them to include "the votes of the person over 60 years of age."[6] According to the instructions, Mrs. Gutiérrez was to make sure every eligible person voted, including people going on vacations, sick at home or in a hospital, and those physically unable to go to the polls.[7]

With five days left before the primary, a worried Johnson sent the following telegram to Judge Bravo: "YOU WILL NEVER KNOW HOW MUCH I APPRECIATE WHAT YOU HAVE DONE IN THIS CAMPAIGN. I WILL BE FOREVER GRATEFUL. BUT THIS IS THE CLIMAX WEEK. THE PAY OFF IS SATURDAY. IF THERE IS A PLACE IN YOUR DISTRICT OR COUNTY NOT BEING THOROUGHLY WORKED, PLEASE SET IT GOING TODAY. THANKS FOR EVERTHING."[8]

While still concentrating on the Senate campaign, Partido Viejo leaders diverted their attention to a political rally scheduled for Wednesday, July 21, in honor of Philip A. Kazen, Democratic candidate for the 15th Congressional District, who had the endorsement of County Judge Manuel J. Raymond and the Webb County Independent Club machine. A day before the event, the Laredo newspaper sensationalized the upcoming event with the headlines, "Greatest Rally in Zapata Co. History Predicted for Kazen Wednesday Night."[9]

An orchestra played to a huge crowd as Kazen and his entourage arrived at the plaza. Judge Bravo, flanked by the other Democratic county leaders, introduced the guests seated in the *kiosco* (gazebo). The local politicos spoke eloquently in Spanish about electing Laredo's favorite son to represent them in their expected difficulty during the course of the upcoming construction of Falcon Dam and the eventual relocation of Zapata—the county seat.[10] Before a record crowd, Kazen assured them of supporting their concerns and vowed to fight for them. One of Kazen's opponents—Lloyd M. Bentsen, Jr.—purposely was not invited mainly because Zapata's Partido Viejo viewed his huge campaign expenditures with suspicion and regarded him as an outsider representing the economic interests of the Lower Río Grande Valley.[11]

As to his own race, Judge Bravo faced some obstacles, but none were directly related to the campaign since he had no opposition. The first developed when J. Luz Sáenz, a Veterans' Vocational Education teacher who had taught in Zapata County for about two years (1947–48)—and whom Bravo considered a close friend—began campaigning for Lloyd Bentsen, Jr. As part of the political machine's patronage, it was customary for the teachers to support the Partido Viejo–endorsed candidate. Fully aware of this local election practice but committed to his own principles, Sáenz opted to support Bentsen.[12] The judge, under direct orders from the political machine, fired Sáenz from the school district with regrets. Several local friends protested Sáenz's dismissal and sent a petition to L. A. Woods, state superintendent of public instruction in Texas, who sternly cautioned Judge Bravo, "May I urge you not to allow politics to get into the G.I. program . . . and cause you to get in trouble with the Federal Government."[13] The political machine ignored the petition and the whole episode passed quietly.

The second incident occurred when Mike López, another public school teacher, voted against the machine's candidate and consequently did not receive the fifty-dollar bonus that all the other teachers got. Infuriated, López demanded an explanation from Judge Bravo: "I am sorry if I voted not according to your will. I do not think that I voted against you. However, I did vote to what I thought was right."[14] The judge apologized for any misunderstandings, explained that the bonus was intended for all teachers who wanted to attend summer college classes, and sent Mike his bonus. It was an established practice in Zapata County that all county employees should be loyal to the political machine in return for patronage. Teachers voted for the Partido Viejo and in turn had college expenses covered.

In the county race for precinct 3, the fifty-two-year-old County Commissioner Guillermo González narrowly defeated his nephew, Santiago González, by three votes. Alleging irregularities in voting, tabulation, and reporting, the defeated Santiago promptly solicited the legal assistance of prominent San Antonio civil rights lawyer Alonso Perales. After studying the allegations, Perales confirmed Santiago's fears: "The evidence before me, however, indicates strongly that Mr. Guillermo González' election was irregular, and that several people voted unlawfully."[15]

Perales suggested to Judge Bravo that perhaps Guillermo should resign and the commissioners' court should appoint the thirty-eight-year-old Santiago as successor. Perales described the following scenario, designed to keep harmony in the family, to the judge. "In this manner both factions might again smoke the pipe of peace and everyone be happy. After all, the uncle would be yielding to the nephew and the Commissionership would remain in the family, so to speak. . . . I shall be very glad to submit any proposition which you might care to make. I feel that I can write to you in this vein because we know each other well and have been friends for a long time."[16] But Perales was innocent to the fact that Guillermo had been a loyal member of the political machine for years. It was not in Bravo's interests to meddle in this family dispute, and the results remained unchanged.

ELECTION RESULTS

When the returns for the 1948 primary election were announced on July 25, Stevenson had won in 168 of 254 counties, Johnson in 72, and Peddy in 14.[17] In the three larger conservative metropolitan counties, Bexar, Dallas, and Tarrant, the voters went for Stevenson with percentages of 56, 45, and 49 respectively. But in South Texas, Johnson, the liberal candidate, carried ten out of fourteen counties; Stevenson, the conservative runner, took the other four.[18]

The race for the 15th Congressional District seat also produced a runoff, as Bentsen garnered 18,913 votes to Kazen's 16,042. An analysis of the thirteen counties comprising the 15th district reveals that the votes were almost evenly distributed: six counties voted for Bentsen and seven went with Kazen. Judge Bravo and his lieutenants supported Kazen for three main reasons. First, Zapata and Webb counties were the only ones in the 75th state congressional district, and the representative there was Abraham Kazen, Jr. Second, Zapata and three other counties (Dimmit, Jim Hogg, and Webb) were in the 49th Judicial District, and Jimmy Kazen was the district attorney. Third, Judge Bravo could count on Kazen's support when the time came for the relocation of so many families. Feeling optimistic about having him in his corner, the judge predicted that Philip Kazen "will not fail us in our battle for justice when the Falcon dam is built, and we dare not entrust our future to promoters from the Lower Valley."[19] The dam was intended to benefit the Lower Río Grande Valley citrus industry.

The border counties of Maverick, Webb, Zapata, and Starr also voted for Kazen, favoring him with percentages of 65, 96, 96, and 59, respectively. Three of Webb County's neighbors, Dimmit, Jim Hogg, and La Salle, similarly voted for Kazen, though Frio, Zavala, and Medina counties did not. Cameron and Willacy, the two counties surrounding Bentsen's Hidalgo County, voted for him.[20] Even though Duval County was not in the 15th District, George B. Parr supported Kazen because he was the border bosses' favorite candidate.

BENTSEN-KAZEN RUNOFF ELECTION

Kazen and Bentsen wasted no time in reflecting on the outcome of their race. Preparing for the upcoming runoff election, Bentsen made the first move, asserting, "The line of battle is now clearly defined. It is a fight of the independent voters against the candidate of the Webb County political machine!"[21] Kazen countered by emphasizing "that a man of humble origin running without the backing of great wealth, can be elected to Congress. . . . There is opportunity for all in this great district of ours, and my purpose will be to make it possible for all, not just a privileged few."[22]

The issue of equal representation to all the 15th Congressional District counties became a hot topic during the runoff campaign in August. Kazen accused Bentsen of serving "only the interests of the Lower Valley land promoters if he goes to Congress and the security and safety of the small farmers and citrus growers of the area would be endangered."[23] Bentsen charged that Kazen harped too much on alleged discrimination issues. Moreover, Bentsen warned that as a member of Laredo's powerful political machine, Kazen would be sure to sway to Laredo's advantage many important decisions pertinent to the economic survival of the Valley.[24]

In the end, official election runoff returns from Zapata County gave Philip Kazen 893 votes and only 167 votes to Lloyd Bentsen, Jr. Along with Zapata County, five other counties voted for Kazen, namely Jim Hogg, La Salle, Maverick, Starr, and Webb. But the remaining seven counties voted for Bentsen, among them Dimmit, which switched loyalties. A resounding victory for Bentsen in Hidalgo, Willacy, and Cameron counties offset a huge turnout in Webb County. Final districtwide election results proclaimed Lloyd M. Bentsen, Jr., the winner with 31,325 votes to Kazen's 21,421. Thus ended a campaign marred by arrests, ver-

Table 8. 15th Congressional District Vote by Counties Runoff Election, August 28, 1948 (unofficial results)

County	Bentsen	%	Kazen	%	Total
Cameron (complete)	8,528	67	4,125	33	12,653
Hidalgo (complete)	13,925	78	3,912	22	17,837
Dimmit (complete)	853	58	623	42	1,476
Frio (complete)	1,275	66	656	33	1,931
Jim Hogg (complete)	190	21	715	79	905
La Salle (complete)	449	48	489	52	938
Maverick	430	37	721	63	1,151
Medina (complete)	1,117	73	412	27	1,529
Starr	1,149	42	1,573	58	2,722
Webb (complete)	618	9	6,204	91	6,822
Willacy (complete)	2,147	75	704	25	2,851
Zapata (complete)	167	16	893	84	1,060
Zavala (complete)	477	55	394	45	871
Total	31,325	59	21,421	41	52,746

Source: United Press County-by-County Tabulation

---

bal attacks, and blustering rallies, so that two days later, on August 30, Judge Bravo forwarded a congratulatory letter to Bentsen.[25] In it he included his concerns about the construction of Falcon Dam and the future for Zapata County.[26]

Bentsen, aware that Zapata County had voted against him, assured Bravo that he was going "to represent *all* of the people in the district equally and fai[r]ly." Cognizant of the county's impending dramatic economic and social changes due to the construction of Falcon Dam, he added, "Call on me if I can be of any service in helping the people of Zapata County."[27]

JOHNSON-STEVENSON RUNOFF ELECTION

Lyndon Johnson had held a special interest in the runoff election between Bentsen and Kazen. As historian Robert Dallek indicated, "a runoff in the Rio Grande Valley ... for a House seat directly benefitted Lyndon. Both men supported Johnson over Stevenson, and their higher respective totals in the run-off translated into more votes for Johnson." [28] LBJ, however, was not one to take chances.

On the day before the runoff election, in fact, Judge Bravo received a telegram from Johnson with last-minute instructions. LBJ expected the judge to campaign until election day, working tirelessly and energetically from dawn to dusk. His final words were, "I HOPE YOU WILL GIVE ME TOMORROW AND WORK AS HARD AND FAST AS YOU CAN AND AS YOU KNOW I WILL FOR YOU WHEN I AM SENATOR. PLEASE WATCH THE POLLS AFTER 7:00 P.M. AND GET US A WIRE OR TELEPHONE CALL TELLING US WE HAVE TAKEN THE LEAD IN YOUR COUNTY." [29]

The 1948 senatorial runoff turned out to be a cliff-hanger, with the final outcome enshrouded in doubt. The telegraph office in Zapata was kept busy during election day of August 28 and even into the night. At 7:00 P.M. that evening, Brad Smith, a Lower Río Grande Valley newspaper reporter who collected election returns from all the counties in the 15th Congressional District for the Texas Election Bureau, sent a telegram requesting the first available report and subsequent totals on the Kazen-Bentsen congressional race.[30] Smith recalled years later that "at the time of the 1948 election, he (Judge Bravo) called me to give what were supposed to be the COMPLETE results. I called them to Dallas about 10 P.M. By that time the race was neck-and-neck between Johnson and Stevenson. . . . Those were the wild days in South Texas. Two hours later, the Judge [Bravo] called back to say [he] had 'found' another 112 votes for Johnson. Then we both laughed like crazy and went home and went to bed!" [31]

A day after the election, on Sunday, August 29, Johnson—obviously concerned about the closeness of the returns but not aware that the Zapata machine had secured his victory—telegraphed Judge Bravo to make sure that all the ballots were carefully checked and error-free. He reminded the Zapata County Executive Committee to canvass and certify the returns by checking the voting lists, because "THE RACE IS SO CLOSE THAT AN HONEST ERROR IN TABULATION COULD EASILY MAKE THE DIF-FERENCE. PLEASE CHECK THE RETURNS NOW IN AND . . . CORRECT ALL DISCOVERED ERRORS BEFORE THE RESULTS ARE CERTIFIED. . . . PLEASE WIRE RESULTS OF THE RETURNS TO ME IN AUSTIN. MANY THANKS FOR YOUR FINE WORK. I AM NOW CALLING ON YOU FOR WHAT IS PROBABLY THE MOST IMPORTANT SERVICE YOU CAN RENDER ME." [32] Hours before receiving Johnson's telegram, the judge had telegraphed the following good news: "THE CITIZENS OF ZAPATA COUNTY HAVE BEEN HAPPY ALL DURING LAST NIGHT AND TODAY ON ACCOUNT OF RESULTS OF ELECTION ASSURING YOUR NOMINATION TO THE U.S. SENATE . . . , FOR IN PREVIOUS CAMPAIGN, WE SUPPORTED YOU WITH ALL OUR MIGHT, BECAUSE WE BE- LIEVE IN YOU."[33]

Upon receiving Johnson's urgent telegram, Judge Bravo responded with another telegram on Monday morning, August 30, notifying John- son that the Zapata County Executive Committee had canvassed the re- turns and that they were being mailed to Robert W. Calvert, chairman of the state Democratic Executive Committee. The results indicated that Johnson had the lead with 711 votes to Stevenson's 158 votes.[34] That evening, at 8:00 P.M., with statewide results changing constantly, Judge J. C. Looney, who chaired the Johnson campaign in Hidalgo County, wanted to make sure that the Stevenson camp engaged in no dubious practices. He requested Judge Bravo by telegram to "BE ON HAND OR HAVE SOMEONE ON HAND AT THE CANVASS OF THE BALLOTS FOR YOUR COUNTY SO AS TO CHECK THE RETURNS CAREFULLY. IF THERE IS ANY CHANGE FROM RETURNS REPORTED TO TEXAS ELECTION BUREAU PLEASE ADVISE ME COLLECT."[35]

George Parr also expressed concern over the changing returns. He called Bravo almost daily, urging him to help Johnson in any possible manner. The judge similarly telephoned Parr, asking him to do more for Johnson, "Hay George, ándale, vámos porque está muy apurado Lyndon Johnson, vámos a ayudarle. El (Johnson) decía ayudenme!, ayudenme!" (Let's go George, let's help Johnson because he is worried. Johnson said, help me, help me!).[36]

The Partido Viejo in Zapata County made certain Stevenson support- ers did not try to pull a fast one on the presiding judges; it instructed Sheriff Martínez and his men to supervise closely the election precincts. Other counties were not so cautious, prompting Johnson's headquar- ters to tell Frank Oltorf, a state house representative who worked with the Johnson campaign, "that they felt that if there were any shenani- gans going on, it was going on the Stevenson camp, and they wanted to alert their people to watch these ballot boxes and make sure that the count was right. It was no suggestion *ever* that we try to pick up an extra vote. The suggestion was that we make sure that the other people didn't do it."[37]

As suspense in the Senate runoff election mounted, the Zapata

Table 9. Runoff Election Results, August 28, 1948

County	Lyndon B. Johnson	Coke R. Stevenson
Zapata	669	71
Starr	3,038	170
Webb	5,554	1,179
Duval	4,622	40
Jim Wells	1,988	770
Hidalgo	10,412	6,851
Cameron	7,276	5,204
Bexar	15,610	15,511
Dallas	17,649	26,263
Galveston	5,992	7,985
Harris	37,377	51,495
Jefferson	15,670	11,801
Tarrant	18,092	22,741

Source: Texas Almanac, 1949–50, p. 474

County Democratic Executive Committee, reviewing its vote totals, reported 619 for Johnson and 121 for Stevenson.[38] For unknown dubious reasons, it took away 92 and 37 votes, respectively. Unofficial results reported by the Texas Election Bureau indicated that within a thirty-hour time span, the lead statewide changed almost every five hours.[39] In some counties, the corrected figures favored Johnson while in others, Stevenson benefitted. For instance, Zapata, Jim Wells, and Duval counties submitted revised ballot figures, but so did another county where Arthur Stevenson, cousin of Coke Stevenson and chairperson of the county Democratic Executive Committee, "made five different returns to the State Executive Committee."[40]

After receiving certified results from county executive committees all over the state, Johnson asked all of them to respond on a form letter. He simply requested them to fill in the total vote count and concluded by stating, "I wish to thank you for all you have done in my behalf and to urge that you send this information back to me as promptly as you can."[41] Judge Bravo immediately reported the revised number of votes, wrote the chairperson's name, initialed the letter, and forwarded it to Johnson's headquarters.

The following day, on September 3, the judge received another letter from Johnson:

> It's still too early to say whether we have won or lost this election, but win or lose, I'll always be grateful from the bottom of my heart for the good people of Zapata County. Whether I am in the Senate or out, I hope that you and the good folks in your county will call on me at any time I can be of assistance to you. I am deeply grateful to you personally for your "all out" efforts in my behalf. . . . When the last votes are counted and the election is over maybe we will have an opportunity to talk together personally and I shall look forward to that time.[42]

Three days before the state executive committee's September 13 deadline for canvassing the election results, Josefa Gutiérrez officially certified to Chairperson Robert W. Calvert that Johnson had gained 50 votes for a new total of 669, and that Stevenson had mysteriously lost the same amount for a revised 71 votes.[43] After all the statewide tallies were counted, Lyndon B. Johnson became the new United States senator with 494,191 votes to Stevenson's 494,104—a difference of just 87 votes! Not willing to accept defeat, Stevenson had his lawyers persuade Judge T. Whitfield Davidson from the U.S. District Court for the Northern District of Texas to intervene. On September 15, 1948, Judge Davidson issued restraining order number 1640 and put into effect an injunction against placing Johnson's name on the ballot for the November 2 general election. Stevenson claimed that alleged voting irregularities had taken place in Zapata, Jim Wells, Webb, Starr, and Duval counties. Johnson's lawyers, on the other hand, argued that Stevenson had received 1,102 fraudulent (tombstone) votes in one county and over two thousand illegal votes in Galveston County.[44]

FEDERAL INVESTIGATION

Judge Davidson scheduled a two-day hearing commencing at 10:00 A.M. on Tuesday, September 21, 1948, in Fort Worth, with both Johnson and Stevenson and their legal counsel present. Former Texas Governor Dan Moody, acting as chief legal counsel for Stevenson, opened by stating that witnesses and notarized affidavits from Zapata County would prove that votes were stolen from Stevenson and given to Johnson.[45] Moody added that he would also provide witnesses and more affidavits from Duval and Jim Wells counties. Johnson's lawyers rebutted by arguing that

Stevenson had not been deprived of any constitutional rights, and that they too were ready to "show that Complainant [Stevenson], himself, has been the beneficiary of frauds, illegal ballots and irregularities in various counties of Texas; and that complainant knows of these frauds in his own behalf which have been widely publicized." [46]

On the following day, at the request of Stevenson's lawyers, witnesses came from Zapata, Jim Wells, and Duval counties to testify against Lyndon Johnson. A total of thirteen witnesses took the stand—nine from Jim Wells County (Harry Lee Adams, B. M. Brownlee, Enriqueta Acero, Mrs. D. Lobrecht, Mrs. Jay Mitchell, Juan R. Martínez, Louis Salinas, Héctor Cerda, and Charles Wesley Price); one from San Antonio (James F. Garner); one from Laredo (Truman Phelps); and two from Zapata (Natividad Porras and L. E. Vela).[47] Not surprisingly, all thirteen witnesses had actively campaigned for Stevenson. S. Truman Phelps, former district attorney for the 49th district, a Stevenson appointee and campaign manager for Bentsen in Webb County, brought four witnesses. M. G. Flores and León Ramírez from Zapata and V. Zepeda from Laredo did not get to testify. Some local politicos from Jim Wells and Duval counties who supported Stevenson came forward to corroborate other evidence and/or to submit affidavits before Judge Davidson.[48]

The two witnesses from Zapata County, Natividad Porras and L. E. Vela, presented evidence before Judge Davidson that Bentsen had appointed both of them as supervisors. Under direct examination by Groce, Vela tried to explain the relationship between the Kazen-Bentsen and the Johnson-Stevenson race.

A: I keep a record of the exact amount that Mr. Bentsen and Mr. Kazen get.

A: It is 59 for Mr. Bentsen and 91 for Mr. Kazen, giving a total of 150.

Q: All right. Now, do you know the ratio of votes between Stevenson and Johnson?

A: There was a difference in the votes that Mr. Stevenson received in comparison with Mr. Bentsen. I was really interested in the Bentsen-Kazen race and I took that in writing, but I have a recollection that there was a difference of 10 votes less received by Mr. Stevenson than by Mr. Bentsen.

Q: In other words, Mr. Stevenson received about ten votes less than Mr. Bentsen did.[49]

Johnson's lawyer argued that Stevenson presented "in a garbled way only a part of the facts; and otherwise show[ed] an absence of frankness and candor. . . . [Stevenson] received more illegal votes in that one county than he claims this Defendant [Lyndon Johnson] received in both Jim Wells and Zapata Counties, the only counties of which he complains; therefore, the result of the election would not be changed." [50]

After two days of testimony, Judge Davidson concluded that alleged voting irregularities existed in Zapata, Duval, and Jim Wells counties. The poll lists, tally, and returns sheets for each of the precincts in question needed to be carefully examined, in particular Box 3 in Zapata County and Box 13 in Jim Wells County. The judge suspected that George Parr had already counted all the living and dead poll tax payers from Duval County. Davidson also believed that, in desperate need of additional votes, Parr had ordered Luis "El Indio" Salas, election judge of precinct 13 in Jim Wells County and one of Parr's henchman, to certify two hundred additional votes for Johnson. Consequently, Judge Davidson appointed two Special Masters and ordered them to conduct an investigation in the three counties where Stevenson claimed fraudulent votes had stolen his election. William R. Smith, Jr., a United States attorney for the Western District, was to go to Jim Wells County and hold hearings on Monday, September 27, at 3:00 P.M. James McCollum Burnett, an associate of Smith, was dispatched to Duval County to hear testimony on Tuesday, at 10:00 A.M. Thence, he was to drive to Zapata County and listen to evidence on Wednesday, at 10:00 A.M. Judge Davidson instructed both Special Masters to "hear witnesses, examine the certified poll lists, the lists of those who voted in said election, the tally sheets and returns sheets made in the conduct of said election, and particularly all the facts in respect to the holding of said election and the returns there from Precinct one (1), two (2), three (3) and four (4) of Zapata County, Texas and Duval County, Texas." [51]

During a half-day briefing in Corpus Christi on the morning of Monday, September 27, the two Special Masters laid out to the attorneys present the legal parameters and the rules of order for the hearings. That afternoon, Smith started the proceedings in Alice, the county seat of Jim Wells County. The probe lasted only a few minutes since none of the key subpoenaed witnesses could be located. Smith rescheduled for 9:30 A.M. the next day. Early on Tuesday morning, September 28, both Special Masters began their investigations on schedule—Burnett in San Diego, the Duval County seat, while Smith continued in Alice. In order to verify the alleged voting irregularities, the Special Masters wanted to examine the poll tax list and the tally sheet from each of the voting precincts. By law, one copy of these two documents was to be inside the precinct ballot box (along with the ballots); another was to be filed with the secretary of the county Democratic executive committee; and a third set should be with the presiding judge of the said precinct.[52]

In Jim Wells County, the situation with the ballot boxes turned into a confusing issue because Deputy Marshall W. W. Ainsworth brought in twenty boxes, but there were only seventeen voting precincts. Some precincts could have had more than one ballot box; however, four boxes were marked "Precinct 14" or "La Gloria, Precinct 14" or "La Gloria School District No. 21."[53] To make matters worse, some boxes were locked with no keys attached, other were unclosed, and one box had had the numbers of the precinct scraped off. In reference to the question of the last 202 names added to Box 13, Everett Looney objected, stating that there was "no law requiring that the poll list be made in any particular ink or by any one particular person."[54] Historian James Reston alleges that John Connally, Philip Kazen, and another person secretly met in Alice, Texas, and added two hundred votes for Johnson and two for Stevenson, all done in alphabetical order with the same color of ink (blue-green).[55]

Key Duval County witnesses had taken vacations in Mexico; consequently, only eight out of fifty persons responded to the subpoena. County Judge Dan Tobin provided evasive answers throughout the Burnett hearing and pleaded ignorance in not remembering the names of the judges or clerks, except for Domingo González—the presiding judge for precinct 1.[56] Burnett adjourned the hearing at about 3:00 P.M. in order to prepare for the court proceeding in Zapata, scheduled to begin at 10:00 A.M. the next day.

On the second floor of the two-story Zapata County Courthouse, Joe G. Montague, F. L. Kuykendall, and Truman Phelps represented Stevenson, while Polk Shelton and Manuel J. Raymond were Johnson's lawyers. Witnesses, family and community members, curious onlookers, and the news media waited anxiously for the hearing to start. Unlike what had occurred in the other two counties, all thirty-one subpoenaed witnesses answered the roll call that morning. The Zapata political machine made sure that all the key people were present. Three days before the subpoenas were issued, Judge Bravo's secretary had notified them to be there.[57]

Both Polk Shelton and Manuel J. Raymond opened the hearing by stating two objections: first, that the Northern District Court of Texas had no jurisdiction in Zapata County, and second, that the temporary injunction established by Judge Davidson was invalid and should be dissolved. Needless to say, Master Burnett overruled both motions. It is interesting to note at this point the different procedural styles of the two Masters. Smith had allowed all the witnesses to stay inside the courthouse during the proceedings in Alice. In Zapata County, Burnett gave specific instructions for all witnesses except the one being interrogated to "remain outside of the courthouse" and wait in an adjacent building.[58] Moreover, he instructed them not to discuss the hearing with anyone else, except with their attorneys.

After U.S. Marshall Joe Davis administered the oath in English and Spanish to all the witnesses, Joe G. Montague, representing Stevenson, called on Leopoldo Martínez, the Zapata County tax assessor/collector and sheriff, to take the stand as the first witness. Martínez provided a list by precincts of all the residents who had paid their poll tax. Montague then called on Matías Cuéllar, the county and district clerk, who testified that all the ballot boxes from the four voting precincts had been turned in and had been safe and secure in the vault since election night.[59]

The attorneys questioned Cuéllar on the different unofficial returns that were first reported to the Texas Election Bureau through Jim Falvella, a newspaper correspondent who represented Zapata and Webb counties at all elections. Cuéllar had telegraphed the following official totals: 711 for Johnson and 158 for Stevenson. He further testified that he had picked up some information "on the court house lawn and out on the street."[60] Being an election night for national, state, and local offices, it was not uncommon for the people to discuss several unofficial voting results.

Josefa Gutiérrez, called to the witness stand after Falvella, stated that just before the hearing, Judge Bravo had given her three envelopes (for precincts 1, 2, and 4) instead of four. But during the executive committee canvassing meeting on September 2, she testified, he had given her four envelopes, which included the one from precinct 3. When I interviewed Mrs. Gutiérrez in 1990, she stood by the statement she had made to Burnett during cross examination, that "I left the four in Mr. Bravo's office after we had the meeting and there were only those three left; I don't know what happened to the other."[61] It was customary in Zapata County for the chairperson of the Democratic Executive Committee to leave all the election returns in Judge Bravo's office for safekeeping. This practice, however, was illegal because the county judge was not authorized by state statute to store this information.

After the noon recess, Judge Bravo took the stand and testified that he had received the election returns from the four voting places in sealed brown envelopes and had kept them in a filing cabinet. Burnett continued to interrogate Bravo about the missing returns from precinct 3 (Lopeño).

Q: And when was the next time that you handled those returns?

A: Sometime last week. I saw in the paper where some of our Republican residents from here were up in Fort Worth testifying. There was a picture of them, referring to the Zapata returns, and so I felt like I should check up. They said something about what votes there were in some precincts. I don't remember which, so I went and checked it, and found the No. 3 was gone.

Q: Have you made a diligent search to find the returns of Precinct No. 3?

A: Yes sir. I checked in all my files and everything in the office, to see if they were misplaced.

Q: Was it the custom and was it followed always that these precinct chairmen would bring the returns and leave them with you for her?

A: Yes.

Q: They did that every year; every election?

A: Yes.[62]

Frustrated over not receiving an answer on the whereabouts of the lost returns, Burnett questioned three other key election officers—Elia González, presiding judge; Anita Ramírez, associate judge; and Sacramento Benavides, election clerk. Elia testified that she had given Judge Bravo all three copies of the returns because she did not keep any backups: "He didn't even notice it [that there were only three copies of the election returns instead of four], I don't think so, because he didn't tell me; otherwise he would have."[63] Moreover, she could not remember what she had done with the keys to the ballot boxes—whether she had given them to Cuéllar or to Bravo.

At this point, Montague suggested to Burnett that the four ballot boxes be impounded in order to find the missing returns. Shelton and Raymond strongly objected, but Burnett overruled them and placed the containers in the custody of the U.S. marshall. Montague proceeded to question Sacramento Benavides, but at that moment Burnett received a telephone call and motioned for a short recess. After a few minutes, he returned and notified the attorneys present that Judge Davidson had just directed him to terminate the investigation in Zapata County immediately and "to close the proceedings at this time and to restore all impounded documents back to the custodian of those respective documents, . . . and the returns shall be returned to the county chairman for Precinct Nos. 1, 2, and 4. . . . Gentleman, that will be the order of the day."[64] And with that announcement, Burnett adjourned the hearing at about 3:00 P.M. Johnson's lawyers, wheeling and dealing behind the scenes, had persuaded Supreme Court Justice Hugo Black to stop Judge Davidson's investigation.

On October 20, 1948, Johnson sent Judge Bravo the following thank-you note: "It is impossible for me to find words to express the thanks of Lady Bird and myself for the time and effort you spent in the primary campaigns.

We now have the opportunity on November 2 to show our strength. Since Stevenson has joined up with the Republican Party and is supporting its nominee, we will roll up a half-million majority and let the country know how Texas stands."[65]

THE GENERAL ELECTION

Johnson defeated the Republican nominee Jack Porter by an overwhelming majority (702,985 to 349,665 votes). In Zapata County, Johnson received 629 votes and Porter garnered 417. As to the 15th Congressional District, Lloyd Bentsen, Jr., easily won since he had no opposition.

In the local elections, things were not as peaceful, for the campaign between the incumbent PV leaders and their opponents escalated intensely. The two parties debated such issues as the educational system, agricultural development, and the role that local civic organizations should play in bettering the county's economic structure. However, the most critical subject was the relocation of the town of Zapata and surrounding communities, given the impending construction of Falcon Dam.[66] This topic will be discussed fully in chapters six and seven.

Despite the PN's heavy propaganda against the PV (in the form of a one-page political leaflet written in Spanish denouncing the alleged evils of bossism) just before the general election, all the incumbents returned to office: Matías Cuéllar as county clerk; Primitivo Uribe as county treasurer; Leopoldo Martínez as sheriff/tax collector and assessor; and as commissioners, Manuel Medina for precinct 1, Proceso Martínez for precinct 2, Guillermo González for precinct 3, and Lizandro Ramírez for precinct 4.[67] Judge Bravo won reelection as county judge over Emilio Dilley by a return of 625 votes to 432, the second time in his career that he had faced a strong Republican opponent.[68] In the bitterly contested race for the post of commissioner in precinct 3, Guillermo again defeated Santiago (115 votes to 105), who had now switched parties to campaign on the Republican ticket. Bravo notified Perales about the outcome: "But the matter is a closed issue and very difficult for friends on either side to solve; you know that political disagreements between blood relatives are the most difficult for any one friend to participate in. I believe that Santiago has finally accepted the results in the spirit of a looser [sic]."[69] The Zapata County newspaper edition of Monday, November 4, 1948, carried the following catchy subheadlines: "Closest Race Since 1940; Old Party Makes Clean Sweep in Zapata County, Election Quiet—No Arrests Made."[70]

Aftermath

With Christmas just two days away, Johnson sent holiday greetings to Judge Bravo, intermingling fond memories from the 1948 Senate campaign. "This time of the year is a happy one for [Lady] Bird and me and both of us know that without your loyal, unselfish hard work through the past months our joy would not be so complete now. As just a very small measure of our very deep gratitude, we have sent you a little package to fit under your Christmas tree. I hope it will add something to your happiness just as your friendship had added so much to ours."[71]

On January 3, 1949, Lyndon B. Johnson was sworn in as United States senator, while Judge Bravo began his sixth term as Zapata county judge. From all the publicity, Johnson must have known that the political machine had gone to great lengths—including revising returns, misplacing information, and weathering a federal investigation—to have him elected. Perhaps for these reasons, Johnson kept expressing his gratitude and appreciation to the judge. For example, on the anniversary of his decision to run for the Senate, he sent the following short note, "May was a mighty important month last year. That's when I decided to run, and I'll never forget what it meant to me to be able to count on Judge Bravo. I'm writing this note just to say 'thank you' for all you did."[72]

The correspondence between Bravo and Johnson continued throughout the year. Often Johnson remembered the judge's support, "Lady Bird and I will never forget that one year ago—in 1948—you did so much, so unselfishly to help make that year and that Christmas the most joyous of our lives." [73] When Johnson wrote to Bravo with news about the Cold War, problems in Europe that threatened world peace, and budget constraints, he somehow found a way to mention the 1948 Senate election. "It is only natural, I suppose to recall occasionally the events of two years ago when we had the opportunity and the pleasure of working together. As I have told you before, I shall never forget all the friends like you who worked so tirelessly for so long. . . . When you find time, let me hear from you. I would like to know from you how the people with whom you talk are feeling these days." [74]

On another occasion (October 20, 1950), Johnson, with vivid memories of that election, offered to compensate Bravo for his service. "Often I think back to those summer days of 1948 when you helped so effectively to give Texas a new Senator. I am thinking of them now, as I write this letter. It gives me a feeling of intense pride to realize that you spared no time and no effort. I hope that since then my work here has justified your confidence. . . . And while I am about it, I want to express the hope once more that you will one of these days give me an opportunity to try and help you personally to the extent of my ability." [75]

Six days later, with the familiar salutation of "Dear Lyndon," the judge responded on behalf of the county residents by expressing total satisfaction with the results of the 1948 election. With Johnson as senator, the citizens of Zapata County could rely on his leadership during the Falcon Dam relocation process. With sincerity and affection, the judge signed the letter, "Su Amigo, M. B. Bravo." [76]

DUBIOUS POLITICAL PRACTICES

Judge Bravo's politicking during the Bentsen-Kazen and Johnson-Stevenson 1948 races gives insight into the less than predictable nature of South Texas politics. Bravo's alliance with neighboring county bosses helped determine the political career of Johnson but not that of Kazen. While the Tejano bloc vote of the boss-controlled counties played a significant part in assuring Johnson a seat in the U.S. Senate, the electorate bypassed Kazen, whose base of support rested with well-known bosses, including George Parr. The Zapata County Partido Viejo needed Johnson and Kazen's leadership to look after the interests of their predominantly Mexican-American constituency. After all, Kazen had closer ties with the county's machine than did Bentsen. But in the end, the same "political quilt" that gave Johnson his narrow victory could not deliver for Kazen. Contrary to what historians have said about boss politics in South Texas, there were times when the electorate could be at odds with the bosses.

Indeed, citizens had voted in opposition to George Parr, despite his alleged control and/or influence over neighboring counties. Only one patch of the political quilt in South Texas, Parr did work with the border bosses, but almost solely through alliances; he was not able to control, dominate, or manipulate them completely. Consequently, he only had so much power to influence other bosses and their constituents, and he could not use his pull (*palanca*) to elect Kazen. In an interview, Josefa M. Gutiérrez remembered: "George Parr did not control Zapata. I never knew that he did. . . . The county political bosses controlled themselves [that is, they were independent of each other]."[77]

More predictable in South Texas post–World War II politics was the chicanery that accompanied the 1948 race. Bravo's role in the election of that year, and especially his collusion with other bosses to get LBJ elected, exemplify the shadier aspects of South Texas bossism. Bravo put into action the entire resources of his political machine to intimidate opposition voters. Moreover, it seems likely that he massaged the final vote figures to hand LBJ a triumph, while his associates misplaced the election returns from precinct 3. No one knows with any degree of certainty what became of the missing envelope that contained the allegedly dubious results. Was it thrown into the Río Grande, as Zapata businessman Ted Treviño speculated ("Lo hecharían en el río?")?[78] An anonymous source indicated that perhaps it was buried in the Arroyo del Burro. Did the heated family feud between the incumbent Guillermo González and his nephew Santiago have anything to do with its disappearance? Santiago even went as far as hiring a prominent San Antonio lawyer to settle the alleged voting fraud.

Bravo's success at getting away with impropriety is testimony to his skill at political gamesmanship. Bravo could cement ties not only with his constituents but also with the high and mighty, among them LBJ. After the August 1948 election, he and Johnson became the best of friends; partly in gratitude, LBJ intervened and stopped the federal investigation into local electoral irregularities. In due course, Bravo would ask LBJ to return the debt the senator owed him for the 1948 victory.

Manuel and Josefa were married in the Sacred Heart Catholic Church, Edinburg, October 24, 1919.

Zapata County Courthouse in old Zapata. This photo first appeared in the *San Antonio Express* newspaper February 4, 1923. *Courtesy of the Institute of Texan Cultures.*

Manuel *(back row, fourth from left)* and fellow Knights of Columbus were elevated to a Fourth Degree during a special ceremony held at St. Peter's Catholic Church in Laredo, Easter Sunday, April 20, 1930.

Judge John A. Valls served as district attorney of the 49th Judicial District for thirty-five years and as district judge from 1938 until his death in 1941.

Family gathering, 1946. Mother Emma surrounded by her four children *(left to right)*: Robert, Louisa, Virginia, and Manuel.

Zapata County veterans attending Vocational Training School established by Judge Bravo in 1947.

Zapata County political leaders showing their support for Laredoan Philip A. Kazen (at the microphone) during the 1948 campaign rally in Zapata. *Left to right:* Leopoldo Martínez, Manuel Medina, Mr. Rodríguez, Leo Buckley, Proceso Martínez, Serafin Martínez, unidentified person, and Judge Bravo.

Webb County Judge Manuel J. Raymond, ca. 1940s, considered to be one of South Texas' most powerful political bosses. *Courtesy of the Institute of Texan Cultures.*

Zapata County officials negotiating with IBWC staff *(left to right):* Guillermo González (standing), Robert L. Bobbitt (sitting), Judge Bravo, Lizandro Ramírez (signing document), two unidentified federal bureaucrats, and Blas Cantú with the IBWC.

Zapata County Republican leaders studying the new townsite of Zapata, ca. 1953. *Seated (left to right):* Rafael San Miguel, H. P. Guerra, J. M. Sánchez. *Standing (left to right):* Conrado Hein, Humberto González. *Courtesy of the Institute of Texan Cultures.*

Señor San José Church in Lopeño was quickly disappearing under the rising waters of the Falcon Dam reservoir. A few hours later, the water was up to the belfry.

Looking down Main Street in old Falcon. Amigo's store is in the background.

Arcadio Vela's family from Lopeño barely had time to escape the rising waters of the Falcon Dam reservoir, 1953.

View of new Zapata, 1953. There was no potable water or sewage available. Note the Red Cross tents set up for temporary living quarters.

Contractors moving an old school building to the new townsite of Zapata to be used as temporary classrooms, 1954.

Zapata County officials, 1953. *Front row, left to right:* Lizandro Ramírez, Guillermo González, Proceso Martínez, and Manuel Medina. *Back row (left to right):* Primitivo Uribe, Judge Manuel B. Bravo, Leopoldo Martínez, and Matías Cuéllar.

Rapidly rising waters of the Falcon Dam reservoir inundated the Zapata County courthouse and jail. The gazebo located in the middle of the plaza is in the left foreground, 1954.

The Bravo family house in old Zapata (1950s) before the construction of Falcon Dam.

Judge Bravo pointing to the ruins of their house after the inundation of the town of Zapata, ca. 1955. For the safety of those fishing close to the submerged buildings, the IBWC dynamited the entire town.

Area *políticos* meet with Governor Allan Shivers during the 1954 Democratic State convention in Mineral Wells. *Left to right:* Governor Shivers, Maverick County Judge R. E. Bibb, Senator Abraham Kazen, Jr., Judge Manuel B. Bravo, Dimmit County delegate Herb Petry, Jr., Zavala County delegate Bob Crawford, and Congressman Joe M. Kilgore.

A rare photograph of Judge Bravo caught in a pensive mood contemplating the future of Zapata County during the construction of Falcon Dam, ca. 1950s.

A postcard to Judge Bravo from Senator and Mrs. Lyndon B. Johnson, August 25, 1955. This was handwritten on the back: "We were thinking about how happy and grateful we are to be back in Texas among our friends and wanted to let you hear from us. Our pleasant association throughout the years has meant so much to us."

President Johnson shaking hands with Mexican President Gustavo Díaz Ordaz at a marker dedication during El Chamizal ceremony, October 28, 1967. Lady Bird Johnson and Judge Bravo (with hardhat) are to the left. *Courtesy of AP/ Wide World.*

Standing outside the White House during a trip to visit President Johnson *(left to right):* Josefa V. Bravo, Gloria Alicia Bravo (granddaughter), and Judge Bravo, September 30, 1968.

President Johnson sent Judge Bravo an autographed photo after they were unable to see each other during a family trip to the White House, September 30, 1968.

INTERNATIONAL DIPLOMACY AND DOMESTIC ISSUES

W e turn now to Judge Bravo's multifaceted approaches to and successes in dealing with issues of national, state, and county significance. Regarding matters of national import, the judge provided leadership by taking direct action during the Félix Longoria incident. Bravo wrote to request Senator Johnson's intervention in finding a suitable burial place for the slain World War II soldier when the funeral home at Three Rivers refused to handle services for him. The judge and other Tejano leaders publicly supported the Longoria family and denounced the evils of racism in South Texas. In the meantime, the final decision of where to bury Private Longoria had the potential of jeopardizing international relations between the United States and Mexico.

Other national concerns relevant to Zapata County dealt with modernizing communications in the area, rallying citizens behind the cause of the Korean War, and planning the effective use of ranch and farm land. Contacting several agencies in Washington, D.C., Judge Bravo obtained federal assistance in providing rural areas with telephone service. Another major relief for the ranchers and farmers was the establishment of a soil conservation district for the county.

As to state matters, the judge kept in touch with prominent politicians such as James V. Allred and Governor Allan Shivers. From the mid-1930s, when Allred won the gubernatorial race, Judge Bravo and the other border bosses had supported his candidacy. Now, the judge had put in a good word for his long-time friend, and both were elated when Senator Johnson recommended Allred for a federal judgeship, even though Zapata County was not in what would be Allred's judicial district. Moreover, Bravo had long supported the political career of Governor Shivers. Thus, he was able to call upon Shivers for assistance during the relocation problems resulting from construction of Falcon Dam. Bravo knew that it was in Shivers's best interests to support the Falcon Dam project because his father-in-law, John H. Shary, operated huge business enterprises in the Lower Río Grande Valley.

At the onset of the Korean conflict, the judge rallied behind the men and women serving in the armed forces by reactivating the USO in Zapata County. Using his experience with this organization during World War II, Judge Bravo formulated successful strategies to surpass state quotas. He solicited the assistance of both political parties to work harmoniously and cooperatively in a unified effort. The true spirit of patriotism and the desire to help the war campaign permeated the entire county.

In trying to work out solutions to the needs of Zapata County citizens, the judge continued fending off the Partido Nuevo at election time and contending with its accusations of corruption and wrongdoing. Indeed, Bravo faced a formidable task that required confrontational diplomacy when he tried keeping the FBI from investigating alleged indiscretions in local politics. Of course, Senator Johnson played a dominant role in convincing the top echelon G-men to stay away from Zapata County.

THE FÉLIX LONGORIA INCIDENT

Not long after Judge Bravo began his seventh term in office on January 1, 1949, he became actively involved with the controversial circumstances surrounding the reburial of Pvt. Félix Longoria. Contrary to the Hispanic custom of holding the wake at home, Mrs. Beatrice Longoria, the widow, decided to hold the service at the Rice Funeral Home Chapel, located in the predominantly Anglo community of Three Rivers. Private Longoria had been killed in the Philippines and his wife wanted to bring the remains to her husband's hometown for proper reburial.

On January 8, Thomas W. Kennedy, Jr., director of the Rice Funeral Home, tried to discourage Mrs. Longoria from using the chapel, stating that "the whites wouldn't like it," and adding, "No, we're not going to let the Mexicans use the chapel of our funeral home."[1] Kennedy later explained to the news media that he refused because of a long-lasting family feud between Mrs. Longoria and her in-laws. However, in an exclusive interview conducted by the *Laredo Times,* Guadalupe Longoria, the private's father, refuted Kennedy's statement.[2] The director's defensive behavior and racist motives became clear when he admitted to George Groh, a reporter with the *Corpus Christi Times,* that "we have never made a practice of letting Mexicans use a chapel and we don't want to start now."[3]

After reading about the incident in the newspapers, Judge Bravo, enraged, immediately sent Senator Lyndon B. Johnson an urgent telegram requesting his intercession in the matter. He expressed his disgust over the racial attitude of the funeral home as "SO ABSURD AND UN-AMERICAN THAT IS A SHAME FOR IT TO HAPPEN IN THE GREAT STATE OF TEXAS."[4] Furthermore, the judge vehemently requested that "IF YOU COULD HAVE THE DAMN OUTFIT COMPELLED TO HANDLE THE SERVICES FOR FELIX LONGORIA, A VETERAN, THE MEXICAN AMERICAN RESIDENTS OF U.S. WOULD EVER BE INDEBTED TO YOU."[5]

In the meantime, Mrs. Longoria, then living in Corpus Christi and at the suggestion of her sister Sara Moreno, related the incident to her friend, Dr. Héctor P. García, president of the G.I. Forum. Without delay, on January 10, Dr. García requested Senator Johnson to take immediate steps and make, "[an] immediate investigation and correction of the un-American action of the Rice Funeral Home. . . . This American soldier made the supreme sacrifice in giving his life for his country and for the same people who now deny him the last funeral rites. . . . This is a typical example of discriminatory practices which occur intermittently in this State despite our efforts to prevent them."[6]

Two days later, Senator Johnson informed Bravo about his jurisdictional boundaries in obligating the funeral home, a private business, to bury Longoria. "I FEEL EXACTLY AS YOU DO REGARDING REFUSAL SERVICES FOR FELIX LONGORIA. HOWEVER NEITHER I NOR FEDERAL GOVERNMENT HAVE ANY CONTROL WHATSOEVER OVER CIVILIAN FUNERAL HOMES. . . . IF YOU HAVE OTHER RECOMMENDATION, PLEASE GIVE IT TO ME."[7]

What began as overt discrimination by Kennedy against the Longorias mushroomed into an international crisis. First, concerned individuals, state agencies, and organizations sympathetic to the Longorias became involved by publicly denouncing the director's brazen actions. LULAC, the Texas Good Neighbor Commission (an agency established by Governor Stevenson in 1943 to foster goodwill between Hispanics and Anglos in Texas), the American Legion, and the political bosses from South Texas expressed their consternation and demanded changes in federal legislation that would prohibit "outrages such as this as well as prohibiting the humiliation of members of our Armed Forces in public business." [8]

Second, the Longoria incident received considerable publicity in all the area newspapers and made national front-page news in the *New York Herald Tribune* and the *New York Times*. When the Mexican newspapers published the story, diplomatic relations with Mexico over a farm labor contract (the *bracero* program) with the United States came to an immediate halt. [9] Paul J. Reveley, head of Mexican affairs for the State Department, the Mexican ambassador, and American Ambassador Thurston supported Senator Johnson's action in trying to work out an amiable solution. Philip Raine, cultural attaché of the U.S. Embassy in Mexico, confided to Tom Sutherland, executive secretary of the Good Neighbor Commission: "of what could have been a far worse incident." [10]

Senator Johnson rendered a solution that gave Mrs. Longoria the option of burying her husband with full military honors either at Arlington National Cemetery or at Fort Sam Houston National Cemetery in San Antonio. She selected the first alternative and asked for the senator's assistance in shipping the body to Washington, D.C. [11] In essence, her decision to bury her husband in Arlington Cemetery actually reopened diplomatic relations with Mexico over the bracero labor contract (though this was unknown to her at the time). The Mexican newspapers, in a timely manner, published the burial site announcement because "the matter was mentioned to our negotiators on several occasions during the course of the negotiations as an example of anti-Mexican feelings in Texas. However, . . . concurrent press publicity accorded the plans for the Arlington burial appear to have a positive counteracting effect." [12]

In Zapata County, Judge Bravo discussed the Longoria events at every opportune time with members of the local American Legion chapter, for he had witnessed discrimination in Central Texas. Support for his stance on discrimination came from many quarters. For instance, the Laredo newspaper published front-page stories on the matter, almost daily. Both the Webb County Chapter of Disabled American Veterans and the local Veterans of Foreign Wars, headed by Juan C. Garza Góngora and A. R. "Tony" Sánchez, Sr., respectively, openly opposed the action taken by the Rice Funeral Home, and they sent telegrams to their state and national offices condemning the incident.[13] Judge Bravo similarly urged leading citizens of Zapata and Webb counties to write to their state representatives denouncing the racist stance taken by Kennedy. Col. Charles G. Pearcy, commander of American Legion Post 59 and a former commanding officer of the Laredo Army Air Field, responded to the judge's plea and declared Kennedy's attitude undemocratic and anti-American.[14] The whole fiasco also prompted Manuel M. García, a wealthy Laredo philanthropist, to offer to pay all the Longoria family travel expenses for attending the funeral services.

On February 16, 1949, Félix Longoria was buried near the grave of Gen. John J. Pershing. Senator Johnson and other top dignitaries from the United States and Mexico attended the gravesite ceremonies. The interment services satisfied the Longoria family wishes, restored a sense of justice in the Hispanic communities, healed the diplomatic friction between the United States and Mexico, and—although temporarily at best—subdued the spectre of racial discrimination in Texas. The senator later commented to Judge Bravo that "I had an opportunity to meet his family [Félix Longoria] and be with them at the funeral. They are very fine people and made me even happier than I could be of some small service in arranging for their son's decent Christian burial here among the heroes of our nation's wars."[15]

On behalf of Zapata County, the judge sent Johnson a lengthy letter expressing his appreciation for taking an interest in this matter. In particular, he thanked Johnson for arranging the much deserved honors and burial place: "In spite of the lame excuses that followed in this case, however, it seems clear that this was just another instance of unreasoned prejudice . . . and that there are at least some outstanding men in public office who have a broader and grander conception of America and what it stands for, and of the respect due its fallen heroes."[16]

BRAVO'S NETWORK IN ADDRESSING COUNTY MATTERS

Bravo's collaboration and friendship with Senator Johnson persisted as they worked together on other issues pertinent to South Texas. Judge

Bravo helped the senator collect valuable information for the establishment of telephone service to families living in isolated county areas. Considering the geographic size of Zapata County and its demographic layout—mostly farms and small communities situated along the Río Grande, and grazing lands away from the river—it was in the county residents' best interest to support the passage of this important rural bill.[17] If approved by Congress, telephone companies could apply for loans to improve and expand their services to rural areas.

Efforts to promote farming—although, as noted, this involved only about 3 percent of the county's total acreage—led Judge Bravo to explore possibilities for improving the county's soil conservation program. The county commissioners voted in 1952 to establish a soil conservation district, a step needed to make the county eligible for technical assistance from area offices of the Department of Agriculture (DOA). For years, local farmers had complained about receiving part-time and poor supervisory service from the DOA, since field agents had to travel from Webb and Starr counties.[18] The judge wrote letters to Congressman Lloyd Bentsen, Jr., Senator Tom Connally, and Senator Johnson, requesting that they get the DOA to assist in opening a Soil Conservation Service office in the county.

Responding to Judge Bravo's numerous letters of concern, C. J. McCormick, undersecretary for the Department of Agriculture, relayed word from the Soil Conservation Service that an agent and an office unit to care for Zapata County matters had already been earmarked in the federal budget. The specific timeline for the Zapata County soil conservation branch to be operational was not defined, except that federal funding had been made available.[19] The slow-moving wheels of the Washington bureaucracy made the waiting period feel like an eternity. Judge Bravo waited patiently, then renewed his letter-writing campaign to friends in Congress; this time, a response from Bentsen's office provided an explanation for the delay.

Several factors compounded the selection of an agriculture representative to operate the new soil conservation agency in Zapata. First, the Soil Conservation Service office wanted a bilingual person with fluency in Spanish. Second, the moving of the town of Zapata due to the construction of Falcon Dam, then under way, created a housing problem for the new agent. Finally, the qualifications for the job required a specialized training course to be completed at a work station in Edinburg.[20]

Toward the end of July, 1952, the Soil Conservation Service approved the appointment of Angel Andrés Vela to the Zapata County Soil Conservation District office on a full-time basis.

The judge also spent considerable time lobbying and networking with key fellow Democrats at the state level to ensure additional legislation that would improve teachers' salaries, roads and bridges, and other state services. Some of these partisan activities, which included attending dinner functions with staunch Democratic leaders from South Texas, greatly enhanced the county's visibility at the state level. One fund-raiser in Corpus Christi on April 8, 1949, and another held a month later in Laredo, helped develop a strong sense of camaraderie between Judge Bravo and other key Democratic leaders.[21]

Shortly after the social gathering held in Laredo in May, 1949, Hugh S. Cluck, mayor of the Gateway City and a member of Governor Shivers's state committee, solicited Judge Bravo's assistance to "accept the chairmanship of your county for the re-organization of U.S.O. for the benefit of the Armed Forces of the United States."[22] Not realizing at the time how critical the reactivation would be, Bravo energetically took charge of the local USO. When President Truman sent American troops to South Korea almost a year later, the USO chapter in Zapata County was prepared for action.

Bravo developed ties with Texas Governor Allan Shivers, successor to Governor Beauford Jester, who had died while in office. Shivers sought Judge Bravo's advice apropos of the restructuring of the Texas Employment Commission. In one letter the governor requested: "Please continue to give me the benefit of your counsel."[23]

Based on Senator Johnson's recommendation, President Truman nominated James V. Allred for the judgeship of the U.S. Southern Texas District; the nominee would have judicial authority over Brownsville, Corpus Christi, and Laredo. Since his defeat in the 1942 Senate election by Pappy O'Daniel, Allred had resumed his private law practice in Houston. But once confirmed by the Senate on October 12, 1949, the exgovernor was ready to resume public life. The swearing-in ceremony was scheduled for Saturday, October 29, 1949, at 11:00 A.M.

Senator Johnson and Judge Bravo immediately began making plans to use this sociopolitical event for a business meeting (this probably would be their first time together since there is no documentation that they actually met face-to-face before this event). Enthusiastically, Johnson informed the judge about his agenda, "I plan to be in Corpus Christi then and it is my hope you may also be there, if at all possible for you to come. If I do not have an opportunity to visit with you then, I hope that you pass along from time to time suggestions and criticisms to help me better serve our State and Nation in my capacity here." [24] After communicating back and forth, and with two days left before the memorable event, Judge Bravo, eager to discuss the economic and political conditions in South Texas, received the following telegram: "DELIGHTED TO SPEND WITH YOU ALL THE TIME YOU NEED WHEN I GET TO CORPUS CHRISTI ON THE 29TH. CAN NOT SAY DEFINITELY WHAT HOUR BUT WILL MAKE MYSELF AVAILABLE AS SOON AS I CAN AFTER YOU ARRIVE." [25]

Numerous high-ranking public officials, influential members of the business community, and many friends from throughout South Texas attended a banquet at the Robert Driscoll Hotel honoring Judge Allred that Saturday night. At the head table, besides the judge and Mrs. Bravo, were Webb County's political boss Judge Manuel J. Raymond and Lyndon Johnson, the keynote speaker. Zapata County was well represented at the occasion, as was Laredo, the delegation for which included Bismark Pope, Philip A. Kazen, Jr., and John E. Fitzgibbon and their wives and Mrs. Abraham Kazen, Jr.[26] The meeting turned out to be an excellent opportunity for Johnson to consult personally with Judge Bravo on matters pertinent to South Texas politics. After their meeting, Johnson kept in contact by sending the judge copies of his talks, speeches, and even a copy of President Truman's message to Congress.[27]

In addition, Judge Bravo periodically received one-page status reports giving crucial information about the outcome of several legislative activities. For example, during the middle of the Korean War, Johnson commented about his duties in chairing the Armed Services Preparedness Subcommittee: they included supervising several defense efforts, expanding the synthetic rubber plants, condemning the British government for "hijacking the U.S. on tin prices," and implementing the first Universal Military Training (UMT) legislation in history.[28] The letters always concluded with a note of appreciation for making his work in the Senate more effective. Perhaps no other county judge was privy to this type of government information.

Regularly, Senator Johnson, directly or through his confidant Hidalgo County Judge J. C. Looney, checked with Judge Bravo to determine "how the people feel he is serving them and how they feel about his standing on various matters . . . and [to] advise him how the people in your particular area feel . . . and also about what he can do for them that he is not now doing." [30] Judge Bravo always conferred with the political machine (the Big Four) before advising Johnson about the economic problems Zapata County and the other border counties faced.

As their friendship grew stronger over the years, Johnson's implicit trust in the judge's opinion became more apparent. Bravo always provided him with an honest and perceptive viewpoint on issues affecting the rural areas in South Texas. Judge Bravo's continued loyalty and support can be seen in several letters Johnson wrote in appreciation for having him in his corner: "I have long been proud of your friendship, and I am especially proud of your fine letter about my work in the Senate. I hope my efforts here will always justify your great faith in me." [31]

THE 1952 DEMOCRATIC PRIMARY

As to county political matters, Judge Bravo was always having to prepare for a new election. The upcoming Democratic primary of 1952 had all the makings of the 1940 primary and the infamous 1948 race. The hot, dry weather in South Texas seemed to fan already hot issues—chiefly the relocation of the town of Zapata and other surrounding communities—and to polarize further the Partido Viejo and the Partido Nuevo. [32] According to plans already in effect, the federal government, working through the International Boundary and Water Commission (IBWC) and with Mexican officials, was building the first international dam on the border between Zapata and Starr counties. Lamentably, the reservoir would inundate the Zapata County seat, several hamlets along the Río Grande, and the Mexican town of Guerrero, Tamaulipas. The construction of Falcon Dam and the moving of the county seat are discussed in more detail in the next two chapters.

Judge Bravo faced tough opposition from his old nemesis, José María (J. M.) Sánchez, a seasoned politician who had served at one time as county judge (1920–26). Campaigning across Zapata County, Bravo confronted with complete aplomb the many questions surrounding the relocation problems. According to his son Eddie Bravo, Sr., it was essential to win over the large working-class families so that "whatever the old man said, the whole family, including nieces, cousins, etc., voted a straight Democratic ticket. Sometimes, an extended family consisted of fifteen or more eligible voters."[33] Judge Bravo's 1952 campaign platform called for having all residents from the smaller communities, along with those living in the county seat, relocate together to one suitable location in the county. This way, all these people would benefit from the improved utilities, public services, and irrigated lands. Moreover, the savings to taxpayers in reconstructing the town would be cost effective. The IBWC had initially recommended this plan and it had been well received by the political machine. However, the Partido Nuevo candidates from Lopeño and Falcon, voting precincts 3 and 4 respectively, disapproved of the proposal and instead wanted to have their own separate communities.

During the 1952 campaign, the Partido Viejo politicians emphasized their past accomplishments based on administrative experience, leadership, and their political connections in dealing with the federal bureaucracies. For the first time in their history, the Big Four published a manifesto. In it, the PV leaders explained to county residents their solutions for coping with the unavoidable problems arising from the construction of Falcon Dam, and they expressed optimism about providing new jobs and a better economic future for the county.[34]

In the meantime, the Partido Nuevo reorganized its campaign strategy and created the New Coalition Party of Zapata (actually, this was the Zapata County Republican Party in another guise). In a political flyer, its leaders blasted Judge Bravo and Leopoldo Martínez, the sheriff/tax assessor and collector, for "attaining greater political power and personal gains"; labeled the judge as an "antiquated Party chief"; referred to his slate of candidates as "merely a bunch of timid sheep, unwilling instruments in the hands of Old Politician Wolves," and urged the voters to support the New Coalition Party because it was for "Progress and Equal Opportunities for all according to the democratic way of life, with a sincere and open spirit, but without false political promises, and above all, WITHOUT THE EVILS OF BOSSISM."[35]

Early incomplete and unofficial returns from two precincts had Bravo trailing by a wide margin. J. M. Sánchez, the gallant PN candidate, celebrated a premature victory with a cavalcade of cars parading through the town: the first car blasted the Republican Party's theme song of "Las Coronelas" through loudspeakers, and an open flatbed truck carried an empty casket symbolizing the defeat of Judge Bravo's Partido Viejo.[36] By early the next morning, however, all four precincts had reported a record voter turnout, perhaps the biggest in the county's history, declaring Judge Bravo the winner over Sánchez by a mere fifty-four votes. Bravo's ticket won every county and precinct office, with the exception of county commissioner for Lopeño (precinct 3).[37] But the Partido Viejo's sordid reputation for tampering with election returns certainly seemed to cast a shadow over the final results.

At least two factors explain why the Partido Viejo lost its grip over Lopeño. First, the faction that supported the challenger Santiago González opposed the incumbent Guillermo González, who favored the political machine's concept of relocating to one townsite. Instead, the pro-Santiago group wanted to have their own separate community (and had received approval for this from the IBWC). Second, the ongoing and well-publicized family feud between the incumbent Guillermo and his insurgent Republican nephew Santiago proved too much for the political machine to handle. This time, the forty-two-year-old Santiago emerged as the victor by a narrow margin of eight votes, ending the Democratic Party's hold in precinct 3 and Guillermo's political career of twenty years.

At the state level, two major races in the 1952 primary attracted Zapata voters to the polls: the Senate seat vacated by Senator Tom Connally, who resigned after an illustrious political career of thirty-five years, and the gubernatorial race between Governor Shivers and Ralph W. Yarborough. In the Senate race, popular contender Price Daniels battled Lindley Beckworth and E. W. Napier. Both Governor Shivers and Attorney General Price Daniels received overwhelming majorities over their opponents, with the three boss-ruled counties of Webb, Zapata, and Starr delivering close to 96 percent of the votes for Shivers and Daniels. George Parr's supposed influence over neighboring counties must not have asserted itself because Duval was the only boss-controlled county that voted for the liberal candidate Yarborough, an outcome that thoroughly flies in the face of the standard interpretation that Parr ruled the other bosses with an iron hand. Adjacent Jim Wells County voted for Shivers (72%), and so did Jim Hogg (77%), Hidalgo (82%), and Cameron (74%).[38] In the Senate race, Zapata, Webb, Starr, and Duval counties overwhelmingly supported Daniels, with margins of more than 90 percent of the votes. Of the four boss-influenced counties, Webb's political machine was the only one that delivered a decisive count of 99 percent.

ELECTION CONTEST SUITS AND THE 1952 GENERAL ELECTION

The dubious-minded J. M. Sánchez, not convinced about the outcome of the race for county judge, filed an election contest suit in the 49th District Court on August 12 against Judge Bravo, alleging that fraud and voting irregularities had marred the final results. In particular, he maintained that "some ballots were not counted, that aliens and non-residents of the county and precinct voted." [39] Two other contest suits followed: one filed by Republican candidate Joaquín Solís against the winner Hilario Domínguez for the office of constable in precinct 2, and the other by fifty-six-year-old Guillermo González against his nephew Santiago. Similar countercharges of voting irregularities added color to a looming courtroom battle and set the stage for an August 18 hearing before District Judge R. D. Wright, a Democrat who had the backing of Webb County's powerful Independent Club. [40]

Because of the enormous amount of publicity, a mutual agreement between the two political parties moved the case from the town of Zapata to the Webb County Courthouse in Laredo. Attorneys Horace P. Guerra and Gordon Gibson represented Sánchez, Solís, and S. González (the plaintiffs), while Bismarck Pope represented Bravo, Domínquez, and G. González. During the eight days of testimony, close to fifty witnesses—those whose questionable ballots were being challenged—provided testimony regarding their residency. [41] In the course of the trial, Judge Wright examined the absentee balloting procedures. Soft-spoken Matías Cuéllar, the district and county clerk, revealed during direct examination that he had failed to detach the stubs from the ballots, a legal issue providing sufficient grounds to declare all the absentee ballots null and void. The plaintiffs' attorney tried to include a motion to disregard all the absentee ballots, but Judge Wright ruled against it "because it wasn't in the pleadings of the [original] case." [42] The outcome of the primary election would have been totally different if the absentee ballots had been thrown out due to a costly mistake by the county clerk!

On Thursday, August 28, a near-capacity crowd filled the courtroom and listened attentively to Judge Wright's decision in favor of Bravo and Domínguez (Guillermo González had withdrawn his suit before the hearing ended). Needless to say, the Partido Viejo and its supporters were elated with the good news. Judge Wright declared the election results

accurate simply because the plaintiffs had failed to show evidence to sub-
stantiate their case.[43] During the proceedings, many of the alleged "illegal aliens" turned out to be American citizens who were so labeled
because they frequently visited Mexican towns along the border.

A few days later, on September 10, at 10:00 A.M., the attorneys for
the plaintiffs filed an appeal in San Antonio's Court of Appeals, Fourth
Supreme Judicial District; the court granted them a hearing within twelve
days. On September 27, the appellate court reviewed the attorneys' briefs
and upheld the decision rendered by Judge Wright. "It also seems that
appellants' [Sánchez and Solís] evidence is insufficient to justify a rever-
sal."[44] In quick succession, therefore, the New Coalition Party contenders had received another political blow, while Judge Bravo and the
Partido Viejo had been given a second victory. Cleared of any political
malfeasance, the judge set his sights on the upcoming November 4 general election.

His defeat at the polls and twice in the courts notwithstanding, J. M.
Sánchez tenaciously sought the county judgeship by submitting his name
as a write-in candidate on the general election ballot. The voters gave a
jubilant Judge Bravo an overwhelming victory over his obstinate opponent by a wide margin of 181 votes, 724 to 543. The closest race was
between sixty-seven-year-old incumbent Proceso Martínez, Jr., who had
occupied the commissioner's post for precinct 2 (San Ygnacio) since
1922, and E. E. Paredes. Martínez won by a mere six votes.[45] All the
other Partido Viejo incumbents returned to public office, with the New
Coalition Party official Santiago González representing precinct 3. The
canvassing returns for Zapata County reported a total of 1,348 votes
cast for national, state, and local offices.[46]

Judge Bravo and his divided political machine barely mustered
enough votes from the Partido Viejo to give Stevenson 54 percent, which
translated into a difference of just 90 votes. Governor Shivers's endorsement of the Republican nominee for president created a rift among the
state's Democrats, and it proved to be a blow against Adlai Stevenson,
who had not supported Texas Democratic Party leaders in their legal
fight over tidelands claims that had historically belonged to the state.
Texas wanted control of the oil deposits extending from the Gulf shore
out ten and a half miles.[47] This is probably why Hidalgo and Cameron
counties did not remain loyal to their party. In the Senate race, Price Daniels received over 90 percent of the votes from Webb, Starr, Duval, and

Jim Wells counties, but in Zapata he only got 59 percent.[48] The same voting results extended to Governor Allan Shivers.

THE FBI'S DILEMMA

J. M. Sánchez, the vanquished write-in Republican candidate, was still obsessed with the belief that voting misconduct had prevented him from defeating Judge Bravo. Unwilling to accept his failure even after four attempts, he was determined to pursue ways to remove Bravo from office. Sánchez now turned to the Federal Bureau of Investigation (FBI) for assistance. A group of federal agents secretly arrived in Zapata County to conduct an investigation into the alleged election fraud. They made the mistake of bypassing local protocol and not consulting with the county judge.[49] Their business attire and cryptic demeanor soon became the talk of the town. Upon discovering the agents' presence (in a small town it is very difficult to conceal strangers or any type of information), Judge Bravo sent a telegram dated March 12, 1953, petitioning for Lyndon Johnson's intercession in what was becoming an unwanted involvement by the federal government in local politics:

> CERTAIN DEMOCRATS DEFEATED IN PRIMARY ELECTION LAST YEAR
> THEN TURNING RENEGADE AND PROCURING WRITE-IN VOTE IN
> GENERAL ELECTION AT WHICH THEY WERE AGAIN DEFEATED NOW
> CLAIMING TO CONSTITUTE REPUBLICAN PARTY. . . . THIS INVESTI-
> GATION NOW IN FORCE AND ONLY VOTERS SUPPORTING REGULAR
> DEMOCRATIC PARTY OF ZAPATA COUNTY BEING INVESTIGATED.
> FBI OFFICIALS REFUSED TO INVESTIGATE QUALIFICATIONS . . . OF
> VOTERS SUPPORTING THESE RENEGADE CANDIDATES. . . . WE DO
> NOT BELIEVE UNITED STATES AUTHORITIES SHOULD INTERFERE IN
> ANY MANNER IN LOCAL AFFAIRS AND SINCE NO NATIONAL OFFI-
> CER WAS ENGAGED IN ANY CONTEST IN ZAPATA COUNTY IN GEN-
> ERAL ELECTION WE SUBMIT THAT NO RIGHT FOR A FEDERAL
> INVESTIGATION EXISTS.[50]

The day after receiving the judge's telegram, Johnson contacted the Attorney General's office and requested a complete report on the FBI's "irregular and illegal" meddling.[51] U.S. Justice Department officials reassured the senator that they had no intentions of prying into local and state politics, and that their initial involvement was purely exploratory in an effort to determine if sufficient cause existed for a full-blown investigation.[52] The federal agents' visit, cut short by Judge Bravo's continuous pressure on Johnson and the Justice Department, rendered Sánchez his final defeat. On a warm and windy afternoon, the dejected Sánchez and his group of supporters sadly watched the agents depart from Zapata County. By the end of March, Bravo apprised Johnson about the status of the situation. "The F.B.I. have not been in Zapata since you went to work for us. . . . The opposition is very persistent but the real trouble with them is that they do not have sufficient voters on their side."[53] At least for now, Judge Bravo kept a tight rein over Zapata politics.

THE MEANS JUSTIFY THE END

Even though historians have generally associated the Félix Longoria episode with Dr. Héctor P. García, the Bravo Papers reveal that the judge and Senator Johnson corresponded on this delicate issue. Judge Bravo felt that this act of discrimination was of utmost seriousness, and as the political boss and Tejano leader of Zapata County, he took immediate action in response. He reacted angrily and publicly condemned the racist actions of the funeral director. As a product of the Mexican-American generation, Judge Bravo was an advocate for civil rights and a champion for equal treatment of Tejanos as first-class citizens, for, as noted, he himself had experienced overt discrimination in South and Central Texas in the 1940s. On a personal level, the judge empathized with the Longoria family because his younger brother Robert had been stationed in the Philippines when Félix was killed.

As the jefe político of the county, the judge provided the necessary leadership in addressing pertinent domestic concerns—telephone service to rural areas, the USO campaign, and soil conservation programs. Judge Bravo further fulfilled his role as a political boss by providing for the social and economic welfare of his constituents—whether of the middle or lower class—in the way of improved education, good roads, and the like. Taking a leadership role in solving pertinent local issues was something inherent in the role of political boss. In turn, the people continued to place their faith in him because he delivered. Indeed, satisfying county needs and maintaining the machine in good standing enabled the judge to defeat the New Coalition Party during the 1952 election campaign.

His domination of Zapata County politics, then, may be attributed in part to his ability to meet his constituents' expectations. But his leadership style in dealing with domestic issues also contributed to his stay in power and to the Partido Viejo's success in every campaign. On the one hand, he did not operate in a greedy manner; he shunned wealth for himself. This mark of honesty earned him the trust and support of the majority of Zapata County voters. Additionally, he relied on his personal and political skills to get the job done. Bravo's bilingual communication abilities enabled him to converse equally well with fellow politicians and with all the people, Democrats and Republicans alike. In short, his resiliency and lack of pretension helped in addressing the concerns that impacted the county.

On the other hand, Bravo could well turn to questionable methods to have his way locally. In the view of the New Coalition Party, he and the Big Four regularly engaged in alleged unethical vote counting, in manipulating final vote tallies, and in non-residents voting. The judge's seamy side is most obviously seen in the way he got the FBI to stop its investigation of local vote fraud. In the judge's estimation, the federal agency had no business investigating him and his administration. Since his political machine had not violated federal laws, he noted, county government had the right to operate local affairs without federal interference. The judge well knew that in a time of crisis, he could play his high card with Lyndon Johnson. When the FBI got too close for comfort, he duly contacted the senator. As a result, Bravo remained the undisputed boss in Zapata County, and the Partido Viejo maintained its dominance over local politics.

Falcon Dam and the Relocation of Zapata

The Water Treaty of February 3, 1944, signed between the United States and Mexico and known formally as the Treaty Between the United States and Mexico Respecting Utilization of the Waters of the Colorado and Tijuana Rivers and of the Río Grande, set into motion a binational agreement that would lead to the construction of three storage dams along the Río Grande. Of utmost concern to both countries was the maximum usage of the Río Grande flow through conservation and storage, so that it could be used for flood control and hydroelectricity, and more water would be available for farms and towns. The first dam would be located between Santa Elena Canyon (Brewster County) and the mouth of the Pecos River (Val Verde County); the second between Eagle Pass and Laredo; and the third below Laredo and close to Roma, Texas. Work on the latter one was scheduled to begin at once, and the two governments had about eight years in which to finish it. Doomed by the construction of Falcon Dam would be the towns of Zapata, Ramireño, Uribeño, Lopeño, Falcon, and several farms on the American side. All were situated parallel to the Río Grande. The Mexican town of Guerrero, Tamaulipas, located along the banks of the Río Salado, would also be inundated by the waters of the reservoir.

During the building of the dam, Zapata officials had to deal with the International Boundary and Water Commission (IBWC), a federal body of long standing, the mission of which had broadened to include the planning, construction, and operation of the three proposed dams; with the Bureau of Reclamation; Corps of Engineers; and with other federal agencies. In such negotiations, which lasted throughout the tenure of Judge Bravo (and even afterward), Zapata County's political machine turned to the capable Bravo for leadership and guidance.

The projects posed a test of technical and diplomatic skills for the forty-five-year-old patrón of the ruling Partido Viejo. To begin with, he had no legal experience in dealing with large government bureaucracies. However, Judge Bravo relied on an old friend who had extensive knowledge of the law—Robert Lee Bobbitt, former attorney general and fellow Democrat—for advice. Also, the judge counted on his political ties with Senator Johnson and Congressmen West and Bentsen to obtain the leverage he needed from Washington. Cleverly, he got the leading citizens of Zapata County to provide input through nonpartisan advisory committees.

A second problem that the Falcon Dam project presented for Bravo was calming the fears of his constituents. Many in Zapata County wondered if the new dam, proposed to be built near the towns of Falcon or Salineño, would inundate their homes. And if so, would they receive fair, equitable, and replacement compensation? Furthermore, there lingered the agonizing chore of relocating or replacing their homes, the *campo santo* (ancestral burial grounds), and public buildings. The harsh reality of having to uproot their historic settlements, social networks, and economic means of survival stared the county residents straight in the face, producing hysteria, confusion, and uncertainty. Since twelve thousand acres of cropland were to be inundated, farmers whose cultivated lands lay adjacent to the Río Grande faced particular worries (ranchers encountered no major trauma as livestock ranges in Zapata County were located away from the rising waters of Falcon Dam). Judge Bravo and the political machine worked unceasingly to see the people through the crisis, though never able to anticipate the real consequences and impact of the massive project.

Another problem for the judge, and perhaps his most difficult one, was accommodating the Partido Nuevo's demands before the IBWC. The IBWC itself faced a delicate situation in having to negotiate with Judge Bravo and the county commissioners—the county's official elected governing body—but needing also to accommodate the Partido Nuevo's demands for equal time in the discussions; they assumed a de facto role of authority. But Bravo handled the Partido Nuevo's insistence by allowing them to serve on committees, meet with IBWC officials, and even attend business trips to Austin—at county expense.

PRELIMINARY PLANS

In 1946, Judge Bravo scheduled a meeting in El Paso between Commissioner Lawrence M. Lawson of the IBWC and Zapata County leaders to discuss the impact that the construction of Falcon Dam would have on the county's citizens. In particular, officials focused on the prospects of saving the town of Zapata and the surrounding communities from inundation—possibly by reducing the size of the dam so that the reservoir would not flood them.[1] Zapata representatives also wanted to inquire of Lawson about what federal assistance the county might receive in the quest for a new townsite with appropriate water facilities and other necessities. To their disappointment, Lawson informed them (at the meetings held on May 2 and 3, 1946, in El Paso), that Congress had authorized the construction of an international dam and that under existing laws, there was "no assurance that we would be given extra assistance for surveying and plotting a new townsite or for moving the city's more than 400 homes and business buildings."[2] Lawson stated that IBWC procedures called for the condemnation of all properties and for providing owners a fair market value for their loss. This latter rule also applied to public and school buildings, except that the appraised amount was based on a replacement cost factor. Lawson informed the Zapata County delegation that IBWC officials could not get involved in the matter of relocating citizens.

At first, the prospective size of the reservoir and the exact position for the construction of the dam were not officially known, except that IBWC engineers and geologists favored either the Falcon or the Salineño site, both close to the Zapata–Starr County line. Damming the river at either site would inundate Zapata. As suspense escalated on the question of location, Valley newspapers carried headline stories focusing on possible alternatives for the dam. In an effort to acquire more information on the project, Judge Bravo and Commissioner Medina met with Congressman Milton West, who represented Zapata County in the 15th Congressional District. They wished to discuss the size of the dam, to ask if it would inundate the county seat of Zapata, and to look into the possibility of getting the U.S. government to compensate the county financially for losses incurred.[3]

While the judge and the political machine pondered the location as well as the effects that the construction of the dam would have on the social and economic future of the county, the Partido Nuevo flung the relocation issue into the political arena, creating unnecessary havoc. At times its tactics proved to be counterproductive to the Partido Viejo's objectives. This factionalism served only to compound the IBWC's dilemma in making preliminary decisions on matters that would ultimately affect the fate of the county. As noted by anthropologist Wilfrid C. Bailey, who spent a year in Zapata County studying the effects that the project would have on the people, "When the Boundary Commission held public meetings, they sometimes found the Old Party supporters gathered in one place and the New Party in another."[4] Consequently, the IBWC found it necessary to schedule two separate meetings every time.

On May 23, 1946, Judge Bravo and County Agricultural Agent J. T. Morrow met with officials from the Bureau of Reclamation in McAllen. One of their planning engineers, John C. Thompson, acknowledged that Zapata County needed assistance but felt that legally (as had Lawson), the IBWC did not have the authority to rebuild towns; consequently, he referred the question to another bureaucratic agency.[5] A week later Judge Bravo approached the Bureau of Reclamation again, asking it to conduct a field survey between Zapata and Lopeño for the purpose of finding a more suitable place for the county seat. Ideally, such a location would be close to an adequate water supply for domestic use and would have about five thousand acres of irrigable land.[6]

On September 12, 1946, in preparation for their negotiations with IBWC, the county commissioners approved two recommendations for the purpose of protecting Zapata County's residents and landowners. First, they unanimously accepted the appointment of a ten-member nonpartisan advisory committee whose role would be to advise the county officials on matters needed to protect and safeguard local interests as the construction of the dam progressed. Second, the commissioners acquired the legal services of Robert Lee Bobbitt, who would attempt to obtain the best allowable compensation for citizens losing their properties. Bobbitt would represent the county's interests in future litigation. The county officials gave Bobbitt wide latitude and discretion to choose technicians and other experts who could provide him with additional assistance to carry out his task.[7]

Two Partido Nuevo members, Rafael San Miguel and Humberto

González, spearheaded a short-lived proposal that momentarily appeared to have the potential to stave off inundation of Zapata and the surrounding communities. This plan would have been more cost effective than relocating an entire town and would have made moot the relocation problems and compensation issues. IBWC Commissioner Lawson apparently liked it, explaining that this alternative idea entailed the construction of three levees around Zapata, leaving open the north side of the town for traffic.[8] Judge Bravo concurred with this plan and as a second option argued for building the dam upriver from the city of Laredo. Another alternative that the judge proposed was to reduce the size of the lake, but IBWC rebutted that a smaller reservoir would reduce the dam's effectiveness. Unfortunately for the county's residents, none of these proposals was ultimately considered.

On Tuesday, August 19, 1947, David Herrera Jordán, commissioner for the Mexican Water Commission, and J. C. Bustamante, consulting engineer for the Mexican Water Commission, recommended to Commissioner Lawson the Falcon site at the Starr–Zapata County line for the construction of the dam. Two days later, the United States engineers met in El Paso and approved this recommendation.[9]

RELOCATION DEBATE OPENS WITH CONDEMNATION PROCEEDINGS

Thus began the tedious process of planning and coordinating the multiple phases of constructing the first international dam at an estimated cost of over $45 million, with the United States assuming 58.6 percent of the cost and Mexico the remaining 41.4 percent. While immediate evacuation plans for the Mexican town of Guerrero were set in motion, in Zapata a cloud of ambiguity and confusion delayed the relocation process. Mainly responsible for this predicament were the Partido Nuevo with its constant meddling and the IBWC's lack of experience in dealing "with public relations, political issues, and administrative policies, where we had little precedent, from previous jobs of a similar nature."[10]

County officials cooperated with IBWC staff by granting them leased office space at forty dollars per month. Judge Bravo accommodated them with a room on the southwest corner of the second floor of the courthouse, just a few feet from his office. From their sixteen- by sixteen-foot office cubicle, modest but comfortable, IBWC workers made paramount decisions that directly changed the lives of all the families living in the path of the huge reservoir.[11]

In the meantime, through condemnation proceedings, the IBWC had acquired 4,908 acres in Starr County and about 85,000 acres in Zapata County for the construction of Falcon Dam and reservoir. Under condemnation laws, government appraisers established a fair market value on each house and then subtracted 20 percent for depreciation and another 20 percent for obsolescence. Such a formula left owners suffering an economic loss. This IBWC policy, based on "fair market value," simply failed to take proper account of circumstances in the county.

Since some of the homes were about one hundred years old, Judge Bravo proposed a more equitable compensation policy, one based on replacement value rather than on fair market monetary projections.[12] For years, Zapata County had had no real estate market—few real property sales—so the appraisal process had to be established on an assumed price for a given buyer. Dissatisfaction with the IBWC's compensation policies continued even into the late 1960s.

On September 26, 1949, a friend of Judge Bravo's, Earl A. Thompson, owner of Abby Drilling Company of San Antonio and heavily involved in the oil and gas business in Zapata County, expressed his concern for the people in a fiery letter to Senator Johnson. He criticized the IBWC's "fair appraisal" methods and practices, adding, "It seems our government has completely forgotten its own people and is spending all its money and time on the Poor Dsitressed [sic] People of other lands."[13] Bitter observations came from another Bravo acquaintance, Gordon Mackenzie, a principal oil and gas lessee from Lopeño, who vehemently opposed the construction of Falcon Dam because of the economically detrimental impact it would have on Zapata County citizens. In a three-page, single-spaced, typed letter to the chairman of the Appropriations Committee, dated August 11, 1950, he questioned the condemnation proceedings and challenged the payment of "just compensation." Moreover, his sentiments reflected Judge Bravo's general attitude toward the IBWC policies. The judge complained: "It is perfectly all right to confiscate the property of the people and put them on the highway barefooted and without just compensation," just so that the federal government can "build a dam to furnish water for the Río Grande Valley, to raise more grapefruit."[14]

Almost two months later, on November 30, Commissioner Lawson defended the IBWC's action to Senator Johnson, stating in part that there was no legal authority "to value the various properties fully and fairly." [15] Moreover, the IBWC clearly outlined the legal procedures available to Zapata landowners should they disapprove of the appraised values. For the local Hispanic residents unaccustomed to litigious activities, however, this questionable alternative was too lengthy and highly expensive. Yet, the judicial process was the only avenue available for them to take on the federal bureaucracy. Humberto González, secretary and general manager of the county's chamber of commerce, was among the first to express dissatisfaction with the legal recourse. In a letter to Lyndon Johnson, he informed the senator that the homeowners did not have enough money for appeals or feel comfortable going to the federal district court to contest the appraiser's decisions. [16]

PARTIDO NUEVO'S DEFENSE COMMITTEE

While the judge grappled with the IBWC, the bureaucracy, and the needs of his constituents, he also fought brush fires with the Partido Nuevo. Predictably, a heated debate broke out on January 3, 1950, at a joint meeting between the county commissioners' court and a recently organized defense committee of the Zapata County Chamber of Commerce over the issues of relocation and the condemnation of more land than the government actually needed. [17] A day after the encounter at the courthouse, Bobbitt expressed a concern to Judge Bravo about continuing as legal counsel. In a hand-delivered letter stamped "Personal and Confidential," Bobbitt noted: "There are many important problems ahead of the people of Zapata County. They seem to be all confused as to what they can or should do for the protection of their own best interests. . . . All people who have any judgement must now realize that the Falcon Dam is going to be built. . . . Any thought or suggestion of 'enjoining the Government from proceeding,' is simply wishful thinking and is a waste of time." [18]

Bobbitt further recommended in his letter to the judge that the relocation matters would best be resolved, from the residents' perspective, if the county officials followed four recommendations: (1) "meet all issues in the Court proceedings. . . . That is, get the highest and best advantage we can through court proceeding"; (2) appeal to Bentsen, Connally, and Johnson to "enact such special laws as may be necessary and appropriate to restore the communities . . . that will bring justice and a fair deal to the people whose lives are being destroyed"; (3) approach the Texas Legislature, "to give the citizens of Zapata County some priority or right in the waters of the lake to be constructed"; and (4) let the whole world know, if necessary, "about the hardships and injustices confronting the people of Zapata County." [19]

On January 26, 1950, another group called the Citizens Committee, created by the chamber of commerce, presented a proposal to Judge Bravo at the commissioners' court meeting demanding that he approve the hiring of another attorney to represent the interests of the citizens better; that he formulate a stern resolution opposing the IBWC's actions; and that there be unanimous support for a protest in the form of a petition against the IBWC's condemnation procedures.[20] But the request, Judge Bravo felt, would be counterproductive at a time when the county was engaged in sensitive negotiations with the IBWC. Without an approved plan of action, the judge declared, any "hastily drawn petitions, phrased in general terms, may later prove to be contrary to the best interests of a majority of the people and the county and hamper the effectiveness of all our efforts toward the attainment of those much-desired goals." [21]

In response to Bobbitt's advice and the work of the chamber of commerce committees, Judge Bravo made two recommendations to the commissioners on March 6, 1950, both of which were approved by the officials. First, Bravo suggested that they should acquire the services of Manuel J. Raymond, who had just retired as Webb County judge, to assist Special Counsel Bobbitt in an effort to strengthen their case against the IBWC. Second, he proposed that the court accept the recommendations of the defense committee. The judge then informed Bobbitt that he should intensify his lobbying efforts with Lawson to help reduce the amount of land actually needed for the reservoir. Initially, the U.S. government had condemned all lands in Zapata County lying below the 325-foot elevation traverse and, above this, lands extending to the proposed route for a relocated Highway 83. In essence, the added acquisition of territory deprived property owners from using acreage that would front on the edge of the reservoir, acreage traditionally used for cattle grazing.

POLITICAL POWER PLOYS

At the behest of Judge Bravo, civil rights activist José T. Canales, a personal friend of the judge, came to represent several Zapata County property owners wanting the IBWC to rethink its policy toward acquiring additional real estate. On February 22, 1950, Canales sent letters to IBWC Project Attorney James Jackson (with copies forwarded to Senator Johnson) accusing the IBWC of "playing political favoritism," as landowners in Starr County were being allowed to retain their lands adjoining the dam (for irrigation purposes), perhaps due to the strong political influence of the Guerra family.[22]

Two days later, obviously perplexed about the allegations presented by Canales, Senator Johnson requested an explanation from Commissioner Lawson.[23] On March 13, the commissioner reported to Johnson and Canales that additional surveys would be taken in porciones 14 through 17. Such surveys were needed to determine if "it will be necessary to amend the petition and declaration of taking which have already been filed covering some of the lands in Zapata County, thus revesting titles [to] the former owners [of] a portion of the lands" in those plots under question.[24]

A total of 31,117 acres were finally returned to the owners in Zapata County, thus leaving 56,520 acres for the dam and reservoir, as opposed to the 87,737 acres of land acquired in the condemnation proceedings.[25] Lawson vigorously disputed the charges of political favoritism being involved as regards landowners of neighboring Starr County.

Such unforeseen problems slowed down negotiations over the important process of relocation of hundreds of citizens and their households. Additional unavoidable steps, such as reconciling the bidding process, detailing architectural plans and designs, and transposing the numerical data into the metric system proved to be tedious and time-consuming since all the necessary documents drafted by the Bureau of Reclamation had to be translated into Spanish.[26] These lulls did not go over well with the politicians and citrus growers of the Lower Río Grande Valley. A two-page resolution, adopted on July 11, 1950, by the Hidalgo County Water Control and Improvement District No. Six, and later copied by neighboring counties, found its way to Senator Johnson's office. Basically, the resolution called for the dam to "be constructed at once and completed in a minimum of time" and blamed the IBWC for slowness, "deploring the long and inexcusable delay in construction of the dam."[27] Johnson assured his old friend and the Valley's Democratic leader, J. C. Looney, that nine million dollars had already been appropriated for the

dam's construction and an additional five million allocated as part of a
pending appropriation bill.[28]

FEDERAL LEGISLATION

At the request of Judge Bravo and with the help of Bobbitt and Raymond,
Congressman Lloyd Bentsen, Jr., drafted legislation that contained specific provisions for relocating communities affected by the Falcon reservoir and for building new towns. Copies of the proposed bill were
distributed to the IBWC and the county's public officials for their perusal.[29] After much deliberation at the local level, and input from the
county commissioners and the Partido Nuevo's chamber of commerce,
Bobbitt and Judge Bravo felt satisfied with the terms of the proposed bill
and forwarded their comments to Bentsen.

On February 27, 1950, Bentsen officially introduced H.R. 7443, also
known as the Bentsen Bill, designed to provide the IBWC with federal
assistance for the establishment of a water and sewer system; for construction of certain public facilities and relocation of movable buildings
and cemeteries; for development of a new townsite that would accommodate citizens of both Zapata and surrounding hamlets; and for
replacement of inundated irrigated lands.[30] Two months later, IBWC
Commissioner Lawson endorsed the provisions of the Bentsen Bill—
which allotted approximately 2.1 million dollars for implementing the
above stipulations and replacing the old irrigated lands—and he so notified Chairman Whittington of the Committee on Public Works.[31]

In the meantime, Elmer B. Staats, director of the Bureau of the Budget, lobbied against the Bentsen Bill and on September 13, 1950, got
Congress to approve instead the Falcon Dam Bill (P.L. 786), also known
as the American-Mexican Treaty Act, which contained provisions for implementing the construction of Falcon Dam as well as for negotiating the
acquisition of properties and the establishment of utilities in the new
county seat of Zapata. The American-Mexican Treaty Act, however, was
unclear concerning the complete replacement of towns, including public
buildings and facilities. The Bureau of the Budget "was in sympathy with
the objectives of the Bentsen Bill, but opposed to the passage of the Bill
itself because it would create an undesirable precedent [for future relocation projects]."[32] The bureau felt by the summer of 1951 that the IBWC

could now proceed "to relocate Zapata under existing authority (Public Law 786)" and to move on the process of erecting the dam.[33]

Not knowing what recourse to take in view of the fast pace of events in Washington, on October 26, 1950, Judge Bravo turned to Senator Johnson for assistance: "The people of this County also feel that when the time comes they will have your Leadership in Congress that laws may be passed where Justice will be given them on account of the losses of their property by the Construction of the Fal [sic] Dam. The Bentsen Bill will be re-introduced in regular session and although it will [not] be an all cure for each individual, it will be of great help to the majority of the people."[34] At this time, the judge and Bobbitt initiated an intensive letter-writing campaign, lobbying for the reconsideration of the Bentsen Bill and the rejection of the Falcon Dam Bill.

On January 17, 1951, Congressman Bentsen reintroduced his bill, now H.R. 1649, which contained the same provisions as the earlier version. Even though the second Bentsen Bill never reached the House floor, it would serve as a blueprint for the course the IBWC would follow between 1950 and 1955 in dealing with the relocation problems. Commissioner Lawson had wanted specific guidelines in relocating the affected communities, but he notified the State Department "that we considered the general provisions of the Bentsen Bill (H.R. 1649) to be desirable."[35] He had some doubts about the American-Mexican Treaty Act, stating "that it was possible that provisions of Public Law 786 were sufficiently broad to permit us to effect the relocation, but [preferring] limitations to be put therein and the authority to be definitely prescribed and limited."[36] However, as the IBWC proceeded with the relocation agreement, officials realized that some of the terms of the Bentsen Bill could not be implemented because the IBWC "in fact 'lacked legal authority' to carry into effect some of the substantial provisions . . . which could, as far as possible, compensate the local government agencies and communities for their destroyed facilities."[37] Nonetheless, both the IBWC and the Zapata County officials would be following the spirit and intent of the Bentsen Bill until Falcon Dam's completion.

Zapata County's hopes for the passage of the Bentsen Bill died on May 16, 1951, when President Truman convinced Congressman Bentsen to retrieve his piece of legislation because "he did not believe it necessary to have special legislation for the relocation of Zapata County residences."[38] The president reasoned that "the best way to accomplish this objective is . . . through general legislative authority which now exists [P.L. 786]. . . . The Commissioner of the United States section of the International Boundary and Water Commission can, and should, furnish all necessary assistance to the residents of the area." [39]

Shortly after President Truman's decision, attorneys Bobbitt and Raymond scheduled a meeting at the Plaza Hotel in El Paso with Judge Bravo, IBWC Commissioner Lawson, Chief Counsel Frank Clayton, and Project Counsel James F. Jackson. In Bravo's opinion, Clayton played a crucial role in getting the IBWC to collaborate with the county officials to plan and prepare a just and equitable compensation proposal. More significantly, the meeting produced an accord favorable to Zapata County. In the judge's words: "After exhaustive discussion, an agreement was reached wherein the Boundary Commission [IBWC] agreed to carry out all the provisions provided in the Bentsen Bill." [40] Unfortunately, Clayton unexpectedly died shortly after the meeting, and his replacement was not as cooperative in adhering to the earlier compromise. [41] During the summer of 1951, in preparation for the relocation process, the IBWC held further planning meetings with Judge Bravo, Bobbitt, the county commissioners, and the chamber of commerce.

PROPOSED NEW TOWNSITE FOR COUNTY SEAT

Judge Bravo and the county commissioners wanted the IBWC to find a suitable new county seat—after all, the county was morally, if not legally, responsible for the damages incurred by the construction of the dam. But the commissioners faced opposition from several quarters as to the placement of the municipality. The residents of Falcon (precinct 4) and Lopeño (precinct 3) wanted to have their own separate communities. The people did not want to move to one location (selected by the IBWC and the county), and placed blame for their problem on the political machine and in particular Judge Bravo, who happened to have been born in the Valley. Later in his personal notes, the judge wrote: "The people felt the county officials should have gotten Congress to disapprove the [American-Mexican] Treaty, or should have gotten them to designate the area upriver from Laredo for the Lower Dam; that the Río Grande Valley interest would be the only people receiving valuable benefits at the sacrifice and total loss of Zapata County properties, without its just cost of restitution." [42]

While Judge Bravo and the public officials favored relocating all the

people of Zapata and of the surrounding communities of Uribeño, Lopeño, Ramireño, and Falcon to one central location, many land- and
homeowners in those localities wanted to receive their monetary compensation and just move to wherever they wished. Then there was the
Partido Nuevo, which agreed on the idea of a central location but bitterly
opposed any designation chosen by the county officials. For a while, the
discussion of several possible sites became a political football between
the ruling Partido Viejo and the Partido Nuevo, creating chaos among
the property owners. The anthropologist Bailey blamed the political interference on the anti-Bravo group—the Partido Nuevo—as a contributing factor to the relocation problems, stating that "factionalism has
made it almost impossible to develop a unified front. . . . The challenge
is being made by a loosely organized group known at various times as
the Chamber of Commerce Party, the Veteran's party, the New Party."[43]
This adversary group, which at times referred to itself as the Zapata
County Land Owners Committee but which in reality consisted of members of the Partido Nuevo, from time to time made certain recommendations (albeit congruent with the ones Judge Bobbitt negotiated with the
IBWC) for the Partido Viejo's consideration.

SELECTING THE NEW TOWNSITE

Without an enticing plan for reconstructing the new town of Zapata—
to be situated at the intersection of the Hebbronville highway (Farm to
Market road 496) and the relocated U.S. Highway 83 (about 3.7 miles
east from the present location)—Judge Bravo predicted that about "two-
thirds to three-fourths of the population will move out of the county,"
with many of the residents preferring either the Lower Río Grande Valley
or Laredo.[44] According to Bailey, it "would have been necessary [if too
many people left] to abolish the county and to divide its lands among
the neighboring counties of Starr, Jim Hogg and Webb."[45] One of Judge
Bravo's priorities was to keep the county seat intact while not losing the
county's boundaries or its historic name of Zapata, adopted in 1898 in
honor of Colonel José Antonio Zapata, a hero of the federalists' wars of
the 1830s along the Mexico-Texas border. The Partido Nuevo had its
own agenda and sought ways to achieve "complete reimbursement
for the flooded properties and homes" because in its estimation, "the
residents of the several towns would prefer to select their own places
of relocation rather than become part of a single community."[46] This

continuing controversy divided the county and stalemated the relocation negotiations.

Later that summer, on August 7, 1951, Judge Bravo scheduled one of
several meetings involving the county commissioners, Bobbitt, chamber
of commerce members, landowners, and the IBWC at the Plaza Hotel in
Laredo. Their purpose was to discuss (1) the relocation of Zapata, Falcon, Lopeño and the cemeteries, (2) the Bentsen Bill as it related to the
replacement of irrigated lands, and (3) the location of the schools.[47] The
IBWC staff presented a map of the proposed new townsite and a meteor-
ological analysis of the prevailing winds, showing that a strong breeze
blew in from a south-southeasterly direction about 40 percent of the
time. The IBWC representatives also made available a topographical survey indicating that the depth of the surface soil was favorable for livelihood. The participants agreed on the planning and platting strategies for
the new county seat and assigned Mercurio Martínez, Juventino Martínez, and Agapito Benavides to conduct house-to-house visits and assist
residents in filling out a questionnaire.[48]

As to the relocation of the cemeteries, church records showed that
the burial grounds belonged either to the nearby ranches or to the county.
Blas Cantú, legal assistant for the IBWC, and James Jackson, project
attorney, reported at the meeting that Bishop Mariano S. Garriga of Corpus Christi recommended that the new campo santo be established about
one mile from the new town.

Prior to the adjournment of the meeting, Judge Bravo received an endorsement from the group to hold an election to determine how people
felt about officially relocating the county seat. The people would have
the final approval. For fear of being criticized by the Partido Nuevo, the
group present went on record stating that all the discussions were unofficial and conducted in a spirit of cooperation.[49]

At another meeting held at Falcon, Texas, on August 14, 1951, signs
of political factionalism resurfaced when Rafael San Miguel—president
of the Zapata County Chamber of Commerce, owner of the local water
plant, and a staunch Partido Nuevo supporter—challenged Jackson during the meeting on the proposed new site for Zapata. San Miguel emphatically stated that the proposed location was "the most favorable
place mentioned by the county commissioners, not by the people," and
that he would schedule another meeting with his chamber of commerce
members before making any decision on the final location of the county

seat.[50] At the chamber's suggestion, the IBWC decided to review four or possibly five other places, even though Judge Bravo and the Partido Viejo publicly supported the proposed location selected by the IBWC.

About twenty-two members of the Zapata County Chamber of Commerce met with IBWC staff on August 24, 1951, at the Rex Theater (owned by Humberto González), to present their rationale for selecting sites other than that proposed by the IBWC. At the onset of the meeting, González stated in unequivocal terms that, "speaking for the whole bunch, we have no political connections, no political ambitions. We are private citizens speaking to improve our lot, not to make it worse where we are going."[51] IBWC representatives, obviously unfamiliar with the history of local politics, were not aware that some of the chamber members had campaigned under the Republican ticket to topple the ruling Partido Viejo. Emilio Dilley, a local farmer, had run for county judge against Judge Bravo in 1948; J. M. Sánchez tried four times to defeat the judge; Humberto González would campaign unsuccessfully against the incumbent judge in 1954; Adán Gutiérrez, a rancher who was highly involved with the cattle industry, had lost for the county commissioner's seat of precinct 1 in 1948 and would do so again in 1952; and H. Cuéllar had suffered a similar fate in pursuit of the same seat in 1926 and 1932.

Lloyd Hamilton, resident engineer, supported the IBWC proposed townsite because it was located on higher ground, with the reservoir just a short distance away—thus making it an attractive place to live. Moreover, the topography at this location made the installation of water pumps along the Río Grande more practical.[52] However, the chamber of commerce came up with five possible sites of their own, all quite close to San Ygnacio: one near Triangulation Station 456, one about three miles from the town, one two and a half miles from the Río Grande, one about a mile from the town, and the fifth near the San Francisco Hills on the boundary between San Ygnacio and the Dolores land grant.[53]

Following the meeting, Jackson, the IBWC project attorney, postponed the door-to-door survey agreed upon more than a fortnight before, as the chamber members wanted an opportunity for the IBWC to review the pros and cons of all the possible sites. A field survey of the five locations, however, found them to be unsuitable for the establishment of a town, because the area was smaller (compared to the original proposed site), rockier (from a topographical perspective), closer to San Ygnacio, or irregular in terrain. "You are sure moving the County Seat to one end of the county," Jackson said. "Yes, . . . They are more likely to come here than to the other location because of the nearness to Laredo," answered chamber member J. M. Sánchez.[54] Such disagreements further slowed down the implementation of the relocation schedule.

Without waiting any longer, Judge Bravo and some Partido Viejo members got 446 Zapata property owners' signatures and presented them to the county commissioners on August 27, 1951. The petition, calling for an election to select the location of the county seat officially, supported IBWC's recommended site.[55] Among the signers was Father Eduardo Bastien, OMI, who liked the proposed location, though not a landowner. He nevertheless remained an outspoken critic of the IBWC's compensation policy. Republican leaders Humberto González and Rafael San Miguel showed their disapproval by not signing the petition.

After some deliberation, Judge Bravo, Bobbitt, Raymond, and the county commissioners unanimously approved the petition and scheduled a special election to take place at all four voting precincts on Saturday, September 29, 1951. Just prior to the election, however, González, in a last-minute desperate attempt to derail the referendum, called a special board meeting of the chamber members to review other alternatives for relocating the county seat.[56] The chamber was particularly infuriated that Commissioner Manuel Medina owned some of the land in the proposed townsite and was making plans to develop a housing project. The objections of the chamber came to naught, for after the smoke cleared, the Laredo newspaper reported that 436 voters approved the relocation of the county seat to the proposed site, while none had voted against it.[57] Shortly thereafter, Judge Bravo scheduled meetings with Bobbitt, IBWC, and local leaders. Agenda items included specific, detailed preliminary plans relating to the moving of homes, construction of streets and utilities, and the replacement of irrigated lands.

The San Ygnacio residents did not give up, however. A few months later, over two hundred landowners organized the Committee for the Preservation of San Ygnacio, under the leadership of Mercurio Martínez. At the suggestion of Judge Bravo, the group submitted a lengthy petition to Lawson, Congressman Bentsen, and Senators Connally and Johnson, vehemently requesting that the town of San Ygnacio and the surrounding lands be spared.[58] The petition pointed out that the level of the Falcon Lake reservoir, even at its maximum elevation, would not cause the flooding of San Ygnacio, so why have people there relocate? Johnson and Bentsen immediately pledged their support to save the old town.[59] If Zapata was to be inundated, then at least San Ygnacio would remain as the only community in the county with its lands and historic homes, dating back to the 1830s, untouched by the path of progress. On June 7, 1951, Lawson reconsidered his original condemnation plan and officially removed the town of San Ygnacio from the relocation schedule.

INUNDATED IRRIGATED LANDS

Without replaceable farming lands, county farmers making their living from some twelve thousand irrigated acres along the river had no other means of economic survival. Judge Bravo knew that the provisions of the defunct Bentsen Bill had not satisfactorily addressed this problem. One solution he mulled over was allowing about twenty thousand acres of land close to the town of Zapata to be set aside for farming, with the government subsidizing an irrigation system. Indeed, the judge made frequent phone calls to Congressman Bentsen to discuss federal assistance.[60]

On Tuesday, August 14, 1951, Judge Bravo and the IBWC held a meeting in Falcon, with about twenty property owners representing the towns of Falcon and Lopeño. Attorneys Harbert Davenport and H. P. Guerra represented these concerned citizens and brought up the following issues: the relocation of these two hamlets to separate locations, an adequate water system to support about eleven hundred persons, the need to exchange land from the old town for a similar lot in the new site, and the replacement of the irrigated lands. As to the issue of farm lands in jeopardy, Humberto González asked Jackson about the provision in the Bentsen Bill authorizing the purchase of acreage outside the reservoir locale for use in irrigation. Jackson quickly gave the IBWC's interpretation: "I do not think that anyone of us would be willing to say that there is going to be irrigation there. It was never attempted in the Bentsen Bill that the Government would obtain water."[61]

In order to have water for the proposed farming lands on the fringes of the reservoir area, an irrigation district would have to be established, at a cost to the county of an estimated six million dollars (based on ten thousand acres of land at $644 an acre). The prohibitive cost of such a district discouraged farmers and made them reluctant to relocate from Falcon or Lopeño to Zapata. The whole idea of an irrigation district, or the IBWC negotiating with the farmers, seemed such a remote possibility that discontented landowners continued to complain.

On Thursday, October 18, 1951, Judge Bravo held still another meeting—in Spanish, as was his method—to explain the provisions in the Bentsen Bill allowing for the exchange of irrigated lands. Almost immediately, Bobbitt questioned the legality of condemning lands from one group of owners to give them to another. Farmers expressed their own worries and raised many questions. Numerous negative comments also came from two Republican leaders—González and San Miguel, self-appointed to represent the farmers. At one point during the discussions, González insisted that his group (as small as it was) would continue to fight the IBWC for the preservation of their riparian rights.[62] At times Bobbitt emphatically enlightened González, explaining that the water rights issue was not up to the IBWC to discuss because the federal government could not interfere in state law. In trying to keep the discussion from getting too heated, Bobbitt reminded González to stay focused and avoid making it a partisan matter by criticizing the opposition party with philippic attacks.[63]

In a desperate attempt to get back to the purpose of the meeting, Judge Bravo made González and San Miguel stop getting into personalities and criticizing the county officials' past actions.[64] He continued the deliberations by reminding those present that Falcon Dam was being built regardless of their opinions or disapproval. The group's purpose was to get ideas from everybody, to find the best possible solutions for all the people, and to accept the reality of what the dam would do to their ancestral homes.[65]

Toward the end of the meeting, Judge Bravo asked the farmers to step forward, give their names, provide the number of acres they had under irrigation, and to vote either "yes" or "no" on whether they wanted the IBWC to obtain new property in exchange for land that would soon be inundated. A total of twenty-seven voted in the affirmative, two were undecided, and three voted against the plan.[66] To comply with the farmers' wishes, the IBWC agreed to carry out the provisions in the Bentsen Bill authorizing the replacement of irrigated lands with lands outside the reservoir area. The tally sheet indicated that Humberto González was not one of the affected landowners and consequently did not vote. Needless to say, San Miguel voted "no," along with Juan de Dios Gutiérrez

and H. Cuéllar. Concepción Salinas and Zaragoza Martínez voted undecided.[67]

FALCON DAM'S ELECTRIC BILL

Unknown to Judge Bravo and the political machine in Zapata County,
in March, 1951, a bill was being prepared in Austin by the law firm of
Looney, Clark, and Moorehead. This piece of legislation, which dealt
with the distribution of hydroelectric power generated by Falcon Dam,
would soon affect the residents of Zapata and other South Texas counties. Everett Looney, a strong supporter of Senator Johnson and his legal
counsel during Judge Davidson's investigation into the 1948 Senate election, was a moving force behind the bill, and he wanted Johnson's political influence to help Lon C. Hill, president of Central Power and Light
Company, purchase this electric energy. Looney cajoled Johnson by reminding him of his services during the federal investigation: "I am . . . as
much interested in . . . the [electric] power as you were in the project
which prompted you to get me out of bed in the latter part of 1948 to
go to Fort Worth when certain folks were engaged in a conspiracy to try
to deny you the right to sit in the Senate. I hope you will as cheerfully
help me on this as I helped you on your project."[68]

A week later, on March 16, Johnson replied to Looney, reaffirming
his previous commitment to support the Rural Electrification Administration (REA) cooperatives instead of private power companies, an assurance that favored and benefitted Zapata County. Since his early years in
Congress, Johnson had found the REA (a New Deal program) a good
way for promoting rural electrification projects and had worked diligently to bring electricity to rural areas in Central Texas. He was a firm
believer in rural cooperatives that offered electrical power (as in the case
of Falcon Dam) for rates lower than those of the private utility companies: "I always want to do that, but if it is a question of private company
or the REA distributing this Government power, I would be less than
frank if I did not repeat again that I have told the several cooperatives I
would favor their distributing it."[69]

COMMUNITY INPUT ON RELOCATION

Judge Bravo scheduled back-to-back open meetings at the Zapata
County Courthouse on October 17 and 18, 1951. The purpose of these
convocations was to discuss the removal of cemeteries, and the substitu-

tion of new land for those condemned by the IBWC. In keeping with his bilingual format for conducting public assemblies, the judge spoke in Spanish. He explained the need for having community input as to the relocation of public facilities (courthouse, fire station garage, and public schools), some twenty-one cemeteries, and the public utilities, as the townsite plan called for the relocation of Zapata and the surrounding hamlets into one modern town, with convenient facilities and utilities.[70] "The way that plat was made is on a basis of 100 percent substitution of Zapata and the other towns," IBWC attorney Jackson explained. Bobbitt added: "certain sections of the town will be turned over to the other small communities to be flooded; for instance, we will have the Falcon section, the Lopeño section, and so forth."[71] Not knowing the estimated number of residents from Zapata, Lopeño, and Falcon who would be relocated made it difficult for Judge Bravo to plan the boundaries of three voting precincts and for the IBWC to estimate the cost of building the new town.

The judge then moved to the question of utilizing a numerical system to identify each lot and respective block, and employing a nomenclature method to avoid confusion during the transferring of property.[72] He also brought up people's concerns about the recent policy regarding cemeteries, which made allowance for the relocation of graves, plus additional plots. Zapata County did not own any of the old burial places but wanted to provide for the upkeep of the new ones. Toward the latter part of the meeting, the county officials asked Judge Bravo to negotiate with attorney Jackson on the practicality of having the county acquire the title for the new campo santo.[73] More important, the IBWC adopted Bravo's recommendation for identifying tracts of real estate (to include homes and public buildings) and even approved his suggestion of photographing each lot from at least two angles.

During the month of November, 1951, Commissioner Lawson solicited the judge's support once again in disseminating a one-page (legal size) questionnaire consisting of six "yes" or "no" general questions. The IBWC would then use the responses as a guide to planning the new townsite, facilities, cemetery, and public utilities. An attached four-page document explained that the IBWC would: (1) pay the owner the fair market value of a lot and dwelling if the owner did not want to relocate, (2) exchange an old lot for another in the new town, (3) reimburse costs involved in relocating a house (if deemed reasonable) in addition to building a new foundation, or (4) remunerate the owner the fair market value for a house, if the owner did not want the house relocated but still wanted to exchange lots.[74]

Landowners had until December 15 to consider the different options. They could consult in the meantime with three previously approved community volunteers and review the new townsite map or, if they needed additional copies of the questionnaire, could go to the courthouse. Judge Bravo and the county commissioners, along with IBWC officials, provided additional assistance by working longer hours. Committed to completing the dam in the spring of 1954, the IBWC had over two years left for coordinating and finishing the relocation process. According to Patsy Jeanne Byfield in her monograph, *Falcon Dam and the Lost Towns of Zapata,* resistance was still coming from the residents of Lopeño and Falcon, who opposed relocating to the county seat because of a deep historical attachment to their respective communities.[75] There was also opposition from the Partido Nuevo, whose members encouraged many people not to answer the questionnaire. According to IBWC officials, this refusal again slowed down the planning process.[76]

Beginning in January, 1952, the negotiations between the residents and the IBWC proceeded at a steady pace. After six months, almost 90 percent had already exchanged lots. At a county commissioners' meeting on June 25, 1952, Commissioner Lizandro Ramírez made a last-minute pitch to have his constituents from the Falcon community permitted to relocate to the new county seat (as previously agreed during the preliminary discussions of the new townsite). However, it was already too late for such a recommendation because the IBWC officials had developed the new town plat based on the results of the questionnaire.[77]

Toward the end of the meeting, Bobbitt requested the approval of a formal order that would officially obligate the IBWC to proceed with the construction of public buildings, utilities, and streets and with the relocation of the cemeteries. Bravo served as translator during the presentation, clarifying and explaining in Spanish Bobbitt's statements, and after a lengthy discussion on the specifications, the county commissioners unanimously voted their approval.[78]

Even though the Bentsen Bill provided for one townsite, residents from Lopeño, Falcon, and Ramireño eventually relocated as separate communities along the relocated Highway 83. In his anthropological study, Bailey found it interesting to note that there was animosity even among the people from Lopeño. The two political factions could not agree on one townsite, so the residents created two separate communities (along party lines) about a mile apart.[79] One housed the post office and the other the school building.

With just over a year left for the inauguration of Falcon Dam, Judge Bravo called a series of meetings with IBWC officials and representatives from the Texas Education Agency (TEA) to discuss the future of the educational system in Zapata County. His concern was replacing old school facilities with modern buildings. To that end, the judge, the school board of trustees, Bobbitt, and Mrs. Jewel Walker—principal of Zapata schools—held an important meeting in Laredo with TEA officials Dr. Joe R. Humphreys and Joe R. Brown. Bravo informed the TEA that he wished to hire an architect and have specifications drawn for new school buildings (all subject to approval by the IBWC).[80]

Since he had taken over as superintendent of schools in 1937, Bravo told the Laredo newspaper in an exclusive interview, the Zapata County School District had experienced remarkable progress.[81] But he now had plans to build an elementary school at San Ygnacio and another one at Zapata, he informed the reporter. The latter facility would accommodate about twelve hundred students. Currently, the district was accredited up to the tenth grade, but the judge hoped to expand the accreditation status to the twelfth grade, pending the hiring of more certified teachers. Unfortunately, his goals for improving the school system were stopped short when the relocation process took a turn for the worse.

IMPACT OF GOP 1952 VICTORY

General Eisenhower's victory during the November general election gave the Zapata County Republican Party an edge in their negotiations with the IBWC. Wasting no time, they flexed their political muscle over the issues that confronted the county's landowners. On January 4, 1953, Jack Porter, GOP national committee chairperson from Texas and Johnson's opponent in 1948, visited Zapata at the request of the local Republican leaders. In him, the local party found the conduit necessary for relaying information to the president on relocation issues. At a local ranch the GOP leaders treated Porter to the unique taste of good old South Texas barbecue cooked over mesquite wood.[82]

A short time after his departure from Zapata County, a brawl took place at the ranch between members of the two political parties. Four participants (all of them Bravo opponents) landed in jail, charged with inciting a riot. The exact cause of the fight remained unknown, but now the four defendants faced the county judge's wrath at a trial scheduled for February. The incident had been brief, but it added fuel to the rift between the two parties. Moreover, it had disrupted work with IBWC officials. Porter now demanded that Attorney General Herbert Brownell stop the construction of the new county seat and he publicly criticized Truman's administration for handling the relocation matters inadequately. He called the whole IBWC program a "dirty mess," but Judge Bravo responded, "Mr. Porter is a good man and we know he wants to help the people of the county, but evidently he is not acquainted with all of the details of the program." [83]

The imbroglio between the Partido Viejo and the Partido Nuevo stoked further petty charges, allegations, and counteraccusations regarding relocation matters. A San Antonio newspaper reporter described the rivalry as perhaps unequaled in South Texas politics. It involved the "ins" led by Judge Bravo (Bravoites), who with Bobbitt were trying to work with IBWC officials, and the "outs" led by San Miguel, González, and Sánchez, who had commissioned the legal services of G. C. Mann and H. P. Guerra. The "outs," the journalist observed, had publicly objected "to the size and location of the New Zapata and predicted the majority of Zapata townfolk will refuse to move there." [84]

While the anti-Bravoites definitely opposed the location of the new townsite, the reporter was incorrect on some points—namely, both groups opposed the IBWC policy of appraising a house at fair market value minus 20 percent for depreciation and another 20 percent for obsolescence. They wanted the IBWC to use the more equitable appraisal formula of replacement value. For instance, a homeowner might receive a fair market value of $8,900, but in reality the appraised value, according to a Laredo contractor, was closer to $10,762. The IBWC offered the Catholic Church $12,500, and a second appraiser estimated a replacement cost of $21,000. Marcelino Peña's house, built in 1900 at a cost of about $3,500, now was valued at $1,200. In contrast, the courthouse cost about $20,000 in 1900, but its replacement value had jumped to $150,000. [85] Incongruent replacement values for public buildings as opposed to fair market values for homes rested with the IBWC appraisal policy, which clearly needed to be reassessed and revised. Area newspapers, as far away as San Antonio, Corpus Christi, and Houston, quickly came to the support of the homeowners in their plight.[86]

Then, on February 16, 1953, progress on the new town received yet another unexpected political attack from the anti-Bravoites when Porter publicly opposed the construction of the new town and the condemnation of some forty-five thousand acres lying close to the reservoir. The occasion was a second visit to Zapata by top national and state GOP leaders accompanying Porter and members of the Zapata County Land Owners Association, led by Republican County Chairperson John Rathmell. In a ranting fashion, Porter said that the new townsite was a waste because it was four or five times too big. Moreover, he again expressed consternation with the IBWC's condemnation policy and the relocation process.[87] Neither Porter or the Republican Party offered any suggestion on doing things differently.

Somber jokes about the Partido Viejo and its alleged collusion with the IBWC were by now being hurled throughout the state. The Laredo newspaper, on April 26, 1953, carried the following sarcastic story: "The stupidest and most arrogant creature in the world is a jackass that cannot bray." A person unfamiliar with this kind of animal then asked for an explanation, to be told: "A jackass that cannot bray is a burro-crat . . . Why, a holdover New Deal bureaucrat who thinks that a courthouse is more valuable than a church and more important than a home." Another gloomy observation went like this: "The dead and the politicians are being given plenty of room in New Zapata, . . . but the plain, living citizens are going to have to squeeze into more cramped quarters." [88]

IRRIGATION PROJECT

In January, 1953, Bobbitt arranged for a meeting with Nebraska Congressman A. L. Miller, who chaired the powerful House Interior and Insular Affairs Committee, Lloyd Bentsen, Jr., Judge Bravo, and some Zapata County officials to discuss the exchange of irrigated lands as provided for in the Bentsen Bill. As a result of that meeting, Commissioner Lawson appointed an ad hoc Zapata County investigating committee for the purpose; it consisted of three IBWC staff members, Ward, Hamilton, and Jackson. Judge Bravo nominated Serapio Vela, Salvador García, Juan M. Vela, Juan G. Benavides, Eddie Bravo, and J. M. Salinas to represent the county on the committee.[89]

Under specific instructions from Lawson, the investigating committee was to review possible lands on the outer rim of the reservoir that might be traded for inundated irrigated lands along the Río Grande. Moreover, it was to interview current owners to see if they would agree to enter into a contract with the IBWC. Once the farmers conceded to exchanging their lands, the United States would obtain an equal amount of acreage outside the reservoir under condemnation proceedings and enter into a written five-page agreement.[90] The IBWC compact, however, contained two provisos that absolved the federal agency of its obligation to the farmers. First, Congress had not appropriated the necessary funds for the project; and second, the federal court had not condemned the exchanged lands.[91] According to Senator Johnson's Senate files, the investigating committee on January 28, 1953, concluded that any irrigated lands needed to receive the state's approval for riparian rights, since the federal government had no authority in this matter.[92] To make matters worse, the ambiguity and confusing condition of some land titles meant that all the owners of a given piece of property needed to sign the contract before exchanging the land.

While land transfers and compensation moved through the negotiation phase, the construction of utilities, streets, and public facilities at new Zapata progressed very slowly. The IBWC periodically provided Judge Bravo with engineering reports of progress, and it estimated that between 60 and 70 percent of the sewer and water lines would be completed by August 1953.[93] Feeling more secure about the status of the developing townsite, the people living in old Zapata, Uribeño, Ramireño, Soledad, Sabinito, and other ranches started making plans to relocate.

APPRAISAL POLICY CONTROVERSY

As the construction of Falcon Dam proceeded apace, the controversy over the IBWC's appraisal policy did not abate. Indeed, the stream of grim jokes continued all over the state: they revolved around archaic laws, the replacement value method to appraise public buildings, and the fair market value system used for assessing homes. Meanwhile, the people of Zapata felt that they were being left out of the decision making on the construction of the dam and that they had no choice but to be uprooted from their ancestral homes.

County officials continued to rely on Judge Bravo's dogged pursuit of Senator Johnson, whose immediate attention to the inequities within the appraisal system and to other relocation concerns was needed. The senator responded by asking Lawson to act expeditiously to solve the many woes confronting the Zapatans. On May 15, 1953, Johnson advised Judge Bravo by telegram that Lawson had clarified the legality of several pending matters at a meeting held in his office with Bobbitt, Bentsen, and the IBWC staff.[94] He informed Bravo that the IBWC had reduced the amount of condemned land by thirty-four thousand acres; that farmers who owned condemned real estate could still farm (for a reasonable rental fee) closer to the reservoir's level; that home appraisal values needed to be reviewed and possibly corrected; and finally, that Lawson ruled that without congressional authorization, the IBWC did not have legal authority to exchange potential irrigated lands outside the reservoir for inundated lands.[95]

Two days later, news about the IBWC's policy revisions hit the area news media, and the Laredo newspaper promptly interviewed Judge Bravo, who stated that changes "were definite steps in the right direction." On the matter of the replacement of irrigated lands, he added, "If you take our people's livelihood away then the other benefits we have been fighting for are small use. . . . There is only one fair basis and that is replacement value. . . . It should be square foot for square foot for homes, and acre for acre of equally good land for farms. . . . For our people must have the chance to earn a living on new farms replacing the ones they are losing. . . . That is the only way to give justice." [96]

Bravo continued the interview in his typical modest manner by claiming no special credit for himself but praising the continuous efforts of both Bentsen and Johnson as well as the local Republican Party for its support in a unified effort to fight for just compensation. In his opinion, "no concessions have been made which haven't been fought for and, judging from the official attitude of the past, it will require a continuing battle [if] the spirit and the law of the constitution are to be lived up to." [97]

For their part, the Zapata County Land Owners Association along with GOP national leader Porter claimed victory in the concessions offered by Lawson. Both praised each other's efforts in getting the IBWC to make policy changes, and Porter used the opportunity to make gibing remarks at the previous White House Administration and the Partido Viejo leaders: "[Zapata GOP leaders] not only had to fight the Truman State Department but also their local county officials who have hallucinations of grandeur about developing a great resort area around this lake." [98] Realizing that concessions by the IBWC were only token in nature, all citizens, including the local priest, braced themselves for more difficult issues yet to be resolved. They felt that with enough perseverance, just compensation for their lands and homes would eventually become a reality.

OBJECTIONS OF THE CHURCH AND AMERICAN LEGION

On June 2, 1953, Father Eduardo Bastien, OMI, pastor of Our Lady of Lourdes Catholic Church in Zapata and an outspoken critic of the IBWC, decided to take his bombastic verbal attacks to the Laredo newspaper. For years, Father Bastien had sent letters to every politician and bureaucrat who was directly associated with the relocation of Zapata. Writing under the pseudonym "I. Poz" (Irate People of Zapata), he penned ten articles for the *Laredo Times,* each stamped with his own brand of witty and caustic sarcasm.[99] Utilizing a vast repertoire of creative writing allusions, Father Bastien's articles achieved his intent of exposing the arrogant behavior of the federal bureaucracy. The initial attacks targeted the unfair market values that Zapata residents were forced to accept, including for his own thirty-year-old Catholic church building. Father Bastien wondered: "Since when . . . have churches become 'obsolete?' A church is forever old and forever new. 'What . . . would you do if you had to appraise the church of St. John outside the walls of the Vatican. The church is over 1,000 years old.' By the methods used to appraise Fr. Bastien's church, the famed church in Rome would owe money." [100]

The priest would at times cross the fine line between attacking government policy and deriding local personalities, as when he ridiculed Sheriff Leopoldo Martínez—a staunch Partido Viejo politico: "Most people don't even stop. You should see them drive through this town. The other day, I was sitting on a porch along the highway with our Sheriff, and we would see streaks of lightening whizzing past our town. Leopoldo, I told him, if you were not as good and kind as you are you could collect enough in fines to give everyone their just compensation. It could take you a little while, but you could do it. He just smiled." [101]

Many of his articles favored the anti-Bravoite group, so that his slanted viewpoint sometimes did not sit well with the ruling political machine. Then, on October 14, 1954, after eight years of caring for the spiritual and temporal needs of his parishioners, Father Bastien received transfer orders to Sacred Heart Chapel in Big Spring, Texas. Eddie Bravo, Sr., recalled that "Father Bastien got too involved with the opposition and used the pulpit to get to the people."[102] Judge Bravo's secretary felt that the prelate's health was slowly deteriorating, as a result of hard work combined with severe allergies. She also remembered that "people would say that he was meddling too much."[103]

Even after his departure, Father Bastien continued getting involved in politics from his new station in Big Spring, despite his ecclesiastical superiors' orders to stop interfering with decisions in Zapata County. On one occasion, he questioned the political machine's judgment on certain legal matters. To this point, Judge Bravo answered:

> With reference to employment of an expensive lawyer, being Hon. R. L. Bobbitt and M. J. Raymond, might say that it is still my judgement that we employed the most influential lawyers. . . . I am sure that neither you nor I would have gotten to first base and much less, with misleading propaganda put out by Humberto and San Miguel, and the untimely interference of Jack Porter during the change of National administration. . . . So many people were misled by Humberto and San Miguel . . . which kept a lot of people from accepting lots in the Town. . . . Of course it now appears that Mr. Humberto [González] also got some very nicely located lots notwithstanding the ill advice he gave to so many people.[104]

In the meantime, Judge Bravo received heat from another front. At their meeting held on July 29, 1953, veterans from Zapata County's American Legion group—headed by two anti-Bravoites, cattleman and rancher Angel Flores and Pedro Ramírez, Jr., a butane gas distributor—blasted the IBWC for giving unjust and unfair appraisal values to homeowners. They criticized the political machine and called for the removal of the IBWC from the appraisal process, stating in the Laredo newspaper that, "the *politicos* and bureaucrats who are rebuilding Zapata . . . are more arrogant and dictatorial than Nero ever dared to be."[105] Specifically, the group detested Congressman Bentsen's lack of support in passing a law that appraised homes by replacement value. Their resolution to use three independent appraisers instead of the IBWC staff received the full endorsement of the legionnaires at the state convention in Houston on August 2, 1953, and again a month later at the national convention in St. Louis.[106] For additional support the Zapata legionnaires sent President Eisenhower a telegram, outlining the same protests and soliciting his intervention with the IBWC.

NATURAL DISASTER HELPS IBWC'S RELOCATION CAUSE

Two months before the scheduled dedication ceremony for Falcon Dam, unforeseen heavy thunderstorms fell on South Texas and northeastern Mexico. These rains in August, 1953, unexpectedly caused the newly finished reservoir to rise very rapidly and in the process totally inundated the villages of Lopeño and Falcon and the ranching communities of Santo Niño, Libertad, and Sabinito—the ones closest to the dam. Emergency evacuation plans forced the residents to flee, many of them leaving behind their personal possessions, furniture, livestock, and, of course, their homes.[107]

Judge Bravo responded to the catastrophe by calling on his county staff to salvage as many of the residents' belongings as possible. With the new town of Zapata only partially completed, Judge Bravo turned for assistance to the Laredo Air Force Base and the American Red Cross. He secured about 115 squad tents, which provided temporary shelter and a safe refuge for about seventy-two families. He also persuaded the IBWC to use its trucks to move stranded families and their possessions.[108]

In Old Zapata, Judge Bravo made available the school auditorium and other public buildings for shelter and storage space. He also was instrumental in providing space for the Red Cross Disaster Relief Office to establish headquarters in the courthouse. Paquita Peña, Viola Martínez, Armando Gutiérrez, and Eugenia Bustamante were especially helpful in running the operation. IBWC Resident Engineer Lloyd Hamilton observed that "about 5:30 P.M. that same evening [September 3, 1953] I returned to Zapata and found the people in a near state of panic—Judge Bravo was standing on the Courthouse steps attempting to organize the movement from Zapata and about 75 to 100 men were gathered about conversing loudly in Spanish." Hamilton assured the judge that "Zapata was still not in any real immediate danger of flooding and then attempted to explain why, but too, [sic] many people were continuing to yell at the judge."[109] The reservoir was able to contain the rising water, which fortunately never seriously threatened to flood the county seat.

By the first weeks of September, some forty-five residents from Old Zapata had wisely moved their frame homes to New Zapata. In the workers' haste to evacuate as many structures as possible in a minimum of time, they severely damaged most of the buildings. By December about 96 percent of the Zapata residents had made their transition to the new townsite; however, the IBWC had to haul water from Old Zapata because the new water plant was not yet operational.[110] Completion of the public utilities and telephone lines and the ongoing construction of the courthouse and elementary school provided much needed encouragement for the recently arrived inhabitants, however.

The unexpected inundation of the several small communities, coupled with the need to get the school facilities ready for the beginning of another year, prompted Judge Bravo to send urgent telegrams to Johnson, Lawson, Bentsen, and Texas Education Agency Commissioner J. W. Edgar. He described the situation as "an extreme emergency" because the new elementary school was still not finished and the old school buildings were "not sufficient or adequate" to meet an increased enrollment.[111] Even if the old buildings could be moved, the establishment of temporary facilities was the only solution.

Via a packet containing newspaper clippings about New Guerrero and the flooding of Lopeño and Falcon, Bravo informed President Eisenhower about the way the Mexican government had completed the relocation of its citizens in a timely manner with modern homes and public facilities, while the American agency, in comparison, had not yet completed the relocation project in Zapata. Furthermore, the Mexican government had taken a more humane approach toward the social, cultural, and economic needs of its citizens. A committee composed of the townspeople (Comité de Orientación y Defensa Pro-Guerrero) had acted as the authorized agent to deal with the Mexican section of the IBWC (Secretaría de Recursos Hidráulicos) and to express citizens' concerns to that body.[112]

On September 23, 1953, Sherman Adams, assistant to the president, responded to the judge's plea: "[The president] asked me to tell you that the matter about which you write is being brought to the attention of the appropriate officials of the Government."[113] A couple of weeks later, on October 7, Senator Johnson informed Bravo that Lawson had agreed to relocate the existing school buildings to New Zapata, effective immediately, so that the students would be able to attend the required nine months of instruction as prescribed by state statutes.[114] As in the case of private houses, some of the two-story school buildings were so badly damaged during the move that it was nearly impossible to prepare them in time for classes in September.

October, 1953: Dam Inauguration Coincides with Compensation Hearings

Two paramount events took place during the middle of October, 1953—the Zapata hearings held on the twelfth and the inauguration of Falcon Dam on the nineteenth. The former resulted from political pressure brought about by the American Legion on behalf of the Zapata veterans, and it led to the establishment of a special three-member commission. Federal Judge James V. Allred appointed John W. Ward and Amando Villarreal of Laredo to serve on the commission, and James C. Abbott from San Benito to chair the panel.

The commission scheduled a series of hearings in Laredo with unhappy property owners to hear complaints that the IBWC had not given them just compensation for their lands and homes. Plans were to complete all commission hearings on personal property before the first of January, 1954, and on all the farm land cases shortly thereafter. And, indeed, during the first three days, the appointed panel settled seventeen cases out of court, including those of Adán Gutiérrez, "who sought higher valuation on his residences and business property"; Pedro Garza, "who claims he should be reimbursed more for his tavern"; Judge Bravo, who was "asking higher compensation on his residence and garage"; Father Bastien, who "appeared . . . with some inquiries and he was heard"; and Mrs. Fortunata Santos de Rosas, a Zapata property owner, who "went before the commission to discuss her title problems."[115]

Lauding it as the first international dam ever built in the United States, area newspapers carried front-page stories during mid-October, 1953, in preparation for the dedication of Falcon Dam by the two heads of state, President Dwight D. Eisenhower and President Adolfo Ruiz Cortines.[116] Notwithstanding the historic and economic significance of the event, the farmers of the Lower Río Grande Valley regarded the dam as their own special economic project. On the day of the inauguration, a San Antonio newspaper headline read, "Dam Bringing Valley Money." [117]

Meanwhile, in Zapata County, the refugees from Lopeño and Falcon were still living in tents. Their harsh reality was reflected not in cheers or applause but in somber signs that greeted President Eisenhower: "We lost our homes to the Falcon Dam. We want to see Justice done," and "Refugees from Falcon Dam." [118]

CHAOS AND NEGLECT

Judge Bravo played a crucial role in resolving the relocation problems that Zapata County residents faced due to the building of Falcon Dam. His proactive stance as the head of the Zapata County political machine enabled him to work collaboratively with Bobbitt, the IBWC, and even the Partido Nuevo. Working together for the most part, they were committed to promoting the county's best interests. In the meantime, Judge Bravo dispatched a spate of letters to public officials in Washington to obtain assistance. But several factors, some of them beyond the control of the judge, of the IBWC, or even of Congress, caused unforeseen bureaucratic confusion and chaos at the local level.

For years in other parts of the United States, the federal government had constructed dams, relocating people and acquiring the necessary lands through the Justice Department. However, the unique situation in Zapata County challenged the government's long-standing condemnation policies. Other entities in the United States, such as the Tennessee Valley Authority, had been friendlier and more sensitive and cooperative in handling land acquisition, using an appraisal policy that "took into consideration actual costs or losses sustained by the owners in the process of getting re-established." [119] Zapata landowners would have received better treatment all around if a TVA-like agency had handled their relocation. The IBWC's interpretation of "just compensation," as applied to Zapata County, meant a fair market appraisal based on a unprecedented assumption of real estate value. It did not take into account the cultural or architectural—let alone the aesthetic—values that these historic buildings represented. To be sure, some of these edifices were more than a century old.

The Bentsen Bill was the only practical solution, and had Congress approved it, the IBWC would have had the legal authority to interpret and implement all of the bill's provisions from the very beginning. Instead, the government's bureaucratic agency was obligated to implement the American-Mexican Treaty Act of 1950, which did not contain the specific provisions of the Bentsen Bill. As if the IBWC's insensitivity were not enough, federal red tape created ill feeling and severe psychological stress on the people. Disruption and disorganization produced havoc in Zapatans' economic lives. Religious stress resulted from efforts to disturb the sacred graves of families' ancestors. A spirit of homelessness haunted many. A total of about six hundred families were forced to leave and/or move their homes. Twelve thousand acres of the county's best fertile cropland along the Río Grande was totally flooded. Farmers were left to fend for themselves in finding new land and irrigation. More than one hundred recorded historic and prehistoric archaeological sites were destroyed.

The IBWC and the Army Corps of Engineers demonstrated a total lack of understanding. None of their members was trained or had any education in dealing fairly, equitably, and knowledgeably with the Hispanic sociohistorical experience of Zapata County. And the adjudication of unsettled claims did not happen until the mid-1960s, and is discussed in the next chapter.

For that matter, these same federal agencies (Bureau of Reclamation and the Corps of Engineers) treated Native Americans in a similar fashion, if not worse. Around the same time that Falcon Dam was being built, Congress approved the construction of several dams inside Sioux reservations in North and South Dakota. Just as they mistreated the Zapata landowners, these bureaucrats "caused more damage to Indian land than any other public works project in America. . . . Approximately 580 families were uprooted and forced to move from rich, sheltered bottomlands to empty prairies. . . . The federal government and the United States Corps of Engineers, in particular, has demonstrated an appalling lack of sensitivity." [120]

The IBWC's obligation was only to replace residents' homes, public facilities, utilities, and streets equivalent to what had existed in the old town. But citizens felt that since they were being forced to move, it was the federal government's responsibility to provide them with a new town that featured modern conveniences. Not only that, but the IBWC and the Corps of Engineers offered no plan to coordinate or implement an effective relocation program. The IBWC claimed that it was the homeowners' responsibility to move on their own. Such irresponsibility further turned people's feelings against the IBWC.

Both the IBWC and Department of Justice insisted on applying the strict interpretation of the willing buyer–willing seller concept—this to a community that for generations did not deal in "fair market value." In preparing the condemnation suits, county residents were asked to give up their homes before even agreeing to a price or to settlement for equitable compensation. Additionally, the lack of experience and expertise among the federal agencies caused many errors in the assessment procedures. Zapata County was never reimbursed for any loss of property tax revenues.

Consequently, the responsibility for most of the county's hardships must rest with the IBWC and its inability to provide a just and humane administrative policy. The lessons learned from the construction of Falcon Dam and the relocation process are numerous and unpleasant, but for the IBWC, they appeared to have been few, insignificant, and inconsequential.

While Falcon Dam was designed to generate hydroelectric power as well as serving other conservation and flood-control functions, the people of Zapata County were the last ones to gain from this venture. A simple question to area bureaucrats in Zapata and Laredo today as to how much electric power the county receives produces mixed and dumbfounded responses. As of this writing, the specific answer remains unknown: it is hidden in a grid system (where the hydroelectric power is combined with coal, gas, and nuclear power) that serves a large portion of South Texas outside Zapata County. The hydroelectric power generated by Falcon Dam has by no means been a major contributing factor in the county's use of electricity.

BROKEN PROMISES: THE IBWC AND BUREAUCRATIC RED TAPE

M anuel Bravo, the resolute political leader of Zapata County, continued to be a driving force in the saga of the unresolved relocation issues following inauguration of Falcon Dam in 1953. During the rest of his years as county judge, he unceasingly fought the IBWC and other federal bureaucracies in an effort to achieve closure in numerous pending matters, among them new parks and recreational areas, public utilities, furniture for public buildings, a desperately needed fire station garage, and a number of other discrepancies related to the completed courthouse and inundated irrigated lands. He also supervised the construction of the elementary school and the planning phase of the high school.

During the summer of 1954, Judge Bravo had to modify his leadership style to deal with a weak interim IBWC staff, a new commissioner (Col. Leland H. Hewitt) who knew nothing about Zapata County's past dealings with the former administrator, and a General Accounting Office (GAO) investigation. It took approximately fifteen years and, ironically, a twist of fate in Judge Bravo's career, before the landowners settled with the IBWC. In November, 1965, the IBWC mailed out the last of the Zapata claims.

Bravo also contended with the Partido Nuevo, whose election campaign against the powerful political machine decried the delays in the relocation settlements. And the judge faced the problem of having to court new political leaders at the national level. In 1955, Judge Bravo's

Table 10. Representatives of the 15th Congressional District

Name	Tenure of Office	Comments
John N. Garner	Nov. 8, 1904 to Dec., 1932	Elected first Representative from the new Congressional district created in 1902.
Milton H. West	April, 1933 to Oct., 1948	Served in Texas Legislature from 1929 to 1933. Re-elected to Congress until his death.
Lloyd M. Bentsen, Jr.	Jan., 1949 to Dec., 1954	Defeated Philip Kazen in 1948. Resigned from public office to pursue business ventures.
Joe M. Kilgore	Jan., 1955 to Dec., 1964	Resigned in 1964, to pursue legal career in Austin.
Eligio "Kika" de la Garza	Jan., 1965 to Dec., 1996	Resigned after thirty-one years of service.
Rubén Hinojosa	Jan., 1996 to present	Elected in 1997

Note: 15th District Counties: Cameron, Dimmit, Frio, Hidalgo, Jm Hogg, La Salle, Maverick, Medina, Starr, Webb, Willacy, Zapata, Zavala.

---

friend in Congress, Lloyd Bentsen, Jr., relinquished his seat in the House of Representatives, and Joe M. Kilgore succeeded him to represent the 15th Congressional District. Over a period of time, the judge was able to develop good relations with Congressman Kilgore, and the two worked jointly on several claims legislation bills that brought relief to the property owners.

INTERIM DELAYS

The retirement of Commissioner Lawson five months after the Falcon Dam inauguration placed a hiatus on negotiations between Judge Bravo and IBWC officials. During the interim, Thurston B. Morton of the State Department and George H. Winters, the IBWC secretary, continued deliberations on unfinished matters with the county attorneys and with Senators Johnson and Price Daniel and Congressman Bentsen. Of utmost importance were unresolved questions pertaining to the recreational and educational life of the new town of Zapata; extension of public utilities to unimproved lots; completion of public facilities and utilities; and compensation values of inundated lands and homes. Judge Bravo's plans to provide a recreational park area along the reservoir were met with an emphatic negative response from the State Department; the only site the State Department allowed for such outings was in the proximity of the new school.[1] Additional efforts by the judge to persuade the IBWC to grant the county the right to utilize the existing condemned lands—lying between the reservoir's 307-foot normal water level and the 314-foot maximum flood height—for recreational and educational purposes were similarily rebuffed. IBWC's revised policy, published in the *Federal Register* (a daily document that contains recently enacted federal rules and regulations) on January 21, 1954, permitted the use of condemned lands in Zapata County only for operating and maintaining Falcon Dam and reservoir.[2]

In March, 1954, Judge Bravo again opened negotiations with the IBWC on the matter of replacing the inundated irrigated lands with tillable acreage located beyond the boundaries of the reservoir. The Bentsen Bill had addressed this particular concern and would have allowed the IBWC commissioner to purchase or acquire the necessary land through condemnation proceedings. However, President Truman felt that under existing federal laws (the Water Treaty of 1944 and the American-Mexican Treaty of 1950), the IBWC had enough authority to exchange new acreage for the inundated farming lands.[3] But the IBWC, now supported by a Republican president, was not sympathetic to the woes of a predominantly Hispanic and Democratic county. Instead of abiding by the spirit of the Bentsen Bill and the compromise reached in El Paso in May, 1951, Secretary Winters, in a seven-page, single-spaced letter to Judge Bravo, explained that neither he nor the Department of State could authorize the IBWC to "purchase or condemn private lands outside the reservoir site to be exchanged in part payment for irrigated lands within the reservoir area"; he concluded by stating that "legislation could not properly be considered without a satisfactory showing of economic feasibility."[4] Moreover, Winters rebutted the intent of the Bentsen Bill, President Truman's views, Public Law 786, and the terms of the Water Treaty of 1944 by noting that "an assumption is wholly unwarranted that the President intended to direct the United States Commissioner to carry out all objectives of a bill which did not become law or, what is more important, that he intended to direct the [commissioner] to undertake anything for which there is no authority in law."[5]

However, it was the general feeling of Zapata County residents that the IBWC was still legally responsible for helping with the inundated irrigation lands and for completing the relocation activities previously agreed upon.[6] Judge Bravo's next step was to hold a meeting of Partido Viejo leaders, nonpartisan community members, IBWC staff, and Zapata's legal counsel. After consulting with the political machine, Judge Bravo and Bobbitt spent May and early June, 1954, arranging and planning a meeting in Washington with Senators Johnson and Daniel, and Congressman Bentsen.[7] But the State Department postponed the scheduled arrangements until after the appointment of a new commissioner. After months of waiting, the county officials were elated when President Eisenhower, on June 17, 1954, named Col. Leland H. Hewitt, an army engineer with experience in dealing with international water disputes, to succeed Lawson as the new IBWC commissioner. Without wasting any time, and exactly a week after Hewitt's appointment, Judge Bravo urged Senator Johnson to communicate with Hewitt and bring him up to date on the relocation process.[8]

Eager to present his case to Hewitt, Judge Bravo prepared a long list of unresolved concerns, which included furniture for the elementary school, construction of a junior-senior school, a fire station, the replacement of irrigated lands, final settlements of the condemned lands above the 314-foot level, and unsettled home claims based on an arbitrary fair market value. On July 22, 1954, Hewitt responded with a five-page, single-spaced letter to Congressman Bentsen. At first, Hewitt admitted that if the Bentsen Bill had passed, all the relocation problems would have been resolved. Next, he applied his own interpretation of the "rigid rules" of eminent domain, explaining that they did not take "into consideration the impact of the project upon the economy of the community nor the consideration of sentimental values which the citizens in the locale of the project rightly attach to their ancestral homes."[9] In reference to the irrigation project, Hewitt felt that the State Department needed to make legal and constitutional regulations with regard to the condemnation of private property for personal use. He would not act on the provision contained in the Bentsen Bill, he advised, until Congress, by special authorization, gave him more definite direction.[10]

PUBLIC SYMPATHY AND SUPPORT

On Wednesday, June 30, 1954, destructive Hurricane Alice's thunderstorms flooded the Río Grande beyond its banks, sweeping the international bridge at Laredo. The following day, the predicted high crest hit Zapata County. Immediate evacuation plans had gone into action the previous Monday for the removal of the remaining residents still living in Zapata, Uribeño, and Ramireño. Within a few hours, the town of old Zapata slowly disappeared from view. The ravaging waters of the Río Grande had submerged it below a big lake. Only the second floor of the courthouse and a few rooftops remained visible. Judge Bravo set up temporary county offices at one of the relocated school buildings, formerly army barracks. But the lack of adequate office space for conducting business and the coming of the scholastic year forced the county commissioners to move into the new courthouse built by the IBWC. They could not officially accept it because the necessary furniture, previously conceded by mutual verbal agreement between Bravo and former IBWC Commissioner Lawson, had not yet been approved in writing.[11]

About two months later, the *Houston Chronicle,* empathizing with the Zapatans' plight, published a series of eight articles and numerous editorials on the recent flooding and relocation problems. Norman Baxter, an inquisitive reporter for the *Chronicle,* visited the county and gained firsthand knowledge of the many problems. He interviewed county officials and residents as well, and his headlines depicted the overall pitiful situation: "Falcon Dam's Refugees Left Holding Bag," "U.S. Failure on Pledges Wrecks Zapata Economy," "Many Falcon Claims Stymied," "U.S. Hedges on Zapata Aid," and "Zapata's Schools Are Old Barracks." [12]

As a result of the articles, there followed an outburst of support, as evidenced by the numerous letters mailed to Senator Johnson. One typical letter, from Helen Graham, a resident of Lake Jackson near Houston, understood the hardships, and pressed Johnson to give a "good speech on the Senate floor . . . These are *Americans* and the fact that their land had to be taken for the general good is no excuse for the treatment they have received." Her postscript said: "Please don't have a secretary send me any 'we will keep it in mind' answer." [13]

Governor Allan Shivers, among many sympathizers, promptly sent President Eisenhower a telegram with an urgent message to reinvestigate and, if possible, readjust the appraised values on the property claims. Senators Johnson and Daniel and Congressman Bentsen also applied pressure upon the president, who finally gave Hewitt specific instructions to review the law and see how things might be rectified.[14] Hewitt wired Judge Bravo asking him to set up a meeting with Bobbitt and all parties concerned, and to schedule it for the middle of September, 1954. In addition, he wanted in advance a bill of particulars on pending matters and unsettled claims that the IBWC had not fulfilled. The people of Zapata saw the meeting as an encouraging sign that the federal agency might change its fair market policy and allow them a replacement value.[15]

BILL OF PARTICULARS

The meeting with Judge Bravo, Leopoldo Martínez, Manuel Medina, Robert Bobbitt, Congressman-elect Joe M. Kilgore, Hewitt, other IBWC members, and Texas Education Agency (TEA) officials took place in San Antonio on September 15, 1954.[16] On behalf of the county, the judge submitted a bill of particulars that included a full and complete chronological listing of relocation activities that had already occurred, including projects awaiting disposition. The three-hour afternoon meeting began with charges and countercharges between Hewitt and Bobbitt, ending with an exchange of verbal jabs. Hewitt claimed that "the county had been slow to provide the IBWC with the information which it had," and Bobbitt replied sharply that "it was the government, not the county, which had been slow to carry out [the] agreement and to provide adequate facilities." He continued, "Four years ago the President of the United States and the Congress set forth a policy for IBWC to follow, and in my opinion, those who were administering the IBWC made up their minds not to follow that policy and not to carry out the wishes of the President. It is time, that the four-year-old mess in Zapata County be cleaned up." [17]

After regaining his composure, Bobbitt, assisted by Judge Bravo, explained in detail all the points contained in their bill of particulars. Hewitt said the requests were too general and insisted on another report with additional specific engineering data as regards the completion of the elementary school, courthouse, water plant, and streets, and with blueprints for a new high school. Before he approved these projects, Hewitt wanted to make sure that they were in accordance with what had originally been understood by the IBWC. The judge expressed dissatisfaction over the extra time, money, and effort it would require to complete such a revised report, suspecting that the additional work was another bureaucratic tactic to delay the settlement process.[18] The increased cost, moreover, placed an unforeseen burden on the Zapata County budget. Hewitt purposely had not invited the original IBWC staff (who knew more about what needed to be done), and had only three staff members in attendance, two of whom were completely new to the negotiations. All this only caused further setbacks for the county.

In order to comply with the commissioner's request, Judge Bravo contracted consulting engineer Frank T. Drought of San Antonio. The revised report drafted by Drought apprised the commissioner of the status of the elementary school, the courthouse and jail, the water plant and sewage system, fire department equipment, and the condition of the streets and roads. Before the county accepted responsibility for the public buildings, however, Bravo wanted to make sure, from an engineering standpoint, that they were completely finished as previously agreed to by the IBWC. Hewitt explained to Senator Johnson that "the United States Section was not prepared to state that it had authority to carry out all of the requests of the residents of Zapata and [the revised report would be reviewed] . . . for decision by higher authority as to exactly what items therein might properly be provided by the [U.S.] Section under existing legislation and what items would have to be covered by special legislation."[19] If any modifications to the existing law needed to be made, Congress would have to enact new legislation.

NEW LEGISLATION NEEDED

At a meeting held on October 5, 1954, Judge Bravo strongly urged Hewitt to reexamine the unsettled private claims and to consider the establishment of an irrigation district to replace the twelve thousand acres of rich farm lands that lay inundated along the Río Grande.[20] Four months later, Senator Daniel and Congressman Kilgore publicly criticized Hewitt for not taking action on these problems. The commissioner, in turn, blamed the Justice Department for its inability to act expeditiously. Daniel retorted, "There was never any doubt as to the legality of the condemnation proceedings, but it was hoped that the agency could, under the law, settle the claims with kindness and a little more equity."[21] Judge

Bravo in the meantime had undertaken an aggressive lobbying effort. In response to Bravo's initiative, Johnson, Daniel, and Kilgore prepared the legislation addressing the areas where the IBWC had no legal authority to comply with the provisions of the Bentsen Bill.

As of the early part of 1955, five years after the relocation process started, many of the projects were only partially completed. The elementary school, albeit finished, had no furniture; the proposed middle-high school was still in the blueprint stages; the courthouse remained unfurnished; exchange of irrigable lands was on the back burner; the old roads that gave landowners access to their property needed repairs; and of course, the question of replacement value of homes was still unresolved. Waiting patiently and feeling frustrated, Judge Bravo, Bobbitt, and the county commissioners attended several meetings in Laredo, Zapata, Austin, and San Antonio with IBWC staff, TEA consultants, and engineer Drought. At their last meeting, held on March 19, the IBWC's proposed specifications for a middle-high school failed to meet TEA's accreditation standards.[22] Consequently, the plans reverted to the drawing board, causing yet another delay.

In a nine-page, single-spaced letter to Kilgore, with courtesy copies to Senators Johnson and Daniel, Judge Bravo outlined the status of the pending projects in terms of which ones needed to be completed via new legislation. Not pulling any punches, the judge placed the blame squarely on the IBWC, accusing it of lack of responsibility in not implementing the policies and arrangements approved earlier by President Truman in the Bentsen Bill. As a result of Hewitt's unresponsiveness to the county's needs, Judge Bravo was reluctant about any future communications with Hewitt; this meant even additional and needless expensive postponements.[23] Unfortunately for the Zapata officials, their high expectations of Hewitt did not materialize and proved fruitless and unproductive. By all indications, the judge had lost all faith and enthusiasm for what Hewitt could deliver. As a follow-up to Bravo's status report, Bobbitt scheduled a meeting in Washington with Johnson, Daniel, and Kilgore for about mid-April.

GAO INVESTIGATION

On March 9, 1955, Hewitt asked the General Accounting Office (GAO) to investigate the legal obligation and responsibility of the IBWC to provide the furniture and equipment for the Zapata County Courthouse, schools, county jail, water treatment plant, and fire department. Pending the outcome of the GAO report, Bobbitt, after consulting with Johnson, Daniel, and Kilgore via letters and telephone calls, recommended to Judge Bravo that the Washington meeting be rescheduled for the week of April 25.[24]

However, Bobbitt moved up the meeting again, awaiting the receipt of engineer Drought's status report on the public facilities and the proposed irrigation district. A reason for the wait was that the United States Office of Education (USOE) in Dallas and TEA had not submitted their recommendations on the educational facilities to Hewitt.[25] Another cause for the delay was that Frank Quinn, chairman of the Texas State Parks Board, had scheduled a meeting in Zapata during the latter part of April, 1955, to discuss the development of a park project for the county.

On May 13, Bobbitt, concerned that the GAO might not have received the complete Zapata County file on the pending projects, advised Kilgore to make sure that Commissioner Hewitt provided the auditing agency with the chronology of the relocation activities, along with the background information on the IBWC's responsibility for furnishing the public facilities.[26] Furthermore, Bobbitt reminded Kilgore that he should check to see if Hewitt had already forwarded the county's report to the GAO attorney; but a week later the GAO had not yet received the data. As late as June 1, Kilgore was still desperately trying to locate the records, but all his efforts proved unsuccessful: "For hours . . . I have sought the report . . . but I have been unable to locate any trace of it up here in Washington."[27]

By the time Kilgore requested another copy of the file, the GAO had already concluded its study. However, he let the USOE know that the missing materials would have been advantageous to the Zapata situation.[28] Notwithstanding the missing file, Joseph Campbell, comptroller general of the United States, submitted a five-page, single-spaced response to Hewitt on June 9, 1955. He cited six court cases and several statutory federal regulations indicating that the U.S. government was required to pay only for real property taken by condemnation proceedings; the law was silent on replacing movable personal property. Campbell followed a strict interpretation of the condemnation laws and ruled that the directions found in President Truman's letter (May 16, 1951) and the provisions contained in the Bentsen Bill could not "be construed as an agreement on the part of the United States, [on] the furniture and equipment. . . . It must be held that the appropriations available for the construction of the Falcon Dam may not be used for expenditures of such nature." [29]

Actually Campbell's report had been influenced by Hewitt's own interpretation of what he considered to be the difference between real and personal property. On the latter issue, Hewitt's definition of personal property extended to movable objects, such as school furniture, equipment, books, and playground equipment. Therefore, Hewitt carefully phrased his questions so that Campbell's ruling answered only real and not personal property. Needless to say, the report clearly stated that under no circumstances would the IBWC replace anything but real property (facilities and nonmovable structures). [30]

Judge Bravo received his copy of the document on June 14, with a cover letter from Hewitt nonchalantly stating, "Now that these questions have been answered, I hope, as I know you do, that the remaining matters relating to this Section's responsibilities in connection with New Zapata can soon be disposed of." [31] Hewitt had also sent copies, for their perusal, to Johnson, Daniel, Kilgore, and Bobbitt. Unfortunately for the people of Zapata County, Hewitt's strict interpretation of the condemnation proceedings was contrary to what the Zapata County officials had agreed upon four years earlier in El Paso. To Judge Bravo the replacement of public facilities with new furniture and equipment would make these buildings serviceable, at an estimated cost of about $30,000. [32] Judge Bravo clearly understood now that under existing laws, there were no written, specific contracts with the IBWC that obligated it to replace the furniture and equipment or that allowed federal funds to be used to pay for these items.

Kilgore, Bobbitt, and Johnson blamed Hewitt for taking it upon himself to determine what course of action was needed for Zapata County. Instead of following the policies already established by his predecessor, Hewitt had made matters worse and "the results had been terrific injuries, losses, damages and inconveniences to the destroyed communities, public facilities and people of Zapata County." [33]

In a letter to Kilgore, with copies to Johnson, Daniel, and Bravo, Bobbitt expressed his own disappointment over the GAO ruling. The comptroller general and the IBWC, he wrote, had never requested information from the judge or from Zapata's legal counsel, nor were Zapata officials given an opportunity to present their case. Without this pertinent information, the GAO had made a decision based on Hewitt's incomplete facts.[34] Now that the IBWC's legal position on the furniture and equipment for the county's public facilities was clear, Bobbitt planned a meeting in Washington with Bravo, Johnson, Daniel, and Kilgore. Their focus was on the legislation needed to furnish the facilities and on other matters still pending.

PRELUDE TO PROPOSED LEGISLATION

Before making additional plans, Bobbitt requested a detailed report from Hewitt on exactly what projects the IBWC planned to finish and their estimated dates of completion. In the middle of the planning stages and just two days before the fourth of July holidays (1955), Johnson suffered a serious heart attack.[35] His able and competent assistant, Arthur C. Perry, fulfilled the senator's business commitments with Judge Bravo, and he followed through on the volumious correspondence associated with the Zapata County dilemma. A scheduled meeting in Washington was postponed and tentatively set for August or September, depending on Johnson's recovery.

As anticipated, the judge received Hewitt's status report on July 12. It indicated the completion of the elementary school, courthouse, raw water intake plant, water treatment facility, water distribution system, sewage collection and treatment center, and all streets and roads.[36] After reviewing the report, Judge Bravo took exception to the approach that the IBWC staff had pursued in determining the status of certain public facilities. To begin with, the judge and legal counsel had not been invited to determine to what degree the facilities should have been completed. Second, the county engineer had not been consulted on improvements done to some buildings. Bravo had hoped that through a collaborative effort among all the parties involved, they would have arrived at a consensus acceptable to all.[37] It is evident that Hewitt never got together with them because the public facilities in his report were not all completed, as previously agreed, and they had not all been approved by Judge Bravo.

Still in the planning stages were the middle-high school, the fire station garage, and the bandstand. The judge reviewed what else needed completion so that Kilgore and the two senators could address these matters in future legislation. Perry kept Johnson, who was still in the hospital, abreast of the developments in Zapata County and on a proposed meeting in Washington.[38]

At this point, Judge Bravo and the county's legal counsel met to discuss strategies for a meeting scheduled before the next legislative session. Their top priority was initiating the necessary legislation to complete the relocation project. Moreover, the judge recommended pursuing a different plan: to wit, have another federal agency complete the tasks left unfinished by the IBWC! It seemed nothing would be gained by continuing their negotiations with Hewitt.[39] In preparation for the meeting, Judge Bravo readied a general list of what the IBWC proposed to accomplish within its legal authority and what else remained to be completed either by Congress or by another federal agency.

Because of depletion of county funds brought on by numerous out-of-town conferences over the past five years, Bravo decided a day before the meeting "not to make the trip with Judge Bobbitt to Washington, as we cannot afford to continue spending County money which is not available. Therefore we will appreciate very much that you and our Senators will try and arrive at a program that will end the continuous expense of Zapata County, and get those things promised us completed."[40]

On July 26, 1955, Bobbitt met in Washington, D.C., with Perry, Daniel, and Kilgore. As a result of the all-day conference, immediate positive moves were agreed upon by all in attendance. The group obtained Judge Bravo's approval via telephone conversations to proceed with a proposed plan that contained a series of steps.[41] First, the IBWC would be permitted to finish the projects it had already started and had legal authority to complete. Second, the judge would accept all the completed facilities, and any projects still pending (including furniture, etc.) would be dealt with in future legislation. Third, the federal government would determine what still needed to be done from the original official policy of relocation (the irrigation district, etc.), for the IBWC lacked legal authority to continue functioning. Fourth, Kilgore, just prior to the second session of the 84th Congress, would introduce a bill in the House and Senators Johnson and Daniel were to do the same in the Senate. The bill would call for completing the facilities and services originally approved by the IBWC as part of its relocation policy.[42]

ZAPATA CLAIMS LEGISLATION

Three days later, Bobbitt sent Senator Johnson a letter expressing optimism about the results of the meeting. Both agreed that once the process started in subcommittees, it would be a matter of time before the displaced people of Zapata County would receive their just compensation.[43]

During the summer of 1956, Johnson, Daniel, and Kilgore pressed ahead, drafting the language of the proposed Zapata claims legislation. From the beginning, Kilgore consulted with Judge Bravo, Bobbitt, Perry, and Jake Jacobson, administrative assistant to Daniel.[44] By early January, 1957, Kilgore and the judge had exchanged notes on the wording of the proposed bill. Judge Bravo offered suggestions and advice on the different updated versions and Kilgore always sent him the latest revisions for his careful and critical observations. On several occasions, Kilgore expressed his appreciation and thanks to Bravo "for all the thoughtful help and generous assistance you have provided on this project. Without it I would not have been able to get even this far with the bill."[45]

The Zapata claims draft bill, after being rewritten several times, contained major modifications from earlier proposals when it was finished on March 1, 1957: it named the Department of Health, Education, and Welfare (HEW) as the responsible agency instead of the IBWC and it added both public and private claims.[46] Kilgore sent copies of the draft to all the parties involved and he awaited their suggestions before presenting the new bill to the legislative council of the House of Representatives for final review. Judge Bravo immediately gave his approval and in the postscript to his letter to Kilgore, he notified the congressman officially about his resignation as county judge, effective October 1, 1957.[47]

On March 20, 1957, Bravo solicited Senator Johnson's support for Kilgore's proposed claims bill: "The greatest thing you could do for Zapata County residents, is the assistance I know you will give our Congressman Kilgore in getting the Zapata County claims Bill approved by Congress at this session."[48] Johnson responded to the judge's plea, "You know I will do my best, working with Joe Kilgore, on the Zapata County claims bill. I am anxious to see justice done our friends there, and I will help in any way I can."[49]

Six months later, on August 21, 1957, Kilgore introduced the Zapata Claims Bill to the House Appropriations Committee, with some minor changes to the final draft. A subcommittee would discuss all the bill's components before the full House Committee would consider it at a later date, presumably before the next legislative session. Kilgore and Bobbitt continued to keep Judge Bravo informed of the bill's status, though by now the judge was free of politics and had secured permanent employment with Brown & Root, Inc., a Houston company involved in the construction of platforms for offshore oil and gas drilling.[50] While Bravo was in Houston training for his new position as office manager for field construction projects, Johnson asked for his advice on Zapata County issues still pending before the next congressional session of January, 1958.[51] Judge Bravo's resignation and the behind the scenes political networking to secure a job in South America are discussed in the next chapter.

As of June 18, 1958, Kilgore's claims bill (H.R. 9383), remained in the Bureau of the Budget awaiting congressional approval, but it was referred back to the Judiciary Committee for additional changes in language. Kilgore reintroduced it during the first session of the 86th Congress, on January 7, 1959, as H.R. 162. The legislation set a maximum limit of twenty-five hundred dollars per claim and gave the people eighteen months in which to file. Again, Kilgore kept the secretary of HEW as the responsible federal agency for receiving, adjudicating, and compensating the filed claims and, if necessary, soliciting the assistance of the IBWC for any records or information needed.[52] A Judiciary Committee subcommittee recommended an amendment deleting the section on the courthouse and school furniture in hope that this change would lead to the bill's approval. Kilgore reintroduced an amended bill, H.R. 684, on January 3, 1961, during the 87th Congress.

Subsequent amendments to the language kept it tied up in the snail-paced bureaucratic workings of the Claims Subcommittee. For example, modifications were made excluding people whose claims had already been heard and settled, and those cases that were pending litigation. Another amendment was inserted to restrict compensation requests directed to state agencies that had assisted in moving the landowners during the emergency evacuations. Other legislators wanted further information on all potential depositions, in order to project appropriations.[53] The revised bill took the responsibility away from HEW and gave it back to the IBWC commissioner, who was authorized to adjudicate and compensate all filed pleadings within one year. All the other provisions of earlier proposed legislation remained the same, except that more specific language classified the types of eligible claims.[54]

It would be three years before President Lyndon B. Johnson signed H.R. 8999 into law as P.L. 88-447 on August 19, 1964. By now, Hewitt was no longer in office and had been replaced by a Democrat and President Kennedy appointee—Commissioner J. F. Friedkin, who appointed a four-member Board of Adjudicators, consisting of Luis J. Cárdenas, a

Laredo banker; Frank Y. Hill, a Laredo attorney; Weldon Armstrong, a Zapata business owner; and Jorge Guerra, a rancher and merchant from Roma. The board was to hear cases of unsettled claims and adjudicate monetarily each one due "to moving expenses and losses of personal property in the sudden floods caused by the filling of Falcon Reservoir in 1953 and 1954." [55] Judge Bravo, by now working for the IBWC, was appointed by the commissioner to assist the new board as a claims expediter. The judge's familiarity with the history of the relocation problems and with the landowners involved placed him in an advantageous position.

The Board of Adjudicators met at the Zapata County Courthouse for three days in March and for five days in October 1965. IBWC legal counsel consulted Bravo regarding certain questionable claims still unfinished by the government. A decision on their validity needed to be made before the filing deadline, which was a year from the date the bill was signed. [56]

In the end, the Board of Adjudicators heard a total of 185 requests. When President Johnson signed the Appropriations Bill on September 2, 1965, the board had awarded a total sum of $255,763.95 in claims. It was a victory that garnered Judge Bravo a lofty commendation from Friedkin: "Your diligence in receiving, processing and investigating the claims, and your fairness in evaluation thereof, enable this expeditious determination of the claims by the adjudicators and approval by me. I thank and commend you for your good work on this assignment." [57] The judge's goal of providing just and fair compensation to the people of Zapata for the unsettled claims finally became a reality.

Within a year, the Board of Adjudicators, through its efficient procedures, reviewed and paid all the valid claims. The last payments were mailed out during the first week of November, 1965. The IBWC efforts did not go unnoticed; Congressman Eligio "Kika" de la Garza publicly praised his predecessor—Joe M. Kilgore—for introducing P.L. 88-447 and for the work his staff had done in processing the necessary paperwork and paying the claimants as soon as funds were received. [58]

Attorney Philip Kazen, who represented over 130 residents, summarized the IBWC's overall humanitarian attitude: "We wish to express our sincere appreciation for the kind, courteous and understanding treatment which all of our clients received during the hearings . . . and particularly the investigators, Mr. M. B. Bravo, and Mr. Blas Cantú, were eminently fair and considerate. . . . Most important, the formal and courteous manner in which the hearings were conducted did much to erase the inevitable bitterness which had been created by the previous condemnation proceedings."[59]

With the Board of Adjudicators' task now completed, the people of Zapata County had at last received compensation for the hardships and losses suffered as a result of the construction of Falcon Dam. As of the early 1990s, IBWC and the U.S. Attorney General's records indicated no pending litigation cases or claims regarding the relocation of Zapata, Lopeño, or Falcon.[60]

WARFARE DIPLOMACY

After the fanfare of the Falcon Dam dedication was over, Judge Bravo had wanted the IBWC to complete all the pending projects as previously agreed under the provisions of existing legislation and the intent of the Bentsen Bill. After Colonel Hewitt was appointed commissioner, however, the judge realized that Zapata County residents were in for a tough fight. If Commissioner Lawson was criticized for being too insensitive and callous in dealing with the people, Hewitt's hard-nosed and by-the-book military mentality made Lawson seem benevolent. Hewitt kept erecting hurdles for Judge Bravo, making it nearly impossible for the county to obtain fair and equitable condemnation benefits. Moreover, the Colonel took it upon himself to apply his own strict interpretation of the law and totally ignored any previous agreements. Hewitt perceived the negotiations as a war mission, and in his trained mind, Zapata County was the enemy.

The judge's persuasive skills were tested to the full in his dealings with Hewitt and IBWC bureaucratic red tape. At first, Bravo tried complying with whatever Hewitt demanded. He even contracted a consulting engineer to prepare a more detailed report of specific facilities that still needed to be completed, hoping that this would meet the IBWC's requirements. Even as Bravo fulfilled all requests, Hewitt's turned to the General Accounting Office and Congress to gain stronger support for his own interpretation of the American-Mexican Treaty of 1950. Aware that Hewitt was turning to other governmental agencies to block Zapata County needs, the judge opted for special legislation to remove the IBWC from any further involvement with Zapata County.

Bravo's appeals to national leaders point to still another of his skills—namely, his ability to maintain contacts outside Zapata County's boundaries. The judge used his political alliances with Senators Johnson and Daniel throughout the Falcon Dam episode, and when Bentsen decided to step down from the 15th Congressional District, Bravo cultivated the support of Congressman Joe M. Kilgore. Through this coalition, Bravo worked incessantly, collaborating and cooperating with Hewitt's mandates to end the several unfinished relocation projects. He negotiated carefully with Washington officials for what was best for the county residents, whatever obstacles the IBWC commissioner presented.

Judge Bravo's political acumen is evident in his consummate ability to hold in steady focus his vision of what he believed was in the best interests of the Zapata community. Throughout the Falcon Dam maze of problems, he remained steadfastly committed to his responsibilities, despite relentless opposition from Hewitt and the IBWC as well as from the Partido Nuevo. In letters to Washington and IBWC officials, members of the Partido Nuevo kept interfering with negotiations. They intervened in sensitive matters by attacking the Partido Viejo's position regarding relocation, just compensation for citizens, and the timetable for finishing Falcon Dam. They sought to destabilize the Bravo machine by launching frivolous lawsuits. Both in the general elections of 1954 and 1956 and then when county officials were in the midst of settling their concerns with the IBWC, Partido Nuevo candidates running as Republicans challenged the returns in federal court, claiming fraud had occurred. On both occasions, the results of the investigations were rulings in Bravo's favor, but he still had to spend considerable time and energy away from the talks with IBWC staff and the county's legal counsel.

The judge's reputation for efficiency gained new strength in his wheeling and dealing to get Zapatans just compensation. He probably could have won reelection in 1958, for he held the trust of the majority of voters, who had always counted on him to deliver services: most Zapata County citizens were hardly ignorant peons ill-informed on politics. To the contrary, they were like other common folks who wanted part of the American dream, and they felt Bravo could help bring it to them.

His style throughout the Falcon Dam project remained what it had always been: using diplomacy, fairness, honesty, and forgiveness. Throughout all the planning and negotiations over the dam, events that spanned almost twenty years, Judge Bravo did not profit personally. Potentially, corrupt politicians might easily have benefitted from graft during the time of the dam construction. But Judge Bravo would have none of that. His track record indicates that he aspired instead to a better lifestyle for his constituents and fair compensation for them. He also strongly believed that the best way to work with the IBWC was through honesty and trustworthiness. His interpersonal skills were demonstrated when he placed partisan and nonpartisan community leaders in several committees. He even went as far as involving Partido Nuevo members in important decision-making tasks and allowing the county to pay their travel expenses to Austin. Such generosity was hardly in keeping with the ruthless persona generally associated with bossism.

After leaving public office in the fall of 1957, Judge Bravo never stopped caring for the welfare of his loyal constituents. He continued corresponding with Johnson, Daniels, and Kilgore throughout his hiatus from work in Zapata County. He had embarked on a new career and could easily have forgotten the county's woes, but instead he chose to return, found employment with the IBWC, and finished what morally and legally should have been done for the county residents from the beginning, bringing to completion the pending claims settlements.

Sphere of Geopolitical Influence

I n the history of bossism in South Texas, no jefe político had more influence over a longer period of time than Judge Bravo. His retirement ended a twenty-year tenure as county judge (1937–57) and an even lengthier career in public service. He had played a dominant role in local politics and influenced state and national matters for almost half a century—a grand total of forty-seven years.

Bravo's strong connections with Lyndon Johnson paid off handsomely in retirement. The senator turned to George Brown, his key financial supporter, to secure the judge employment with Brown & Root in 1957. Then in 1964, LBJ used his influence to get the IBWC to hire Bravo. President Johnson never forgot what Bravo had done for him in the 1948 Senate election.

Even in retirement, the judge made contributions to public life, casting a much longer shadow than his modest stature of five feet nine inches might suggest. Politicians sought him not only because of his reputation as a border leader but also for his sage counsel and the proven trust he had established over the years. From his different assignments in South America, El Paso, and Zapata, people kept him informed on issues. He obliged them by advising certain politicos about local problems.

In 1962, Judge Bravo returned to Zapata at the request of some old allies hoping to save the crumbling political machine. But it was too late. In just five years, his absence had produced economic and political turmoil. He attempted to run for his former post and recapture the Partido

Viejo's power, but things were not the same. Alliances had changed and a new breed of hungry politicians had emerged. The machine and boss-style politics had come to an end in Zapata County with the judge's departure in 1957.

RETIREMENT FROM PUBLIC OFFICE

After serving Zapata County for twenty years, Judge Bravo, in consultation with his wife Josefa and family members, decided to resign as county judge and pursue private employment. His decision to leave the political arena, at the age of fifty-six, first emerged during the fall of 1956 when he quietly confided to Kilgore that "he was somewhat tired of political wrangling and would like some sort of a job overseas."[1] Subsequent conversations during the spring of 1957 with Kilgore over the possibility of working for Brown & Root led the congressman to discuss the matter with Senator Johnson. During George Brown's visits to Washington, Johnson discussed Bravo's interest in working in Spain.[2] However, because of a prior agreement with the Spanish government, allowing only key engineering personnel and local Spanish citizens to work for Brown & Root, LBJ could not recommend the judge. Brown suggested the possibility of an assignment in Mexico or Central or South America.[3]

On April 9, 1957, Kilgore submitted Bravo's application for federal employment to Walter Jenkins, administrative assistant to LBJ, who in turn forwarded it to Brown at the Ambassador Hotel in Washington, D.C. A day later, Jenkins assured Kilgore, that "It had been put in the proper hands."[4] Almost three months later, D. E. Warfield, an agent for Brown & Root, contacted Bravo about his interest in working with the company and scheduled an interview in Houston for the middle of July. After the meeting, Judge Bravo returned home completely elated that he had found employment. He quickly notified Johnson that "Mr. Warfield was very nice to me and I have the impression that he thinks I can fulfill the work I will have to perform for them. . . . And I also want you to know that I shall never forget what you have done for me."[5] Johnson expressed his congratulations: "I am as pleased as can be with the news. . . . Your plans sound fine—just fine!"[6] Kilgore echoed these sentiments to the political warrior: "I think its wonderful—but it's bad too. This means you will leave our part of South Texas—and Zapata County will lose its Judge and I will lose a dear friend."[7]

Two months before his departure for Houston, Bravo had officially announced his retirement from public office, effective October 1, 1957. The commissioners' court, at the recommendation of Judge Bravo, appointed Santos Medina—a fellow Democrat, precinct judge for many years, and a loyal supporter of the Partido Viejo—to complete the remainder of Bravo's unexpired term. According to Eddie Bravo, Sr., the judge's oldest son, "He made a deal with Santos Medina to come in as county judge in his place."[8] Bravo reminded Medina to work unceasingly hard to serve the needs of the people by "conserving and protecting their public properties, and working for the prosperity of all the people in the County, regardless of party affiliations. It will be a great satisfaction to me that these things shall happen."[9] Before his departure, he briefed the county judge and the commissioners in a detailed report, arranged in chronological order, describing all the relocation negotiations the county had had with the IBWC up to the time of his resignation. He also gave them a master key to the new junior high school building and the warranty deeds to the facilities and public sites in the relocated town.

Local newspapers and others as far away as San Antonio and Corpus Christi carried the news of his retirement. A spate of farewell letters from friends, political allies, and business associates poured into the judge's office. None summarized Bravo's career better than that of the former state representative and district attorney for the 49th Judicial District, Oscar Laurel: "You will long be remembered as being the most outstanding public official in its long and colorful political history. You have always unflinchingly championed the cause of the people in Zapata and your well-known stand against the unreasonableness of the 'taking' by the United States government of Falcon Dam, will never be forgotten by those who greatly benefitted from your actions."[10] The judge, in turn, sent letters of appreciation to all the county officials, to personal friends, and to political foes.

BROWN & ROOT VENTURE

On September 30, 1957, Judge Bravo departed for Houston for a six-month training period in the management of a field construction office. Shortly after his arrival, he found a modest apartment and made final moving arrangements before Josefa joined him. Several times, the Bravos traveled to Zapata and Laredo on weekends to visit friends and relatives. During this period, Johnson assured Bravo that he had made the right decision: "I am happy you are enjoying it and hope you will have many pleasant years in the new association. It is a fine company with a great deal of interesting work going on." [11]

Once he had passed his physical examination and completed the training period, Brown & Root notified Judge Bravo about his assignment as office manager of Paría Operations at Guiria, Venezuela. On March 6, 1958, the judge wrote a jubilant letter informing Johnson about his trip to South America. [12] His dream of working abroad had finally become a reality, thanks to his two political allies, Johnson and Kilgore. Josefa's most memorable impression of their arrival in Guiria was having to climb twenty-four steps to their apartment. [13] In the meantime, a new house for the Bravos was under construction.

The Bravos spent three years in Venezuela before receiving a transfer to Panama, where they stayed for a few months. In May, 1961, Bravo's contract terminated and a new reassignment sent them to Medellín, Colombia, for over a year; there, the judge worked as a payroll clerk and labor-relations consultant. From August to December, 1962, he remained in Colombia, working with the Zapata Offshore Company, an oil drilling operation owned by future president George Bush; the two men had become friends during Bravo's training in Houston. Bush wrote to Bravo later: "Just a note to thank you for the services which you rendered to the company during your employment with us. . . . And please stop by to say hello when you come back to Houston." [14]

While the Bravos lived in Medellín, one of Bush's sons visited the drilling company and stopped by at the Bravos' home several times for homemade meals. Manuel B. Bravo, Jr., remembered that "my mother fed him *tortillas* and *arroz* and *frijoles;* he didn't want to go back home. . . . He would say that this is the best food I ever had." [15] Josefa vividly recalled Bush expressing his gratitude when the Bravos returned to Houston—"Mrs. Bravo, I want to thank you for being so nice with my boy." [16]

Judge Bravo continued corresponding with the future president well into Bush's congressional campaign for the Seventh District, which included Houston. A few weeks after his victory in the November, 1966, general election, Bush wrote Bravo the following typed note: "Thanks for your wonderful letter. . . . I would have answered your letter sooner, but Barbara and I went to Washington to hunt for an apartment, then on to Florida for a four-day rest." As a postscript, he noted in cursive, "*Great* to hear from you again. I had lost track of you, and now I am happy. Come see us if you get to D.C." [17]

INFLUENCE FROM AFAR

On March 10, 1962, the company assigned Bravo to a short-term project in Louisiana. He remained there until the following December when complications from a serious bout with diabetes forced his early retirement.

During his four years with Brown & Root, the judge's influence over political matters had transcended the geopolitcal limits of South Texas. His cohorts in Zapata County continued to keep him informed on local politics, while he in turn provided pertinent and timely advice. For instance, when LBJ made plans to attend the LULAC convention in Laredo during the latter part of June, 1958, Bravo warned him about the newly developed political schism between the two powerful families—the Martins and the Kazens, who controlled Webb County's Independent Club. Bravo forewarned the senator: "Feeling that you may not be fully aware of this situation, I felt that maybe I should mention it to you so that you may avoid a slip of the tongue or any other act that may affect you adversely. You have always had the good will and esteem of all the people of Webb County, hence the reason for my words of caution." [18]

Three days later, Johnson replied, "I will certainly be guided by your judgement as to my activities there. And, you can be certain that I will be very careful. Please know that I appreciate very deeply your letting me have the benefit of your information." [19] Johnson was a close friend of both families and needed their support in South Texas if he decided to run for the presidency in 1960. Thus, he could not afford to alienate either one.

During the 1958 Democratic primary, the judge also alerted Senator Ralph Yarborough and Congressman Kilgore to the rivalry going on within the Independent Club in Webb County. The Reform Party, a splinter faction of the Independent Club headed by former Independent Club member Jimmy Kazen, had taken a stand behind Yarborough. The Independent Club proper, however, ruled by the Martins, was opposing the junior senator. Cautiously, Judge Bravo advised Yarborough: "I believe you can get a great majority of the votes in Webb County if they don't place you as a protege of either faction. However, if the opportunity would present itself whereby some friends of yours that are influential with the Martins would get their backing I would certainly do so." [20] Yarborough kindly responded to the judge's inside scoop, "I am indebted to you, not only for this information, but for your interest and thought in conveying it to me. I shall certainly follow through on your suggestions." [21] Yarborough could not afford to lose the support of either the Independent Club or the Reform Party. He needed to be careful that neither group used him to destroy the other.

He followed Bravo's advice and carried Webb County for the first time. From Venezuela, the judge personally paid for Yarborough's political ads in the Laredo newspaper. The judge, in the meantime, reminded the senator to solicit the new county judge's support for the primary Democratic election: "Don't fail to write Santos Medina [County] Judge and tell him you are counting on Zapata Co's vote. He is our mutual friend." [22]

In Kilgore's case Judge Bravo offered another kind of advice. "I sincerely hope you remain out of Laredo and away from the local squabble so that you will be able to retain the same friends even though on opposite sides. Things will not be the same, even after the elections, because both factions have gotten too rabid on the issue. It might be best if you don't get back to Texas . . . until after August 1st." [23] Kilgore replied, "I sure thank you for your note of the 16th and I appreciate the friendly advice and the information." [24] He was up for reelection and needed to keep both families on his side; he might lose if either faction publicly supported him.

From time to time, Kilgore communicated with Bravo regarding South Texas politics and requested his sage advice, "I suppose it's too early to tell how Zapata County's politics, or Webb's for that matter, will shape up in the next election. As a matter of fact, you probably know more about this, all the way down where you are, than I do up here. And speaking of politics, I'll be sure to tell Lyndon you asked to be remembered to our future President." [25]

After a long and heated summer campaign for the judgeship position of the 49th Judicial District, Jimmy Kazen, who campaigned without the support of any political group, defeated the incumbent, Judge R. D. Wright (backed by Webb County's Independent Club), in the July 26, 1958, primary. In Zapata County, the political machine gave Kazen 696 votes to Wright's 246. In his congratulatory letter to Kazen, Judge Bravo acknowledged their mutual friendship, "A sus ordenes—su compadre" (At your service—your compadre).[26] The Republican Party in Zapata had supported the incumbent judge, but their efforts fell short of clinching a victory.

Throughout Judge Bravo's stay in South America, both Kilgore and Bobbitt continued to keep him up to date on Zapata County's relocation problems, sending him copies of Kilgore's proposed claims bill for perusal and advice. Likewise, the judge conveyed to Bobbitt information he obtained from other sources. In one communiqué, dated 1958, the judge snarled "that the S.O.B. at El Paso [Commissioner Hewitt] had determined not to go ahead and deed Zapata County all town lots which they have left over or which have not been assigned to owners of lots in the Lake Area prior to condemnation. And I am wondering if he is going to put anything over on the Coiisioner [sic] Court by getting them to accept the conveyance and signing some RELEASE that might affect claims which Zapata County should carry on in Federal Court."[27]

From his vantage point in Venezuela, the judge was still able to exercise political influence over several local matters. For instance, Armando López, a friend and resident of Zapata County, serving time in 1958 in Huntsville, sought Bravo's help in obtaining parole; the López family had been longtime supporters of the judge. Bravo communicated with Governor Price Daniel, obtaining the executive's permission to try to help, pending a favorable ruling by the Board of Pardons. Assured of the propriety of the overture, Judge Bravo pleaded the case with Jack Ross, chairman of the Board of Pardons.[28] The parole was granted, and Armando, expecting to be released by early August of 1958, sent a letter of gratitude to the judge.[29]

When not campaigning for his friends, the judge continued to recommend political allies for positions of influence and authority. During March, 1961, a federal judgeship position became available, and Bravo at once persuaded Kilgore to put in a good word for Judge E. Salinas from Webb County. By now, rumors had spread through the grapevine that Senator Yarborough was interested in another candidate, and since the appointment was considered "Senatorial patronage," Kilgore did not pursue the matter any further.[30]

All the way from Venezuela, Bravo financially supported the Kennedy-Johnson presidential ticket in 1960. Knowing that the election could go either way, Johnson, through calculated planning, made an effective campaign tour through the South during the middle of October in 1960, being careful not to alienate the northern liberals.[31] Though historian Robert Dallek argues that the Democratic headquarters in Texas feared a Republican win, LBJ had a more positive view and shared his reflections on the political strategy with Bravo on October 21, 1960: "The Democratic ticket is winning nationally and Texas will win with it. We have made great strides this year toward ending the prejudice against our region and state. I believe we are on the threshold of new influence and opportunity—and a Texas-sized majority for the 'Texan's Ticket' will open the door to the future for the goals we have so long sought."[32] In Zapata County, the Kennedy-Johnson ticket garnered 675 votes, while the Republican ticket of Nixon and Lodge received only 260 votes.

DECLINE OF ZAPATA COUNTY'S MACHINE

Without the leadership at the top to keep the Partido Viejo working together, the political machine slowly disintegrated after Judge Bravo resigned. On July 19, 1961, a day after the unincorporated Bank of Zapata closed its doors and declared bankruptcy, Bravo's successor, forty-six-year-old Santos Medina, abruptly withdrew as county judge. Santos and his brother Manuel had owned and operated the bank since 1930. The people of Zapata County lost their life-long savings in the mishap, while the investments of ranchers and other business establishments also suffered. The bank's failure proved a severe blow to the residents and to the county's economy.

Judge Bravo returned to Zapata County in 1962, only to find it in political and economic turmoil. Since his resignation as county judge, three of the county's stalwart Democrats who had kept the Partido Viejo in power since the early 1920s had resigned—Proceso Martínez, Manuel Medina, and Leopoldo Martínez.

The Democratic Party was experiencing for the first time in its history internal disagreements and a lack of unity. This split had surfaced in 1961 when the county commissioners' court sought to replace the disgraced Medina. County commissioner for precinct 2, Delfino Lozano, nominated Sheriff Conrado Hein, an educator, and the Republican commissioner for precinct 3, Santiago González, seconded the motion. But Hein failed to win a majority as the commissioners split their votes (2-2). After much discussion, the county commissioner for precinct 4, Lizandro Ramírez, nominated county Republican chairperson and well-known

rancher Jacob G. Rathmell; the commissioner for precinct 1, Derly Villarreal, seconded the motion. Once more, a split vote denied Rathmell
the county judgeship.[33] The commissioners then adjourned for the day
and that evening, both factions presumably did much wheeling and dealing over dinner and late into the night. On the following day, July 20,
1961, Derly Villarreal nominated Pedro Ramírez, Jr.; Lizandro Ramírez
seconded, and Ramírez received unanimous approval (4-0) as the next
county judge. All three contenders—Hein, Rathmell, and Ramírez—
came from prominent middle-class families.

It is interesting to note that in the first nomination the Republican
González supported Sheriff Hein—a Democrat—but voted against fellow party member Rathmell. Why he did not vote for Rathmell and for
an opportunity to have two Republicans on the commissioners' court is
baffling. Perhaps it was because Rathmell was Leopoldo Martínez's son-
in-law, and Martínez had long been associated with Zapata County machine politics. Seemingly, Zapata County residents no longer wanted to
tolerate Democratic party bossism.

BRAVO RUNS FOR REELECTION

The Democratic faction led by Commissioners Derly Villarreal and fifty-
seven-year old Lizandro Ramírez, a rancher and a political veteran who
had served the Falcon area for over twenty years (since 1942 when he
defeated the incumbent Santos Yzaguirre), convinced Judge Bravo to try
and mend the party's internal problems by campaigning for county
judge. At the age of sixty-one, and against his better judgment, Bravo
accepted the challenge to run in the May 5, 1962, Democratic primary.
In his acceptance speech before a large gathering of loyal supporters, he
pledged to bring economic stability to the county, "observing the condition that county affairs are in at the present time, . . . and believing that
an efficient, experienced, harmonious, courageous and honest administration will remedy this situation, . . . in the hope that I can serve and
help all the citizens of Zapata County, particularly those whose life savings have been so adversely affected by recent occurrences here."[34]

The other Democratic faction, headed by Commissioners Lozano and
González, supported the incumbent, Judge Pedro Ramírez, Jr. Its slate of
candidates included both incumbents and new aspirants, as did that of
Bravo's faction.

Several things put Bravo at a disadvantage. His physical absence from county politics for almost five years had greatly diminished his visibility among voters. Moreover, the upstart politicians brought with them a different breed of supporters, most of them loyal to the leaders who had replaced the old guard since 1957.

Indeed, Judge Bravo's longtime political associates who had supported him for twenty years were no longer in power, except for Lizandro Ramírez, the commissioner for precinct 4. But he later resigned his post. Leopoldo Martínez and Proceso Martínez had given up politics in 1955 and 1958 respectively; Manuel Medina left in 1959; and Primitivo Uribe had passed away in 1955. Both J. M. Sánchez and Ygnacio Sánchez had left the political scene altogether. The powerful Big Four no longer existed as an influential force. With Lizandro, last of the Partido Viejo diehards, gone, the judge's former strong and solid political power base vanished. To exacerbate matters, many of his supporters, although they had requested his comeback, unexpectedly switched sides and campaigned against him.

Family members knew well that Judge Bravo did not have the backing to defeat the incumbent Ramírez. The judge received sound advice from his youngest son, Manuel Jr.: "I asked him not to run. . . . He consulted with us and talked about it. There is a time and place that people have used to learn when to quit, when to leave, and it is not the same as when you have your finger in the pot all the time." [35] Eddie, the oldest son, also provided wise counsel: "The old politicians wanted him, but had no control anymore. . . . Don't believe anything that they tell you, these people are not with you anymore, they are already obligated. . . . You are going to lose, you are going to lose face." [36]

The judge felt uneasy about the smoldering personal hatreds among the Democrats; such feelings, which had not existed during his tenure, had been brought on by a lack of leadership at the helm of the Democratic Party. During the many heated and bitter earlier campaigns between the Partido Viejo and the discontended Democrats who ran as Republicans, Judge Bravo's diplomatic skills had made it possible to mend relationships shortly after an election. As county judge, Bravo had firmly believed that both factions should bury the hatchet after a hard-fought election campaign, and he had not allowed bitterness or hatred to carry over past election day. "With this in mind and hoping to bring harmony to the people of the county, . . . and not hatred for each other [the judge announced just prior to the Democratic primary], I have decided to withdraw from the race." [37]

As predicted, the incumbent Judge Ramírez received a landslide victory. Bravo managed to garner one vote, while another candidate, Angel Flores, got two. In the other races, Nicasio González, who ran unopposed, gained the seat vacated by Lizandro Ramírez. Popular incumbent Arturo L. Benavides solidly defeated Humberto González, Jr., for county treasurer. In the November 6, 1962, general election, Angel Flores, who had campaigned as a Democrat in the primary, now ran under the Republican banner against Judge Ramírez, but he lost by a margin of 2 to 1. [38]

Following the debacle of 1962, Judge Bravo took a year off to spend visiting family and friends in Zapata, Laredo, and the Río Grande Valley. On one occasion, the Bravos toured the East coast, visiting his first cousin Elías Cavazos, who was then living in New York, and later stopping by the White House to visit with Vice President Johnson and Congressman Kilgore. "We had a very nice trip to the Capitol but the greatest satisfaction was to meet with you [Kilgore] and our beloved Veep. The Tonic of life for me, is when I am among friends," the judge recalled when he returned home. [39] His youngest son, Manuel Jr., vividly remembered another trip to the White House, after Johnson became president. The young Bravo recalled the scene at the Oval Office: "Lyndon, what he did, he put like a pillow or cushion on one end of the couch and lay down, put his hands behind his head, looked over and said, okay Bravo, tell me what's going on in South Texas." [40]

SLEEPING WITH THE ENEMY: BRAVO JOINS IBWC

During a Christmas holiday visit to Laredo in 1964, the judge visited his old-time political ally, Philip A. Kazen, to explore the possibility of getting gainful employment. At Kazen's recommendation, Judge Bravo sent a letter to Cliff Carter, one of President Johnson's assistants, inquiring into work opportunities, either at home or abroad. [41] In the meantime, Kazen spoke to Carter about the judge's qualifications and his eagerness to find employment. In a follow-up letter, dated March 6, 1964, Kazen reminded Carter about the judge's longtime friendship with President Johnson:

I am writing you on behalf of M. B. Bravo, who was County Judge of Zapata County when the President won his Senate seat over Coke Stevenson in 1948. . . .

Cliff, this man has been the President's loyal and devoted friend throughout the years. We worked shoulder to shoulder together and with others back in 1948 when the Stevenson crowd wanted to nullify the hard won victory of Lyndon Johnson for a Senate seat. . . . Trusting that you may pass the word on to the Chief and that something might be done.[42]

At the age of sixty-three and with only an eighth-grade formal education, Bravo found getting work difficult. Hence, he turned to political patronage, hoping to find something. The good news came in April, 1964, when IBWC Commissioner J. F. Friedkin notified Judge Bravo that he needed him as a realty assistant in nearby Falcon Village.[43] Again, President Johnson came through for his friend and former ally.

With over thirty years' experience dealing with land titles, deeds, landowners, and the relocation problems, Judge Bravo was well qualified for the job, regardless of the president's influence. He knew the geographical terrain and clearly understood the landowners' plight. Under the supervision of Project Superintendent N. H. Scoggins, he oversaw a study of the leasable parcels in the Falcon Reservoir area.[44]

With the passage of Kilgore's H.R. 8999 (P.L. 88-447) on August 19, 1964, Judge Bravo's contract with the IBWC was extended so that he could assist the Board of Adjudicators in negotiating and adjusting unsettled claims following the construction of Falcon Dam. In his capacity as a claims expediter, the judge performed his duties meritoriously, gaining recognition for his laborious work from Commissioner Friedkin. Consequently, he received a promotion to GG-6, and an assignment to the Chamizal section at the IBWC headquarters in El Paso, effective October 25, 1965.[45] "We regret losing the services of Mr. Bravo, . . . I want you to be fully aware of the excellent work which Mr. Bravo did at this office. . . . He has been faithful, energetic, thorough, and loyal in the special assignment which we gave him," former Project Superintendent Scoggins told Commissioner Friedkin.[46] In response, Friedkin stated, "This is not the first time his good performance had been brought to my attention. Nevertheless, your letter confirmed, and rightfully so, the fine job Mr. Bravo has done while in our employment at Falcon Dam."[47]

From a modest apartment in El Paso, located at 3600 La Paz, Bravo commuted to the IBWC's office for three years. His mission was to negotiate a fair market value with landowners, to inspect and prepare inventories of houses and properties purchased by the IBWC, and to carry out the tenets of the Chamizal convention. Due to an international century-old dispute that arose when the Río Grande changed courses (caused by natural occurrences), the issue was settled when Mexico received 366 acres of the Chamizal area and 71 acres east of Córdova Island. In exchange, the United States obtained monetary compensation and 193 acres of the same island. In addition, Bravo and his staff meticulously prepared the final arrangements for the official ceremony of the El Chamizal settlement, set for October 28, 1967, between President Johnson and Mexico's President Gustavo Díaz Ordaz. Friedkin praised Bravo's efforts, "I wish to express my personal thanks to you for your assistance and the fine manner in which you placed and replaced the flags, photos and other decorations along the route of the motorcade [vandals had destroyed and stolen many of the flags and photos the night before]. I was pleased to see that everything had been restored to its original condition and the decorations looking fine. Your willingness and the efficient manner in which you discharged your responsibility deserve a special recognition." [48]

During his three-year stay in El Paso, the judge kept abreast of current political affairs with state officials. On December 7, 1965, at a breakfast he attended in honor of Senator Yarborough, he expressed his satisfaction that the senator was not seeking the governorship. "I believe we need you more in the U.S. Senate at this time when the peace of the world is at stake and the rights of our citizens are being questioned by Birchites and what have you." [49] A week later, Yarborough responded, "Although I have not made any decisions about the political situation in Texas for 1966, I shall keep your advice in mind. It was good of you to write and share your thoughts with me." [50]

FALCON VILLAGE PROJECT

After completing his assignment in El Paso, Bravo returned to Zapata, where he was again assigned to Falcon Village. Before assuming his new duties, the judge traveled with his wife and granddaughter Gloria Alicia to Washington, D.C., during the latter part of September, 1968, for a sight-seeing trip and, among other things, to stop by and visit with President Johnson. Unfortunately, the president was in a cabinet meeting all day and did not get to see them. The following day Johnson said, "When I learned you had been to The White House and didn't wait to see me, I sent out a search warrant. . . . Since I didn't have the chance to visit with you today, you will have to keep your word and come see me someday at the LBJ Ranch or in Austin Office."[51] Johnson later informed Judge Bravo that he would have made time for the threesome, regardless of demands made by the cabinet meetings.

SPECIAL CONSULTANT ASSIGNMENT

After his retirement from the IBWC in the summer of 1969, the judge received a warm letter of appreciation from Commissioner Friedkin. "You helped very much in getting our leasing program at Falcon straightened out and properly functioning. You played a very important part in our Chamizal settlement. . . . Your good spirit was catching, it was important to our project."[52] He continued doing consulting work for the agency, generally around Zapata County. In his capacity as advisor, he prepared for the commissioner a special report in July, 1970, dealing with the economic future of San Ygnacio. As we have seen, this was a historic town settled in the mid-nineteenth century. The special legal assistant for the IBWC, M. H. Raney, cautiously counseled Judge Bravo to "make your inquiry in a discreet manner so as to avoid causing any suspicions or to arouse questions about your inquiry."[53] The study would help determine the cost of relocating movable structures from San Ygnacio to Zapata. It also proposed making use of empty lots in the town of Zapata for the possible relocation of San Ygnacio families. Another more cost-effective alternative involved leaving the town where it was and constructing a six-foot protective levee around it.

The IBWC was concerned with the impact of flooding on San Ygnacio, which was located about fifteen miles north of the relocated county seat on U.S. Highway 83. In the early part of 1970, the IBWC commissioner had reviewed engineering reports indicating that silt accumulation at Falcon Dam posed a potentially serious flooding problem to the old settlement. The projections, based on a fifty-year lifespan for the reservoir, predicted that such danger could occur by the year 2003.[54] However, Amistad Dam, which had been built in 1969 in southern Val Verde County, could prolong the survival of San Ygnacio by controlling the amount of water that flows towards the Falcon reservoir. If heavy rains fell below Amistad, then all the border towns along the river would be subject to flooding.

Judge Bravo completed the report for Friedkin in about three weeks and concluded that "since the Amistad Dam is now completed and since heavy floods are not expected between the Amistad and Falcon Dams, it is believed that San Ygnacio is not in danger of being flooded any-more. . . . San Ygnacio will continue to exist, in a gradually declining state, because of tradition and because of larger landholders."[55] Satisfied with the report, Commissioner Friedkin agreed with the judge, "I ap-preciate very much your report. . . . You have surveyed the situation very thoroughly and I think your conclusions are all very sound."[56]

For five years, Judge Bravo contributed significantly to the work of the IBWC. Most important, his own experience in fighting the same fed-eral agency more than a decade ago helped to adjudicate, in a spirit of fairness, cooperation, and understanding, the claims of so many county residents whose lives were affected by the construction of Falcon Dam and the relocation process. Judge Bravo never dreamed that during his lifetime, he would be given an opportunity to assist the IBWC in helping the Zapata County landowners with their negotiations. Being able to obtain a just compensation for his people was the real climax of the judge's career. No one else could have done it so well as Judge Bravo.

EVER THE COMMUNITY LEADER

Every election year, Judge Bravo kept busy by supporting local and state Democratic candidates, scrounging from his Texas Retirement System savings and from Social Security benefits so that he could support them financially. He also helped them by writing numerous letters and making an untold number of telephone calls. Whether from Falcon Village, El Paso, or his home in Zapata, he remained involved in partisan politics and in many different issues, as evidenced by the substantial number of letters in the Bravo Papers. At the request of Zapata County landowners, for example, he pleaded their case in 1965 for federal assistance for drought relief, corresponding with "Kika" de la Garza several times and with the state director for the U.S. Department of Agriculture.[57]

He also assisted Senator Ralph Yarborough during his three reelec-tion campaigns and State Senator Franklin Spear during the latter's 1966 bid for attorney general of Texas. After winning the 1964 senatorial Democratic primary, Yarborough confided in Bravo, "Half of the war is over; the first battle is won. Before the smoke clears away my thoughts turn to you. . . . When the opposition was seeking to destroy me by the foulest means, your loyalty and confidence meant [much] to me." [58] Just before the general election, Yarborough said, "It is my hope that you will continue to keep me advised of the political situation in your area." [59] After his triumphant victory in November, Yarborough expressed his gratitude to the judge: "Please accept my warmest appreciation . . . for your outstanding leadership of the Democratic Party in your County . . . and for your help, friendship and loyalty over the years." [60]

In 1968 Bravo actively campaigned for the Humphrey-Muskie ticket, and four years later he supported the McGovern-Shriver campaign. Never did he hesitate to express his views and let the candidates know how he felt about the issues. Texas Representative Ralph ("Skip") Scoggins, in seeking reelection, commented that "you were one of the many interested citizens of our community who took time out from their busy schedule to write to me and express your views on pending legislation. Your ideas aided me to become properly informed on the subject you were interested in and also gave me an indication of the people's feelings back home." [61] On another occasion, Bravo took time to discuss with Congressman Henry B. González the proposed minimum wage legislation pending congressional hearings and the impact the law would have on the South Texas economy. [62]

Judge Bravo's fast pace slowed down considerably in the early 1970s following corrective surgery to restore the blood flow of the carotid arteries. Even during his convalescence, however, he managed to keep in touch with his political connections. Kika de la Garza, openly concerned about the judge's health, responded in one missive, "I was particularly grateful that you could take the time, during your own recuperation, to write me about my seeking re-election. Along with you, I hope I don't have any opposition because, as you so aptly observed, it leaves me much more time to tend to my duties, and saves much expenses." [63] He ended the letter with the postscript, "to speed along your recovery, I hope, I am sending you separately today, a pictorial calendar."

Following his recuperation, Bravo resumed his involvement with several projects. He did consulting work for John F. Williams, a distant cousin employed with an architectural firm in San Antonio that needed expert advice on a school building contract. [64] At the recommendation of Ralph Yarborough in 1973, Judge Bravo accepted an appointment to serve with Robert W. Calvert as a member of the Texas Constitutional Revision Commission for South Texas.[65] In his own hometown, there were also urgent matters that required his attention. In the mid-1970s, the local school superintendent, about to lose federal funds, turned desperately to Bravo, hoping that the judge's recollections of county history could help. The school board needed additional documents to make Zapata County School District eligible for funding. Bravo, the only person who had any knowledge of the records lost during the 1954 flood, interceded on behalf of the school district and provided the missing information.[66] Also during this time, the Zapata County Commissioners' Court appointed the judge to act as the administrator of the Rose A. Laurendeau estate, consisting of more than sixty thousand dollars' worth of personal and real property.[67] The court considered Bravo the best qualified person because of his knowledge in probate and estate matters and appraisal values of county property. For two years (1975–77), he administered the disposition of the estate, receiving about two thousand dollars for his services.[68]

On the twentieth anniversary of the construction of Falcon Dam, George and Bonnie Carmack, a writer-and-photographer duo from the *San Antonio Express* newspaper (known also for their weekly series in Texas history) visited Zapata and interviewed the Bravos. The Carmacks' report appeared on October 13, 1973, under the appropriate headline, "The Tale of 2 Cities: One Is Old, Other New." In reference to the construction of Falcon Dam, they concluded that the new town of Zapata was much better off economically than its predecessor would have been: "Time had proven him [Judge Bravo] right and the area is far more prosperous than before." [69]

LAST YEARS

By the early 1980s Judge Bravo's health was deteriorating. Complications from diabetes coupled with minor strokes left him speech impaired and bedridden. The inability to continue his active involvement in politics by speaking or writing left an indelible impression of frustration on his face. His mental acumen enabled him to know exactly what was taking place, but his incapacity to express himself produced a sense of hopelessness and frustration. At times, his family members felt that Bravo, Zapata County's patriarch, had resigned himself to whatever the Lord might allow. In 1983, Michael L. Gillette, chief of acquisitions for the LBJ

Library, sent the judge a letter expressing an interest in obtaining his personal papers.[70] Apparently, Bravo was never aware that his political career had meant so much to President Johnson. The judge never responded to the request made by the archival depository in Austin. Years later, Gillette's letter was found in the judge's filing cabinet.[71]

Manuel Jr. sadly remembered his father's last days. "It was a shame to see this giant of an individual, just lying in bed and not able to communicate, and that's what he liked to do. At first, I used to guess a lot of what he wanted to say, and he just smiled and moved his hands. . . . But then later, I couldn't understand what he wanted to say, and he became angry all the time."[72]

Painstakingly and with faith and courage, Josefa nurtured the judge and attended to all his physical, emotional, and spiritual needs. On Josefa's eighty-sixth birthday, September 18, 1984, Judge Manuel Box Bravo passed to his eternal reward at the age of eighty-three. Many family members had gathered at the Bravo household that morning to prepare for a small but festive birthday celebration. Then, following one of Josefa's periodic checks on the judge's needs, family members in the home were alerted by a soft whimpering sound from Judge Bravo as he passed away. His last breath signaled the end of the life of one of the most colorful political figures in South Texas. Two days later, on a sunny morning, a mile-long funeral procession slowly and solemnly made its way from Our Lady of Lourdes Catholic Church to the Zapata County Cemetery. The townfolk gathered to bid farewell to their benevolent *patrón.*

EPILOGUE: *EL JEFE POLÍTICO,* DON MANUEL B. BRAVO

Since Judge Bravo's retirement, eight different county judges have been elected to run the Zapata County government over a forty-year period (1957–99), but none has ruled for twenty years. In 1975, the Duke of Duval, George B. Parr, already in trouble with the Internal Revenue Service for income tax fraud, committed suicide at his Los Horcones Ranch. Three years later, the last of South Texas political machines—Webb County's powerful Independent Club—came tumbling down when Mayor J. C. "Pepe" Martin, Jr., resigned amid a grand jury investigation.

In part, the end of political bossism in South Texas occurred due to a sequence of events that began during the late 1950s. These developments included the sense that "politics as usual" should no longer continue; the growing influence of the Republican Party; civil rights movements calling for more representative government; the 1975 Voting Rights Act; and general acceptance by mainstream society that political reform ought to be part of the contemporary era. Even Bravo found himself caught out of place at a time of flux when he sought a comeback in 1962. In other words, the circumstances present along the border up until the 1950s explain Bravo's tenure as jefe político. Once things changed in Zapata County and South Texas, bossism and Bravo became remnants of a glorious past for which there was little room in the modern political age.

Bravo's biography offers several historical lessons, therefore. Funda-

Table 11. County Judges of Zapata County, 1858–2003

1858–1860	Henry Redmond[a]
1860–1862	Ysidro Vela[a]
1866–1868	Henry Redmond[a]
1869–1872	D. D. Lovell and Laureano Vidaurri
1873–1878	Theodore S. Dix
1879–1882	William D. Langston
1883–1898	J. Antonio G. Navarro[b]
1899	Angus Peter Spohn
1899–1900	A. P. Spohn and Mercurio Martínez
1901–1920	A. P. Spohn
1921–1928	José M. Sánchez
1929–1936	A. V. Navarro
1937–1957	Manuel Box Bravo[c]
1957–1961	Santos Medina[d]
1961–1970	Pedro Ramírez, Jr.
1971–1974	Angel A. Flores
1975–1986	Jake Rathmell
1987–1990	Angel A. Flores
1991–1994	José Luis "Pepe" Guevara
1995–1998	Norma Villarreal-Ramírez
1999–2003	David Morales

Source: Jean Y. Fish and Robert Fish, *Elected Officials of Zapata County, 1858–1986*
[a]County judges were called Chief Justice
[b]Resigned on September 12, 1898
[c]Resigned on October 1, 1957
[d]Resigned on July 19, 1961

---

mentally, it buttresses the description other students of Mexican-American political history have given of particular counties in South Texas. David Montejano notes, for instance, that Zapata County was one of the "ranch counties," or so-called "Mexican counties," where Tejanos dominated much of the political system.[1] Indeed, Mexican Americans in Zapata held many if not all of the local offices: county judge, county commissioners, hide and animal inspector, sheriff, district and county clerk, tax assessor and collector, county treasurer, justices of the peace, constables, and chairpersons for the different voting precincts.

Many of these officials were educators (intellectuals in some cases), merchants who dealt with mainstream businesses, landowners, journalists, or ranchers, and they even included an activist priest with a social justice agenda. Their influence extended beyond the geopolitical boundary of the area since many of them had economic and family ties with neighboring counties.

Scholars like Montejano note further that the Tejano electorate voted "freely," unfettered by such obstacles as were found in the "farm counties"—racial prejudice, the "White Man's Primary," landowner interests, gerrymandering, and the like.[2] In part, this access to the political forum in the ranch counties, in contradistinction to farm or "Anglo" counties, was due to the existence of a bond among citizens, a sense of peoplehood (*la raza*), or a unified consciousness of *nosotros* (us). Most residents in Zapata County shared a similar heritage of values, customs, rituals, language, and religion. Despite social differentiation, overt or covert "racial" dominance was seldom an issue in Zapata County, even though members of the middle class came from the families who had established the *ranchos* in the mid-eighteenth century. Many middle-class Tejanos never considered themselves "whites," for example, and they treated others whose skin color was darker with respect and decorum. Given this unique set of circumstances, Hispanic leaders ostensibly pursued goals beneficial to the common good—providing education, a modern infrastructure, and job opportunities. Whether well-off or poor, the majority of voters felt confident, based on prior political experiences, that the Partido Viejo provided the best for them and their children by way of improvements in county programs, more jobs, government assistance (soil conservation, drought relief, rural telephone service, etc.), and a better educational system.

The Bravo story does much to bolster the case that bossism was rooted more in historical situations than anything inherent to ethnic culture. Unique circumstances in Zapata County helped promote and nurture this type of political governance. A major contributing cause of bossism was Zapata County's isolation from the hustle and bustle of South Texas social and economic activities. Geographically speaking, the county seat was not located directly across the Río Grande from a Mexican border town (unlike Laredo, Eagle Pass, Hidalgo, or Brownsville). In addition, the lack of a railroad system and a modern highway helped to perpetuate a strong sense of local identity and control. Zapata County's political history served further to perpetuate bossism, as people had long relied on the institution as a practical way of conducting county business. Closely associated with this specific setting were the demographics of the area as a whole, almost 100 percent Hispanic, and in particular, the ruling families' longtime loyalty and support of the Partido Viejo. This state of affairs had been in place for several generations.

To be sure, machine politics were a national phenomenon. Patronage, graft, and voting irregularities were to be found in Chicago, New York, Baltimore, New Orleans, St. Louis, San Francisco, and other places. Bossism provided political stability, economic well-being, and other positive benefits to particular locales. In getting projects completed and fulfilling the needs of the people, it cut straight through the red tape of the cumbersome bureaucratic echelons.

As in the case of Zapata County's missing returns in Box No. 3, and Jim Wells County's infamous Box No. 13, similar activities had been occurring in northern cities. Gary W. Cox and J. Morgan Kousser, in their study on "Turnout and Rural Corruption: New York as a Test Case," cite newspaper reports showing that the political machine provided "free transportation to the polls, the use of repeaters, the illegal naturalization of foreigners, the election-day importation of voters from other states, the padding of registration rolls, fraudulent counting, and most interestingly, payments to citizens not to vote." [3]

As far back as the presidential election of 1860 between Republican Abraham Lincoln and the Democrat Stephen A. Douglas, a partisan Ohio newspaper warned its readers "to ignore propaganda from the opposition and to watch for tricks at the polls." [4] During the presidential campaign of 1876 between Rutherford B. Hayes and Samuel J. Tilden, thousands of Democratic votes were declared illegal by an electoral commission in three southern states—South Carolina, Florida, and Louisiana. The ensuing political maneuvering that gave Hayes the election led historian Samuel Eliot Morison to conclude, "There is no longer any doubt that this election was 'stolen.'" [5]

Precinct election judges throughout the big cities of the United States, under strict orders from the bosses, were known to hold back election results from key precincts until the opponent had reported the returns first, especially in close contests. This was considered an established and acceptable practice and deeply rooted in the American political system. The key issue was when to report, albeit in a timely manner, all the official returns to the state executive committee. Such a decision affected the 1941 special Senate election between Lyndon Johnson and Lee O'Daniel when LBJ submitted vote totals prematurely. Upon Johnson's return to Washington, President Roosevelt advised him to sit on the ballot boxes at the next election.[6] Johnson made a vow that he would do just that.

Bravo's biography, then, indicates that a boss's politics reflected existing American political practices, even when activities extended to using the more questionable machinations associated with that tradition. Indeed, Bravo's own political thinking, his blueprint for governance, and his expectations for Zapata County all reflected an upbringing in American constitutional principles. Like Bravo, most Tejano bosses and leaders in South Texas had received a public education in U.S. schools, and they believed firmly in their country's tenets of democracy, freedom, and human rights. Some tried to volunteer for the armed services during World War II, as Bravo did, but because of personal circumstances were not eligible to be drafted. Many more went on to serve heroically in Europe and Asia.

While prepared to take up arms as Americans against the enemies of democracy, Bravo and his generation of Tejano leaders were bicultural individuals highly sensitive to their Mexican heritage and thus also predisposed to fighting ethnic battles. They were committed "to achieving first-class integration and a new identity for Mexican Americans in a period shaped by the Great Depression and World War II."[7] Their approach was to take a proactive stance through civil rights movements and to encourage fellow Mexican Americans to participate in the electoral process. In this way, they hoped to achieve first-class citizenry for their constituents. Most of them—Judge Bravo was one—probably had little interest in radical philosophies, such as those advocated by Emma Tenayuca, a labor union organizer in San Antonio during the 1930s, or by other militant groups in the United States. They did, however, support the political agendas of activists like José T. Canales, Alonso Perales, Dr. Héctor P. García (the GI Forum founder), and others.

If the political tenure of Judge Manuel Bravo makes clear that he had the same ideological outlook and patriotic sentiments as his generational cohorts, it also provides a more precise picture of the human dimensions characteristic of Tejano leaders. According to Gómez-Quiñones's description of Mexican-American leaders during the 1940s and 1950s:

They were also more likely to participate in several organizations and civic projects concurrently, to be competently bilingual, church-affiliated, married and with children, and decorous in their behavior. A rule was pronounced commitment to civic equities and to organizational action. Formal organization was understood to be the basis for the advancement of goals. The practiced mode was negotiation. Among the formal leadership, responsibility, accountability, and public discourse were consensual duties. Leaders were invariably criticized, but this was part of the leadership experience and a usual part of organizational life.[8]

Bravo and his contemporaries in Texas who made up the leadership cast certainly fit this description, but the jefe político often had to have more than an understanding of the values of organization as a means for getting things done. Many were instinctively paternalistic and altruistic human beings, as was Judge Bravo. Like Bravo, they often possessed special strengths (a *don*) or unique skills. They had the capacity to develop and nurture political connections, which came in handy during occasions requiring wheeling and dealing (*movidas chuecas*—shady deals) or dictating cooperation with other bosses, as part of the political quilt, to elect certain candidates for statewide office. The Tejano patrón could be as slick, clever, and cunning as Anglo bosses.

Further, Tejano bosses, like their white counterparts, acquired political powers that extended beyond county limits. As the example of Bravo shows, they generally were well-informed leaders who attended state and sometimes national party conventions, and whose personal networks kept them abreast of interstate and intrastate events. Certainly, Anglos looked up to Tejano leaders just as they "respected" white bosses. Mexican-American leaders had a talent for working harmoniously and effectively with Anglos, even high-powered Anglo figures such as governors, senators, congressmen, judges, and many others. Due to alliances, mutual relationships of trust, hard-working campaigns and political favors, often they were just a telegram away from Lyndon B. Johnson, Lloyd Bentsen, Jr., Joe M. Kilgore, Ralph W. Yarborough, and other top-level politicians.

Still, politics in Zapata County from 1937 to 1957 embraced things other than the coordination of county matters, political campaigning, and power wielding on the part of the elites. There, as elsewhere, rank-and-file folks, both from the working class and the well-to-do, acted out their vested interests, independent mindedness, philosophical stands, patriotic duties, and civic responsibilities. In short, people were active agents in the events that unfolded around them.

Equal to the task of engaging in petty politics, just as the bosses were, Zapatans at times turned to unorthodox or frivolous ways to have a say-so in politics, as when unknown parties turned off the lights during the Kazen rally of July, 1940, or when factions took conflicting stands on the Falcon Dam issue merely to embarrass the opposition. On the more serious side, voters could buck the system. While people generally remained loyal to the machine, they might bolt for a candidate other than the boss-supported contender, as occurred when the charismatic Philip Kazen ran as an independent during the 1940 Democratic primary. Eight years later, however, the Tejano constituency failed to give Kazen the necessary votes and instead went with Lloyd Bentsen, Jr., even if the latter was not the boss's favorite.

Stands taken on county political issues stemmed from information sifted at a grassroots level, perhaps away from the watchful eye of the bosses. Voters habitually discussed problems, viewpoints, or a candidate's qualifications during informal gatherings at the main plaza, the local taverns, the barbershop, or the beauty salon. Judgments made rested on the populist conception of democracy, acquired by way of contacts with the church, school, employers, the *mayordomo* (ranch foreman), the local newspaper, and the middle class as well as through the Partido Viejo and Partido Nuevo's political propaganda. Common laborers might have had a vague and abstract notion of democracy, but they took their cues from a number of sources. Tejano voters knew that the vote, persuasion, propaganda, and movidas could produce patronage, work opportunities, and other benefits.

Both political parties realized the voting power of the citizenry. At every election campaign, political factions vied for the people's vote, running on different platforms and taking contrasting positions on the several issues. Victories were not always a sure thing. That is why Judge Bravo had to campaign hard during elections and count on every vote, especially absentee ones, and had to visit even the most remote ranchos. But as long as the Democratic Party kept meeting their expectations and demands, voters continued supporting the political machine at every election; as the faithful supporters used to say, *malo por conocido, que bueno por no conocer,* which translates loosely as "better the devil you know . . ."

The political setting that explains the Bravo era ceased to exist by the last four decades of the twentieth century. After Bravo's departure from Zapata County politics, the changing social, educational, and economic demographics of South Texas and the electoral changes brought on by legislation and court orders made it highly improbable for any ambitious politician to become a boss, much less for a political machine to operate. The age of bossism in the trans–Nueces River area has passed into the history books as an interesting and colorful era that once enlivened the pageant of Texas politics.

NOTES

PREFACE

1. Juan Gilberto Quezada, "Judge Manuel B. Bravo: A Political Leader in South Texas, 1937–1957," *Journal of South Texas* 5 (Spring 1992): 51; J. Gilberto Quezada, "The Box Family Roots and South Texas Politics: Judge Manuel Box Bravo," *East Texas Historical Journal* 34, 2 (Aug. 1996): 21.

INTRODUCTION

1. Raymond A. Mohl, *The New City: Urban America in the Industrial Age, 1860–1920*, pp. 83–85, 106; Robert W. Cherny, *American Politics in the Gilded Age, 1868–1900*, pp. 6–8.

2. Mohl, *The New City*, pp. 83–84.

3. Frank R. Kent, *The Great Game of Politics*, p. 76.

4. Ibid., p. 65.

5. Robert Merton, *Social Theory and Social Structure*, pp. 126, 128.

6. Ibid., p. 128.

7. Evan Anders, *Boss Rule in South Texas: The Progressive Era*, p. 281.

8. John Closner resigned as Hidalgo County treasurer for stealing $160,000. In Cameron County, the Democratic party leaders had embezzled $38,000. Anders, *Boss Rule*, p. 282.

9. Evan Anders, "James B. Wells and the Brownsville Patronage Fight, 1912–1917" (M.A. thesis, University of Texas at Austin, 1970), pp. 6–9, 31.

10. Seymour J. Mandelbaum's 1965 study of the notorious William Marcy Tweed, *Boss Tweed's New York*, added other attributes to the repertoire of the political boss. Mandelbaum described Tweed as "a master of the strategy of the leadership which succeeds," "a master communicator," a skillful manipulator with an "ability to ingratiate himself with men of respectability and with law politicians," a visionary with a "breadth of political imagination," and a person who "was predictable." Tweed's other practices involved cor-

ruption at election time. His personal goal of attaining huge amounts of wealth was made possible through alliances with other influential entrepreneurs (Seymour J. Mandelbaum, *Boss Tweed's New York,* pp. 67–75). Joel A. Tarr's 1971 work, *A Study in Boss Politics: William Lorimer of Chicago,* concisely conceptualized into a three-tier model the operations of an urban boss and his political machine. In the first level, the boss sought the voters' loyalty by providing social welfare through jobs, loans, and small favors from law enforcement agencies. At the second tier, Boss Lorimer offered patronage for the members of the machine; and finally, the political machine worked with business interests "to exploit the economic opportunities presented by the growing city" (Joel Arthur Tarr, *A Study in Boss Politics,* pp. 72–76). Zane L. Miller, in *Boss Cox's Cincinnati: Urban Politics in the Progressive Era,* described his subject as "an evil genius, a master at the manipulation of men who possessed an almost magical power to inspire trust and secure obedience from his followers." Through a series of alliances with other bosses and with the business world, Cox accumulated vast amounts of personal wealth. His bon vivant living style was reflected in a mansion decorated with expensive works of art, good cigars, and a true philanthropic philosophy (Zane L. Miller, *Boss Cox's Cincinnati,* pp. 91–92).

11. Mohl, *The New City,* pp. 100–107. For an in-depth analysis of machine politics, refer to Peter McCaffery, *When Bosses Ruled Philadelphia,* and Oliver E. Allen, *The Rise and Fall of Tammany Hall.*

12. Douglas O. Weeks, "The Texas-Mexican and the Politics of South Texas," *American Political Science Review,* 24, 3 (Aug. 1930): 613. During the depression, the boss provided some relief, either with money by way of loans or in food commodities. In a personal type of a relationship, the *patrón* became the godfather (*el padrino*) for many children, delivered countless eulogies, attended numerous weddings, and financially helped many young Tejanos when they celebrated a daughter's *quinceañera* (a traditional ritual for Hispanic girls celebrating a fifteenth birthday).

13. Edgar G. Shelton, *Political Conditions among Texas Mexicans along the Río Grande,* p. 32.

14. Ibid., p. 35.

15. Quotation cited in Anders, *Boss Rule,* pp. 59–60.

16. Douglas E. Foley et al., *From Peones to Politics: Ethnic Relations in a South Texas Town,* pp. 25–26.

17. Shelton, *Political Conditions among Texas Mexicans,* pp. 106, 74.

18. John R. Peavey, *Echoes from the Río Grande,* p. 46.

19. Peavey does point out that both political parties accommodated the votes of the Tejano and Anglo illiterate laborers alike. To simplify the election process for them, the Democratic Party chose blue as their color and the Republican Party selected red, except in Starr County, where the parties reversed their colors. This practice was prevalent during the Progressive era, and in some counties lasted until the 1930s. Peavey, *Echoes,* pp. 46–49.

20. John E. Clark, *The Fall of the Duke of Duval: A Prosecutor's Journal,* p. 23.

21. Cherny, *American Politics,* pp. 7–8.

22. Wilfrid C. Bailey, "Problems in Relocating the People of Zapata, Texas," *Texas Journal of Science* 7 (March 1955): 29.

23. Manuel B. Bravo, Jr., interview with author, Laredo, Dec. 24, 1990, tape recording.

24. Ibid. Many leaders of the Democratic Party justified the spoils system as a means of retaining "huge armies of loyal retainers to identify and turn out voters and to distribute party tickets at polling places." Cherny, *American Politics,* pp. 15–16.

25. Seth Shepard McKay, *Texas and the Fair Deal, 1945–1952,* p. 240.

26. George Norris Green, *The Establishment in Texas Politics: The Primitive Years, 1938–1957,* p. 5. The Río Grande Valley was known for being boss dominated, mainly by the "Big Four *patrons* [sic], whose territory stretched out along the Río Grande from Eagle Pass to Brownsville." See Joe Phipps, *Summer Stock: Behind the Scenes with LBJ in '48 — Recollection of a Political Drama,* p. 238.

27. Quoted from an interview by Dugger with Judge Bravo on Nov. 20, 1969, in Ronnie Dugger, *The Politician: The Life and Times of Lyndon Johnson,* p. 323. Seven years later, in 1989, James Reston in his biography of John Connally claimed that Parr ruled over Duval, Jim Wells, Starr, Zapata, and Webb counties and that his machine "had gained its outrageous dimensions over four decades, and could deliver scandalously lopsided votes." James Reston, Jr. *The Lone Star: The Life of John Connally,* p. 142.

28. Robert A. Caro, *The Years of Lyndon Johnson: Means of Ascent,* p. 187.

29. Ibid; Robert A. Caro, *The Years of Lyndon Johnson: The Path to Power,* pp. 720–23.

30. Robert Dallek, *Lone Star Rising: Lyndon Johnson and His Times, 1908–1960,* p. 222; Phipps, *Behind the Scenes with LBJ,* p. 238.

31. Dallek, *Lone Star Rising,* p. 340.

32. Judge Bravo used the word *compadre* as a term of friendship and as a reference to close working relationships among elected officials in South Texas. In the 1940 Democratic primary, Duval County gave O'Daniel 3,728 votes; seven other contenders got 181. In the 1944 Democratic primary, Coke Stevenson took Starr County with 1,396 votes, while eight other candidates collectively received 16. John Gunther, *Inside USA,* p. 844.

33. During the Democratic primaries, Sheriff Martínez assigned additional bodyguards or *pistoleros,* not only to maintain order but also to intimidate the opponents.

34. For a detailed study of bossism in Hidalgo County and the Lower Río Grande Valley, see Ruth Griffen Spence's work, "The Nickel Plated Highway to Hell: A Political History of Hidalgo County, 1852–1934."

35. Spence, "The Nickel Plated Highway to Hell," p. 38. Baker and his cronies, with the political muscle and support of Jim Wells, controlled and manipulated county politics. The alliance among Baker, Parr, and Wells solidified the important and decisive Tejano bloc votes that held the balance of power in many border counties, especially when State Senator Archie Parr represented Cameron, Hidalgo, Starr, Zapata, Webb, Duval, and ten other South Texas counties, from about 1915 to 1934. This may very well be where the myth of the regionally powerful Parr got started, except that his son George is credited with controlling these many counties.

36. A. W. Cameron to Archie Parr, July 29, 1933, Manuel B. Bravo Papers (hereafter cited as MBBP).

37. "Reception Line Will Greet Visitors at the Bank," *Edinburg Valley Review,* Feb. 25, 1927, Pan American Library, University of Texas (hereafter cited as PAL).

38. Josefa V. Bravo, interview with author, Zapata, Dec. 24, 1990, tape recordings.

39. Ibid.

40. James "Eddie" Bravo, Sr., is the oldest son of Judge Bravo and Josefa Villarreal Bravo. During the 1960s, he served as chair of the Zapata County Democratic Party. J. E. Bravo, Sr., interview with author, Zapata, July 5, 1991, tape recording.

41. Estate of Manuel B. Bravo, Sr., Judge's Probate Docket, vol. 4, no. 891, Aug. 14, 1984, Zapata County Courthouse (hereafter cited as ZCC), pp. 601–603.

42. James C. Parish to author, Feb. 8, 1996 (copy in possession of the author).

43. Mario T. García, *Mexican Americans: Leadership, Ideology, and Identity, 1930–1960*, pp. 19–22.

44. Bravo and other Tejano leaders of this epoch became "a political generation of middle-class and working-class leaders who were determined to wage protracted struggles for change in the Mexican communities and who demanded a rightful place for Mexican Americans in U.S. society. This was the Mexican-American Generation." García, *Mexican Americans*, pp. 16–20.

45. Kenneth L. Stewart and Arnoldo De León, *Not Room Enough: Mexicans, Anglos, and Socio-Economic Change in Texas, 1850–1900*, pp. 51, 52.

46. Ibid.

47. "Otras 2 Causas De Mandamus," *El Día* (Laredo), Nov. 1, 1940, MBBP; "La Falta De Representación," *El Día*, Nov. 2, 1940, MBBP; "Carta Abierta—Open Letter," MBBP.

CHAPTER 1

1. Quezada, "Box Family Roots" pp. 18–19.

2. Marriage License of David Bravo and Emma Box, issued on May 24, 1900, Hidalgo County, book 2, Hidalgo County Marriage Records, p. 261. In a sociological/demographic study, Dr. James A. Sandos concluded that intermarriages in Hidalgo County in 1900 accounted for nearly 47 percent of the total population: "The mingling of families through intermarriage and godparenthood up to 1900 produced a precarious but real social balance." James A. Sandos, *Rebellion in the Borderlands: Anarchism and the Plan of San Diego, 1904–1923*, pp. 63–64; *U.S. Census, 1900* (microfilm), San Antonio Public Library (hereafter cited as SAPL).

3. Elías Cavazos, a first cousin, grew up with Manuel in El Rancho Sauz. Elías Cavazos, interview with author, Zapata, Sept. 29, 1990, tape recording.

4. Ibid.

5. Quezada, "Box Family Roots," p. 19.

6. The schooling practices in McAllen resembled similar ones throughout other Lower Río Grande Valley school districts. Manuel's early learning experience was a true reflection of the larger societal attitude Anglos had toward Tejano students. Many Valley Anglos farmers and educators held the same pervasive attitude about the superiority of white children over those with Mexican ancestry. As sociologist/historian David Montejano noted, "Mexican schools were substandard, with inadequate supplies and poor facilities. Their Anglo teachers, who frequently shared the common Anglo belief about Mexican biological and intellectual inferiority, received lower salaries. . . . And politics in the farm counties, the [school district] trustee explained, meant that the Mexican school policy was influenced by the needs of local growers." David Montejano, *Anglos and Mexicans in the Making of Texas, 1836–1986*, pp. 192–94; Arnoldo De León, *They Called Them Greasers: Anglo Attitudes toward Mexicans in Texas, 1821–1900*, p. 105.

7. The segregated school system in Hidalgo County in 1928 included 71 percent Tejanos, with Anglo students constituting the other 29 percent. Few Tejanos made it beyond the elementary or the middle school level; however, once that number started increasing during the 1920s, the segregation of classes extended to the high school. Montejano, *Anglos and Mexicans*, p. 169. Ironically for the few Tejano students who attended the McAllen public school system, the name of the school's yearbook had a Spanish name— *El Espejo* (The Mirror). All the prestigious titles of "Most Beautiful Girl," "Most Hand-

some Boy," "Most Popular Girl," "Most Popular Boy," "Best All Around Girl," and "Best All Around Boy," were won by Anglo students. *El Espejo, 1937* (copy in possession of the author).

8. Just nine years before, a group of politicians—County Judge Chapin; County Treasurer A. Y. Baker, Sheriff John Closner, County Clerk A. E. Chávez, and Tax Assessor and Collector Joe Alamía—had relocated the county seat from Hidalgo to its present location in Edinburg. Spence, "The Nickel Plated Highway to Hell," pp. 17–18.

9. Ibid., p. 122. Luis de la Rosa and Aniceto Pizaña are credited with initiating the revolutionary plan in San Diego, Texas. Their recruits came mainly from northern Mexico and South Texas. The movement sought to create a new republic constituted of the states of Texas, New Mexico, Arizona, Colorado, and California. For detailed accounts of the plan, refer to chapter 5 in Sandos, *Rebellion in the Borderlands,* pp. 79–100.

10. Emma Box de Bravo to Inspector of Immigration, Feb. 23, 1917. Letter in possession of Virginia Bravo López, Mission, Texas.

11. Anti-Tejano incidents escalated to what Montejano described as "a virtual war zone during 1915–1917," when "between 1907 and 1912 sixteen Mexicans were killed by Rangers and peace officers in Hidalgo and Cameron counties." Montejano, *Anglos and Mexicans,* pp. 116–17.

12. When the city of Edinburg was incorporated on September 9, 1919, A. Y. Baker was elected mayor by 53 votes. Marshall McIlhenny and J. W. Heacock won as city commissioners. "Edinburg Voted a City in 1917," *Daily Review,* May 18, 1954; Paul Jackson and Harry Quin, eds., *Edinburg: A Story of a Town,* pp. 26, 48.

13. *The New Handbook of Texas,* vol. 1, p. 342.

14. Ibid., p. 343; Allan Engleman, "A. Y. Baker, Political Ruler–1920," *Valley Review,* Dec. 7, 1952; Izora Skinner, "A. Y. Baker Home," *Edinburg Daily Review,* June 27, 1976; "Death Claims A. Y. Baker, Millionaire Sheriff and Political Power in Río Grande Valley," *Uvalde News,* Nov. 7, 1930.

15. "Millionaire Hidalgo Sheriff, Political Storm Center, Dies Following Stroke of Apoplexy," *Daily Review,* Nov. 3, 1930.

16. Weeks, "The Texas-Mexican," p. 620; Anders, *Boss Rule,* p. 281; Peavey, *Echoes,* pp. 46–49.

17. Brad Smith, "One Night That Averted Civil War in Hidalgo County," unpublished essay, Hidalgo County Historical Museum, Mar. 6, 1989, p. 2.

18. Ibid., p. 7.

19. Josefa V. Bravo interview.

20. "Reception Line Will Greet Visitors at the Bank," *Edinburg Valley Review,* Feb. 25, 1927, PAL.

21. Quezada, "Judge Manuel B. Bravo," p. 53.

22. Josefa V. Bravo interview. Manuel B. Bravo Baptism Certificate, Our Lady of Guadalupe Church, Mission, Texas, vol. 1, no. 237, p. 171.

23. *Saint Martin Council Year Book,* Nov., 1930, p. 41, MBBP; "Se Forma Una Nueva Asociación Católica en Edinburg," *El Defensor* (Edinburg), Feb. 14, 1930, Barker Texas History Center (hereafter cited as BTHC), The University of Texas, Austin; Bravo to Arturo Z. Flores, June 20, 1964, MBBP; "Convención De La Orden De Los Caballeros De Colón," *El Defensor,* Feb. 21, 1930, BTHC; "Por La Orden de los Caballeros de Colón," *El Defensor,* Mar. 21, 1930, BTHC; "Sociales y Personales—Viajeros," *El Defensor,* Oct. 3, 1930, BTHC. The Spanish newspaper *El Defensor* considered itself to be the "official organ of the LULAC."

24. The three members from McAllen included Manuel Box Bravo, Thomas J. Baker, and E. B. Reyna. "110 To Be Raised to 4th Degree," *San Antonio Express*, April 20, 1930, SAPL; "K.C. Degrees Conferred on 110 Here Sunday," *Laredo Times*, April 20, 1930, Laredo Public Library (hereafter cited as LPL).

25. "Convention of the LULAC, May 18–19, 1929," Oliver Douglas Weeks Collection, box 1, folder 6, Benson Latin American Collection (hereafter cited as BLAC), The University of Texas, Austin. In developing their constitution and by-laws, the League of Latin-American Citizens borrowed the format from the already established group, the Order of Sons of America. Robert A. Cuéllar, *A Social and Political History of the Mexican American Population of Texas, 1929–1963,* p. 10.

26. Oliver Douglas Weeks Collection, box 1, folders 4 and 6, BLAC; De León, *They Called Them Greasers,* pp. 92–93. For a descriptive narrative of the evolution of the LULAC in South Texas, refer to chapter 2 in Benjamin Márquez, *LULAC: The Evolution of a Mexican American Political Organization,* pp. 15–38.

27. "Convention of the LULAC, at Corpus Christi, Texas, May 18 and 19, 1929," Oliver Douglas Weeks Collection, box 1, folder 6, BLAC.

28. Ibid.

29. "Special Meeting of the LULAC, at McAllen, Texas," Oliver Douglas Weeks Collection, box 1, folder 6, BLAC.

30. "Latin American League to Hold Edinburg Meeting," *Brownsville Herald,* May 2, 1931, MBBP.

31. Data contained in a federal application that Judge Bravo submitted in 1964 to the International Boundary and Water Commission. Application for Federal Employment, Form 57, April 12, 1964, Lyndon B. Johnson Library (hereafter cited as LBJL), Austin.

32. Shelton, *Political Conditions among Texas Mexicans,* p. 77; Montejano, *Anglos and Mexicans,* pp. 147–48.

33. Spence, "The Nickel Plated Highway to Hell," pp. 55, 88–89.

34. Ibid., pp. 38, 53, 73–75; Peavey, *Echoes,* p. 38; Montejano, *Anglos and Mexicans,* pp. 147–48.

35. Spence, "The Nickel Plated Highway to Hell," p. 38; Milo Kearney and Anthony Knopp, *Border Cuates: A History of the U.S.-Mexican Twin Cities,* p. 210.

36. Spence, "The Nickel Plated Highway to Hell," pp. 73–75.

37. Clyde W. Norris, "History of Hidalgo County," M.S. Thesis, Texas College of Arts and Industries, 1942, pp. 69–70.

38. Spence, "The Nickel Plated Highway to Hell," pp. 103–106.

39. Application for Federal Employment, Form 57. Alfredo N. Vela, Sr., Chief Deputy District Clerk since 1910 and a Baker follower, exiled himself to Brownsville when the GGL took over all county offices in 1930.

40. For a genealogical study of Lina H. Box, refer to Quezada, "Box Family Roots," pp. 17–19.

41. Spence, "The Nickel Plated Highway to Hell," pp. 109–110.

42. "Candidacy of Bravo Filed," *Edinburg Valley Review,* Apr. 8, 1932; Josefa V. Bravo interview.

43. Josefa V. Bravo interview; "Programa del Club Demócrata Femenil Latino-Americano," *El Defensor,* May 6, 1932, BTHC. Political rallies for the candidates were announced in the county's Democratic bilingual newspaper. "Celebró Una Junta el Partido Demócrata en Mercedes, Texas," *Hidalgo County Democrat,* July 15, 1932, BTHC.

44. Griffin received 1,273 votes and Merts garnered 1,213. "Complete Returns in

Demo Primaries are Compiled," *Edinburg Valley Review,* July 27, 1932; "Completion of Political Tickets Shows 106 Candidates in Hidalgo County Primary Races This Year," *Edinburg Valley Review,* June 25, 1932.

45. "Elect These Democrats for a New and Better Deal in Hidalgo County," *Edinburg Valley Review,* Oct. 26, 1932.

46. "Old Ring, New Bosses vs Uncontrolled Democratic Party." (Paid Political Advertisement), *Edinburg Valley Review,* 1932; second quotation cited in Spence, "The Nickel Plated Highway to Hell," p. 108.

47. "Sweeping Demo Victory on Tuesday Seen by Chairman," *Edinburg Valley Review,* Nov. 7, 1932.

48. "Final Ballot Returns Show G.G.L. Victory," *Edinburg Valley Review,* Nov. 11, 1932; *Texas Almanac, 1933,* pp. 264–88.

49. Josefa V. Bravo interview.

50. Manuel had sold their first house and purchased a bigger one with "oak floors, French doors, big hallways, etc." Josefa V. Bravo interview; J. E. Bravo, Sr., interview.

51. A. W. Cameron to Hon. Archie Parr, July 29, 1933, MBBP.

52. Hesiquio Cuéllar, a first cousin of Antonio Martínez Cuéllar (the patriarch of the Martínez family, who started his political career in 1900 as county commissioner of precinct 2 [San Ygnacio]), owned three mercantile stores in the county. He was the hide and animal inspector in 1918, but in the next election he lost his post to Gilberto González. Hesiquio ran unsuccessfully at least three times for county commissioner of precinct 1 (the town of Zapata) from 1926 to 1932. Though his political career was short-lived, he remained actively involved with the Democratic Party and in civic activities. His parents, Felipe Cuéllar, Sr., and Albina Cuéllar de Cuéllar, were direct descendants of the original Cuéllar pioneer settlers. *Record of Election Returns,* vol. 1., ZCC, pp. 39–87; Davis, *Historical Encyclopedia of Texas,* p. 1007.

53. Josefa V. Bravo interview; J. E. Bravo, Sr., interview.

54. Webb County is the largest county in South Texas at 3,295 sq. mi., followed by Hidalgo County at 1,541 sq. mi., and Starr County at 1,207 sq. mi. *Texas Almanac 1936,* pp. 232–33; *1939–40,* p. 465.

55. *The Texas Almanac, 1936,* pp. 138, 161.

56. Ibid., pp. 141–42.

57. *Texas Almanac, 1941–42,* pp. 105–107; *1956–57,* pp. 134–36; *1961–62,* p. 65; *1990–91,* pp. 197–267.

58. *Texas Almanac, 1952–53,* p. 619; *1956–57,* p. 720; *1947–48,* p. 535; *The New Handbook of Texas,* vol. 6, p. 1143; J. E. Bravo, Sr., telephone interview, July 11, 1997.

59. *Texas Almanac, 1939–40,* p. 465; *1941–42,* p. 522.

60. *Texas Almanac, 1939–40,* p. 465; *1943–44,* p. 152; *1947–48,* p. 220; *1956–57,* pp. 720–21.

61. *Texas Almanac, 1943–44,* pp. 166–69.

62. *Texas Almanac, 1947–48,* pp. 237, 240.

63. Virgil N. Lott and Mercurio Martínez, *The Kingdom of Zapata,* pp. 22–27, 84–91; J. E. Bravo, Sr., telephone interview, July 11, 1997.

64. A brief discourse on the "Old and New Towns of Zapata," prepared by Judge Bravo for IBWC Commissioner J. F. Friedkin, July 3, 1969, MBBP.

65. *Texas Almanac, 1939–40,* p. 465; *1941–42,* p. 522; *1947–48,* p. 535; *1949–50,* p. 607.

66. *Texas Almanac, 1945–46,* p. 512; *1947–48,* p. 535.

67. During the Progressive era, County Judge Angus Peter Spohn led a Republican Party–controlled county for over twenty years, 1898–1921. Lott and Martínez, *Kingdom of Zapata*, p. 64.

68. Lott and Martínez, *Kingdom of Zapata*, pp. 53, 62, 188, 199; *U.S. Census, 1920* (microfilm), SAPL.

69. David Montejano, *Anglos and Mexicans*, pp. 246–47.

70. William Curtis Bryson, "The Social Basis of South Texas Bossism" (B.A. Thesis, Harvard University, 1969), pp. 6–7.

71. The other eight counties were Brooks, La Salle, Dimmit, Willacy, Kleberg, Zavala, Frio, and Jim Wells. Bryson also categorized Jim Hogg and Maverick as "moderately boss-run" counties. Bryson, "South Texas Bossism," p. 26.

72. Ibid., pp. 28, 33, 110; Montejano, *Anglos and Mexicans,* pp. 246–49.

73. Henry Redmond was the first county judge in 1858 and served for about six years. D. D. Lovell followed him from 1869 to 1873 and he was succeeded by Theodore S. Dix, 1873–78; W. D. Langston, 1878–80; and John Orismus, 1880–82. Jean Y. and Robert W. Fish, comp., *Elected Officials of Zapata County, Texas, 1858–1986,* pp. 1–8.

74. Lott and Martínez, *Kingdom of Zapata*, pp. 2, 64; Bryson, "South Texas Bossism," p. 61. A study by Paul Casdorph, *A History of the Republican Party in Texas, 1865–1965,* revealed that of seventeen counties in Texas that voted for Rutherford B. Hayes in 1876, only Zapata and Starr of the border counties voted for the new president (ch. 3, fn. 34, p. 277). In 1884, Zapata was the only Tejano county out of nineteen to support James G. Blaine (ch. 4, fn. 21, p. 279). Zapata and Webb were the only two border counties to carry William McKinley in 1896 (ch. 4, fn. 124, p. 282), and Cameron County joined the former two counties for McKinley in 1900 (ch. 5, fn. 30, p. 283). In 1904, out of ten counties, Zapata, Webb, and El Paso went with Teddy Roosevelt (ch. 5, fn. 58, p. 284). In the 1912 presidential election, Zapata and Webb voted for Taft, and four years later, Zapata and Maverick were the only two counties to support Charles Evans Hughs, pp. 108–16.

Spohn and his machine had a unique political understanding with the Democratic Party in Zapata County. From 1896 to 1920, the people voted unanimously in the national and county general election for the Republican ticket and gave the same lopsided votes to the Democratic candidates for state and district offices. It was not until the 1928 election that Zapata County went with Alfred E. Smith, a Democrat, over Herbert C. Hoover. During these same election years—and in contrast to Webb and Zapata counties—Starr, Hidalgo, and Cameron voted steadfastly for the Democratic presidential candidate (J. Will Falvella, "Kingdom of Zapata Now at Peace with the World," *San Antonio Express,* Feb. 4, 1923, SAPL). According to historian Jerry D. Thompson's explanation of why Webb County supported the Republican Party from 1896 to 1912: "The romance with the Republicans was consummated . . . when an agreement was reached in which the Independent Club would support Republican candidates for state and national offices, and the Republicans would help elect Independent Club candidates locally. It was indeed a marriage of convenience." Jerry D. Thompson, *Warm Weather and Bad Whiskey: The 1886 Laredo Election Riot,* p. 148.

75. State Representative D. W. Glasscock is credited with initiating legislation to create Jim Hogg County in an effort to have mostly Anglo ranchers control the county. Montejano, *Anglos and Mexicans,* pp. 134, 139–40.

76. Fish and Fish, *Elected Officials of Zapata,* pp. 20–23.

77. Leopoldo Martínez's wife, María Benavides, came from a prominent border family; her father, José Benavides García, served as justice of the peace for precinct 3 (Lopeño),

for two years (1898–1900). Then for the next ten years, 1906–16, he served as the county's district and county clerk. José M. Sánchez, Leopoldo's uncle, followed García for the next four years. In 1921, Sánchez became the county judge, a post he held for eight years. It was this political move that allowed his twenty-year-old nephew, Leopoldo, to succeed him as district and county clerk. Another uncle, Ygnacio Sánchez (José's brother) was tax assessor in 1912, and in 1928, he doubled as sheriff/tax collector, a position he held for twelve years. In 1940, Leopoldo left his post and took over Ygnacio's job as sheriff/tax collector for the next eighteen years. In the meantime, Leopoldo's brother, Juventino Martínez, had a short stint in politics, serving as county commissioner for precinct 1 (Zapata) from 1928 to 1932. Another brother, Francisco, served as chair of the Zapata County Democratic Executive Committee and was succeeded in the early 1940s by his sister, Josefa.

Manuel Medina, another influential businessperson and staunch Democrat, was actively involved in civic affairs. Valentín Medina, Manuel's father and a leading merchant, purchased the bank of Zapata in 1930, where his two sons, Manuel and Santos, handled the business transactions. The Medinas were descendants of Pedro Bustamante, who received a Spanish land grant in 1802. Manuel's first introduction to politics happened on February 23, 1932, when the commissioners' court appointed him to the vacant post of county commissioner of precinct 1. The following November, he ran for this post and won. Two years later, Manuel resigned as commissioner and accepted a position in one of President Roosevelt's relief programs in the county. The commissioners' court appointed Adán Gutiérrez, a prominent businessperson, to succeed him. In 1937, the commissioners' court created a position for Manuel as the official road superintendent of Zapata County. About a year later, during the 1938 Democratic primary, at the age of twenty-seven, he won back his county commissioner's seat by defeating the incumbent Gutiérrez, a seat he would hold for the next twenty-two years.

After his defeat, Adán Gutiérrez retired from public office and dedicated his life to the business of livestock and agriculture. Both of his parents, Evaristo Gutiérrez and Josefa Bustamante, came from South Texas' oldest pioneer families and used their large landholdings for ranching. Throughout the years, the Gutiérrez family continued to remain influential in the social and civic affairs of the county.

Santos Yzaguirre was county commissioner for precinct 4—the Falcon area—and served in this capacity from 1928 until 1942. He was a lifetime resident of the county, getting involved in the cattle industry and in ranching. His parents, Tomás Yzaguirre and Crecencia Ramírez, were considered to be among the early settlers of the county. The Yzaguirres have been involved in local politics since about 1894.

Primitivo Uribe, one of the politicians of longest standing in Zapata County's political history, was county treasurer when Bravo took office as county judge in 1937. Born in San Ygnacio (political precinct 2) to Trinidad Uribe and Francisca Garza, Primitivo came from a pioneer Zapata County ranching family heavily involved in civic and community activities. At the age of eighteen, Primitivo was elected to the post of district clerk in 1899. He subsequently held several public offices, ranging from notary public and justice of the peace to county commissioner of precinct 2. In 1920, he won the Democratic Party seat for sheriff and tax collector, an office he held for six years. He remained with the political machine as county treasurer from 1926 until about 1956.

Another native of San Ygnacio was Proceso Martínez, Jr., a lifelong supporter of the Democratic machine. He came from a family involved in politics, ranching, and business, and is considered the don of Zapata politicians, having served as county commissioner of precinct 2 from 1910 to about 1958—a total of forty-eight years of public service. A teacher by profession, Don Proceso received his preparatory training at St. Edwards University, the University of Texas at Austin, and Southwest Texas State Teachers College in San Marcos.

Proceso's older brother, Mercurio Martínez, was also involved in county politics. In 1899, he served for one year as county judge and then as notary public and justice of the peace for precinct 2. From 1912 to 1916, he served as the county treasurer. Even though Mercurio never ran for public office again, he remained a strong influence within the Democratic Party. In the spring of 1951, the county commissioners contracted him to coauthor *The Kingdom of Zapata* as a tribute to the historical, cultural, social, and political heritage of an area where settlement dated back to the eighteenth century. He was the father of Mercurio Martínez, Jr., the county judge of Webb County during the 1990s.

Both Mercurio and Proceso learned to serve the public and to become actively involved in county affairs from their father, Don Proceso, Sr. In 1859, Don Proceso, Sr., helped his father (Don Cósme Martínez) expand the family's farming and cattle operations in a large tract of brush country that had originally been part of a Spanish land grant. During and after the Civil War, Don Proceso, Sr., engaged in a successful mercantile business that involved the exportation of Mexican products to markets in Laredo, San Antonio, and Corpus Christi. In 1870, Governor Edmund J. Davis appointed him to the Board of Appeals, a body responsible for reviewing land titles and other matters during the Reconstruction period of Texas history. The following year, Don Proceso, Sr., was appointed district clerk, and he also served as county commissioner of precinct 2 for five years. In 1882, he was elected again to the same post and served the county until 1894. He died in 1937, at the age of ninety-six.

In precinct 3 (Lopeño), the González family dominated in the political arena from the early 1900s. The Ramírez family, however, had created the town after the Spanish land grant (porción 21) given to Ysabel María Sánchez in 1761 had passed on to them. Then, in 1918, the Ramírez family took over the political reins, when Leandro Ramírez won the election for county commissioner. Four years later, Ildefonso Ramírez was elected but lost to the Benavides family. Ildefonso's economic influence extended to his cattle and ranching interests, and he also operated a large cotton gin. On February 23, 1932, the county commissioners accepted the resignation of S. G. Benavides as county commissioner, and appointed thirty-six-year-old Democrat Guillermo González, a rancher and farmer. During that election year, Guillermo won his own seat, a public office he held for eighteen years. His nephew, Santiago González, a well-known Republican, took over that post for the next twenty years, 1952–72.

Precinct 4 (Falcon) also has a rich history embedded in Spanish legacy. Initially, the area (porción 15) was granted by the Spanish crown to José Clemente Ramírez on July 7, 1757. Through the years, as the title of the original grantees passed to other Ramírez heirs, the hamlet came to be called Ramireño. It was not until establishment of a post office in 1915 that the name changed to Falcon, even though the Ramírez family still controlled the economic, social, and political life of the town. From about 1898, the county commissioner's seat changed families several times, alternating between Miguel de la Garza and Andrés Salinas. In 1914, Leandro Ramírez won the post, and in 1924, Regulo Ramírez, a distant relative, succeeded him. Eduardo Yzaguirre controlled the 1922 election, and in 1928, Santos Yzaguirre, another relative, won that political seat. The Yzaguirres' stranglehold was broken during the 1942 election, when Lizandro Ramírez (Leandro's son), a descendant of the original Spanish grantees, became county commissioner and held that office for the next twenty-two years. Fish and Fish, *Elected Officials of Zapata*, pp. 13–34; Record of

Election Returns, vol. 1., ZCC, pp. 39–87; Ellis Arthur Davis, *The Historical Encyclopedia of Texas,* pp. 905–1009; Lott and Martínez, *Kingdom of Zapata,* pp. 6–7, 118, 165, 166; Zapata County Commissioners Court Minutes (hereafter cited as ZCCCM), Feb. 23, 1932, vol. 5, ZCC, pp. 55–56; ZCCCM, Feb. 12, 1932, vol. 5, ZCC, pp. 54–55; ZCCCM, July 10, 1934, vol. 5, ZCC, p. 94; ZCCCM, Nov. 8, 1937, vol. 5, ZCC, pp. 236–37.

78. After several unsuccessful attempts to defeat his uncle—including the notorious 1948 election—Santiago finally won in 1952 by a landslide, 192 votes to only 2. ZCCCM, Nov. 7, 1952, vol. 7, ZCC, pp. 186–89.

79. Lott and Martínez, *Kingdom of Zapata,* pp. 65–68; unpublished speech by Judge Bravo, 1962, MBBP.

80. "Al Pueblo del Condado de Zapata," by Trinidad Uribe, Aug. 1938, MBBP; "Al Pueblo de Zapata," Jan. 1938; "Al Pueblo de Zapata," Nov. 1937, MBBP. (These flyers were paid political propaganda distributed by the Partido Nuevo.)

81. Fish and Fish, *Elected Officials of Zapata,* pp. 23–29.

82. ZCCCM, Feb. 8, 1937, vol. 5, ZCC, pp. 157, 435–36.

83. Leo J. Leo to Bravo, Oct. 10, 1957, MBBP.

84. Josefa V. Bravo interview.

85. The commissioners' court consisted of County Judge A. V. Navarro, Adán Gutiérrez, co. comm. #1; Proceso Martínez, co. comm. #2; Guillermo González, co. comm. #3; Leopoldo Martínez, co./dist. clerk; and Ygnacio Sánchez, sheriff/tax collector. ZCCCM, Jan. 11, 1936, vol. 5, ZCC, p. 125.

86. Texas Planning Board, box 017-22, folder 22-36, IV 894, RG 017, Records, 1914–39, Texas State Archives (hereafter cited as TSA); ZCCCM, vol. 5, Apr. 10, 1936, Aug. 10, 1936, ZCC, p. 131. Bravo accepted the appointment of road supervisor at a monthly salary of $90.

87. Josefa V. Bravo interview; Josefa M. Gutiérrez, interview with author, Zapata, Dec. 28, 1990, tape recording. During the 1940s, Mrs. Gutiérrez served as chair of the Zapata County Democratic Executive Committee.

88. "County Judge Navarro of Zapata County Withdraws from Race on Election Eve," *Laredo Times,* Nov. 2, 1936; "Navarro Still Out of Race at Zapata," *Laredo Times,* Nov. 3, 1936; ZCCCM, Jan. 1, 1937, vol. 5, ZCC, p. 143. Manuel's salary increased from $90 to $150 per month, a jump of $60.

89. "County Judge Navarro of Zapata County Withdraws from Race on Election Eve," *Laredo Times,* Nov. 2, 1936.

90. *U.S. Census, 1920* (microfilm), SAPL. Besides Navarro, two of the four county commissioners spoke only Spanish.

91. Since 1934, surveyors and engineers had been studying the Río Grande from Zapata to Roma for a possible site for the construction of an international dam. Lott and Martínez, *Kingdom of Zapata,* pp. 14–15.

92. Márquez, *LULAC,* p. 21.

93. Ibid., p. 22.

CHAPTER 2

1. The county officials included the following: commissioners Adán Gutiérrez, precinct 1; Proceso Martínez, Jr., precinct 2; Guillermo González, precinct 3; Santos Yzaguirre, precinct 4. Also serving the county were Leopoldo Martínez, county/district clerk; Ygnacio Sánchez, sheriff/tax assessor and collector; and Primitivo Uribe, county treasurer.

2. *Board of County School Trustees Minutes* (hereafter cited as *School Trustees Minutes*), vol. 1, Jan. 1, 1937, Zapata ISD Administration Office, pp. 1–3.

3. Ibid., Jan. 12, 1937, p. 5.

4. Jovita González, "Social Life of Cameron, Starr, and Zapata Counties," M.A. thesis, University of Texas at Austin, 1930, pp. 78–79.

5. *School Trustees Minutes,* Oct. 4, 1937, pp. 11–12; Davis, *Historical Encyclopedia of Texas,* p. 1193.

6. Under reclassification, Common School District No. 1 embraced fourteen schools, with a total student enrollment of 746, while Common School District No. 2 encompassed five elementary schools, with a smaller enrollment of 337 students. *School Trustees Minutes,* May 10, 1937, pp. 6–9.

7. The county proposed a thirty-cent tax on a hundred-dollar valuation of taxable property and the issuance of bonds in the aggregate amount of $100,000. *School Trustees Minutes,* Aug. 27, 1941, pp. 57–59.

8. Bravo to G. W. Foster (Texaco Petroleum Products), Sept. 22, 1942, MBBP.

9. *School Trustees Minutes,* Oct. 12, 1942, p. 84. Both courts stated "that Common School District No. One, as described in the order of August 4, 1941, . . . does not legally exist, and the alleged bonds, in the sum of $100,000.00, . . . are likewise illegal and void." Case No. 11165 in Court of Civil Appeals, 4th Supreme Judicial District, San Antonio, Texas, pp. 1–4; Case No. 11165 in the Court of Civil Appeals, 4th Supreme Judicial District, San Antonio, Texas, *Appellee's Brief,* pp. 29–63; Transcript of Case No. 11165, 49th Judicial District of Texas, Laredo. Texas State Library (hereafter cited as TSL), San Antonio Branch.

10. J. A. Prickett (Magnolia Petroleum Company) to Bravo, Sept. 14, 1942, MBBP.

11. P. W. Pitzer (Pitzer & West Oil Producers) to Bravo, Sept. 19, 1942, MBBP. The Bravo Papers contain correspondence on this matter from the following oil companies, all of which expressed willingness to cooperate: Magnolia Petroleum Company, Texaco Petroleum Products, Pitzer & West Oil Producers, H-Y Oil Company, Humble Oil Company, Humble Pipe Line Company, and Interstate Minerals, Inc.

12. Carlton Meredith (geologist and engineer) to Paul Pitzer (Pitzer & West Oil Producers), Sept. 16, 1942, MBBP.

13. Ibid.

14. Lott and Martínez, *Kingdom of Zapata,* pp. 56–66.

15. *School Trustees Minutes,* Aug. 2, 1949; Aug. 3, 1949, pp. 184–85.

16. "Al Pueblo de Zapata" (To the People of Zapata), political circular, Comité Propaganda del Partido Nuevo, Zapata, Jan. 1938, MBBP.

17. ZCCCM, Aug. 12, 1940, vol. 5, ZCC, p. 454.

18. Ibid., p. 456.

19. Charles D. Turner to Manuel Medina, Oct. 23, 1940, MBBP.

20. Turner to Bravo, Nov. 8, 1940, MBBP.

21. Ibid.; Turner to Bravo, Nov. 15, 1940, MBBP. Why did Philip Kazen get involved in this local dispute? Medina was co-owner of the only Zapata bank, and could Turner have found some questionable bookkeeping practices that involved county funds? Perhaps, since Zapata County was in his 49th District, Kazen wanted his brother appointed as the auditor.

22. King to Matías Cuéllar, April 4, 1942, MBBP.

23. Ibid.; Bravo to King, April 16, 1942, MBBP; King to Bravo, April 30, 1942, MBBP.

24. ZCCCM, Feb. 18, 1929, vol. 5, ZCC, pp. 6–7.

25. In addition, if the taxpayers could not make any financial arrangements within the thirty-day period, then they would be served with notice for a court appearance, at which time, specific steps for collecting and/or selling the property would be spelled out. More troubling to the Partido Nuevo, Kazen would collect, under the Partido Viejo recommendation, a 15 percent fee over and above all outstanding taxes, including interest and penalties incurred (to be paid by the taxpayer in default). "Al Pueblo de Zapata," Comité Propaganda del Partido Nuevo (a one-page political announcement paid by the Republican party), Nov., 1937, Zapata, MBBP.

26. Ibid. Two years later, in 1940, the county commissioners replaced Kazen with another Laredo attorney, Horace C. Hall, to continue the work already in progress. ZCCCM, Sept. 23, 1940, vol. 5, ZCC, p. 460. Even today, the collection of delinquent property taxes in Zapata County, as elsewhere, continues to be a financial nightmare for school and county administrators. Public institutions continue to seek collection agencies for assistance.

27. The public officials approved the petition for bonds to be issued for $500,000 at an annual interest rate not to exceed 5 percent, and the levy of an ad valorem tax on all taxable property. ZCCCM, Nov. 11, 1940, vol. 5, ZCC, p. 494.

28. ZCCCM, Feb. 8, 1937, May 14, 1940, vol. 5, ZCC, pp. 157, 435.

29. Ibid., May 10, 1937, vol. 5, ZCC, p. 184.

30. The State of Texas had assumed the indebtedness of the county's road and bridge fund, and the commissioners court wanted to transfer the surplus funds to the general fund. Philip A. Kazen (Kazen and Kazen Law Firm) to J. M. Sánchez, Aug. 4, 1937, MBBP; Davis, *Historical Encyclopedia of Texas,* p. 1193.

31. "Al Pueblo de Zapata," Nov., 1937; "Al Pueblo de Zapata," Jan. 1938, MBBP.

32. Ibid.

33. Bismark Pope to Bravo, June 23, 1938, MBBP.

34. Buckley to Bravo, July 15, 1938, MBBP.

35. George H. Sheppard to Bravo, July 18, 1938, MBBP.

36. "Zapata Names Old Officers Again," *Laredo Times,* July 25, 1938, LPL.

37. Mike Kingston et al., *The Texas Almanac's Political History of Texas,* pp. 224–27.

38. Ibid.

39. "New Webb Political Boss," *Laredo Times,* July 24, 1938, LPL.

40. "Zapata Names Old Officers Again," *Laredo Times,* July 25, 1938, LPL.

41. "Zapata Vote," "Incomplete Returns Given," *Laredo Times,* Aug. 28, 1938, LPL.

42. "Divided on District Attorney Job," *Laredo Times,* Nov. 9, 1938, LPL; "May Break Deadlock of Valls-Raymond-Martin Combination," *Laredo Times,* Nov. 10, 1938, LPL.

43. "May Break Deadlock," *Laredo Times,* Nov. 10, 1938, LPL.

44. "Allred Appoints Valls, Kazen—as District Judge and Attorney," *Laredo Times,* Nov. 11, 1938, LPL.

45. "Frontier Hilation—New Era for Zapata County," *Laredo Times,* July 14, 1940, LPL; "Zapata Will Stage Great Celebration," *Laredo Times,* July 17, 1940, LPL. Jack Yeaman, staff writer for the Laredo newspaper, coined the cognomen "Hilation," a combination of *hilarious, highway,* and *celebration.* "It'll Be Hilarious 'Hilation'—Zapata Road Fete Is Publicized Here," *Valley Evening Monitor,* April 4, 1940, MBBP. The Zapata County Commissioners Court authorized funds for the expenses and appointed John H. Yeaman to coordinate the event. ZCCCM, May 13, 1940, vol. 5, ZCC, pp. 430–31.

46. "Judges, C of C Managers to Meet," *Laredo Times,* Apr. 7, 1940, LPL; "Zapata Will Stage Great Celebration," *Laredo Times,* July 17, 1940, LPL; "At Zapata July 20 Is Date," *Laredo Times,* July 7, 1940, LPL.

47. "Zapata to Get Most of Them Saturday," *Laredo Times,* July 15, 1940, LPL; "Zapata Host to Texas Saturday," *Laredo Times,* July 19, 1940, LPL; "Among Political Leaders to Be at Hilation," *Laredo Times,* July 14, 1940, LPL; "Hilation Program Thrill Filled," *Laredo Times,* July 18, 1940, LPL; Bravo to Lamar Seeligson, May 3, 1940, MBBP.

48. "Thompson and Hines Also Speak," *Laredo Times,* July 21, 1940, LPL; "Old Style Show Promises Fun," *Laredo Times,* July 14, 1940, LPL; "At Zapata July 20 Is Date," *Laredo Times,* July 7, 1940, LPL. Having the momentum of the successful Frontier Hilation, Judge Bravo and the county commissioners passed a road bond election of five hundred thousand dollars on December 12, 1940. The results were 240 votes for and 27 against. ZCCCM, Dec. 12, 1940, vol. 5, ZCC, pp. 494–504.

49. "Politics!—An Editorial," *Laredo Times,* July 18, 1940; July 22, 1940; July 24, 1940, LPL.

50. "Lights Out after Threat of Old Party," "Politics!—An Editorial," *Laredo Times,* July 22, 1940, LPL.

51. Ibid.

52. Ibid.

53. "D.A. Speaks, San Agustin Plaza at 8," "Politics!—An Editorial," *Laredo Times,* July 11, 1940, LPL.

54. "Carries Three of Four Counties; Judge Valls Takes All; His Majority 2761," "Results by Counties in District Race," *Laredo Times,* July 29, 1940, LPL.

55. "Carries Three of Four."

56. Bravo et al. to Philip Kazen, July 29, 1940, Western Union telegram, MBBP.

57. "People's Choice!—Kazen Shows that the Feet of the Leaders of the Old Party are Clay," *Laredo Times,* July 28, 1940, LPL.

58. Robert Engler, *The Politics of Oil: A Study of Private Power and Democratic Directions,* pp. 350–51.

59. Oscar A. Riley, Tyler County Superintendent, to Bravo, June 5, 1940, MBBP; Pierce Brooks to Bravo, June 5, 1940, MBBP; Lamar G. Seeligson et al. to Bravo, n.d. (letter seeking endorsement of Pierce Brooks), MBBP.

60. Lamar Seeligson et al. to Bravo, n.d., MBBP; Bravo to Lamar Seeligson, May 3, 1940, MBBP.

61. J. R. Hill to Bravo, Aug. 14, 1940, MBBP.

62. Bravo to L. A. Nordan, Aug. 15, 1940, MBBP; Bravo to J. R. Hill, Aug. 15, 1940, MBBP.

63. Bravo to L. A. Nordan, Aug. 15, 1940, MBBP; L. A. Nordan to Bravo, Aug. 13, 1940, MBBP.

64. J. R. Hill to Bravo, Aug. 17, 1940, MBBP.

65. Ron Tyler, ed., *The New Handbook of Texas,* 2:436–37.

66. Bravo to J. R. Hill, Aug. 15, 1940, MBBP.

67. "For General Election in November," *Laredo Times,* Aug. 5, 1940, LPL.

68. Adelina Garza to Bravo, Oct. 25, 1940, MBBP; Virginia Bravo (and other teachers) to Leopoldo Martínez, July 18, 1940, MBBP; Judge Bravo's personal notes on the election campaign itemized in detail all the contributions and expenses.

69. Affidavit from the Zapata County Democratic Party Executive Committee, signed by chairperson, Franciso J. Martínez, et al., Oct. 5, 1940, MBBP. Hesiquio Cuéllar's

brother, Felipe Cuéllar, Jr., was the father of Matías, who held the office of county and district clerk for forty-two years. Matías was married to his distant cousin Elena Cuéllar, daughter of Jesús Cuéllar. She worked in the courthouse as Judge Bravo's secretary for many years. Lott and Martínez, *Kingdom of Zapata*, p. 166.

70. Juan Avalos (Palo Blanco Ranch) to Bravo, Nov. 1, 1940, MBBP.

71. Report entitled, "Disastified [sic] as per conversation on 1st visit asking their support," n.d., MBBP.

72. Josefa V. Bravo interview; Santos Medina, interview with author, San Antonio, Sept. 4, 1991, tape recordings.

73. "Mandamus Denied to Zapata Republicans," *Laredo Times*, Oct. 31, 1940, LPL.

74. Ibid.; Bravo to Hershel Hunt (*Laredo Times*), Nov. 1, 1940, MBBP. The Zapata County Commissioners Court approved payment of $150 for legal fees. ZCCCM, Nov. 11, 1940, vol. 5, ZCC, p. 495.

75. The newspaper compared Bravo's administration to the totalitarian governments in Nazi Germany, Fascist Italy, and Communist Russia, and labeled him a *"hampón político"* (a roguish politician). "Otras 2 Causas de Mandamus Presentadas en Contra de los 'Gangsters' Políticos de Zapata," *El Día*, Nov. 1, 1940, MBBP.

76. Ibid.

77. "La Falta de Representación Es la Causa de Toda Tirania," *El Día*, Nov. 2, 1940, MBBP.

78. Judge Bravo's personal notes, 1940 election, MBBP.

79. Ibid.

80. "Democrats Win in Zapata in All but One Precinct," *Laredo Times*, Nov. 6, 1940, LPL. Meanwhile, Zapata voters, along with the rest of the state's Democratic supporters, kept President Roosevelt in the White House, with 784 to 495 votes over Wendell L. Wilkie. ZCCCM, Nov. 5, 1940, vol. 5, ZCC, pp. 489–90.

81. ZCCCM, Nov. 11, 1940, vol. 5, ZCC, p. 495. The case docket no. 369 was filed in 49th District Court on December 3, 1940, by Bismark Pope, attorney representing Juan Manuel Vela, Zapata County Courthouse (hereafter cited as Case No. 369).

82. Mandamus Bond Documents, Dec., 1940, 49th District Court, Zapata County, MBBP; Case No. 369. The court named Judge Bravo, the county commissioners, other public officials, and the county clerk as contestees. The court set bonds of $7,600 for Judge Bravo, $1,200 for the county commissioners, and $8,000 for the county clerk. On January 9, 1941, in preparation for the upcoming trial, the Zapata political machine again contracted the law services of Raymond, Algee and Alvardo. The three attorneys met with the Zapata County officials and urged Bravo to make available the official election results. The highest bond was for the office of sheriff/tax assessor, set at $14,000, with $8,000 set for the office of county treasurer. Raymond, Algee, and Alvardo to Bravo, Jan. 9, 1941, MBBP.

83. Raymond, Algee and Alvardo to Bravo, Feb. 4, 1941, MBBP.

84. 49th District Court Minutes, vol. 2, ZCC, p. 227.

85. Ibid., pp. 250–51. "Funeral for Judge Valls," *Laredo Times*, Aug. 14, 1941, LPL.

86. Seth Shepard McKay, *Texas and the Fair Deal*, pp. 154–55; Jimmy Banks, *Money, Marbles and Chalk: The Wondrous World of Texas Politics*, p. 82.

87. Hofheinz to Bravo, n.d., MBBP. Judge Hofheinz, a strong supporter of Lyndon Johnson, campaigned actively all over the state. Caro, *The Years of Lyndon Johnson: Means of Ascent*, p. 192; Dallek, *Lone Star Rising*, p. 214.

88. LBJ to Bravo, June 11, 1941, MBBP. Dr. Claudia Anderson, archivist at the LBJ Library, conducted an inquiry on John Duncan and "found nothing" after reviewing the

House folder title list, Johnson's Senate year file, the 1941 campaign files, and the name indexes for the Senate from 1949 through 1954. Anderson to author, June 20, 1991, Oct. 27, 1992 (letters in possession of the author).

89. Bravo to Hofheinz, June 13, 1941, MBBP.

90. Bravo to LBJ, June 16, 1941, MBBP.

91. Bravo to Mose J. Harris, June 16, 1942, MBBP; Mose J. Harris to Bravo, June 13, 1941, MBBP; Merritt H. Gibson to Bravo, June 12, 1941, MBBP.

92. Bravo to Mose J. Harris, June 16, 1941, MBBP.

93. Bravo to LBJ, June 16, 1941, MBBP.

94. LBJ to Bravo, June 19, 1941, MBBP. A San Antonio Spanish newspaper, *Alma Latina,* carried a one-page pro-Johnson political advertisement entitled "Quien Es Lyndon B. Johnson" (Who Is Lyndon B. Johnson). "Quien Es Lyndon B. Johnson," *Alma Latina,* June 23, 1941, MBBP.

95. LBJ to Bravo, June 20, 1941, MBBP.

96. Judge Valls to Leopoldo Martínez, June 22, 1941, MBBP.

97. Leopoldo Martínez to Judge Valls, June 25, 1941, MBBP.

98. Ibid.

99. Shelton, *Political Conditions among Texas Mexicans,* p. 45; McKay, *Texas and the Fair Deal,* p. 156; *Texas Almanac, 1943–44,* p. 259; Kingston et al., *Political History of Texas,* pp. 146–49.

100. Caro, *The Years of Lyndon Johnson: Means of Ascent,* pp. 4, 184–90, 265; Dallek, *Lone Star Rising,* p. 222.

101. Belia Peña Cooper, interview with author, Zapata, July 13, 1993.

102. Santos Medina interview.

103. Josefa V. Bravo interview.

104. Bravo to LBJ, July 3, 1941, MBBP.

105. LBJ to Bravo, July 10, 1941, MBBP. Many years later, in an interview with Professor Lewis L. Gould, Mrs. Johnson still remembered the day when Congressman Johnson flew back to Washington, D.C., after his defeat: "And a memory of him I will always have and be very fond of is the way he looked walking off to catch the plane to go to Washington defeated after having been announced Senator and practically hired a staff and had about 3,000 congratulatory telegrams. But then the majority dwindled away by miraculous means and we woke up one day about five days later with O'Daniel having won. And I still see him walking off toward that plane looking very jolly and putting extra verve into walking, with his head up and just stepping along real sprly [sprightly]" (Interview with Mrs. LBJ by Lewis L. Gould, Lewis Gould Papers, 516-AC, 85–54, LBJL, p. 23).

106. Johnson to Bravo, Aug. 7, 1941, MBBP; Johnson to Bravo, Aug. 19, 1941, MBBP.

107. Major Grubbs to Bravo, Aug. 15, 1941, MBBP. During the summer of 1940, Major Grubbs swore Judge Bravo's two older sons, Eddie and Adolph, into the army air force.

108. Vance D. Raimond to author, Nov. 19, 1992 (letter in possession of the author).

109. Mrs. Alex Champion to Bravo, June 19, 1941, MBBP. Judge Bravo responded in a tactful and kind tone, apologizing for being unable to help her after running an expensive election campaign. Bravo to Mrs. Alex Champion, June 27, 1941, MBBP.

110. Mana Mejia to Bravo, Jan. 6, 1941, MBBP; Bravo to Agustina Mejia, Jan. 29, 1941, MBBP.

111. Amando H. López to Bravo, Jan. 26, 1941, MBBP; Bravo to Amando H. López, Jan. 31, 1941, MBBP.

112. Arturo Paredes to Bravo, n.d., MBBP; Bravo to Arturo Paredes, Jan. 20, 1941, MBBP.

CHAPTER 3

1. "Zapata County Raises U.S.O. Quota; In Excess of Allotment," *Laredo Times,* Oct. 2, 1942, pp. 1, 5, MBBP.

2. "Zapata County Makes Fine War Bond Record," *Laredo Times,* Aug. 23, 1942, LPL.

3. Ibid.

4. Bravo to Headquarters, First Military Area, San Antonio, Mar. 11, 1942, MBBP.

5. Bravo to Eddie, May 18, 1942, MBBP; Capt. W. F. Schreiner to Bravo, n.d., MBBP.

6. Judge Bravo to Eddie Bravo, May 18, 1942, MBBP.

7. West to Bravo, Oct. 28, 1941, MBBP.

8. Capt. Schreiner to Bravo, n.d., MBBP.

9. Bravo to Paul H. Figg (District Manager, Civil Service Office) May 25, 1942, MBBP; Internal Revenue Service, Individual Income Tax Return for 1942, MBBP.

10. Hill to Bravo, Dec. 5, 1942, MBBP.

11. Mark McGee to Bravo, April 9, 1942, MBBP.

12. ZCCCM, Oct. 12, 1942, vol. 6, ZCC, p. 66.

13. "Stevenson, Smith Blame New Deal Bungling for Election Turnover and Losses," *Laredo Times,* Nov. 6, 1942, LPL.

14. Bravo to Homer Garrison, April 15, 1942, MBBP; Garrison to Bravo, April 24, 1942, MBBP; Garrison to Bravo, April 28, 1942, MBBP; Bravo to Senator Tom Connally, Jan. 12, 1942, MBBP. The Southwest Customs Patrol was created in 1853 and used mounted customs inspectors to enforce the tariff laws along the frontier. The agency went through several changes until an executive order in 1948 abolished it. Lott and Martínez, *Kingdom of Zapata,* pp. 181–90.

15. She may well have been the only Hispanic female in Texas elevated to head the county executive committee of a political party. The judge faced no opposition from the PN, but the rest of his Democratic allies braced themselves for a long hot summer, as they expected strong opposition. The voter turnout in Zapata County was not predicted to be heavy—except the slot for county commissioner in precinct 3, where the Democratic candidate, Guillermo González, fought to regain his position from the incumbent, Salvador García. Bravo to Kelley, June 5, 1942, MBBP.

16. Thompson to Bravo, May 29, 1942, MBBP.

17. Smith to Bravo, May 8, 1942, MBBP.

18. Allred to Bravo, June 2, 1942, MBBP; Green, *The Establishment in Texas Politics,* p. 41.

19. McKay to Bravo, June 3, 1942, MBBP.

20. Bravo to Allred, June 5, 1942, MBBP.

21. Allred to Bravo, June 12, 1942, MBBP.

22. Bravo to Eddie, July 23, 1942, MBBP; Elena González to Bravo, July 15, 1942, MBBP. Elena, selected to assist in the election of precinct 3 (Lopeño), notified Judge Bravo about her bout with the flu but indicated that she would vote absentee.

23. Democratic Primary Official Ballot for Zapata County (includes the number of votes cast for each candidate), attached to a letter from Bravo to Kelley, Aug. 1, 1942, MBBP (hereafter cited as Democratic Primary Official Ballot); "Zapata Votes Very Light,"

Laredo Times, July 26, 1942, LPL; *Texas Almanac, 1942–44,* p. 252; Alexander Heard and Donald S. Strong, *Southern Primaries and Elections 1920–1949,* p. 179; Kingston et al., *Political History of Texas,* pp. 126–29.

24. "Kazen to Speak in Five Cities for Judge Allred," *Laredo Times,* July 19, 1942, LPL; "Give Allred 2,611 of Total," *Laredo Times,* July 26, 1942, LPL.

25. Green, *The Establishment in Texas Politics,* p. 41.

26. "Polls Showing Allred Leads," *Laredo Times,* July 21, 1942, LPL. In the governor's race, six candidates placed their names on the Democratic ballot. It was obvious at the end of the primary election that Coke Stevenson was the boss's favorite candidate. This time, all the border counties voted overwhelmingly for Stevenson, along with Duval, Jim Wells, Dimmit, and Jim Hogg counties. All the South Texas county bosses supported Stevenson over his next closest opponent, Hal H. Collins. Statewide results showed Stevenson with 651,218 votes to Collins's 272,469. Kingston et al., *Political History of Texas,* pp. 228–31.

27. "Give Allred 2,611 of Total," *Laredo Times,* July 26, 1942, LPL; "Zapata Votes Very Light," *Laredo Times,* July 26, 1942, LPL.

28. Bravo to Kilday, July 29, 1942, MBBP.

29. Ibid. Jimmy's younger brother, Congressman Paul J. Kilday, who won without opposition in the 20th Congressional District, sent Bravo a thank-you letter "for the fine work in Jim's behalf. We all appreciate it very much." Paul J. Kilday to Bravo, Aug. 13, 1942, MBBP.

30. Democratic Primary Official Ballot. The Zapata County Democratic Party Executive Committee planned to spend about thirty dollars for the cost of the July 25, 1942, primary election. Josefa M. Gutiérrez to Bravo, June 20, 1942, MBBP. Final tabulations from Zapata County showed the following unopposed candidates to have received over five hundred votes: State Senator Rogers Kelley, Representative Milton West, State Representative B. J. Leyendecker, 49th District Judge R. D. Wright, and 49th District Attorney Philip A. Kazen.

31. Charles Deutz to Bravo, May 13, 1942, MBBP; Bravo to Deutz, June 11, 1942, MBBP.

32. Maddox to Bravo, Aug. 9, 1942, MBBP.

33. Transwestern Oil Company to Bravo, Oct. 23, 1942, MBBP; Bravo to Pitzer & Sons, Sept. 22, 1942, MBBP; Bravo to Transwestern Oil Company, Nov. 9, 1942, MBBP.

34. Internal Revenue Service, Individual Income Tax Returns for 1942 and 1944, MBBP.

35. Allred to Bravo, Aug. 17, 1942, MBBP.

36. Bravo to Kelley, Aug. 26, 1942, MBBP. Over 100 more votes were cast in the runoff election than in the July primary. "Zapata Raises July Vote," *Laredo Times,* Aug. 23, 1942, LPL.

37. "Less Than One Percent Is Margin as O'Daniel Holds Lead of 11,979 at 1:30 Sunday Morning," *Laredo Times,* Aug. 23, 1942, LPL.

38. Minutes of the Zapata County Convention of the Democratic Party, held at the county courthouse on August 1, 1942, MBBP.

39. O'Hern to Bravo, Aug. 21, 1942, MBBP.

40. ZCCCM, Sept. 10, 1942, vol. 6, ZCC, MBBP.

41. Laura K. Saegert, archivist, to Gilberto Quezada, Oct. 2, 1992 (letter in possession of the author); J. E. Bravo, Sr., interview, MBBP. According to local World War II veterans, the Zapata Selective Service Board consisted of Humberto González, Lulu Vela, J. M. Sánchez, and John Rathmell (telephone interviews with Rubén Salazar, July 15, 1992, and

Salvador García, July 13, 1992). The official SSB membership roster for Zapata County listed J. M. Sánchez, Julian Wallis, and John Rathmell (C. A. Fuller, Major, National Selective Service System, to State Director of Selective Service, Oct. 29, 1953, Texas State Archives [hereafter cited as TSA]).

42. Bravo to Zapata County Local Board, Aug. 28, 1942, MBBP.

43. Buckley to State Headquarters, Selective Service System, Aug. 31, 1942, MBBP.

44. Upchurch to Buckley, Sept. 3, 1942, MBBP.

45. "La Voz del Amo y Don Leopoldo," political propaganda flyer, 1942, MBBP.

46. Ibid.

47. "El Partido Nuevo de Zapata en la Lucha," political propaganda flyer, 1942, MBBP.

48. Bravo to Miss Florine Baker, Nov. 23, 1942, MBBP; ZCCCM, Nov. 9, 1942, vol. 6, ZCC, pp. 60–61, 70; "Incumbents Win in Zapata," *Laredo Times,* Nov. 4, 1942, LPL. Affidavit signed by Santos Yzaguirre and notorized by Judge Bravo, Zapata County, Texas, Oct. 2, 1942, MBBP. Bravo prepared an itemized analysis of expenses that totaled $116. The list included expenditures for a calf (dinner), six musicians, the rental fee for a dance hall, and mileage used to transport voters to the polls. Gastón de Elección del Pto. No. 3 (Lopeño), Nov. 3, 1942 (Election Expenses for Precinct 3), MBBP.

49. Bravo to Coke R. Stevenson, n.d., MBBP; J. T. Canales to Bravo, Nov. 25, 1942, MBBP.

50. Bravo to Stevenson, n.d., MBBP. Green, *The Establishment in Texas Politics,* pp. 80–81; Guadalupe San Miguel, Jr., *"Let All of Them Take Heed": Mexican Americans and the Campaign for Educational Equality in Texas, 1910–1981,* p. 68; Montejano, *Anglos and Mexicans,* pp. 168, 286.

51. Bravo to Canales, Dec. 4, 1942, MBBP. The incident at the barbershop occurred around Oct. 10, 1942.

52. *House Concurrent Resolution 105,* May 6, 1943 (approved by Governor Coke R. Stevenson), MBBP. Governor Stevenson was more agreeable toward Tejanos in establishing the Good Neighbor Commission: "Meskins is pretty good folks. If it was niggers, it'd be different" (Green, *The Establishment in Texas Politics,* pp. 80–81). Montejano, *Anglos and Mexicans,* pp. 286–69; San Miguel, *Let All of Them Take Heed,* p. 93.

53. Canales to Bravo, Sept. 3, 1943, MBBP.

54. Ibid; Resolution adopted by Commissioners' Court of Cameron County, Aug. 23, 1943, MBBP.

55. Resolution adopted by Commissioners' Court, Aug. 23, 1943, MBBP.

56. ZCCCM, Sept. 13, 1943, vol. 6, ZCC, p. 139.

57. Stevenson to Bravo, Oct. 7, 1943, MBBP.

58. Bravo to Canales, Oct. 12, 1943, MBBP. Judge Bravo closed the letter in Spanish, stating, "Bueno, agradecido como siempre, y con mis mejores deseos para Ud. y su familia, su amigo." (Well, grateful as always, and with my best wishes to you and your family, your friend.)

59. Perales to Bravo, Mar. 6, 1946, MBBP; "Anti-Discrimination Treaty Suggested," *Laredo Times,* July 29, 1946, LPL.

60. Perales to Bravo, Mar. 6, 1946, MBBP.

61. Bravo to West, Nov. 24, 1942, MBBP; West to Bravo, Nov. 30, 1942, MBBP.

62. K. P. Aldrich, First Assistant Postmaster General, to West, Aug. 25, 1943, MBBP; Bravo to West, Jan. 16, 1943, MBBP; West to Bravo, Jan. 20, 1943, MBBP; Ambrose O'Connell, First Assistant Postmaster General, to West, Jan. 25, 1943, MBBP; West to Bravo, Jan. 26, 1943, MBBP; West to Bravo, Aug. 31, 1943, MBBP.

63. Lott and Martínez, *Kingdom of Zapata,* pp. 38–41.

64. West to Bravo, Dec. 9, 1943, MBBP.

65. For a detailed analysis of the origins and historical background of the Independent Club's gradual rise to power in Laredo and Webb County, see Thompson's *Warm Weather and Bad Whiskey.*

66. Kazen to Bravo, Jan. 28, 1943, MBBP; "Kazen Takes Over," *Laredo Times,* Sept. 2, 1942, LPL; "To Washington for War Duty Assignment," *Laredo Times,* Aug. 30, 1942, LPL; "Kazen's Appointment Confirmed by Senate," *Laredo Times,* Jan. 22, 1943, LPL.

67. Allred to Bravo, Mar. 16, 1943, MBBP.

68. R. R. Gilbert, Chair to Bravo, 1943, MBBP.

69. American National Red Cross citation, MBBP.

70. Bravo to Commander/Officer, April 15, 1943, MBBP.

71. West to Bravo, Feb. 10, 1944, MBBP; Richard Critz to Bravo, May 23, 1944, MBBP; Grover Sellers to Bravo, May 1944, MBBP.

72. Bravo et al. to Francis Biddle, U.S. Attorney General, Jan. 12, 1944, MBBP; Linton M. Collins, Acting Assistant to the Attorney General, to Bravo, Jan. 19, 1944, MBBP.

73. Joseph to Bravo, n.d., MBBP. The previous day Eddie and a group of soldiers stationed at Laughlin Field in Del Rio traveled across the border to play baseball against a Mexican team and upon their return learned of the news of the invasion, which caught all of them by surprise (Eddie to Bravo, June 6, 1944, MBBP). As the Roosevelt-Truman campaign gained momentum for the Democratic primary, Josefa M. Gutiérrez, chair of the Zapata County Democratic Executive Committee, conferred with Judge Bravo and his supporters on the nomination of the precinct chairpersons. They selected Abel Ramírez for precinct 1, Juventino Martínez for precinct 2, Aurelio López for precinct 3, and Crisóforo Ramos for precinct 4 (Josefa M. Gutiérrez to Charles E. Simons, State Democratic Executive Committee, Jan. 25, 1944, MBBP).

74. Bravo et al. to Sgt. Cuéllar, June 11, 1944, Western Union telegram, MBBP.

75. Bravo et al., to Sgt. Cuéllar, June 16, 1944, Western Union telegram, MBBP.

76. Bravo to Critz, July 17, 1944, MBBP.

77. As a matter of record, Stevenson received huge victories from all the counties. He amassed a total of 696,586 votes statewide and the nearest opponent, Minnie F. Cunningham, got 48,029 votes. Other state candidates winning big majorities included John Lee Smith for lieutenant governor, Grover Sellers for attorney general, George H. Sheppard for comptroller, Beauford Jester for railroad commissioner, J. E. McDonald for agricultural commissioner, and Jesse James for treasurer. Kingston et al., *Political History of Texas,* pp. 232–35; "Zapata County Gives Incumbents Majority," *Laredo Times,* July 23, 1944, LPL; Heard and Strong, *Southern Primaries and Elections,* pp. 158–60; "Webb Goes All Out for State Incumbents," *Laredo Times,* July 23, 1944, LPL.

78. Myron G. Blalock to Bravo, Oct. 3, 1944, MBBP; Blalock to Bravo, Oct. 10, 1944, MBBP; Blalock to Bravo, Oct. 14, 1944, MBBP.

79. Seay to Mrs. Gutiérrez, Oct. 4, 1944, MBBP.

80. "Political Leaders Here Urge Democratic Vote" and "Ballot of the Democratic Ticket," *Laredo Times,* Nov. 5, 1944, LPL.

81. Bravo to Blalock et al., Oct. 21, 1944, MBBP. Both Blalock and Harry L. Seay acknowledged Judge Bravo's unflinching support and cooperation to the Democratic Party. Blalock to Bravo, Oct. 24, 1944, MBBP; Seay to Bravo, Oct. 27, 1944, MBBP.

82. Certificate of Election and Qualification of County and Precinct Offices, January 1, 1945, MBBP. President Roosevelt received 821,605 votes, and Dewey garnered 191,425.

83. Blalock to Bravo, Mar. 16, 1945, MBBP.

84. Ibid., Mayor Tom Miller to Bravo, April 4, 1945, MBBP.

85. "Politicos Pick State Slate," *Laredo Times,* July 18, 1946, LPL. Parr had stated that if Jester and Rainey met in a runoff he would back Jester, even though he supported Sellers in the primary. In Jim Wells County, Parr predicted a split between Sellers and Jester. "George Parr Gives Views on Primary," *Laredo Times,* July 26, 1946, LPL.

86. Statewide results showed a runoff election between Jester, with 443,804 votes, and Dr. Rainey, with 291,282 votes. Also in a runoff were Allan Shivers versus Boyce House for lieutenant governor, and incumbent West against Colonel J. T. Ellis. It was a close race as Zapata and Webb counties led the border counties for West with 10,647 votes, while incomplete returns from eleven counties gave Ellis 6,535. West to Bravo, Mar. 27, 1946, MBBP; "West Leads Race for Representative," *Laredo Times,* July 28, 1946, LPL; "Border Counties Are Represented at Party Here," *Laredo Times,* Aug. 11, 1946, LPL; Heard and Strong, *Southern Primaries and Elections,* pp. 162–65.

87. "Rainey Fires Third Blast at Jester," *Laredo Times,* Aug. 2, 1946, LPL; "Rainey's Plan for Schools Hailed by Woods," *Austin American,* June 14, 1946, BTHC; "What Homer Rainey Stands For," *Wichita Falls County News,* July, 1946, BTHC.

88. Kingston et al., *Political History of Texas,* pp. 236–39.

89. "Webb Voters Give Margin to Incumbent," *Laredo Times,* Aug. 25, 1946, LPL. Zapata County's Partido Nuevo faction, led by L. E. Vela and J. M. Salinas, publicly announced its support for Ellis ("Zapatans Annouce They'll Back Ellis," *Laredo Times,* Aug. 12, 1946, LPL). At a political rally for Ellis in Zapata, Humberto González led the attack on Milton West ("Zapata Rally Scores West," *Laredo Times,* Aug. 21, 1946, LPL).

90. The importation of 120 infected Brahma bulls from Brazil to the Mexican port of Veracruz on October 10, 1945, despite protests by the United States, led to the spread of foot-and-mouth disease throughout southeastern and central Mexico (U.S. Department of Agriculture, *Campaign in Mexico Against Foot-and-Mouth Disease, 1947–52,* pp. 7–10).

91. Bravo to Kelley, Jan. 18, 1947, Western Union telegram, MBBP.

92. Because of the imminent danger to the cattle industry of Texas in particular, and to the southwestern United States in general, alarming news of the infectious disease spreading from central Mexico inspired a concerted effort among the border states' political leaders. By January 1947, Governor Jester had established a three-member Livestock Sanitary Commission, designed to coordinate the monumental task of working with county judges, state representatives, and national legislators.

93. Many returning World War II veterans found employment with the U.S. government as paymasters, appraisers, livestock inspectors, and in other types of fieldwork.

94. Kelley to Tom M. Lasater, Member, Livestock Sanitary Commission, Feb. 19, 1947, Western Union telegram, MBBP; Kelley to Lasater, Feb. 19, 1947, MBBP. Judge Bravo, with the assistance of Senator Kelley, sought employment for Rodolfo Muñoz and Aurelio Gutiérrez from Zapata and for Horacio Treviño from Los Sáenz.

95. Kelley to Bravo, Feb. 20, 1947, MBBP.

96. Bravo to West, Feb. 27, 1947, MBBP. The state appropriation, earmarked to implement a quarantine on livestock from Mexico, complemented actions taken by the border states of New Mexico, Arizona, and California. U.S. Dept. of Agriculture, *Campaign in Mexico,* p. 14.

97. Bravo to West, Mar. 11, 1947, MBBP.

98. West to Bravo, June 30, 1947, MBBP; West to Rathmell, July 3, 1947; West to Bravo, July 10, 1947, MBBP; S. O. Fladness (Bureau of Animal Industry) to West, July 11, 1947, MBBP; West to Rathmell, July 15, 1947, MBBP.

99. West to Bravo, June 30, 1947, MBBP.

100. Bravo to West, July 7, 1947, MBBP.

101. Ibid.

102. LBJ to Bravo, Jan. 25, 1949, Western Union telegram, MBBP; LBJ to Bravo, Jan. 26, 1949, Western Union telegram, MBBP; LBJ to Bravo, Aug. 20, 1949, Western Union telegram, MBBP.

CHAPTER 4

1. According to political analysts, the field of candidates could have been divided into two groups: the major and the minor ones. Lyndon Johnson, Coke Stevenson, George Peddy, and Martin Dies fell into the former category (McKay, *Texas and the Fair Deal,* p. 164).

2. E. James Kazen to Bravo, Jan. 28, 1943, MBBP; "Laredo Boasts Three Brother Team Winners in Election," *Laredo Times,* July 28, 1946, LPL; Caro, *The Years of Lyndon Johnson: Means of Ascent,* p. 190; Dallek, *Lone Star Rising,* p. 330; Dugger, *The Politician,* p. 322; Lott and Martínez, *Kingdom of Zapata,* pp. 168–69. Several leading historians have indicated that Governor Stevenson nominated S. Truman Phelps over Jimmy Kazen for a vacancy in the D.A.'s office of the 49th Judicial District. But according to the *Laredo Times,* in August 1942, Philip Kazen, then D.A., resigned to accept employment with the Board of Economic Welfare. So Stevenson immediately appointed Philip's brother—E. James ("Jimmy")—effective September 1 of the same year. On January 22, 1943, the Senate confirmed Jimmy's appointment. Further research in this area may clarify how and when Phelps became D.A. "To Washington for War Duty Assignment," *Laredo Times,* Aug. 30, 1942, LPL; "Kazen Takes Over," *Laredo Times,* Sept. 1, 1942, LPL; "Kazen's Appointment Confirmed by Senate," *Laredo Times,* Jan. 22, 1943, LPL.

3. LBJ to Bravo, June 16, 1948, House Papers, Container no. 94, LBJL; LBJ to Bravo, June 23, 1948, House Papers, Container no. 94, LBJL.

4. Brooks to Gutiérrez, June 23, 1948, House Papers, no. 110, LBJL. In an interview with Dr. Lewis L. Gould, Lady Bird Johnson stated, "Mrs. Max Brooks, a very good friend, and I set up an organization, got as many volunteers as we could. She began to make lists of all the club women she knew all over the state that might be friendly and help." Interview with Lady Bird Johnson conducted by Dr. Lewis L. Gould, Lewis Gould Papers, box 1 of 2, LBJL, p. 32.

5. Brooks to Gutiérrez, June 23, 1948, House Papers, 110, LBJL.

6. Beeman to Gutiérrez, July 10, 1948, House Papers, no. 110, LBJL.

7. Ibid.

8. LBJ to Bravo, July 19, 1948, Western Union telegram, MBBP; Quezada, "Judge Manuel B. Bravo," p. 57.

9. "Greatest Rally in Zapata Co. History Predicted for Kazen Wednesday Night," *Laredo Times,* July 20, 1948, LPL.

10. "Zapata County Voters Promise Kazen Loyalty at Large San Ygnacio Rally," *Laredo Times,* July 23, 1948, LPL.

11. Ibid.

12. J. Luz Sáenz to Bravo, July 24, 1947, MBBP. Sáenz was Bravo's protégé but also his mentor. After LULAC's founding in 1929, they were involved in establishing LULAC councils in South Texas, and now Judge Bravo gave him a job administering vocational classes.

13. L. A. Woods to Bravo, July 6, 1948, MBBP.

14. Mike López to Bravo, July 27, 1948, MBBP; Bravo to López, July 30, 1948, MBBP.

15. Perales to Bravo, Aug. 27, 1948, MBBP; Quezada, "Judge Manuel B. Bravo," p. 58.

16. Ibid.

17. McKay, *Texas and the Fair Deal*, pp. 218–19.

18. The Tejano bloc vote in Duval, Zapata, Starr, and Webb gave Johnson a landslide victory with 98%, 95%, 93%, and 92% of the votes respectively. Two of the other border counties—Hidalgo and Cameron—voted for Johnson with margins of 47%. With Parr's influence in Jim Hogg and Jim Wells, Johnson got a close victory with 50% of the votes. Brooks and Nueces counties also went with Johnson, with 59% and 53% respectively. Voting for Stevenson, Kenedy, Dimmit, Willacy, and Kleberg counties provided 77%, 47%, 47%, and 46% margins respectively. Without a clear majority for either Stevenson or Johnson, election officials scheduled a runoff for Saturday, August 28 (*Texas Almanac, 1949–50*, pp. 462–64; "Independent Backs Kazen, Johnson," *Laredo Times*, Aug. 13, 1948, LPL; Kingston et al., *Political History of Texas*, pp. 130–33). When the polls closed, Governor Stevenson led Congressman Johnson with enough votes to achieve a majority, 477,077 votes to 405,617, and George Peddy, an attorney from Houston, came in third with 237,195 votes.

19. "Greatest Rally in Zapata Co. History Predicted for Kazen Wednesday Night," *Laredo Times*, July 20, 1948, LPL.

20. "Bentsen Leads Kazen 1512 votes in District Race," *Laredo Times*, July 26, 1948, LPL.

21. "Sees Election as Victory of Independents," *Laredo Times*, July 26, 1948, LPL; "No Boos, No Heckling at Kazen Mission Rally," *Valley Evening Monitor*, Aug. 17, 1948, PAL.

22. "Kazen Thanks His Many Supporters," *Laredo Times*, July 26, 1948, LPL.

23. "Kazen Winds Up Campaign at Big Rally," *Laredo Times*, Aug. 27, 1948, LPL.

24. "Ellis to Support Bentsen; Cramer Urges His Election," *Valley Evening Monitor*, Aug. 26, 1948, PAL; "Harlingen Kazen Club Head Quits, Will Back Bentsen," *Valley Evening Monitor*, Aug. 25, 1948, PAL.

25. "15th District Vote by Counties," *Laredo Times*, Aug. 29, 1948, LPL; "Bentsen Winner by 10,000 Votes," *Valley Evening Monitor*, Aug. 29, 1948, PAL; "Arrests Mark Laredo Voting," *Valley Evening Monitor*, Aug. 29, 1948, PAL; "Celaya Says Uproar at Rally 'Will React' against Kazen," *Valley Evening Monitor*, Aug. 15, 1948, PAL; "Kazen Tactics Like Hitler's Bentsen Says," *Valley Evening Monitor*, Aug. 19, 1948, PAL; "Port Isabel Officer Arrests Kazen for Disturbing Peace," *Valley Evening Monitor*, Aug. 22, 1948, PAL.

26. Bravo to Bentsen, Aug. 30, 1948, MBBP.

27. Bentsen to Bravo, Sept. 3, 1948, MBBP.

28. Dallek, *Lone Star Rising*, p. 347.

29. LBJ to Bravo, Aug. 27, 1948, Western Union telegram, MBBP.

30. Brad Smith to Bravo, Aug. 28, 1948, Western Union telegram, MBBP.

31. Brad Smith to author, May 21, 1992 (letter in possession of the author).

32. LBJ to Bravo, Aug. 29, 1948, Western Union telegram, MBBP.

33. Bravo to LBJ, Aug. 29, 1948, MBBP.

34. Caro, *The Years of Lyndon Johnson: Means of Ascent*, p. 309.

35. Looney to Bravo, Aug. 30, 1948, MBBP.

36. Josefa V. Bravo, interview. Parr and Bravo were good political friends and relied on each other for favors. At one time, Parr wanted the judge to find employment for Isidoro Garza, "one of my friends. . . . So if there is any thing that you can do to help him—please

do so. Any thing that you may be able to do will be greatly appreciated by me." As a postscript, Parr noted, "Eres puro! Ya sabes que." Parr to Bravo, Jan. 16, 1953, MBBP.

37. Frank Oltorf, Ac78–53, Oral History, interview by David G. McComb, Aug. 3, 1971, LBJL.

38. Bravo to LBJ, Aug. 30, 1948, Western Union telegram, House Papers, no. 124, Folder Title Z, LBJL.

39. For example, on Sunday, August 29, 1948, at 3:00 P.M., Stevenson led by 315 votes. Two hours later, his lead was down to 8 votes, and by 8:00 P.M. Johnson was ahead by 717 votes. At noon the next day, Stevenson had gained the lead by 210 votes. McKay, *Texas and the Fair Deal,* pp. 237–40.

40. "Defendant Lyndon B. Johnson's Opposition to Granting of Temporary Injunction," sec. 9, Federal Archives and Records Center (hereafter cited as FARC), Records of the U.S. District Court, Northern District of Texas, Fort Worth, vol. 1, pp. 5–7. ("Vote Probe Asked in Zapata, Duval, Webb and Starr," *Laredo Times,* Sept. 3, 1948, LPL).

41. LBJ to County Judges, n.d. House Papers, Container no. 124, Folder Title Z, LBJL.

42. LBJ to Bravo, Sept. 3, 1948, MBBP.

43. Josefa M. Gutiérrez to LBJ, Sept. 9, 1948, LBJL.

44. Reference is made to the September 22, 1948, affidavit submitted by Walter W. Jenkins, who was present at the state's Democratic subcommittee canvassing when the results for Jack County were announced: Stevenson 894 and Johnson 879. The actual results should have been Johnson 894 and Stevenson 879, but "the error was not corrected later" ("Defendant Lyndon B. Johnson's Opposition to Granting of Temporary Injunction," Sec. 9, FARC, vol. 1, pp. 5–7). A friend of Johnson's who tried to vote in Dallas encountered the following experience, "I tried to pull the lever down over Johnson, and it was locked. I called the instructor, and asked him why the lever over Johnson's name was locked. He dident [sic] answer me, but stepped in[to the] booth and released the lever, then I voted." This same person told Johnson that later on in the day, a friend of his had faced a similar problem. Sam Allen to LBJ, Sept. 9, 1948, Pre-Presidential Confidential File, box 6, LBJL.

45. "Judge T. Whitfield Davidson holding court in Fort Worth, Texas, Sept. 21, 1948—Morning Session," FARC, vol. 1, p. 5.

46. Ibid., pp. 5–7. The Pre-Presidential Confidential File at the LBJ Library contains thirty cases of alleged election fraud: "Possible Election Irregularities Which Benefitted Coke Stevenson," Box 6, LBJL.

47. "Johnson Lawyers Rush Appeal," *San Antonio Evening News,* Sept. 23, 1948, SAPL; Fort Worth Hearing, Sept. 21–22, 1948, FARC, vol. 1, pp. 48–58.

48. Fort Worth Hearing, pp. 48–50; Caro, *The Years of Lyndon Johnson: Means of Ascent,* pp. 360–62; Dallek, *Lone Star Rising,* p. 338.

49. Fort Worth Hearing, pp. 51–55; Green, *The Establishment in Texas Politics,* pp. 114–15. L. E. Vela, a staunch supporter of the Republican Party for many years, also campaigned for Democratic candidate Bentsen ("Bravo Re-Elected," *Zapata County News,* vol. 3, no. 45, Nov. 4, 1948, MBBP).

50. "Defendant Lyndon B. Johnson's Opposition to Granting of Temporary Injunction," No. 9, Fort Worth Hearing, FARC, vol. 1, pp. 5–7; Dallek, *Lone Star Rising,* p. 338; Caro, *The Years of Lyndon Johnson: Means of Ascent,* pp. 363–64.

51. "Civil Action No. 1640 Appointing Special Masters," FARC, pp. 1–2; Dallek, *Lone Star Rising,* p. 338; McKay, *Texas and the Fair Deal,* pp. 241–42; Caro, *The Years of Lyndon Johnson: Means of Ascent,* pp. 364–74; Green, *The Establishment in Texas Poli-*

tics, pp. 115–16. Special Master J. M. Burnett appointed J. L. McAtee and M. I. Mondshine from Houston to serve as official court reporters in Duval and Zapata counties. For a detailed account of the legal maneuvering employed by Johnson's attorneys to overturn Judge Davidson's injunction in Jim Wells, Duval, and Zapata counties, see Caro, *The Years of Lyndon Johnson: Means of Ascent,* pp. 362–84, and Dallek, *Lone Star Rising,* pp. 331–42.

52. Caro, *The Years of Lyndon Johnson: Means of Ascent,* p. 375.

53. "Jim Wells County Hearings Being Heard by W. R. Smith, Sept. 28, 1948," FARC, vol. 1, p. 18.

54. Ibid., p. 62.

55. Reston, *The Lone Star,* p. 145; Green, *The Establishment in Texas Politics,* pp. 114–15. According to Luis Salas, Deputy Sheriffs Willie Mancha and Ygnacio Escobar were the ones who added the names. Caro, *The Years of Lyndon Johnson: Means of Ascent,* p. 393.

56. "Duval County Hearings Being Heard by James M. Burnett, Sept. 28, 1948 at 10:00 A.M.," FARC, vol. 2, pp. 18–20; Banks, *Money, Marbles, and Chalk,* pp. 88–94; Wilbur Matthew, *San Antonio Lawyer,* pp. 101–108; Philip Reed Rulon, *The Compassionate Samaritan: The Life of Lyndon Baines Johnson,* pp. 103–104.

57. "Zapata County Hearings, Sept. 29, 1948," vol. 2, FARC, pp. 116–17.

58. "Zapata County Hearings, Sept. 29, 1948," vol. 2, FARC, pp. 116–17; Santos Medina, interview with author, San Antonio, Sept. 4, 1991, tape recordings. Medina, the presiding judge for precinct 1, was also one of the subpoenaed witnesses. Santos and his brother, Manuel, had established economic dominance over the county through large-scale investments in the only bank, the international bridge, and real estate.

59. "Zapata County Hearings, Sept. 29, 1948," vol. 2, FARC.

60. "Zapata County Hearings, Sept. 29, 1948," p. 127.

61. Ibid., p. 177; Josefa M. Gutiérrez interview; Green, *The Establishment in Texas Politics,* pp. 115–16; "Probe Chief Told Zapata Returns Lost," *Laredo Times,* Sept. 29, 1948, LPL.

62. "Zapata County Hearings, Sept. 29, 1948," pp. 188–93; Caro, *The Years of Lyndon Johnson: Means of Ascent,* p. 377; Dugger, *The Politician,* p. 336; Dallek, *Lone Star Rising,* p. 340.

63. "Zapata County Hearings, Sept. 29, 1948," p. 210.

64. Ibid., p. 234; Dallek, *Lone Star Rising,* pp. 340–42; Caro, *The Years of Lyndon Johnson: Means of Ascent,* pp. 383–84. I attempted to locate the 1948 election returns but the county clerk's office was unable to locate them. Belinda Bravo to Gilberto and Jo Emma Quezada, Jan. 18, 1991 (letter in possession of the author).

65. LBJ to Bravo, Oct. 20, 1948, MBBP.

66. Josefa V. Bravo interview; Lott and Martínez, *Kingdom of Zapata,* p. 243; James Rowe, "Efforts Being Made to Save Zapata County Seat, Towns," *Corpus Christi Caller-Times,* June 9, 1946, Corpus Christi Public Library (hereafter cited as CCPL); George Carmack, "The Tale of 2 Cities: One is Old; Other New," *San Antonio Express–News,* Oct. 13, 1973, SAPL.

67. "Bravo Re-Elected," *Zapata County News,* vol. 3, no. 45, Nov. 4, 1948, MBBP. Judge Bravo kept an itemized list of all the expenditures incurred during the campaign. Costs included beer party, $164; Aguilar Orchestra, $50; typists, $20; Stamps, $23. His total expenditures amounted to about $1,000. Document on file in MBBP.

68. "Bravo Re-Elected," MBBP.

69. Bravo to Perales, Sept. 17, 1948, MBBP; Quezada, "Judge Manuel B. Bravo," p. 62.
70. "Bravo Re-Elected," MBBP.
71. LBJ to Bravo, Dec. 23, 1948, MBBP.
72. LBJ to Bravo, May 6, 1949, MBBP.
73. LBJ to Bravo, Dec. 20, 1948, MBBP.
74. LBJ to Bravo, June 9, 1950, MBBP.
75. LBJ to Bravo, Oct. 20, 1950, MBBP.
76. Bravo to LBJ, Oct. 26, 1950, MBBP; Quezada, "Judge Manuel B. Bravo," p. 63.
77. Josefa M. Gutiérrez interview.
78. Ted Treviño, interview with author, Zapata, July 16, 1991, tape recording.

CHAPTER 5

1. *Minority Report on the Longoria Investigation,* submitted by committee member Representative Frank C. Oltorf, n.d., Pre-Presidential Confidential File, LBJL (hereafter cited as *Minority Report*); Dr. Héctor García Oral History Transcript, p. 6, LBJL; "Nazisim in Texas?—Three River Undertaker Refuses to Bury Latin American Soldier," *Laredo Times,* Jan. 11, 1949, LPL; George Norris Green, "The Félix Longoria Affair," *Journal of Ethnic Studies* 19 (Fall 1991): 23–34.
2. Star Castillo, "Grief-Stricken Father Tries to Find Respite from Sorrow," *Laredo Times,* Jan. 17, 1949, LPL.
3. "Minority Report"; "Texans Try to Make Amends for Slur on Dead War Hero," *Laredo Times,* Jan. 13, 1949, LPL.
4. Bravo to LBJ, Jan. 11, 1949, Western Union telegram, LBJL.
5. Ibid.
6. Dr. García to LBJ, Jan. 10, 1949, Pre-Presidential Confidential File, LBJL.
7. LBJ to Bravo, Jan. 12, 1949, Western Union telegram, MBBP.
8. R. A. Cortéz (President, League of United Latin American Citizens) to LBJ, Jan. 12, 1949, Western Union telegram, LBJL; Dr. García to Thomas Sutherland, Executive Secretary, Good Neighbor Commission, Jan. 31, 1949, LBJL; Memorandum to the Press from the Good Neighbor Commission, Feb. 11, 1949, TSA.
9. Philip Raine (Cultural Attaché, United States Embassy in Mexico, State Department) to Sutherland, Jan. 18, 1949, TSA; Dallek, *Lone Star Rising,* p. 369; Memorandum to the Press from the Good Neighbor Commission, Feb. 11, 1949, TSA; Charles Cinnamon to Sutherland, June 14, 1949, TSA; Sutherland to R. E. Smith, Chair, Good Neighbor Commission, Feb. 25, 1949, TSA.
10. Philip Raine to Sutherland, Jan. 18, 1949, TSA.
11. Ibid.; Mrs. Longoria to LBJ, Jan. 12, 1949, LBJL; LBJ to Dr. García, Jan. 11, 1949, LBJL; "Widow Decides on Arlington Burial for Returned Soldier," *Laredo Times,* Jan. 14, 1949, LPL.
12. "Widow Decides on Arlington Burial"; Paul J. Reveley (Chief, Division of Mexican Affairs) to LBJ, Mar. 8, 1949, LBJL. The Longoria incident was more than just a discrimination issue between the Longoria family and the Rice Funeral Home. It seriously strained international diplomatic ties with Mexico. Sutherland to R. E. Smith, Feb. 28, 1949, TSA.
13. "Rites Set for Latin American GI Hero in Arlington Cemetery," *Laredo Times,* Jan. 12, 1949, LPL.
14. Pearcy to Bravo, Nov. 13, 1943, MBBP; "Widow Decides on Arlington Burial."
15. LBJ to Bravo, Feb. 21, 1949, MBBP. Some of the government officials who attended

the gravesite services included Paul J. Reveley of the State Department; Mr. Sierra, first secretary of the Mexican Embassy; a Mexican army official; a Mexican naval officer; and Major General Harry Vaughn, aide to the president (Memo for the files, Re: Félix Longoria, by John B. Connally, Feb. 25, 1949, LBJL).

16. Bravo to LBJ, Feb. 16, 1949, MBBP. Johnson's staff delivered to Mrs. Longoria the official date and time of the funeral service, scheduled for Wednesday, February 16 at 2:00 P.M. (LBJ to Mrs. Longoria, Feb. 1, 1949, Western Union telegram, LBJL). The Webb County Chapter of Disabled Veterans also sent Senator Johnson a congratulatory telegram. "Johnson is Praised for Reburial Stand," *Laredo Times*, Jan. 13, 1949, LPL; "Three River Soldier Is Buried Today in U.S. Cemetery Near Pershing," *Laredo Times*, Feb. 16, 1949, LPL.

17. LBJ to Bravo, April 4, 1949, MBBP; LBJ to Bravo, April 15, 1949, MBBP.

18. Bravo et al. to Connally, June 6, 1952, Tom Connally Papers, container 382, TLC.

19. McCormick to LBJ, June 21, 1952, MBBP; McCormick to Connally, June 21, 1952, MBBP; Connally to Bravo et al., June 24, 1952, Tom Connally Papers, The Library of Congress (hereafter cited as TLC); LBJ to Bravo et al., June 24, 1952, MBBP.

20. Bentsen to Bravo, July 21, 1952 (submitted by Bentsen's secretary); Robert Salter (Chief, Soil Conservation Service) to Bentsen, July 17, 1952, MBBP.

21. Wright Morrow, National Committee person, to Bravo, May 2, 1949, MBBP. The event in Laredo commemorated the election of Bryson Skelton to the post of National Committee person from Texas. E. James Kazen, district attorney for the 49th Judicial District, to Bravo, May 5, 1949, MBBP.

22. Cluck to Bravo, July 18, 1949, MBBP.

23. Governor Shivers to Bravo, Dec. 15, 1949, MBBP.

24. LBJ to Bravo, Oct. 18, 1949, MBBP.

25. LBJ to Bravo, Oct. 27, 1949, Western Union telegram, MBBP.

26. "Raymond to Speak at Allred Banquet," *Laredo Times*, Oct. 23, 1949, LPL. Judge Allen Hannay of Houston administered the oath of office. "J. V. Allred Sworn in as U.S. Judge," *Laredo Times*, Oct. 30, 1949, LPL.

27. LBJ to Bravo, Jan. 17, 1949, MBBP.

28. LBJ to Bravo, Sept. 24, 1951, MBBP.

30. Looney to Bravo, Nov. 27, 1950, MBBP.

31. LBJ to Bravo, Nov. 27, 1950, MBBP.

32. Lott and Martínez, *Kingdom of Zapata*, p. 252.

33. J. E. Bravo, Sr., interview.

34. *Manifiesto al Condado de Zapata*, July 5, 1952 (published by the Partido Viejo), MBBP.

35. Carta Abierta/Open Letter (published by the New Coalition Party, Zapata) n.d., MBBP; Lott and Martínez, *Kingdom of Zapata*, p. 252; J. E. Bravo, Sr., interview.

36. J. E. Bravo, Sr., interview; "Incumbents Are Trailing in Zapata County," *Laredo Times*, July 27, 1952, LPL. For example, J. M. Sánchez polled 316 and Judge Bravo had 211; Leopoldo Martínez, incumbent candidate for sheriff had 238, while his opponent, Trinidad Uribe, polled 265.

37. "Bravo Ticket Wins in Zapata County," *Laredo Times*, July 28, 1952, LPL; Lott and Martínez, *Kingdom of Zapata*, p. 253.

38. Kingston et al., *Political History of Texas*, pp. 244–47; "6,000 Voters Cast Ballots in Webb County," *Laredo Times*, July 27, 1952, LPL.

39. "Zapata Co. Election Suits Hearing Set," *Laredo Times*, Aug. 13, 1952, LPL. Starr

County also made headlines in the Laredo newspaper when fifteen Old Party candidates who had lost filed against the New Party incumbents who won every county office. "Election Fraud Charged by Starr Primary Losers," *Laredo Times,* Aug. 10, 1952, LPL; "Starr County Election Fraud Battle Looms," *Laredo Times,* Aug. 14, 1952, LPL.

40. The Zapata County Democratic Executive Committee met on July 29, 1952, to canvass final election results: Bravo received 768, Sánchez 714; Domínguez had 194, Solís 189; Guillermo González garnered 141, and Santiago González 149 votes.

41. Transcript No. 12499, 49th District Court, Webb County, TSL, p. 42; "Zapata County Old Party Winner in Election Suit," *Laredo Times,* Aug. 29, 1952, LPL. Some of the fifty witnesses included Pedro García, Oscar and Ernestina Treviño, Guadalupe López, Eusebio López, Mr. and Mrs. Lauro Garza, Salvador Garza, Mario Flores, Carmen Flores, Concepción Bustamante, Jacinto García, Mr. and Mrs. Tomás Yzaguirre, Abel Ramírez, Dagaberto López, Filiberto Treviño, Manuel M. López, and Amando Vela.

42. "Absentee Votes Highlight Zapata Co. Election Trial," *Laredo Times,* Aug. 20, 1952, LPL; Transcript No. 12499, pp. 6–42, TSL.

43. Transcript No. 12499, p. 42.

44. Court of Civil Appeals, Fourth Supreme Judicial District, Case No. 12499, TSL, San Antonio Regional Office, p. 8; Lott and Martínez, *Kingdom of Zapata,* p. 253; "Zapata Election Suits Decision Upheld," *Laredo Times,* Sept. 28, 1952, LPL.

45. Lott and Martínez, *Kingdom of Zapata,* pp. 253–54; ZCCCM, Nov. 7, 1952, vol. 7, ZCC, pp. 186–89; "Bravo Wins over Write-In Opponent," *Laredo Times,* Nov. 5, 1952, LPL.

46. At the national level, Republican candidate General Dwight D. Eisenhower earned a landslide victory over Democrat Adlai E. Stevenson, 442 to 89 electoral votes. At the state level, Eisenhower received 53 percent of the popular vote, while Stevenson garnered 47 percent. The five border counties split their party allegiance, with Webb, Zapata, and Starr remaining loyal to the Democratic Party while Hidalgo and Cameron opted for the Republican candidate, with 62 percent and 65 percent of the votes respectively. None of the boss-ruled counties, including Duval and Jim Wells, gave Stevenson the usual one-sided returns of over 90 percent of the votes. Kingston et al., *Political History of Texas,* pp. 88–91.

47. Robert A. Calvert and Arnoldo De León, *The History of Texas,* p. 385.

48. Kingston et al., *Political History of Texas,* pp. 151–53, 297–99.

49. Warren Olney III, Assistant Attorney General, to LBJ, Mar. 20, 1953, Senate files, container 1191, LBJL.

50. Bravo to LBJ, Mar. 12, 1953, Western Union telegram, Senate files, container 1191, LBJL.

51. LBJ to the Attorney General, Mar. 13, 1953, LBJL; LBJ to Bravo, Mar. 13, 1953, LBJL.

52. Warren Olney III, Assistant Attorney General, to LBJ, Mar. 20, 1953, Senate files, container 1191, LBJL.

53. Bravo to LBJ, Mar. 28, 1953, LBJL.

CHAPTER 6

1. Congressman West discussed with Commissioner Lawson the judge's idea of lowering the height of the dam wall. West felt optimistic that the IBWC engineers could

make the necessary adjustments. West to Bravo, April 9, 1946, MBBP; Bravo to Lawson, April 12, 1946, MBBP.

2. Accompanying Judge Bravo were County Commissioner Manuel Medina and Rafael San Miguel, Jr. Judge Bravo, "Falcon Dam—Zapata County," unpublished personal notes, p. 1., MBBP (hereafter cited as Judge Bravo—Personal Notes); James Rowe, "Efforts Being Made to Save Zapata County Seat, Towns," *Corpus Christi Caller-Times,* June 9, 1946, CCPL; Lewis Carter, "Zapata to Be Inundated, Still Has No Place to Go," *Evening Valley News,* May 7, 1946, PAL. With the passage of the American-Mexican Treaty Act of 1950, the IBWC's authority expanded to include the relocation of towns and cemeteries as well as schools and public buildings. It was also to oversee the extension of public services. Adela Isabel Flores, "Falcon International Dam and Its Aftermath: A Study of United States–Mexico Border Policy Making and Implementation," p. 75 (hereafter cited as "Falcon International Dam").

3. "Probable Dam Site 65 Miles from McAllen," *McAllen Monitor,* Mar. 6, 1946, PAL; "U.S.–Mexico Select Tentative Site of Dam on Río Grande," *Evening Valley News,* Mar. 6, 1946, PAL; "Two Sites for Dam Still Being Studied," *McAllen Monitor,* Mar. 25, 1946, PAL; "Two Proposed Sites for Dam Inspected," *Valley Star,* Apr. 12, 1946, PAL; ZCCCM, Jan. 14, 1946, vol. 6, ZCC, p. 286.

4. Bailey, "Problems in Relocating," p. 28; Patsy Jeanne Byfield, *Falcon Dam and the Lost Towns of Zapata,* p. 20.

5. "Reclamation Agency to Study Zapata's Plight," *McAllen Monitor,* May 24, 1946, PAL; "Zapata Citizens Seek New Site for Town," *Valley Star,* May 25, 1946, PAL; "Zapata Officials Seek New Location," *Brownsville Herald,* May 24, 1946, PAL.

6. ZCCCM, June 10, 1946, vol. 6, ZCC, p. 308; Judge Bravo—Personal Notes, pp. 1–2.

7. The county commissioners representing Zapata were Manuel Medina, precinct 1; Proceso Martínez, precinct 2; Guillermo Gonzáles, precinct 3; and Lizandro Ramírez, precinct 4. Members of the advisory council included Serapio Vela, Juan M. Vela, L. J. Ramírez, J. M. Sánchez, C. P. Flores, E. H. Cunningham, Salvador García, L. E. Vela, Rafael San Miguel, and Fernando Garza (ZCCCM, Sept. 12, 1946, vol. 6, ZCC, pp. 332–34; Judge Bravo—Personal Notes, p. 2). According to county records, the political machine refused to award $3,000 to an outside contractor to fix the Veleño bridge (which was located on U.S. Highway 83 and provided transportation over the Arroyo Veleño) but instead gave the money to County Commissioner Manuel Medina for the said purpose. They also hired Jesús L. Cuéllar to serve as County Service Officer at $30 per month, but provided no job description for him.

8. "Levees Studied as Means of Protecting Zapata," *McAllen Monitor,* Nov. 6, 1946, PAL; "Levee May Save Zapata," *Laredo Times,* Nov. 8, 1946, LPL; "Economy Favors Zapata Levees, Says Lawson," *McAllen Monitor,* Dec. 6, 1946, PAL. Even in August 1947, Commissioner Lawson still contemplated the notion of building levees to protect Zapata, agreeing that moving the entire town would be more expensive. Judge Bravo—Personal Notes, n.p.

9. "Engineers to Recommend Dam Sites," *Valley Evening Monitor,* Aug. 20, 1947, PAL; "U.S. Engineers Approve Falcon Site for Dam," *Valley Evening Monitor,* Aug. 21, 1947, PAL; "IBWC Engineers Select Falcon for Dam Site," *Valley Star,* Aug. 22, 1947, PAL. The cost projections, fine-tuned as construction plans became finalized, amounted to over $46 million, to be divided proportionately between the two countries. Joint press statement of Senator Connally, Johnson, and Representative Bentsen, Oct. 5, 1949, LBJL.

10. Lloyd W. Hamilton, *A Report on Procedures Used in Planning New Zapata,* 1955, p. i (hereafter cited as *Planning New Zapata*).

11. Judge Bravo—Personal Notes, p. 3. With congressional approval, the IBWC established its main headquarters in a historic building located inside the compound of Fort McIntosh in Laredo. Congressman West spearheaded the bill through Congress. West to Bravo, June 25, 1947, MBBP.

12. Flores, "Falcon International Dam," pp. 81–82. For an in-depth study of the compensation issues with respect to the IBWC replacement values, see Byfield, *Falcon Dam,* pp. 16–50.

13. Thompson to LBJ, Sept. 26, 1949, LBJL.

14. Gordon MacKenzie to Chairman of the Appropriation[s] Committee, House of Representatives, Aug. 11, 1950, LBJL; LBJ to MacKenzie, Aug. 17, 1950, LBJL.

15. Lawson to LBJ, Nov. 30, 1949, LBJL. One major problem as regards implementation of the IBWC regulations was that the land titles, based on the Spanish land grant *porción* system, had sometimes been transferred to more than one family owner. Bailey, "Problems in Relocating," pp. 25–28; Byfield, *Falcon Dam,* pp. 15–18, 39, 49.

16. Humberto González to LBJ, Nov. 15, 1949, LBJL. Local real estate appraisers Blas Cantú and Mercurio Martínez, aided by Dr. H. H. Power and Wallace W. Wilson of the Department of Petroleum Engineering of the University of Texas, William H. Spice of San Antonio, and Howard L. Bass of Río Grande City determined the property valuation in Zapata County.

17. Members of the defense committee included, for precinct 1, Rafael San Miguel, J. M. Sánchez, C. P. Flores, Humberto González, and H. Cuéllar; precinct 2, Trinidad Uribe, Guadalupe Martínez, Amado Ramírez, Mercurio Martínez, and Arturo Benavides; precinct 3, L. J. Ramírez, Serapio Vela, Santiago González, Salvador García, and Juan G. Benavides; and precinct 4, Flumencio Muñoz, Atilano Ariaza, Crisóforo Ramos, Rafael Guerra, and Tomás Ramírez. ZCCCM, Jan. 3, 1950, vol. 6, ZCC, pp. 631–32.

18. Bobbitt to Bravo, Jan. 4, 1950, MBBP.

19. Ibid.

20. ZCCCM, Jan. 26, 1950, vol. 6, ZCC, pp. 639–40. The results of the petition, published in a Valley newspaper, requested a reevaluation and reclassification of the condemned lands. "Zapatans Ask Resettlement," *Valley Morning Star,* Feb. 9, 1950, PAL.

21. ZCCCM, Jan. 26, 1950, vol. 6, ZCC, p. 640.

22. Canales to James F. Jackson, IBWC Project Attorney, Feb. 22, 1950, LBJL; Canales to LBJ, Feb. 22, 1950, LBJL.

23. LBJ to Lawson, Feb. 24, 1950, LBJL.

24. Lawson to LBJ, Mar. 13, 1950, LBJL; LBJ to Canales, Mar. 21, 1950, LBJL.

25. Byfield, *Falcon Dam,* pp. 14, 52; "IBWC Reduces Land Taking in Zapata County," *Valley Morning Star,* Feb. 27, 1950, PAL.

26. Lawson to LBJ, Aug. 1, 1950, LBJL.

27. Copy of resolution adopted by the Hidalgo County Water Control and Improvement District No. Six, July 11, 1950, LBJL; Looney to LBJ, April 7, 1950, LBJL; LBJ to Looney, April 12, 1950, LBJL; Looney to LBJ, July 20, 1950, LBJL.

28. LBJ to Looney, July 25, 1950, LBJL.

29. Hamilton, *Planning New Zapata,* p. 2.

30. Ibid., pp. 2–3; Judge Bravo was not totally satisfied with the provisions contained in the Bentsen Bill. He was adamant about having the IBWC establish an irrigation system, an enterprise that "would cost $4,000,000 to $5,000,000 but water would not necessarily

have to come from the new Falcon Lake. Either Tigre Creek or Beleno [Veleño] Creek could be dammed up to furnish cosiderable irrigation water" ("Judge M. B. Bravo Says Zapata Relocation Bill Is Inadequate," *Laredo Times,* Feb. 20, 1950).

31. Hamilton, *Planning New Zapata,* p. 4.

32. Ibid., p. 6.

33. Ibid.

34. Bravo to LBJ, Oct. 26, 1950, MBBP; LBJ to Bravo, Nov. 27, 1950, MBBP. Four days later, on October 30, 1950, Walter Jenkins, administrative assistant to Johnson, responded to Bravo's request: "I am sure that Senator Johnson will give his very best attention to the Bentsen Bill when and if it is brought to the Senate for consideration." Jenkins to Bravo, Oct. 30, 1959, MBBP; Hamilton, *Planning New Zapata,* p. 5.

35. Hamilton, *Planning New Zapata,* pp. 5–6; HR 1649, 1st session, 82nd Cong., Jan. 17, 1951; Bailey, "Problems in Relocating," p. 23; Flores, "Falcon International Dam," p. 77. Bentsen's proposed legislation resulted from several meetings among Judge Bravo, the county attorneys (Raymond and Bobbitt), and LBJ and John Connally. Judge Bravo—Personal Notes, n.d.

36. Hamilton, *Planning New Zapata,* p. 6.

37. Memorandum to Our Friends of the Texas Press Regarding Zapata County–Falcon Dam Relocation Problems, n.d., LBJL; Joseph Campbell to Hewitt, June 9, 1955, LBJL; ZCCCM, Jan. 10, 1956, vol. 7, pp. 334–40.

38. Hamilton, *Planning New Zapata,* p. 7.

39. Joseph Campbell, Comptroller General of the United States, to L. H. Hewitt, IBWC Commissioner, June 9, 1955, LBJL. President Truman felt that because the provisions of the Water Treaty of 1944 invested authority in the IBWC, no need existed for new legislation. "Treaty, Bill Provide for Zapata Relocation," *Laredo Times,* May 21, 1951; "Bentsen Talks on Zapata, Airfield, Washington," *Laredo Times,* May 31, 1951.

40. Judge Bravo—Personal Notes, n.p.

41. According to Judge Bravo, the IBWC had failed to implement the provisions of the Bentsen Bill and "on account of their evasive actions," the legal fees and travel expenses paid to Bobbitt to attend meetings in El Paso, Austin, and Washington, D.C., had already totaled over $40,000. Judge Bravo—Personal Notes, p. 23.

42. Judge Bravo—Personal Notes, n.p. Since the passage of the 1944 Water Treaty, the business communities of Laredo and Nuevo Laredo had been lobbying for the construction of the middle dam upriver from Laredo. Judge Bravo wanted the IBWC engineers to build this middle dam first, then see if Falcon Dam could be built at a lower height so that it would not inundate the several hamlets. The Laredo Chamber of Commerce appointed a committee headed by A. E. Guajardo to collect, study, and disseminate information about the middle dam and its impact on Laredo and Nuevo Laredo. As Falcon Dam was nearing completion in 1952, the campaign for the said middle dam intensified. Former County Judge M. J. Raymond, Mayor Hugh A. Cluck, Governor Shivers, Lyndon Johnson, and Lloyd Bentsen pledged their support for the appropriate federal legislation that would begin such a project. A middle dam, they felt, would help both cities in providing flood control, quality water supply, and some irrigation on the U.S. side. For over twelve years, the people waited for funds to become available, but the IBWC finally placed the construction preliminary blueprints on permanent hold. Strong opposition to the middle dam came from Gordon D. Jackson, manager of the Lower Río Grande Valley Water Conservation Association, whose argument—that the evaporation losses would be too great—significantly influenced the IBWC staff. "Joint CC Meeting Pushes Dam Work," *Laredo Times,*

Jan. 26, 1949; "Middle Dam Would Improve Water Supply in Big Area," *Laredo Times,* Aug. 25, 1950; "Judge Urges All Laredo Leaders to Work for Progress," *Laredo Times,* Mar. 21, 1951; "Johnson Asked for Assistance," *Laredo Times,* June 12, 1953; "Valley Group Fights Middle Dam Above Laredo," *Laredo Times,* July 11, 1950.

43. Bailey, "Problems in Relocating," p. 28; Byfield, *Falcon Dam,* pp. 20–21; Harrison Lilly, "Bitter South Texas Political Rivalry Springs to Life in Fight over Land Needed for Completion of Falcon Dam," *San Antonio Light,* Feb. 1, 1953.

44. "County Doomed, Zapatans Fear," *Valley Evening Monitor,* Feb. 10, 1950.

45. Bailey, "Problems in Relocating," p. 23.

46. "Falcon Lake to Cover Towns," *San Antonio Express,* Aug. 20, 1950.

47. At the suggestion of Lloyd Hamilton and Judge Bravo, Bobbitt prepared a press release stating the purpose of the meeting, "I want to get the atmosphere cleared up. We all know that in a project like this you have to necessarily meet with promoters and trouble-makers and people that want to get something for nothing, that want to criticize the public officials and it is generally done for their own selfish welfare, we know that, and we have to face it." Typed transcript of "Meeting held at the Plaza Hotel, Laredo, Texas between Representatives of the County of Zapata and Representatives of the International Boundary and Water Commission, on the 7th Day of August, 1951, at 9:00 A.M.," pp. 2–10, MBBP (hereafter cited as Plaza Hotel Meeting); "Meeting Will Be Held on Re-Location of Towns," *Laredo Times,* Aug. 3, 1951, LPL; "Relocation of Zapata Is Discussed at Meeting," *Laredo Times,* Aug. 7, 1951, LPL.

48. Plaza Hotel Meeting, pp. 10–40; a document entitled, "To the Residents of the Towns of Zapata, Falcon, Ramireño, Uribeño, Lopeño and to the Persons Now Residing within the Lands to be Acquired for the Falcon Dam and Reservoir, Nov. 1951, MBBP (hereafter cited as Towns of Zapata).

49. Plaza Hotel Meeting, pp. 10–40.

50. Typed transcript of meeting held at Falcon, Texas, Aug. 14, 1951, p. 3, MBBP (hereafter cited as Falcon Meeting). The political rivalry became a major stumbling block that "contributed to the slowness and difficulty in achieving satisfactory solutions to these major problems. Factionalism has made it almost impossible to develop a unified front" (Bailey, "Problems in Relocating," p. 28).

51. Typed transcript of "Meeting Held with Officers and Directors of the Zapata Chamber of Commerce, at the Rex Theater Zapata, Texas, on the 24th day of August, 1951, 10 o'clock A.M.," p. 8, MBBP (hereafter cited as Chamber of Commerce Meeting).

52. Ibid.

53. Ibid., pp. 15A–17.

54. Ibid., p. 18.

55. ZCCCM, Aug. 27, 1951, vol. 7, ZCC, pp. 107–18.

56. "Special CC Meeting of Zapata to Be Set," *Laredo Times,* Sept. 29, 1951, LPL.

57. The voting results indicated that precinct 1 had 249 votes; precinct 2, 80; precinct 3, 78; and precinct 4, 29. "Zapata Voters Okay New Seat Location," *Laredo Times,* Sept. 30, 1951, LPL; ZCCCM, Oct. 1, 1951, vol. 7, ZCC, p. 121; Bailey, "Problems in Relocating," p. 24.

58. "200 Sign Petition to Preserve San Ygnacio," *Laredo Times,* May 23, 1951, LPL; "San Ygnacio Residents Will Not Have to Move," *Laredo Times,* June 7, 1951, LPL; "San Ygnacio Elated over Decision of IBWC," *Laredo Times,* June 10, 1951, LPL.

59. "Lyndon Johnson Pledges Support for San Ygnacio," *Laredo Times,* June 3, 1951,

LPL; "Bentsen Promises to Aid San Ygnacio to Keep Site," *Laredo Times,* May 29, 1951, LPL; Byfield, *Falcon Dam,* p. 17.

60. "Land Lacks Irrigation, Judge Says," *Valley Evening Monitor,* Feb. 17, 1950.

61. Falcon Meeting, pp. 8–9; "Falcon, Lopeño Citizens Seek Separate Townsites," *Laredo Times,* Aug. 14, 1951, LPL.

62. Bobbitt publicly admitted the IBWC's lack of experience in dealing with the relocation and irrigation issues, confessing in part that this "is a very new and unusual procedure . . . had no experience in relocating a number of communities." Typed transcript of "Meeting Held at Courthouse in Zapata, Texas, on the 18th Day of October, 1951, in Response to Notice Given by Commissioners' Court to All Owners of Irrigated Land in the County to Appear and Make Their Wishes Known Regarding Substitution of Their Irrigated Acreage," pp. 3–4, MBBP, (hereafter cited as Substitution Meeting); "IBWC Will Help Zapata Farm Owners Get Irrigable Land," *Laredo Times,* Oct. 19, 1951, LPL.

63. Substitution Meeting, pp. 3–4.

64. Ibid., pp. 5–13.

65. Ibid., pp. 10–13; "IBWC Will Help Zapata Farm Owners Get Irrigable Land."

66. Ibid.

67. Ibid. Originally the IBWC had planned to condemn about 125,000 acres, but Judge Bravo, through lobbying efforts, had the amount reduced to about 85,000 acres. The Republican faction, working under the veneer of the Zapata Land Owners Committee and the Chamber of Commerce, also submitted a petition, signed by five hundred landowners. "Petition Is Sent to Boundary Commission," *Laredo Times,* Oct. 24, 1951; "Sen. Johnson Promises Aid to Zapata Co. Land Owners," *Laredo Times,* Nov. 15, 1951, LPL.

68. Looney to LBJ, Mar. 10, 1951, LBJL. Two years earlier, according to historian Dallek, Looney had tried to persuade Lyndon Johnson to intervene on a business arrangement with the Budweiser beer distributorship in Austin—a venture that would be profitable to Looney's law firm. Dallek, *Lone Star Rising,* p. 359.

69. LBJ to Looney, Mar. 16, 1951, LBJL; Dallek, *Lone Star Rising,* pp. 177–84.

70. Typed transcript of "Meeting Held at Courthouse in Zapata, Texas, on the 17th Day of October, 1951, Called by the Commissioners' Court of Zapata County for the Purpose of Discussing Problems Relating to Re-Location of Zapata and Removal of Graves from Affected Cemeteries, pp. 1–5, MBBP (hereafter cited as Relocation Meeting).

71. Ibid., pp. 3, 5.

72. Ibid., pp. 8–9.

73. To facilitate relocating the graves, the cemetery map broke the cemetery up into a grid. Each section in the grid accommodated about 192 graves, and each grave was assigned a letter. The actual measurement for the old graves was three and a half feet by seven, but the proposed new graveyard allowed for five- by eleven-foot graves, thus permitting room for a headstone or marker. Before a grave could be transferred, the local priest made the ground hallow by blessing it with holy water, according to Catholic ritual. Relocation Meeting, pp. 13–16.

74. Towns of Zapata; Byfield, *Falcon Dam,* p. 17. "People who had sold their homes were allowed to buy back their house as salvage. The salvage price was figured by deducting cost of moving and damages from the value of the house and selling it back at one-half of the remainder" (Bailey, "Problems in Relocating," pp. 33–34).

75. Byfield, *Falcon Dam,* pp. 17, 34.

76. Hamilton, *Planning New Zapata,* p. 107.

77. Residents from Falcon later changed their minds and wanted to relocate, but only 10 percent of the lots were available to them, and the properties were scattered throughout the new town. Minutes of a Special Meeting of the Commissioners' Court of Zapata County, June 25, 1952, pp. 6–11, MBBP (hereafter cited as Special Meeting).

78. Ibid., p. 12; ZCCCM, June 25, 1952, vol. 7, ZCC, pp. 162–65.

79. Bailey, "Problems in Relocating," p. 35; "José Sánchez donated enough land to keep Lopeño a separate town," J. E. Bravo, Sr., interview; Hamilton, *Planning New Zapata*, p. 114.

80. "Zapata County Public School System Making Fine Progress," *Laredo Times*, Oct. 21, 1951; "Modern School Plant Will Replace Zapata Facilities," *Laredo Times*, April 16, 1952.

81. "Zapata County Public School System Making Fine Progress," *Laredo Times*, Oct. 21, 1951.

82. Lilly, "Bitter South Texas Political Rivalry"; Bailey, "Problems in Relocating," p. 28.

83. Lilly, "Bitter South Texas Political Rivalry"; "Would Halt All Work on New Town," *Laredo Times*, Jan. 26, 1953.

84. Lilly, "Bitter South Texas Political Rivalry."

85. "Taxpayers' Money Plentiful for Big Public Buildings," *Laredo Times*, Apr. 26, 1953; Byfield, *Falcon Dam*, p. 19; Bailey, "Problems in Relocating," pp. 25–28; "Land Values Set by U.S. Agents," *San Antonio Express*, May 3, 1953; Flores, "Falcon International Dam," p. 84.

86. Examples of headlines that appeared in newspapers throughout the state included "County Doomed, Zapatans Fear"; "Zapatans Need Help, Not Obvious Legal Alibis by Government"; "Zapatans Feel They Were Sold Down River"; "Falcon Dam's Refugees Left Holding Bags"; "U.S. Failure on Pledges Wrecks Zapata Economy"; and "Zapata Residents Want Just Compensation for Homes."

87. "Porter Says He's for Falcon Dam," *San Antonio Express*, Feb. 19, 1953; "Texas GOP Leader Will Visit Dam Site," *Laredo Times*, Feb. 15, 1953.

88. "Taxpayers' Money Plentiful for Big Public Buildings," *Laredo Times*, April 26, 1953.

89. "Progress Made on Zapata County Relocation Problems," *Laredo Times*, Jan. 18, 1953.

90. Arthur C. Perry, Memorandum for the files, Re: Zapata County, Falcon Dam, Jan. 28, 1953, Senate Files, container 1194, LBJL; "Contract between the United States Section of IBWC and Irrigated Landowners within the Falcon Reservoir Site," Jan. 29, 1953, LBJL.

91. "Contract between the United States Section of IBWC and Irrigated Landowners within the Falcon Reservoir Site," Jan. 29, 1953, LBJL.

92. Perry, "Memorandum for the files."

93. Hamilton, *Planning New Zapata*, pp. 100–11.

94. LBJ to Bravo, May 15, 1953, LBJL; Lawson to LBJ, May 14, 1953, Western Union telegram, LBJL.

95. LBJ to Bravo, May 15, 1953, LBJL. Initially, the federal government, through condemnation proceedings, had planned to take all the lands lying between the edge of the lake and the relocated U.S. Highway 83. After much protesting by Judge Bravo and the county attorneys that all this acreage was not needed for the Falcon Dam project, the IBWC dropped the maximum flood elevation to 325 feet. As a result, a total of about 43,000 acres were returned to the previous owners. Then, in 1953, the maximum flood line was

lowered further to 314 feet, making another 34,000 acres available to the farmers and ranchers for a nominal rental fee. In essence, the IBWC had condemned more land than was necessary to operate and maintain the reservoir. "Appraisals Slated for Reviewing," *Laredo Times,* May 17, 1953; "Judge M. B. Bravo Reviews Zapata County Objectives," *Laredo Times,* May 18, 1953.

96. "Appraisals Slated for Reviewing," *Laredo Times,* May 17, 1953; "Judge M. B. Bravo Reviews Zapata County Objectives," *Laredo Times,* May 18, 1953.

97. "Judge M. B. Bravo Reviews Zapata County Objectives," *Laredo Times,* May 18, 1953.

98. "Jack Porter Praises Work of Zapatans," *Laredo Times,* May 17, 1953; "Zapata Landowners Group Pleased with Policy Change," *Laredo Times,* May 18, 1953.

99. Copies of these articles are available in the Father Joseph Narcisse Edourd Bastien, OMI Newspaper file, Oblate Provincial Archives, San Antonio.

100. "Church Typifies Fate of Town Facing Death," *San Antonio Express,* May 4, 1953.

101. "Old Adage, Every Man's Home Is His Castle, Ignored by IB & WC In Zapata," *Laredo Times,* June 8, 1953.

102. J. E. Bravo, Sr., interview.

103. Belia Peña Cooper interview.

104. Bravo to Bastien, Mar. 5, 1955, MBBP; Bastien to Kilgore, LBJ, and Daniel, Mar. 25, 1955, LBJL; LBJ to Bastien, Mar. 29, 1955, LBJL; Kilgore to Bastien, Mar. 7, 1955, Joe M. Kilgore Papers, BTHC (hereafter cited as JMKP).

On another occasion, the relocated padre questioned the judge's presumed harassment of the county doctor, Dr. A. M. Figueroa. The defiant priest accused Judge Bravo of trying to persecute Dr. Figueroa over the legality of the physician's license and his right to practice at the hospital. The judge refuted the allegations with specific citations of the law applicable to the case in point. He ended his letter with: "Father, I forgive you, for you know not what you do." Afterward, an apologetic note from Father Bastien humbly stated that "I note you appreciate human frailty even in the members of the cloth. I hereby retract anything that was not true in my insinuations."

105. "Appraisals Are Illegal, Leaders Say," *Laredo Times,* Aug. 2, 1953; "Legion Post Seeks New Appraisers," *Laredo Times,* Aug. 3, 1953; "Zapata Vets Ask Ike to Oust IBWC," *Laredo Times,* Aug. 10, 1953.

106. "Zapata Vets Ask to Oust IBWC," *Laredo Times,* Aug. 10, 1953.

107. According to IBWC Resident Engineer Hamilton, the residents of Lopeño and Falcon had been told to move out of the reservoir area as early as January, 1953. However, the families delayed their move because the new townsite was not yet completed, and because the appraisal process on their homes was still ongoing. Hamilton, *Planning New Zapata,* pp. 113–15.

108. Ibid.; Bailey, "Problems in Relocating," p. 24; Flores, "Falcon International Dam" p. 101; "Families Begin Move from Falcon Lake Area," *Laredo Times,* Aug. 26, 1953. According to the weather report, "The water was rising at the rate of six or eight inches an hour. . . . Depth of the water in the town [Lopeño] itself ranged up to 50 feet." ("Lopeño Swallowed Up by Lake Water," *Laredo Times,* Aug. 28, 1953).

109. Hamilton, *Planning New Zapata,* p. 115.

110. Ibid., p. 116.

111. Bravo to LBJ, Sept. 23, 1953, Western Union telegram, LBJL; Bravo to Edgar, Sept. 22, 1953, LBJL. Judge Bravo and J. W. Edgar were good friends. Whenever the judge

visited Edgar, he "took couple of bottles of tequila, because Edgar liked tequila and with the two bottles, I think he got more out of Edgar than a lot of people got out of the Education Department." M. B. Bravo, Jr., interview.

112. Flores, "Falcon International Dam," p. 93.

113. Adams to Bravo, Sept. 23, 1953, White House Central Files, box 394, Dwight D. Eisenhower Library (hereafter cited as DDEL).

114. LBJ to Bravo, Oct. 7, 1953, LBJL; Lawson to LBJ, n.d., LBJL.

115. "Owners Ask for Just Appraisals," *Laredo Times,* Oct. 12, 1953; "Two Zapata Land Cases Are Settled," *Laredo Times,* Oct. 13, 1953; "17 Cases Are Settled out of Court," *Laredo Times,* Oct. 14, 1953; "Zapata Land Case Decisions to Be Next Week," *Laredo Times,* Nov. 22, 1953.

116. The upper dam in southern Val Verde County was finished in November, 1969, and was officially named Amistad Dam. It is owned by the United States and Mexico and operated by the IBWC. The middle dam between Eagle Pass and Laredo was never constructed.

117. J. E. Bell, Manager, Harlingen Chamber of Commerce, to LBJ, June 5, 1953, Western Union telegram, LBJL; "Dam Bringing Valley Money," *San Antonio Express-News,* Oct. 19, 1953.

118. "Signs Greet Ike in Zapata," *Laredo Times,* Oct. 19, 1953.

119. Bailey, "Problems in Relocating," p. 27.

120. Michael L. Lawson, *Damned Indians: The Pick-Sloan Plan and the Missouri River Sioux, 1944–1980,* pp. xxi–xxii, 29.

CHAPTER 7

1. Thruston B. Morton, Assistant Secretary, Department of State, to LBJ, Feb. 12, 1954, LBJL; Bravo to LBJ, Feb. 2, 1954, LBJL; LBJ to Bravo, Feb. 9, 1954, LBJL.

2. George H. Winters, Secretary, IBWC, to Bravo, Mar. 19, 1954, LBJL; Morton to LBJ;, Mar. 24, 1954, LBJL; LBJ to Bravo, Mar. 29, 1954, LBJL.

3. HR 7443 2nd Sess., 81st. Cong., Feb. 27, 1950, later reintroduced by Congressman Bentsen as HR 1649, 82nd Cong., 1st. Sess., 1951. Senator Bentsen to author, Sept. 26, 1990 (letter in possession of the author); Winters to Bravo, Mar. 19, 1954, LBJL.

4. Winters to Bravo, Mar. 19, 1954, LBJL; LBJ to Bravo, Mar. 29, 1954, LBJL.

5. Winters to Bravo, Mar. 19, 1954, LBJL.

6. Bobbitt to LBJ, June 5, 1954, LBJL; Bobbitt to Bentsen, June 5, 1954, LBJL; Arthur Perry to LBJ, June 9, 1954 (office memorandum), LBJL.

7. Bobbitt to LBJ, June 5, 1954, LBJL; Bobbitt to Bentsen, June 5, 1954, LBJL; Arthur Perry to LBJ, June 9, 1954 (office memorandum), LBJL.

8. LBJ to Hewitt, June 29, 1954, LBJL.

9. Hewitt to Bentsen, July 22, 1954, LBJL.

10. Ibid.; LBJ to Bobbitt, July 29, 1954, LBJL.

11. The commissioners' court received a bid from the Steck Company to furnish the new Zapata County Courthouse. The said bid was filed in the county judge's office for future settlement with IBWC. Judge Bravo—Personal Notes, May 12, 1954, pp. 14–15; ZCCCM, July 22, 1954, vol. 7, ZCC, p. 250.

12. Jean and Robert Fish, *Journalistic Overview of Refugees in Their Own Land,* n.d., pp. 41–53.

13. Graham to LBJ, Aug. 16, 1954, LBJL; Perry to Graham, Aug. 31, 1954, LBJL; Hewitt to LBJ, Aug. 24, 1954, LBJL.

14. Hewitt to LBJ, Aug. 24, 1954, LBJL; "Ike Urged to Push Relief for Zapatans," *Houston Chronicle,* Aug. 26, 1954; "President Moves to Aid Refugees of Falcon Dam," *Houston Chronicle,* Aug. 27, 1954; "Zapata Dam Land Rates Study Asked," *San Antonio Express,* Aug. 27, 1954.

15. An estimated eighteen hundred county residents needed their appraisal claims reviewed. Herman Phleger, State Department legal adviser, made a new interpretation of IBWC regulations, stating that homeowners could purchase back their condemned homes for salvage (instead of taking the original appraised value of their houses). But salvage was established first at half the appraised value, then later at one-third. Even with the adjusted factor—designed for the benefit of sellers—many residents were still short of funds. For example, Lela Garza, a thirty-five-year-old disabled woman, received $1,500 for her home but discovered that this amount was not enough to install the plumbing and sewage lines. Baxter, "Falcon Dam Miscue Is Costing Taxpayers," *Houston Chronicle,* Aug. 19, 1954; Baxter, "Many Falcon Claims Stymied," *Houston Chronicle,* Aug. 20, 1954.

16. Joe M. Kilgore, who now represented Zapata County in the 15th Congressional District, defeated Brownsville attorney Hubert Hudson in the Democratic primary of July 24, 1954. Former Representative Bentsen retired from public office at the end of his third term, and his father (Lloyd Bentsen, Sr.) wholeheartedly endorsed and financially supported Kilgore, who won unopposed in the November general election.

17. Jack Yeaman, "Hewitt Says All Claims to Be Examined," *Laredo Times,* Sept. 16, 1954. "It was necessary to work out arrangement with the IBWC condemnation proceeding which differed from ordinary proceedings. . . . This is not appropriate nor adequately compensate a public agency . . . , simply because the market value of a school or a courthouse would not adequately compensate the public agency for the loss of that facility" (Robert L. Bobbitt, Jr., interview with author, San Antonio, June 19, 1992).

18. Bravo to Kilgore, Mar. 31, 1955, LBJL.

19. Hewitt to LBJ, Sept. 16, 1954, LBJL.

20. Perry to Bravo, Oct. 5, 1954, LBJL.

21. Baxter, "U.S. Delay in Paying Zapata Claims Rapped," *Houston Chronicle,* Dec. 29, 1954. An editorial in the Houston newspaper blasted Hewitt for stating, "in effect, that since the law had not been broken, there is nothing the government can do. But with the United States shelling out billions of dollars to foreign countries, it is a sorry affair when the government relies on legal technicalities to refuse to give its own citizens what they are rightfully due" ("Zapatans Need Help, Not Obvious Legal Alibis by Government," *Houston Chronicle,* Jan. 2, 1955).

22. Bravo to Kilgore, Mar. 31, 1955, LBJL.

23. Ibid.; Bravo to Kilgore, Feb. 8, 1955, LBJL; LBJ to Bravo, Feb. 14, 1955, LBJL; Kilgore to Bravo, Feb. 18, 1955, JMKP; Bobbitt to Bravo, April 1, 1955, LBJL.

24. Bobbitt to Bravo, April 16, 1955, LBJL; Bobbitt to LBJ, April 16, 1955, LBJL; Kilgore to Bobbitt, April 19, 1955, JMKP.

25. Bobbitt to Bravo, April 28, 1955, LBJL; Bobbitt to Kilgore, April 28, 1955, LBJL; LBJ to Bobbitt, May 3, 1955, LBJL; Kilgore to Bobbitt, April 29, 1955, JMKP.

26. Bobbitt to Kilgore, May 13, 1955, LBJL; Kilgore to Bobbitt, May 5, 1955, JMKP; Bobbitt to Bravo, May 13, 1955, LBJL; LBJ to Bobbitt, May 17, 1955, LBJL. The Zapata County Commissioners' Court accepted Drought's report on the needed furniture for the

courthouse and forwarded a copy to Commissioner Hewitt. ZCCCM, May 13, 1955, vol. 7, ZCC, p. 301.

27. Kilgore to Bravo, June 1, 1955, JMKP.

28. Kilgore to J. H. Bond, Regional Director, H.E.W. (Dallas office), June 6, 1955, JMKP.

29. Joseph Campbell to Hewitt, June 9, 1955, LBJL.

30. Ibid.

31. Hewitt to Bravo, June 14, 1955, LBJL; Kilgore to Bravo, June 10, 1955, JMKP; Bobbitt to LBJ, June 13, 1955, LBJL; Perry to Bobbitt, June 17, 1955, LBJL.

32. Campbell to Hewitt, June 9, 1955, LBJL.

33. Bobbitt to Kilgore et al., June 28, 1955, LBJL; Bobbitt to LBJ, June 28, 1955, LBJL; Kilgore to Bobbitt, July 6, 1955, JMKP.

34. Bobbitt to Kilgore, July 13, 1955, LBJL.

35. Dallek, *Lone Star Rising,* pp. 485–87.

36. Hewitt to Perry, July 12, 1955, LBJL; Kilgore to Bobbitt, July 11, 1955, JMKP; Perry to Bobbitt, July 14, 1955, LBJL. "Falcon Dam was completed around 1953 or 1954. At the time, the engineers for the IBWC were of the opinion that it would take several years for the reservoir to fill up. Consequently, there was no real hurry about getting these things done" (Robert L. Bobbitt, Jr., interview).

37. Bravo to LBJ et al., July 23, 1955, LBJL.

38. Bravo to Hewitt, July 23, 1955, LBJL.

39. Bravo to LBJ et al., July 23, 1955, LBJL.

40. Bravo to Kilgore, July 25, 1955, LBJL; ZCCCM, July 21, 1955, vol. 7, ZCC, p. 313.

41. Arthur C. Perry to Bravo, July 27, 1955, LBJL; Bobbitt to Kilgore et al. (personal memo) July 27, 1955, LBJL; Perry to Bravo, July 27, 1955, LBJL.

42. Bobbitt to Kilgore et al. (personal memo), July 27, 1955, LBJL. On September 8, 1955, Judge Bravo accepted deeds to the park areas, county hospital, streets, county cemetery, courthouse, water distribution system, and sewage treatment plant.

43. Bobbitt to LBJ, July 30, 1955, LBJL; Kilgore to Bravo, Aug. 1, 1955, JMKP; Kilgore to Bravo, Aug. 8, 1955, JMKP.

44. Kilgore to Bravo, June 5, 1956, JMKP; Kilgore to Bravo, June 13, 1956, JMKP; Kilgore to Bravo, June 15, 1956, JMKP. When Johnson was hospitalized, historian Robert Dallek writes how politicians and journalists, regardless of their political affiliation, sent letters of encouragement and support. Judge Bravo was no exception, dispatching the following note: "The majority of the people of Zapata County have always admired your ability in handling the office of Senator, and as a friend you have been considered in the highest esteem and regarded as a sincere and great Texan" (Bravo to LBJ, Aug. 9, 1955, LBJL). Johnson sent Judge Bravo a lengthy letter, thanking him for his cooperation and strong support, "I will never forget your warm friendship for me and the debt I owe you. It is a source of supreme satisfaction that I can call you my friend" (LBJ to Bravo, Sept. 17, 1955, LBJL). Included with the letter was a black and white photo postcard of LBJ standing next to Lady Bird, just as they were disembarking at Fredericksburg airport. According to Dallek, the senator traveled from Washington to Texas on this particular day in order to "complete his recovery." LBJ to Bravo, Sept. 27, 1955, MBBP; Dallek, *Lone Star Rising,* pp. 487–88.

45. Kilgore to Bravo, Aug. 22, 1957, MBBP; Kilgore to Bravo, Jan. 9, 1957, MBBP.

46. Kilgore to Bobbitt, Mar. 1, 1957, JMKP.

47. Kilgore had learned of the judge's decision ten days earlier when he received a telephone call from Walter Jenkins.

48. Bravo to LBJ, Mar. 20, 1957, LBJL.

49. LBJ to Bravo, Mar. 27, 1957, LBJL.

50. Kilgore to Bravo, Dec. 17, 1957, MBBP; LBJ to Bravo, Dec. 23, 1957, MBBP; Bobbitt to Bravo, Nov. 26, 1957, MBBP.

51. LBJ to Bravo, Dec. 23, 1957, MBBP.

52. Kilgore to Bravo, Jan. 7, 1959, MBBP; copy of the Zapata Claims Bill, introduced by Kilgore as H.R. 162, 1st Sess., 86th Cong., Jan. 7, 1959, MBBP.

53. Kilgore, typed and handwritten notes, JMKP; H.R. 8999, 2nd., 88th Cong., Dec. 19, 1963, JMKP.

54. Persons could receive compensation if they met one of the following conditions: (1) if damage or loss of personal property occurred between August 27, 1953, and before September 1, 1954 (during the two big Río Grande floods); (2) if any welfare agency, municipal government, or political subdivision had provided assistance "in the emergency relocation of any person or his personal property by reason of the floods"; or (3) if a person had incurred expenses "in the process and as direct result of moving, himself, his family, and their possessions" during relocation (H.R. 8999, 2nd., 88th Cong., Dec. 19, 1963, JMKP).

55. "Zapata Countians Due Payment for Property," *Laredo Times,* n.d., MBBP.

56. Special Legal Assistant Morris H. Raney to Legal Assistant Blas Cantú, Jan. 20, 1965, MBBP; Raney to Project Superintendent N. H. Scoggins, July 21, 1965, MBBP.

57. Friedkin to Bravo, Nov. 5, 1965, MBBP. The amount paid for the claims did not include the legal and court fees the people of Zapata still had to pay for presenting their case before the Board of Adjudicators. Byfield, *Falcon Dam,* p. 50.

58. "Zapata Countians Due Payment for Property." After representing the 15th Congressional District for ten years, Joe Kilgore opted not to seek reelection in the Democratic primary of May 2, 1964. Instead, Eligio "Kika" de la Garza became the next congressman from this district.

59. Kazen to Friedkin, Oct. 11, 1965, MBBP; Friedkin to Kazen, Oct. 15, 1965, MBBP.

60. Reinaldo Martínez, IBWC Director, Administration, to author, July 20, 1993 (letter in possession of the author).

CHAPTER 8

1. Kilgore to LBJ, Mar. 2, 1957, LBJL. The judge also confided in State Representative Oscar Laurel about his future plans: "But then, I remember that you had told me in confidence that you wanted to do this for quite some time for the best interests of yourself and your family" (Laurel to Bravo, Sept. 12, 1957, MBBP). Josefa V. Bravo interview.

Judge Bravo left the political cauldron for health reasons. Both the 1954 and 1956 primary and general elections resulted in federal investigations, and the judge had to appear in court defending the Partido Viejo against alleged voting irregularities. Even though Judge Bravo and the machine were cleared of any wrongdoing, the mental and physical stress were too much for the man and his family. "Judge Winder Impounds All Ballot Boxes," *Laredo Times,* Nov. 3, 1954; "Federal Judge Orders Zapata Ballots Held," *Laredo Times,* Nov. 6, 1956; "FBI Checking on Counting of Zapata Absentee Votes," *Laredo Times,* Nov. 8, 1956; "Allred Orders Zapata Co. Ballots Returned to Court," *Laredo Times,* Nov. 13, 1956; ZCCCM, Nov. 12, 1956, vol. 8, ZCC, pp. 21–22.

2. Kilgore to Bravo, Mar. 14, 1957, MBBP; Bravo to Kilgore, Mar. 25, 1957, MBBP.

3. Kilgore to Bravo, Mar. 14, 1957, MBBP.

4. Kilgore to Bravo, Apr. 9, 1957, MBBP; Kilgore to Jenkins, Apr. 9, 1957, LBJL; Jenkins to Brown, Apr. 10, 1957, LBJL; Jenkins to Kilgore, Apr. 10, 1957, MBBP; Kilgore to Bravo, Apr. 12, 1957, MBBP.

5. Warfield to Bravo, June 13, 1957, MBBP; Bravo to Warfield, June 19, 1957, MBBP; Bravo to LBJ, Aug. 1, 1957, MBBP.

6. LBJ to Bravo, Aug. 9, 1957, MBBP.

7. Kilgore to Bravo, Aug. 9, 1957, MBBP.

8. J. E. Bravo, Sr., interview.

9. Bravo to Santos Medina, Sept. 30, 1957, MBBP.

10. Quotation cited in Quezada, "Judge Manuel B. Bravo," p. 63. The judge's resignation made front-page headline news in the Sept. 10, 1957 of the *Laredo Times:* "Judge Bravo Resigns Zapata Co. Post." A personal friend wrote, "As for the Zapata politics, they are going to know what it is to do without you now. I am afraid their roof is liable to fall in on them" (Leo J. Leo to Bravo, Oct. 10, 1957, MBBP). The district manager for the South Texas Central Power and Light Company said, "Zapata has come a long way during the tenure of your office and I hope that it shall continue to prosper in the future" (Chester C. Wine to Bravo, Sept. 12, 1957, MBBP). ZCCCM, Oct. 2, 1957, vol. 8, ZCC, p. 85.

11. LBJ to Bravo, Oct. 18, 1957, MBBP. Judge Bravo left an extensive paper trail. A handwritten note, dated September 30, 1957, indicated, "On this date, I left Zapata for job with Brown & Root at Houston—Brought along $140.00." (Judge Bravo note, MBBP). See also Bravo to LBJ, Jan. 15, 1958, LBJL; LBJ to Bravo, Jan. 23, 1958, LBJL.

12. Bravo to LBJ, Mar. 6, 1958, LBJL; LBJ to Bravo, Mar. 14, 1958, LBJL.

13. Josefa V. Bravo interview.

14. Bush to Bravo, Nov. 7, 1960, MBBP. The nomenclature given to Bush's company (Zapata Off-Shore) bears no relation either to Zapata County or to the person for whom the county was named, Col. José Antonio Zapata. Instead, Bush and his business partners chose to name it after the Mexican revolutionary hero Emiliano Zapata. Fitzhugh Green, *George Bush: An Intimate Portrait,* pp. 67–68; President Bush to author, July 22, 1991 (letter in possession of the author).

15. Manuel B. Bravo, Jr., interview.

16. Josefa V. Bravo interview.

17. Bush to Bravo, Nov. 23, 1966, MBBP; Green, *George Bush,* p. 95.

18. Bravo to LBJ, June 16, 1958, MBBP.

19. LBJ to Bravo, June 19, 1958, MBBP.

20. Bravo to Yarborough, June 16, 1958, MBBP.

21. Yarborough to Bravo, June 27, 1958, MBBP.

22. Bravo to Yarborough, June 16, 1958, MBBP; Yarborough to Bravo, Sept. 2, 1958, MBBP.

23. Bravo to Kilgore, June 16, 1958, MBBP.

24. Kilgore to Bravo, June 18, 1958, MBBP.

25. Kilgore to Bravo, Dec. 1, 1959, MBBP.

26. Bravo to Kazen, July 31, 1958, MBBP.

27. Bravo to Bobbitt, July 31, 1958, MBBP; Bobbitt to Bravo, Oct. 20, 1958, MBBP. In reference to the reintroduction of a Zapata claims bill (H.R. 162), Kilgore assured Judge Bravo, "and you know I'll stay in touch with you" (Kilgore to Bravo, Jan. 7, 1959, MBBP).

See also correspondence in MBBP: Bobbitt to Bravo, Oct. 16, 1957; Kilgore to Bravo, Oct. 21 and Dec. 17, 1957.

28. Bravo to Jack Ross, 1958, MBBP. In the latter part of 1953, in a street brawl in Zapata between Armando López and Leonel Presas over some personal family matters, Armando had killed Presas with a knife.

29. López to Bravo, Dec. 16, 1957, MBBP; López to Bravo, July 12, 1958, MBBP.

30. Kilgore to Bravo, Mar. 20, 1961, MBBP.

31. Dallek, *Lone Star Rising,* pp. 582–87.

32. LBJ to Bravo, Oct. 21, 1960, MBBP.

33. ZCCCM, July 19 and 20, 1961, vol. 8, ZCC, pp. 450–52. Judge Bravo's allies kept him informed on the political situation while he worked for Brown & Root. One of them wrote: "Don Mercurio told me that Don Proceso was not going to run for commissioner this year. It seems that Delfino Lozano is taking his place and Proceso will be appointed to some post in Zapata, probably that of probation officer. Proceso seems to be happy with the whole idea since he is getting along in years and prefers to live a more peaceful and sheltered life" (Blas Cantú to Bravo, April 22, 1958, MBBP). Also, Commissioner Manuel Medina notified the judge about Don Proceso's decision and the political arrangement he consummated with Delfino Lozano. Medina to Bravo, n.d., MBBP.

34. "M. B. Bravo Enters Race for Zapata Judge," *Laredo Times,* March 16, 1962.

35. Manuel B. Bravo, Jr., interview.

36. J. E. Bravo, Sr., interview.

37. "Bravo Withdraws from Zapata County Campaign," *Laredo Times,* n.d., MBBP.

38. Zapata County Election Returns, May 5, 1962, Nov. 6, 1962, vol. 2, ZCC, pp. 34–40. Judge Bravo actively campaigned for Preston Smith in Zapata County and tried to solicit the support of leaders in Webb and Starr counties, but they had already committed their support to another candidate. In the general election in November, Smith won the seat for lieutenant governor. Smith to Bravo, June 20, 1962, MBBP.

39. Bravo to Kilgore, Aug. 8, 1962, MBBP.

40. Manuel B. Bravo, Jr., interview; Josefa V. Bravo, interview.

41. Bravo to Carter, Jan. 15, 1964, MBBP.

42. Kazen to Carter, Mar. 6, 1964, MBBP.

43. Bravo to Ivan Sinclair (assistant to LBJ), April 12, 1964, LBJL.

44. Working for the civil service, Judge Bravo received a GG-5 grade with an annual salary of $4,690. Blanche M. Burns (IBWC Personnel Officer) to Bravo, April 23, 1964, MBBP; Sinclair to Bravo, April 29, 1964, LBJL. Even though Judge Bravo could not attend the presidential inauguration, in a letter to Senator Yarborough he expressed his gratitude to LBJ for the job with the IBWC. Bravo to Yarborough, Dec. 10, 1964, MBBP.

45. John B. Moore (IBWC Comptroller) to Bravo, Oct. 20, 1965, MBBP.

46. Scoggins to Friedkin, Oct. 28, 1965, MBBP.

47. Friedkin to Scoggins, Nov. 2, 1965, MBBP.

48. Friedkin to Bravo, Nov. 9, 1967, MBBP.

49. Bravo to Yarborough, Dec. 7, 1965, MBBP.

50. Yarborough to Bravo, Dec. 13, 1965, MBBP. There is a substantial number of letters from Yarborough in the Bravo Papers. In the last letter, Yarborough wrote the following postscript, "Judge, we have fought many battles together for the people. Your name stirs memories of great efforts for everybody. You aided me over and over on this heavy debt." Yarborough to Bravo, Aug. 9, 1973, MBBP.

51. LBJ to Bravo, Oct. 1, 1968, MBBP.

52. Friedkin to Bravo, July 9, 1969, MBBP; Reinaldo Martínez, IBWC Director, Administrative Services, to author, Sept. 18, 1990 (letter in possession of the author).

53. Raney to Bravo, July 22, 1970, MBBP; Purchase Order document, IBWC, payment to M. B. Bravo for $500, July 17, 1970, MBBP.

54. C. E. Dyer to the Commissioner, Feb. 26, 1970, MBBP.

55. Bravo to Friedkin, Aug. 13, 1970, MBBP; Bravo to Raney, Aug. 13, 1970, MBBP.

56. Friedkin to Bravo, Oct. 9, 1970, MBBP.

57. "Kika" de la Garza to Bravo, Oct. 5, 1965, MBBP; W. Lewis David, State Director (USDA), to De la Garza, Oct. 1, 1965, MBBP; De la Garza to Bravo, Oct. 7, 1965, MBBP; Bravo to De la Garza, Oct. 12, 1965, MBBP.

58. Yarborough to Bravo, May 4, 1964, MBBP.

59. Yarborough to Bravo, Oct. 14, 1964, MBBP; Bravo to Yarborough, Nov. 9, 1964, MBBP.

60. Yarborough to Bravo, Nov. 30, 1964, MBBP.

61. Ralph ("Skip") Scoggins to Bravo, April 25, 1972, MBBP. The judge learned about it via a speech State Senator Joe J. Bernal gave in Laredo. The local newspaper carried the speech and Bravo offered his comments on the matter. Bernal to Bravo, Mar. 15, 1971, MBBP; De la Garza to Bravo, 1969, MBBP.

62. González to Bravo, May 26, 1967, MBBP.

63. De la Garza to Bravo, Jan. 26, 1970, MBBP.

64. In the salutation, Judge Bravo is affectionately referred to as "Mel"—a sobriquet used by close family members. John F. Williams to Bravo, June 19, 1970, MBBP.

65. Yarborough to Bravo, May 28, 1973, MBBP; Robert W. Calvert (Chair of the Constitutional Revision Commission) to Bravo, May 30, 1973, MBBP.

66. Antonio Molina, Superintendent, to Dr. John A. Bell, Office of Civil Rights, Mar. 10, 1977, MBBP; Bravo to Molina, Mar. 10, 1977, MBBP.

67. Judge Bravo kept a hefty folder filled with meticulous notes, receipts, letters, bank statements, and other documents. (hereafter cited as Laurendeau Estate).

68. Ibid.

69. George Carmack, "The Tale of 2 Cities; One Is Old; Other New," *San Antonio Express,* Oct. 13, 1973, MBBP; "We could not have had a finer guide to Zapata—or a finer historian of the area" (George Carmack to Bravo, Oct. 19, 1973, MBBP).

70. Gillette to Bravo, Oct. 20, 1983, MBBP.

71. Claudia Anderson (LBJ archivist) to author, Feb. 3, 1991 (letter in possession of the author).

72. Manuel B. Bravo, Jr., interview.

Epilogue

1. Montejano, *Anglos and Mexicans,* pp. 246–50.

2. Ibid., p. 252. In South Texas, the White Man's Primary was a legal method of preventing Tejanos from participating in the electoral process. In essence, they could not vote in the Democratic primary. Tyler, *The New Handbook of Texas,* vol. 6, p. 940.

3. Gary W. Cox and J. Morgan Kousser, "Turnout and Rural Corruption: New York as a Test Case," *American Journal of Political Science* 25 (Nov. 1981): 654–55; James MacGregor Burns, *Roosevelt: The Lion and the Fox,* p. 104. For an analytical historical

study of how a political machine system works, see Eric McKitrick, "The Study of Corruption," *Political Science Quarterly* 72 (Dec. 1957): 502–14.

4. Michael E. McGerr, *The Decline of Popular Politics: The American North, 1865–1928*, p. 18.

5. Samuel E. Morison, *The Oxford History of the American People*, pp. 733–34.

6. Dallek, *Lone Star Rising*, p. 224.

7. García, *Mexican Americans*, p. 19.

8. Juan Gómez-Quiñones, *Chicano Politics: Reality and Promise, 1940–1990*, p. 85.

BIBLIOGRAPHY

ARCHIVES

Alamo Research Library, San Antonio. Zapata County File.

API Wide World Photo Archives, New York.

Barker Texas History Center, University of Texas, Austin. Lloyd M. Bentsen, Jr., File. Joe M. Kilgore Papers. Homer P. Rainey Files. Francis William Seabury Papers, 1914–46. Texas Newspaper Collection. James B. Wells Papers, 1863–1926. Zapata County Scrapbook.

Benson Latin American Collection, Austin.

Bravo, Manuel B., Papers (in possession of the Bravo family), Zapata, Texas.

Dwight D. Eisenhower Library, Abilene, Kansas. White House Central Files.

Hidalgo County Courthouse, Edinburg, Texas. Office of the County Clerk, Marriage Records 2:261.

Institute of Texan Cultures, San Antonio. Webb County Photo File. Zapata County Photo File.

International Boundary and Water Commission Archives, El Paso. Falcon Dam Files.

Laredo Public Library, Laredo, Texas. Newspaper Collection (microfilm).

Laredo State University, Laredo, Texas. Newspaper Collection (microfilm).

Legislative Reference Library, Austin. General and Special Laws of Texas, 1941.

Library of Congress, Washington, D.C. Tom Connally Papers.

López, Virginia Bravo, Collection, Mission, Texas.

Lyndon B. Johnson Library, Austin. Robert Dallek Notes. Dr. Héctor García Oral History. Lewis L. Gould Papers. House Papers, Rivers and Harbors Files. LBJ Photo Collection. Master File Index. Frank Oltorf Oral History. Pre-Presidential Confidential Files. Senate Files.

Oblate Provincial Archives, San Antonio. Father Edourd Bastien, O.M.I. Newspaper File.

Railroad Commission of Texas Archives, Austin. Motor Transportation Division Files.

Records of the United States District Court, Northern District of Texas, Fort Worth. Federal Archives and Records Center (microfilm).

San Antonio Public Library, San Antonio. United States 1920 Census (microfilm). Newspaper Collection (microfilm).

School District Administration Office, Zapata, Texas. Board of County School Trustees Minutes, vol. 1.

State Bar of Texas Archives, Austin. Supreme Court Records, 1870.

Texas State Archives, Austin. Good Neighbor Commission Files. Hidalgo County Election Returns, 1866–69. Railroad Commission Motor Transportation Files. Texas Education Agency Files. Texas Selective Service Administration File.

Texas State Archives Office, San Antonio. Court of Civil Appeals. Fourth Supreme Judicial District. Case No. 12499. The 49th District Court Records, Transcript No. 12499.

University of Texas at Pan American, Edinburg. Falcon Dam Photo Collection. Newspaper Collection (microfilm).

Zapata County Courthouse, Office of the County Clerk, Zapata, Texas. County Commissioners Court Minutes, vols. 5–7. 49th District Court Records, Case No. 369. Probate Records. Record of Election Returns, vols. 1, 2.

Zapata Public Library, Zapata, Texas. Relocation of Cemeteries Inventory. Zapata County Scrapbook.

INTERVIEWS AND MANUSCRIPTS

All interviews were with the author.

Anders, Evan Marcus. "James B. Wells and the Brownsville Patronage Fight, 1912–1917." M.A. thesis, University of Texas at Austin, 1970.

Bobbitt, Robert Lee, Jr. Interview. San Antonio. June 10, 1992.

Bravo, J. E. (Eddie), Sr. Interview. Zapata, Tex. July 5, 1991.

Bravo, Josefa V. Interview. Zapata, Tex. December 24, 1990.

Bravo, Judge M. B. "Falcon Dam-Zapata County." Unpublished personal notes arranged in chronological order.

Bravo, M. (Manuel) B., Jr. Interview. Laredo, Tex. December 24, 1990.

Bryson, William Curtis. "The Social Basis of South Texas Bossism." B.A. thesis, Harvard University, 1969.

Cavazos, Elías. Interview. Zapata, Tex. September 29, 1990.

Cooper, Belia Peña. Interview. Zapata, Tex. July 13, 1993.

Flores, Adela Isabel. "Falcon International Dam and Its Aftermath: A Study of United States-Mexico Border Policy Making and Implementation." M.A. thesis, University of Texas at Austin, 1985.

García, Salvador. Interview. Zapata, Tex. July 13, 1992.

Gonzáles, Jovita. "Social Life of Cameron, Starr, and Zapata Counties." M.A. thesis, University of Texas, 1930.

Gould, Lewis L. Interview. Austin. February 29, 1992.

Gutiérrez, Josefa M. Interview. Zapata, Tex. December 28, 1990.

Hamilton, Lloyd W. "A Report on Procedures Used in Planning New Zapata." International Boundary and Water Commission Office, 1955.

Kilgore, Joe M. Interview. Austin. September 23, 1993.

Laurel, Oscar M. Interview. Laredo, Tex. July 6, 1993.

López, Virginia Bravo. Interview. Zapata, Tex. July 17, 1990.

Martínez, Camilo Amado. "The Mexicans' and Mexican Americans' Contribution to the

Development of the Lower Rio Grande Valley of Texas and Its Citrus Industry." M.A. thesis, Pan American University, 1982.

Medina, Santos. Interview. San Antonio. September 4, 1991.

Norris, Clyde W. "History of Hidalgo County." M.S. thesis, Texas A&I College, 1942.

Quezada, Juan Gilberto, and Jo Emma Quezada, comps. "The Box Family Trek to South Texas, 1691–1866." Vol. 1. 1992.

Salazar, Rubén. Interview. Zapata, Tex. July 15, 1992.

Smith, Brad. "One Night That Averted Civil War in Hidalgo County." Hidalgo County Historical Museum, March 6, 1989.

Spence, Ruth Griffin. "The Nickel Plated Highway to Hell: A Political History of Hidalgo County, 1852–1934." Hidalgo County Museum, 1986.

Treviño, Ted. Interview. Zapata, Tex. July 16, 1991.

Villarreal, Aminta Ramírez. Interview. Zapata, Tex. July 8, 1994.

PUBLISHED SOURCES

Allen, Oliver E. *The Rise and Fall of Tammany Hall.* Reading, Mass.: Addison-Wesley, 1993.

Anders, Evan. *Boss Rule in South Texas: The Progressive Era.* Austin: University of Texas Press, 1982.

Avery, C. E., and Gilberto Quezada. "Confederate Images: 5th Sgt. Lina H. Box." *Confederate Veteran Magazine,* March–April, 1993, p. 5.

Bailey, Wilfred C. "Problems in Relocating the People of Zapata, Texas." *Texas Journal of Science* 7 (March, 1955): 20–37.

Banks, Jimmy. *Money, Marbles, and Chalk: The Wondrous World of Texas Politics.* Austin: Texas Publishing Company, 1971.

Bourgeois, Christie L. Review of *The Years of Lyndon Johnson: Means of Ascent* by Robert A. Caro. In *Southwestern Historical Quarterly* 94 (January, 1991): 471–72.

Burns, James MacGregor. *Roosevelt: The Lion and the Fox.* New York: Harcourt, Brace, 1956.

Byfield, Patsy Jeanne. *Falcon Dam and the Lost Towns of Zapata.* Austin: Texas Memorial Museum, 1966.

Calvert, Robert A., and Arnoldo De León. *The History of Texas.* Wheeling, Ill.: Harlan Davidson, 1996.

Caro, Robert A. *The Years of Lyndon Johnson: Means of Ascent.* New York: Alfred A. Knopf, 1990.

———. *The Years of Lyndon Johnson: The Path to Power.* New York: Alfred A. Knopf, 1982.

Casdorph, Paul. *A History of the Republican Party in Texas, 1865–1965.* Austin: Pemberton Press, 1965.

Cherny, Robert W. *American Politics in the Gilded Age, 1868–1900.* Wheeling, Ill.: Harlan Davidson, 1997.

Clark, John E. *The Fall of the Duke of Duval: A Prosecutor's Journal.* Austin: Eakin Press, 1995.

Cox, Gary W., and J. Morgan Kousser. "Turnout and Rural Corruption: New York as a Test Case." *American Journal of Political Science* 25 (November, 1981): 654–55.

Cuéllar, Robert A. *A Social and Political History of the Mexican American Population of*

Texas, 1929–1963. M.A. thesis, Texas State University, 1969. Reprint, San Francisco: R & E Research Associates, 1974.

Dallek, Robert. *Lone Star Rising: Lyndon Johnson and His Times, 1908–1960*. New York: Oxford University Press, 1991.

Davis, Ellis Arthur, ed. *The Historical Encyclopedia of Texas*. Austin: Texas Historical Society, 1937.

De León, Arnoldo. *Mexican Americans in Texas: A Brief History*. Wheeling, Ill.: Harlan Davidson, 1993.

———. "A People with Many Histories: Mexican Americans in Texas." In *The Texas Heritage*, edited by Archie P. McDonald and Ben H. Proctor, pp. 150–66. 2d ed. Wheeling, Ill.: Harlan Davidson, 1992.

———. *The Tejano Community, 1836–1900*. Albuquerque: University of New Mexico Press, 1982. Reprint, Dallas: Southern Methodist University Press, 1997.

———. *They Called Them Greasers: Anglo Attitudes toward Mexicans in Texas, 1821–1900*. Austin: University of Texas Press, 1983.

De León, Arnoldo, and Kenneth L. Stewart. "Lost Dreams and Found Fortunes: Mexican and Anglo Immigrants to South Texas, 1850–1900." *Western Historical Quarterly* 14 (July, 1983).

Dugger, Ronnie. *The Politician: The Life and Times of Lyndon Johnson*. New York: W. W. Norton, 1982.

Engler, Robert. *The Politics of Oil: A Study of Private Power and Democratic Direction*. New York: MacMillan, 1961.

Fish, Jean, and Robert Fish. *Elected Officials of Zapata County, Texas, 1858–1986*. Zapata: Zapata County Historical Commission, 1988.

———. *Journalistic Overview of Refugees in Their Own Land*. n.p., n.d.

Fish, Jean Y. *Zapata County Roots Revisited*. Edinburg, Tex.: New Santander Press, 1990.

Foley, Douglas E., Clarice Mota, Donald Post, and Ygnacio Lozano. *From Peones to Politics: Ethnic Relations in a South Texas Town, 1900–1977*. Austin: Center for Mexican American Studies, University of Texas, 1977.

Frantz, Joe B. *Texas: A Bicentennial History*. New York: W. W. Norton, 1976.

García, Mario T. *Mexican Americans: Leadership, Ideology, and Identity, 1930–1960*. New Haven, Conn.: Yale University Press, 1989.

George, Eugene. *Historic Architecture of Texas: The Falcon Reservoir*. Austin: Texas Historical Commission, 1975.

Gómez-Quiñones, Juan. *Chicano Politics: Reality and Promise, 1940–1990*. Albuquerque: University of New Mexico Press, 1990.

Gould, Lewis L. *Progressives and Prohibitionists: Texas Democrats in the Wilson Era*. Austin: Texas State Historical Association, 1992.

Green, Fitzhugh. *George Bush: An Intimate Portrait*. New York: Hippocrene Books, 1989.

Green, George N. "The Félix Longoria Affair." *Journal of Ethnic Studies* 19 (Fall, 1991): 23–34.

Green, George Norris. *The Establishment in Texas Politics: The Primitive Years, 1938–1957*. Westport, Conn.: Greenwood Press, 1979.

Gunther, John. *Inside U.S.A.* New York: Harper & Bros., 1947.

Heard, Alexander, and Donald S. Strong. *Southern Primaries and Elections, 1920–1949*. University, Ala.: University of Alabama Press, 1950.

Jackson, Paul, and Harry Quin, eds. *Edinburg: A Story of a Town*. Edinburg, Tex.: Bicentennial Heritage Committee, 1976.

Kearney, Milo, and Anthony Knopp. *Border Cuates: A History of the U.S.-Mexican Twin Cities*. Austin: Eakin Press, 1995.

Kent, Frank R. *The Great Game of Politics*. New York: Doubleday, Doran, 1930.

Kingston, Mike, Sam Attlesey, and Mary G. Crawford. *The Texas Almanac's Political History of Texas*. Austin: Eakin Press, 1992.

Lawson, Michael L. *Damned Indians: The Pick-Sloan Plan and the Missouri River Sioux, 1944–1980*. Norman: University of Oklahoma Press, 1982.

Lott, Virgil N., and Mercurio Martínez. *The Kingdom of Zapata*. San Antonio: Naylor, 1953. Reprint, Austin: Eakin Press, 1983.

Lott, Virgil N., and Virginia M. Fenwick. *People and Plots on the Río Grande*. San Antonio: Naylor, 1957.

McCaffery, Peter. *When Bosses Ruled Philadelphia: The Emergence of the Republican Machine, 1867–1933*. University Park: Pennsylvania State University Press, 1993.

McGerr, Michael E. *The Decline of Popular Politics: The American North, 1865–1928*. New York: Oxford University Press, 1986.

McKay, Seth Shepard. *Texas and the Fair Deal, 1945–1952*. San Antonio: Naylor, 1954.

McKitrick, Eric. "The Study of Corruption." *Political Science Quarterly* 72 (December, 1957): 502–14.

Mandelbaum, Seymour J. *Boss Tweed's New York*. New York: John Wiley and Sons, 1965.

Márquez, Benjamin. *LULAC: The Evolution of a Mexican American Political Organization*. Austin: University of Texas Press, 1993.

Matthew, Wilbur. *San Antonio Lawyer*. San Antonio: Corona, 1983.

Merton, Robert K. *Social Theory and Social Structure*. New York: Free Press, 1968.

Miller, Merle. *Lyndon: An Oral Biography*. New York: G. P. Putnam, 1980.

Miller, Zane L. *Boss Cox's Cincinnati: Urban Politics in the Progressive Era*. New York: Oxford University Press, 1968.

Mohl, Raymond A. *The New City: Urban America in the Industrial Age, 1860–1920*. Arlington Heights, Ill.: Harlan Davidson, 1985.

Montejano, David. *Anglos and Mexicans in the Making of Texas, 1836–1986*. Austin: University of Texas Press, 1989.

Morison, Samuel Eliot. *The Oxford History of the American People*. New York: Oxford University Press, 1965.

Peavey, John R. *Echoes from the Río Grande*. Brownsville, Tex.: Springman-King, 1963.

Phipps, Joe. *Summer Stock: Behind the Scenes with LBJ in '48: Recollections of a Political Drama*. Fort Worth: Texas Christian University Press, 1992.

Pycior, Julie Leininger. *LBJ and Mexican Americans: The Paradox of Power*. Austin: University of Texas Press, 1997.

Quezada, Juan Gilberto. "The Box Family Roots and South Texas Politics: Judge Manuel Box Bravo." *East Texas Historical Journal* 34, no. 2 (August, 1996): 17–24.

———. "Judge Manuel B. Bravo: A Political Leader in South Texas, 1937–1957." *Journal of South Texas* 5 (Spring, 1992): 51–67.

———. "Manuel Box Bravo." In *The New Handbook of Texas*, edited by Ron Tyler, vol. 1, p. 707. Austin: Texas State Historical Association, 1996.

Reston, James, Jr. *The Lone Star: The Life of John Connally*. New York: Harper and Row, 1989.

Royko, Mike. *Boss: Richard J. Daley of Chicago*. New York: E. P. Dutton, 1971.

Rubel, Arthur J. *Across the Tracks: Mexican-Americans in a Texas City*. Austin: University of Texas Press, 1966.

Rulon, Philip Reed. *The Compassionate Samaritan: The Life of Lyndon Baines Johnson*. Chicago: Nelson-Hill, 1981.

Sandos, James A. *Rebellion in the Borderlands: Anarchism and the Plan of San Diego, 1904–1923*. Norman: University of Oklahoma Press, 1992.

San Miguel, Guadalupe, Jr. *"Let All of Them Take Heed": Mexican Americans and the Campaign for Educational Equality in Texas, 1910–1981*. Austin: University of Texas Press, 1987.

Shelton, Edgar G. *Political Conditions among Texas Mexicans along the Río Grande*. M.A. thesis, University of Texas at Austin, 1946. Reprint, San Francisco: R & E Research Associates, 1974.

Simmons, Ozzie G. *Anglo-Americans and Mexican Americans in South Texas*. New York: Arno Press, 1974.

Stambaugh, Lee J., and Lillian J. Stambaugh. *The Lower Río Grande Valley of Texas*. San Antonio: Naylor, 1954.

Stewart, Kenneth L., and Arnoldo De León. *Not Room Enough: Mexicans, Anglos, and Socio-Economic Change in Texas, 1850–1900*. Albuquerque: University of New Mexico Press, 1993.

Tarr, Joel Arthur. *A Study in Boss Politics: William Lorimer of Chicago*. Chicago: University of Illinois Press, 1971.

Texas Almanac and State Industrial Guide. Dallas: A. H. Belo, 1933, 1936, 1939, 1940, 1941–42, 1943–44, 1945–46, 1947–48, 1949–50, 1952–53, 1956–57, 1961–62, 1990–91.

Thompson, Jerry D. *Warm Weather and Bad Whiskey: The 1886 Laredo Election Riot*. El Paso: Texas Western Press, 1991.

Treaty between the United States and Mexico Respecting Utilization of Waters of the Colorado and Tijuana Rivers and of the Río Grande. Treaty Series 994. Washington, D.C.: GPO, 1946.

Tyler, Ron, ed. *The New Handbook of Texas*. Vols. 1, 2, 6. Austin: Texas State Historical Association, 1996.

U.S. Congress. H.R. 7443. 81st Cong., 2d sess., February 27, 1950.

U.S. Congress. H.R. 1649. 82d Cong., 1st sess., January 17, 1951.

U.S. Congress. H.R. 8999. 88th Cong., 2d sess., August 4, 1964.

U.S. Department of Agriculture. *Campaign in Mexico against Foot-and-Mouth Disease, 1947–52*. Washington, D.C.: Agricultural Research Service, 1954.

U.S. House. *Report of the American Section of the International Water Commission, United States and Mexico*. 71st Cong., 2d sess, House Document No. 359. Washington, D.C.: GPO, 1930.

U.S. Senate. *Hearing on Treaty with Mexico Relating to the Utilization of Waters of Certain Rivers*. 79th Cong., 1st sess., March 16 to April 18, 1945.

Vento, Adela Sloss. *Alonso A. Perales: His Struggle for the Rights of Mexican-Americans*. San Antonio: Artes Gráficas, 1977.

Weeks, Douglas O. "The Texas-Mexican and the Politics of South Texas." *American Political Science Review* 24, no. 3 (August, 1930): 606–27.

INDEX

Pages containing illustrations or tables appear in italics.